Studies in the Eighteenth Century

This volume of essays, from the Third David Nichol Smith Memorial Seminar, continues the valuable and lively tradition established in the two earlier seminars and volumes.

The essays, by distinguished international scholars, range over many of the topics that make the eighteenth century a rich area of study: the burgeoning of ideas about man and his place in the world, social history, philosophy and literature, literary criticism and traditions, the poetry and prose of the giants of the age.

For all students of eighteenth-century studies this book will be vital reading.

R. F. BRISSENDEN is Reader in English at the Australian National University. He has published a number of articles and monographs in the field of eighteenth-century studies, most recently Virtue in Distress: Studies in the Novel of Sentiment from Richardson to Sade and has also written on Australian and American literature.

J. C. EADE is Research Assistant in English at the Australian National University. He is the editor of a Bibliographical Essay on Eighteenth-Century Studies in Australia.

Studies in the Eighteenth Century

III

Papers presented at the Third David Nichol Smith Memorial Seminar, Canberra 1973

Edited by
R. F. Brissenden and J. C. Eade

University of Toronto Press
Toronto and Buffalo

© 1976 R. F. Brissenden and the several authors, each in respect of the paper contributed by him; for the full list of the names of such copyright owners and the papers in respect of which they are copyright owners see the Table of Contents at p. vii of this volume.

First published in Australia 1976

First published in 1976 in Canada and the United States by University of Toronto Press, Toronto and Buffalo.

This book is copyright. Apart from any fair dealing for the purpose of private study, research, criticism, or review, as permitted under the Copyright Act, no part may be reproduced by any process without written permission. Inquiries should be made to the publisher.

Reprinted in paperback 2014
ISBN 978-0-8020-2205-9 (cloth)
ISBN 978-1-4426-5228-6 (paper)

Preface

THE THIRD OF the Seminars in Eighteenth-Century Studies designed to honour the memory of David Nichol Smith took place in Canberra from Thursday 23 to Wednesday 29 August 1973. It was sponsored by the Australasian and Pacific Society for Eighteenth-Century Studies, the National Library of Australia, the Australian National University and the Australian Academy of the Humanities. This is the first of the Seminars, now established as triennially recurring conferences, that APSECS has assisted in sponsoring.

The Seminar was officially opened by Professor Joseph Burke, President of the Academy, at the National Library Theatre. During the proceedings which followed twenty papers were delivered dealing with various aspects of the eighteenth century, with particular emphasis being given to the French enlightenment, Johnson and Boswell studies, and eighteenth-century English poetry. Papers were also delivered dealing with architecture and town-planning, opera, the history of ideas, fiction—English, French and Russian—and bibliography. A selection of these papers has been brought together in this volume.

One hundred and sixteen people registered as members of the Seminar. Most Australian and a number of New Zealand universities were represented, and there were a number of members from overseas universities. Some undergraduate honours students and some post-graduate students also took part. The international character of the gathering is indicated by the fact that among the members of the Seminar were the President and the Secretary of the International Society for Eighteenth-Century Studies and the President and two past Presidents of the American Society.

As part of the proceedings associated with the Seminar the National Library published *French Plays, 1701-1840, in the National Library of Australia*, edited by Mr Ivan Page, Curator of Rare Books.

The National Library also mounted an exhibition of books, prints and photographs. The themes of the exhibition were the French Revolution, theatre in eighteenth-century France and the Rediscovery of Classical Architecture.

During the Seminar a Soirée Musicale was staged in the Hall of University House. The program featured Nicolas Bernier's cantata, *The Forges of Lemnos*, sung and acted in an authentic eighteenth-century style by Miss Gaye Macfarlane. The music was under the direction of Mr Richard Divall, Musical Director of the Victorian Opera Company, and the whole performance was produced by Mr Dene Barnett of Flinders University.

The organisation of the Seminars is made possible only through the help given by a number of institutions. It is a pleasure to express our grateful appreciation in particular to the Australian-American Educational Foundation, the Pro Helvetia Foundation, the Modern Languages Association of America, the American Council of Learned Societies and the Australian Vice-Chancellors Committee. We must also thank the Ian Potter Foundation for assisting us in the publication of this volume.

The David Nichol Smith Memorial Seminars provide a unique opportunity for those of us in Australia and New Zealand who are interested in the eighteenth century to meet, talk and exchange ideas with each other and with scholars from other parts of the world. The Third Seminar, like the first two, was stimulating and informative—but it had an extra dimension provided by continuity. To see people—especially people from other countries—at the Third Seminar who had been present in 1966 at the first was a source of delight and satisfaction. We can now be confident the 'DNS' will continue to play a most significant role in the professional life of the international community of scholars.

Canberra, 1975   R.F.B.
                                                                J.C.E.

Contents

Preface		v
Notes on Contributors		ix
Problems of Johnson's Middle Years—the 1762 Pension	*James L. Clifford*	1
Boswell's Ebony Cabinet	*Mary Hyde*	21
Bath: Ideology and Utopia, 1700-1760	*R. S. Neale*	37
Social Stratification and the Obsequious Curve: Goldsmith and Rowlandson	*Robert H. Hopkins*	55
Rousseau and the Common People	*L. G. Crocker*	73
Jacques le Fataliste: un problème de cohérence structurelle	*François Van Laere*	95
The Fortunes of Voltaire's Foppington	*Colin Duckworth*	121
Nerves, Spirits, and Fibres: Towards Defining the Origins of Sensibility	*G. S. Rousseau*	137
Philosophie et Littérature	*Yvon Belaval*	159
Nichol Smith's *Oxford Book* Reappraised	*William B. Todd*	171
Integrity and Life in Pope's Poetry	*S. L. Goldberg*	185
Allusion: The Poet as Heir	*Christopher Ricks*	209
Augustan Prose Fiction and the Romance Tradition	*Henry Knight Miller*	241
Index		257

Illustrations

		Facing page
I	Anonymous Letter to the 3rd Earl of Bute	20
II	Boswell's Ebony Cabinet	21
III	Map of Bath 1723	52
IV	(a) Vitruvian Figure from Cesariano (b) Queen Square, Bath	53
V	(a) Vitruvian Figure, Leonardo's version (b) The Parades, Bath	84
VI	The Circus, Bath	85
VII	The Circus, Bath	116
VIII	Thomas Stothard, 'Rescue of Sophia from Drowning', *The Vicar of Wakefield*, London, 1792 edition	117
IX	Thomas Rowlandson, Frontispiece to *The Vicar of Wakefield*	148
X	William Hogarth, 'The Industrious 'Prentice Lord-Mayor of London', *Industry and Idleness* (Plate 12)	149
XI	Thomas Rowlandson, 'The Departure from Wakefield' (Plate 3)	180
XII	Thomas Rowlandson, 'The Welcome' (Plate 5)	181
XIII	Thomas Rowlandson, 'The Lord of the Manor receiving his Rents', Drawing	200
XIV	Thomas Rowlandson, 'Attendance on a Nobleman' (Plate 18)	201
XV	Thomas Rowlandson, 'The Vicar Preaching to the Prisoners' (Plate 23)	232
XVI	Thomas Rowlandson, 'The Weddings' (Plate 24)	233

Notes on Contributors

BELAVAL, Yvon, Professor of Philosophy at the Sorbonne (Paris I), Vice-President of the Leibniz-Gesellschaft (Hanover), President of the Société Française d'Etude du dix-huitième siècle. Has published numerous studies and editions. On the eighteenth century: *L'esthétique sans paradoxe de Diderot, Au siècle des Lumières, Jacques le Fataliste.*

CLIFFORD, James L., William Peterfield Trent Professor of English, Emeritus, Columbia University. Professor Clifford is author of *Hester Lynch Piozzi (Mrs Thrale)* and *Young Samuel Johnson*. He has been editor of the *Johnsonian News Letter* since its beginning in 1940. He is now working on a study of Johnson's middle years.

CROCKER, Lester G., M.A., PH.D., Kenan Professor of French and Chairman of the Department, University of Virginia. A graduate of New York University and the University of California at Berkeley, Professor Crocker is the author of numerous books on the eighteenth century including *An Age of Crisis* and *Nature and Culture*. His recent publications include a two-volume biography of Rousseau and *Diderot's Chaotic Order, Approach to Synthesis*.

DUCKWORTH, Colin, M.A. (B'ham), PH.D. (Cambridge), Professor of French, Auckland University, has written on aspects of French Drama in the eighteenth, nineteenth and twentieth centuries (especially Tardieu and Beckett), as well as on Flaubert, Renan, Thibaudet and Lèon Bopp. Having completed two critical editions for *The Complete Works of Voltaire*, he is now working on the semi-autobiographical writings of d'Antraigues and on a study of *French Drama in Performance*.

GOLDBERG, S. L., B.A., B.LITT., Robert Wallace Professor of English, University of Melbourne, and editor of *The Critical Review*. His publications include *The Classical Temper: A Study of James Joyce's 'Ulysses'*, *Joyce*, and *An Essay on 'King Lear'*. He is at present working on Shakespeare and seventeenth-century poetry; Pope; and the English novel from George Eliot to D. H. Lawrence.

HOPKINS, Robert, B.A., M.A., PH.D., Professor of English, University of California, Davis. Professor Hopkins is a graduate of Kalamazoo College and the University of Pennsylvania. He is the author of *The True Genius of Oliver Goldsmith* and a founding editor of *Eighteenth-Century Studies*.

HYDE, Mary, PH.D., LITT.D. Trustee of the Pierpont Morgan Library, Member Harvard Visiting Committees of Library and English Department; Member Princeton Advisory Councils Library and English Department, Past President Johnson Society, Litchfield (England); Member Editorial Committee Yale Works of Samuel Johnson and Private Papers of James

Boswell. Her publications include *Playwriting for Elizabethans, Johnson's Diaries, Prayers and Annals* (with Donald Hyde and E. L. McAdam); *Four Oaks Farm and Its Library*; and *The Impossible Friendship* (Boswell and Mrs Thrale). Mrs Hyde is at present working on a book about the Thrales and their children.

MILLER, Henry Knight, B.A., PH.D. Professor of English, Princeton University. Professor Miller is a member of the editorial board of *The Wesleyan Fielding*; his publications include studies in prose-fiction and other genres, and critiques of literary history and the history of ideas in the eighteenth century.

NEALE, R. S., B.SC. (Econ) (London), M.A. (Bristol). Professor of Economic History, University of New England, N.S.W. He is author of *Class and Ideology in the Nineteenth Century* (1972) and co-editor with Eugene Kamenka of *Feudalism, Capitalism and Beyond* (1975). He has published many articles on the economic and social history of England in the eighteenth and nineteenth centuries and contributed to several collections, among them *Rural Change and Urban Growth, 1500-1800*, ed. Chalkin and Havinden (1974). He is currently working on an economic and social history of Bath, 1700-1850.

RICKS, Christopher, M.A., B.LITT., Professor of English, University of Cambridge. From 1958 to 1968, he was a Fellow of Worcester College, Oxford; and from 1968 to 1975, Professor at the University of Bristol. He is the author of *Milton's Grand Style, Tennyson*, and *Keats and Embarrassment*, and the editor of *The Poems of Tennyson*.

ROUSSEAU, George S., B.A., M.A., PH.D., Associate Professor of English Literature, University of California, Los Angeles. Professor Rousseau was trained by Marjorie Hope Nicolson, Louis A. Landa and others in the history of ideas. He is author of *This Long Disease, My Life: Alexander Pope and the Sciences* (with Marjorie Hope Nicolson), and editor of *Tobias Smollett, English Poetic Satire, Organic Form: The Life of an Idea*, and *Goldsmith: The Critical Heritage*.

TODD, William B., B.A., M.A., PH.D., Professor of English in the University of Texas at Austin. Professor Todd, though the author of many studies on the eighteenth century, including bibliographies of Edmund Burke and David Hume, has also ranged indiscriminately from an account of the *Nuremberg Chronicle* (1493) to an analysis of the White House Transcripts (1974). Since 1967 he has been Editor of the Bibliographical Society of America, and in 1969-70 was J. P. R. Lyell Reader in Bibliography at Oxford University as well as Visiting Fellow at All Souls College.

VAN LAERE, François. Born in 1934 in Brussels. His first career was as a social worker, but he soon discovered a passionate interest in literature. He took his degree at the University of Brussels, studied under Maurice-Jean Lefebve and was appointed to a teaching position in the same university. In 1970 he took up his appointment as a Professor of French at Monash University and was chairman of the French Department in 1973. He resigned in September 1974 and returned to Belgium. François Van Laere died in Brussels on 25 April 1975, at the age of forty. He left a widow and a son, Jacques-Stephane, aged 11. His published work includes a monograph on *Jean-Jacques Rousseau—de phantasme à l'écriture—Les révélations du 'Lévite d'Ephraïm'*, Paris, 1967, and a book, *Une lecture du temps dans 'La Nouvelle Héloïse'*, Neuchâtel, 1968, as well as a considerable number of articles on eighteenth-century French literature, Balzac, modern French poetry and the French 'new novel'. His last article was a substantial study on Vivant Denon, ' "Fortunes" de *Point de lendemain*', in *Australian Journal of French Studies*, XI (1974), 149-68.

Problems of Johnson's Middle Years—the 1762 Pension

James L. Clifford

The topic of this paper has been thoroughly covered by James Boswell, as well as by twentieth-century scholars annotating Boswell. What need is there for any further biographical work on Johnson? Do we not know everything that is important? And what new information that is really important can possibly turn up at this late date?

The answer to the first question I made clear some twenty years ago in my *Young Samuel Johnson*.[1] Boswell did not meet Johnson until the latter was in his fifties, when the greater part of his important writing was done, and had to rely for information about earlier years on what he could glean from those of Johnson's friends whose memories were reliable and who were willing to talk. Johnson himself did not like to reminisce about his past troubles. As a result, there are great blanks in our knowledge of Johnson's early life, and the same can be said about his middle years. Boswell cleverly covered up his ignorance as to just what Johnson was doing during long periods by extensive discussions of his works—*The Rambler, Dictionary, Rasselas,* etc.—but in places his biographical information was scanty. For example, in one year, 1761, Boswell had available only one long letter from Johnson to Baretti, and had a few details concerning minor works. And for 1760, in his first edition, he complained that he had been unable to find a single private letter written by Johnson to any of his friends. Later he found one to Langton, but the account for the year is very sparse.[2]

If Boswell was unable to find much that was useful for these years, is it possible for us to do better? He was there on the ground, and

---

[1] New York and London, 1955. (The N.Y. edition has the title *Young Sam Johnson*.)
[2] *Life of Johnson*, ed. G. B. Hill, rev. L. F. Powell, 6 vols., Oxford, 1934-50, I, 354, 357-66. (Cited hereafter as *Life*.)

had friendly connections with people who had known Johnson intimately during these years. The answer is that Boswell did not really try. He had in his own files so much fascinating material concerning Johnson's later years, which he knew to be accurate, written down right at the time, that he decided to move speedily through Johnson's early life and to concentrate on what he knew best. Moreover, almost everyone would agree that we are the richer for this decision. Boswell's long accounts of Johnson's conversation are better than anything he could have secured from others. No other biographer had available so much detailed and fascinating material to work with. And so the fact that the first two-thirds of Johnson's life occupies only about one-sixth of the total work, while the last third occupies five-sixths, and that the final eight years take up almost half the pages, does not trouble most readers. Although the work is obviously ill-balanced, what we have is a unique personal account of a great colourful figure. Nevertheless, for many modern readers there is a desire to know something more about how Johnson actually lived while he was producing his major works.

There are large blanks to fill, but is there any chance of doing so at this late date? How can a modern scholar do the job? I would be the first to answer that it is not an easy task. Without doubt there are very perplexing problems which are virtually unsolvable. But the modern scholar does have a wealth of information unavailable to Boswell. There are diaries of people who knew Johnson—some only recently discovered—which Boswell could not have consulted. There is the journal of Thomas Hollis, now at Harvard University,[3] and still not published, and only a few years ago there were discovered in a Scottish bank over fifty letters and documents once in the possession of Charlotte Lennox, one of Johnson's good friends during his middle years, none of which had ever been seen by scholars before 1964.[4] Of the thirteen letters of Johnson, at least eight were written before 1763. Indeed, the Lennox collection is a treasure trove. And there are other correspondences, such as that of Thomas Birch in the British Museum, which have never thoroughly been studied by active Boswellian editors.

Another mammoth source of information, never completely used by Birkbeck Hill and other eminent scholars, is the wealth of surviving newspapers from London and the provinces during the

---

[3] See my essay 'Some Problems of Johnson's Obscure Middle Years', in *Johnson, Boswell and Their Circle. Essays Presented to L. F. Powell*, ed. Mary Lascelles and others, Oxford, 1965, pp. 101-6.

[4] All the letters have been printed by Duncan Isles in 'The Lennox Collection', *Harvard Library Bulletin*, XVIII (October 1970), 317-44; XIX (January, April, October 1971), 36-60, 165-86, 416-35.

1750s.[5] Boswell obviously did not have easy access to them, but these papers contain many contemporary facts which can be related to Johnson's life during the middle years.

Furthermore, as I have complained many times, there are other major sources of information which I believe do still exist, but which we cannot find. There are the papers of John Newbery, the publisher, which we know were in family hands late in the nineteenth century, and perhaps even up to 1929, but which now have completely disappeared.[6] They may be gathering dust in a closet or attic in some English country house. And there are the originals of the letters of Elizabeth Carter, censored and mangled by her nephew, their first editor, who candidly admitted that he left out all personal details. These may well contain much that is new about Johnson in the 1750s. I still hope to find them some day.

And merely as a digression, addressed to those who think that almost everything of importance which may have survived is now easily available, let me point out that despite all the fabulous discoveries of Boswell manuscripts what must have been his most prized possession, the originals of his letters from Johnson, have still not been found. All these letters he printed in the *Life*, but with some excisions, indicated by ellipses. What did he feel he had to leave out? We will never know unless the originals turn up in some solicitor's office, or some hidden recess at Malahide Castle or Auchinlech. Boswell would hardly have destroyed these priceless treasures. But what did he do with them?

I should have cited enough to reflect the excitement of the search for lost manuscripts, and the accompanying frustrations. Sometimes when my friends ask when my account of Johnson's middle years will be published, I use as an excuse for the long delay the hope that some of these caches of documents will come to light. There is always the fear that the day after I send in final corrected page proofs someone will write me that he has discovered the Newbery papers, including much about Samuel Johnson. It could happen. But let me assure you that I do mean finally to complete my account of the fourteen years of the Great Cham's life from 1749, where I left him in *Young Samuel*, to 1763, when he met Boswell in Tom Davies's back parlour.

This discussion of the many reasons why a biographer's work is never done leads me to my principal subject—an example of how

---

[5] See for example, Roy M. Wiles, 'The Contemporary Distribution of Johnson's *Rambler*', *Eighteenth-Century Studies*, II (1968-9), 155-71; and his *Freshest Advices: Early Provincial Newspapers in England*, Columbus, Ohio, 1965.

[6] See *Johnson, Boswell and Their Circle*, pp. 101-6.

newly-discovered evidence may tend to complicate rather than simplify a biographer's existence. My special topic is the pension of £300 a year which Johnson received from King George III in July 1762. It was the granting of this award which produced the Johnson so perfectly described by Boswell in the *Life*. Released from financial pressures and the necessity to earn a living doing all kinds of journalistic chores, Johnson could become the relaxed, eccentric talker whom all of us know.

But who first thought up the idea of giving Johnson a pension? Who convinced the Earl of Bute, the first minister, that this would be a wise move? What were the various problems involved? In the *Life* Boswell sums up the principal facts, insofar as he could discover them, and gives us the basic story.[7] But since Boswell's day much new evidence has turned up.

Perhaps one should begin with Johnson's *Dictionary* in 1755, since it could be cited as the basic cause for the pension as well as of some of the difficulties. These two great folio volumes certainly became the foundation of Johnson's reputation—'Dictionary Johnson' he was called—and although many at the time admired him more for his moral essays in the *Rambler* and *Idler* and for his eastern tale, *Rasselas*, it was chiefly as a lexicographer that his reputation spread. More and more foreign visitors to London wished to meet the man who had, almost single-handed, produced the first authoritative dictionary of the English language.

In the *Dictionary*, however, Johnson showed clearly his own personal prejudices, his scorn of the Hanoverian régime, and his dislike of the whole pension system, as it was being practised in his time. 'Pension' he defined as 'an allowance made to any one without an equivalent. In England it is generally understood to mean pay given to a state hireling for treason to his country'. And 'pensioner' had two meanings: (1) 'one who is supported by an allowance paid at the will of another; a dependant', and (2) 'a slave of state hired by a stipend to obey his master'. To be sure, the infinitive 'to pension' is merely described as 'to support by an arbitrary allowance', but even here the adjective 'arbitrary' is pejorative. Among the quotations used to illustrate these meanings are two from Pope's satires. Johnson is clearly allying himself with the Opposition writers, who watched the cynical use of the system by George II and his ministers. There could be no mistaking where Johnson stood in 1755.

As long as George II remained on the throne no one would have thought it possible for Johnson himself to be considered for a pen-

---

[7] See *Life*, I, 372-7.

sion. He hardly satisfied the usual requirements. To be sure, there were some who wished that there were some way it could be accomplished. In the 1759 *Annual Register*, when reviewing *Rasselas*, Edmund Burke closed with the sad observation that the author, Johnson, had 'done so much for the improvement of our taste and our morals, and employed a great part of his life in an astonishing work for the fixing the language of this nation; whilst this nation, which admires his works, and profits by them, has done nothing for the author'.[8]

But with the accession of George III in the autumn of 1760, there was a new spirit abroad. Here was a young ruler, born and educated in England, who kept insisting that he was above party domination; with a chief minister, the Earl of Bute, who did not belong to the old Whig oligarchy. Some people obviously decided that the time was ripe to push Johnson for a pension. And at least one person decided to do something about it.

When I was in London in 1965, one day I chanced to find in the British Museum manuscript room a 'Register of Correspondence' of the Earl of Bute from 1739 through 1762.[9] In 1761, for 15 November, is listed 'Anonymous to the Earl of Bute Recommends Mr. Sam Johnson to the Notice of His Majesty as Being worthy of a Pension'. Just that! At once I wrote to the present Marquess of Bute asking if this letter was in his collection, and received a friendly reply from his librarian saying that she could not find the manuscript, and assumed that it had been sold or disposed of in some way in the nineteenth century. But she did send me everything she could find in the archives relating to the affair. And so, reluctantly, I was forced to give up any hope of ever seeing what was in that anonymous epistle. Meanwhile I had no inkling of the fact that hidden away in the Boswell Papers at Yale there was a copy sent to him by Bute's son, which Boswell had never used or mentioned.[10]

Then a little over a year ago, without any warning, I received another letter from the librarian referring to our earlier correspondence and saying that a few days before, when looking for something else completely unrelated to Johnson, she had stumbled on the anonymous letter of 1761, and was sending me a copy.[11] After

---

[8] II (1759), 479.
[9] In British Museum, Add. MS 36, 796.
[10] MS Yale C 3182. Printed in full in Marshall Waingrow, *The Correspondence and other Papers of James Boswell Relating to the Making of the Life of Johnson*, New York and London, 1969, pp. 512-15.
[11] Letter from Catherine Armet, of Mount Stuart, Rothesay, Isle of Bute, 18 May 1972. Her original letter was of 1 November 1965. There are a few minor differences between the original text of the anonymous epistle and the copy sent to Boswell.

almost seven years, purely by chance, the original manuscript was now available (Plate I).

What is it like? Does it settle anything? Frankly, I must confess that at first it seemed to set up more problems than it settled. But the more one studies it the more interesting it becomes. Briefly, it is a rather wordy and repetitious letter of some seven pages, and one wonders if the Earl ever had the patience to read it through. Dated from Cambridge, 15 November 1761, it was apparently delivered to Bute's office in London by hand, with a note on the outside indicating that it was for the minister's eyes alone. Although the writer confesses that he has never met Johnson, and does not know any of his Lordship's close associates, he insists that he is writing in a feigned hand so that his identity can never be discovered. Over and over he reiterates that he has no personal involvement in the suggestion, and is only making it for the reputation of England, to enhance his Lordship's own reputation, and to save a worthy man from penury and want.

After a somewhat flowery beginning, where he points out that England is now the happiest nation in the world, with the best of rulers, and the most liberty for individuals, he maintains that the one thing wanting to ensure national glory is some patronage for those who have 'distinguished themselves in the literary way'. And specifically he points to Samuel Johnson, a 'truly great author', who nevertheless has been exposed to the 'conflicts of indigence, & want'; Johnson has 'not only immortalized as it were our language: but in every work that he has produced has done his utmost to the promotion of every moral, & religious duty'. Yet this virtuous man 'still remains unpensioned, & left to procure himself a precarious subsistence by the bounty of booksellers'.

The writer makes clear that he is well aware of a possible objection to any help for Johnson, a well-known Tory, with reputed Jacobite sympathies, but tries to get around this difficulty in a strange manner. 'If it be objected that his political principles render him an unfit object of his majestys favour, I would only say that he is to be the more pitied on this account, & that it may sometimes happen that our opinions however erroneous are not always in our own power.' But remembering the King's well-publicised plan to do away with party distinctions, he suggests that help for Johnson might be a way of accomplishing such a transformation.

The writer keeps emphasising his admiration for Johnson as a truly great man, 'tho' tarnished with some human failings', and points out that others less worthy have been given pensions. His Majesty was reputed to have conferred a pension of £200 on an Oxford biblical scholar, Benjamin Kennicott, who was collating various ancient manuscripts. Yet without calling into question such an award, the writer could not resist making an obvious comparison.

> Yet what are the merits of this man compared to those of Johnson? Will the world be in possession of any one undiscovered moral or religious truth, when he [viz. Kennicott] has completed his scheme? but with respect to the other, I may venture to say, that he hath done more by his writings to the advancement of real piety, & valuable learning than almost any other man now living.

How much better it is, the writer continues, to reward a worthy man while he is living and not merely to pay empty tributes after his death. Then comes a rather devious insinuation. If only Johnson could be given a pension of £200 or £300 a year it would 'deliver this great author from every fear of penury, & indigence, would fill his heart with gratitude, & at the same time instigate him to shew himself worthy of the royal favour by every means in his power'. Is the writer really suggesting that once given financial support Johnson might even voluntarily come around to supporting the King in various ways? To be sure, the writer makes clear that he has no illusions that Johnson could be hired to do any particular jobs. And there follows a fascinating kind of excuse and explanation.

> I am told that his political principles make him incapable of being in any place of trust, by incapacitating him from qualifying himself for any such office.—but a pension my Lord requires no such performances—& my Lord it would seem but a just condescension to human infirmity, that the man, who has endeavoured in such a forcible manner to correct all our failings, & errors, should be excused one himself.

Having now made his chief point, the writer apologises profusely for keeping his Lordship so long from his public business, expresses the hope that what he has said may not sound like the outpourings of a madman, and concludes with the claim that his only desire has been to help a good man.

And so the long epistle ends. For the modern scholar there are many important questions which at once stand out, some of which may be answered eventually, and others which may be unsolvable. Obviously any complete identification of the anonymous writer, who insists that he has never met either Johnson or Bute, and who claims to be using a disguised handwriting, would appear to be very difficult. Without some later confession, which appears never to have been made, all we can do is guess. Still, there are many clues. And I do have a number of possible suspects.

If we may believe the anonymous writer's claim that he is writing from Cambridge, and I somehow think that we may, this narrows the field considerably. Johnson in 1761 had never been to Cambridge, but his published work could obviously have inspired admiration there as elsewhere. And when Johnson four years later, in 1765, did finally visit Cambridge, he was well received. Could the anonymous writer have been one of those who met Johnson then? It certainly is a possibility.

When I was first faced with this problem, I came up at once with what seemed to me to be an excellent solution. This was Richard Farmer, an active young classical tutor at Emmanuel College. In the autumn of 1761 he was twenty-six years old and had achieved considerable local reputation as a scholar and antiquary. An enthusiastic Shakespearian, he later published in 1767 an *Essay on the Learning of Shakespeare*, still read with interest by twentieth-century scholars. In 1775 he became Master of Emmanuel, was later Vice-Chancellor of the university, and refused a bishopric.

Although Farmer had not met Johnson in 1761, he probably had read the *Rambler* and *Idler* essays, had used the *Dictionary*, and was eagerly awaiting Johnson's edition of Shakespeare.[12] Moreover, in the late summer of 1761 he must have heard a lot about Johnson from Thomas Percy, who came to Cambridge in August to copy old ballads. From Percy's diary we know that he met Farmer at Emmanuel, and later they became good friends. Their surviving correspondence has been edited by Cleanth Brooks. Amusingly enough, Brooks in his Introduction points out the Johnsonian qualities of young Farmer. 'He possessed a powerful and vigorous mind coupled with a carelessness that could be taken for indolence. . . . His books, like Johnson's were often to be seen scattered upon the floor . . . He even had Johnson's habit of muttering to himself as he walked.'[13] There can be little doubt that in Farmer's long talks with Percy at this time, and possibly later in the autumn of 1761, Johnson must have often been discussed—his great gifts, his sad financial plight, and his inability to move forward with his Shakespeare edition. Percy could well have passed on to his new scholarly friend many details very similar to those which appear in the anonymous letter in November. Indeed, Percy may unwittingly have been the starting point of the whole episode. If only a guess,

---

[12] Unfortunately in the Catalogue of the sale of Farmer's library after his death, *Bibliotheca Farmeriana*, London, 1798, there are listed no early copies of works written by Johnson before 1761, but he did have many later copies and a complete edition of Johnson's works. I owe this information to Paul Korshin and Thomas Treadwell.

[13] *The Percy Letters: the Correspondence of Thomas Percy and Richard Farmer*, ed. Cleanth Brooks, Baton Rouge, La., 1946, pp. vi, 12-13.

it does appear to make sense. But I doubt that Farmer would have told Percy what he was doing.

All that we know next about Farmer is that a year or so later, after Johnson had received his pension, Percy wrote to his Emmanuel friend on 9 October 1762:

> I have lately heard an account how Johnson came by his Pension: It seems my Lord Bute had procured a pension of the same value for Hume: and some of his friends (my Lord Melcome, say some) remonstrating, that to prevent an odium he ought [e]qually to distinguish English Literati: he t[hought] it necessary to do this for one of the most eminent, & at the same time, most necessitous of them.[14]

Had Farmer possibly asked Percy if he knew just what had happened? It almost sounds as if he had. Percy at least sensed Farmer's intense interest.

It was not until almost three years later that Farmer met Johnson in the flesh, when the latter made his first and only trip to Cambridge. Their meeting, so the Reverend B. N. Turner described it, was 'uncommonly joyous on both sides'.[15] On 25 February 1765 Farmer described the meeting in a letter to Percy, exhibiting the same kind of split that had appeared in the anonymous letter—admiration offset with some doubts, respect for intellectual capacity balanced by 'pitiable infirmities both in body and mind'. In writing to Percy the emphasis was on Johnson's 'dogmatisms' and 'prejudices' and his extraordinary character, but Farmer was writing to someone who already knew all this, and there was no need to stress Johnson's merits, as would have been necessary when writing to the principal minister. The point I am making is that Farmer's reaction was essentially what one might have expected, assuming that he did write the anonymous letter in 1761.

Unfortunately, there is one major difficulty in this ascription of the letter to Farmer—the handwriting. Now, of course, the writer insists that he is disguising his handwriting. But various scholars to whom I have shown the letter and authentic letters of Farmer have insisted that it was highly unlikely that the same man could have written both.[16] Farmer's real handwriting is so distinctive that he could hardly have produced the more regular and consistent hand that was used by the anonymous writer. To be sure, Farmer might

[14] B.M. Add. MS 28,222, f.4.
[15] *Life*, I, 518. For John Sharp's account of the visit, see pp. 517-18.
[16] For help in attempting to identify the writer I am deeply indebted to J. C. T. Oates and E. S. Leedham-Green of Cambridge, Frederick and Marion Pottle and Cleanth Brooks of Yale, Marshall Waingrow of Claremont, and others.

have used a friend or an amanuensis to do the writing. Just the same, I keep hoping to find someone whose handwriting seems to fit. Amusingly enough, Thomas Percy's is much closer. Could he have written the letter, claiming not to know Johnson, put Cambridge at the top, and sent it to Bute? Or what about the other men at Cambridge who met Johnson in 1765—Baptist Noel Turner, John Sharp, and others?

And might the watermarks of the paper used in the original letter help? Frederick Pottle seems to think so.[17] And why did Boswell never mention that he had a copy of the letter, and never refer to it in his revised third edition? Could it be that he suspected that Percy was involved, and he knew how averse Percy was to any publicity, Percy having forced Boswell to take out various things about him in the first edition of the *Life*?[18] And finally did the letter have any influence at all on the final decision?

To the last question the answer must be, regrettably, that it is impossible to tell. No accounts of the episode ever mention it, though at least it could have prepared the way in Bute's mind. When others later brought up the proposal he was ready to consider the possibility seriously.

Unfortunately there the matter stood, with nothing done, during the winter, and spring of 1762. But apparently some of Johnson's close friends were thinking of possible ways to put pressure on those in charge. Exactly what happened will probably never be known. There are too many conflicting stories, none of them easy to substantiate. And whether Johnson himself had any knowledge of what was going on is also a mystery. Both Arthur Murphy and Thomas Sheridan later claimed to have talked to him about the possibility,[19] though Johnson may well have never taken their remarks seriously. Certainly Johnson had no great admiration for the Earl of Bute. James Elphinston claimed that once when dining with Johnson, not long before the pension was given, he asked his host why he so obviously disliked Bute. 'Because', Johnson replied, 'he gave the king a wrong education. He had only taught him', added Johnson, 'to *draw a tree*'.[20] Nevertheless, like most others of the day, Johnson had great hopes of what the new King might do for the country.

[17] Suggested in a letter of 12 April 1973. Through the kindness of Miss Armet I have seen a photograph of the watermark, which is a Lion 'VRYHEYT' on standard Dutch foolscap, similar to No. 84 in W. A. Churchill, *Watermarks in Paper in the XVII and XVIII Centuries*, Amsterdam, 1935. My Cambridge correspondents tell me that this was a popular paper; thus it can probably be of little help in identifying the anonymous writer.
[18] See Waingrow, *Correspondence*, pp. 597-8, 310, 313-14, etc.
[19] *Life*, I, 374.
[20] William Shaw, *Memoirs of the Life and Writings of Samuel Johnson*, London, 1785, pp. 135-6.

What started the final sequence of events is again far from clear. Later writers, perhaps using *post hoc* reasoning, suggested that it was the bad reputation produced by Bute's many grants to his Scottish supporters which gave his close associate Alexander Wedderburne the idea that a pension for someone like Johnson, a well-known hater of the Scots, might be a clever way to offset these sniping attacks. Surviving satirical prints of the spring of 1762 show clearly that Bute's preference for his northern followers was already a popular theme.[21] As a character in one of the prints (No. 3865) puts it, 'I wish I had been born in a colder Climate for I find Merit lies North'. Moreover, in other prints which appeared somewhat later the term 'Scotch pensioners' is often used. Undoubtedly the widespread dislike of some of Bute's recent actions had something to do with the decision to reward the compiler of the English Dictionary. Thomas Percy certainly thought so.[22]

If Wedderburne saw the possible value of such an award, he also was clearly aware of some difficulties. He knew Johnson's prejudices and his occasional violence. Whether Bute had ever shown him the anonymous letter received the preceding autumn can never be established, but I suspect that he had. Wedderburne's way of proceeding suggests as much. In any event, he moved cautiously and with great skill.

Once Bute and the King had agreed on the general idea, probably some time in early July, the sequence of events was something like this. Because of Johnson's known independent spirit and intransigence at times, it was thought best to approach him carefully. Wedderburne himself preferred not to be the one who made the offer, for he feared that if Johnson should be uncertain of just what was meant he might knock his visitor down with a huge folio, as he had done the bookseller Osborne. Consequently Wedderburne asked Arthur Murphy to be the emissary. At least so Murphy claims.[23]

Exactly what happened after that is not certain, one reason being that Murphy's account was written long afterward, with no contemporary records to consult. But it is clear that Murphy was delighted by his assignment and on the week-end 16-18 July he

---

[21] See the *Catalogue of Prints and Drawings in the British Museum. Division I: Political and Personal Satires*, ed. F. G. Stephens, London, 1883, Vol. IV: No. 3843, 'The State BALLANCE'; No. 3865, '*Britannia guided by Justice &c.c.c.*'; and later ones—No. 3844, 'The Hungry Mob of Scriblers and Etchers' (conjecturally dated 26 May 1762, but must be after July, since Johnson is included); No. 3885, 'A Wonderful Sight'; No. 3979, 'John a Boot's Asses'; and No. 4068, 'THE IRISH Stubble alia(s) Bubble GOOSE'.

[22] B.M. Add. MS 28,222, f.4.

[23] *An Essay on the Life and Genius of Samuel Johnson*, London, 1792; repr. in *Johnsonian Miscellanies*, ed. G. B. Hill, 2 vols., Oxford, 1879. Here I, 417-19.

went to see Johnson in his chambers in Inner Temple Lane, and 'By slow and studied approaches the message was disclosed. Johnson made a long pause: he asked if it was seriously intended? He fell into a profound meditation, and his own definition of a pensioner occurred to him'.[24] When Murphy insisted that Johnson certainly did not fit the well-known definition, Johnson suggested that they meet again at the Mitre Tavern, at which time he would deliver his decision.

From other accounts we know that Johnson at once consulted Joshua Reynolds and other close friends, seeking their advice as to the propriety of his accepting this royal favour, remembering his definitions in the *Dictionary* and his known anti-Hanoverian position.[25] Reynolds at once told him that he could see no objection at all, since this was a reward for literary merit. The definitions were not applicable to his situation. Evidently Johnson did not hesitate any longer, and by Sunday, 18 July, he had given up 'all his scruples' and decided to accept the award. The next day, Monday, 19 July, Murphy was at Johnson's chambers soon after nine o'clock in the morning, 'got Johnson up and dressed in due time', took him to see Wedderburne, who showed him the documents, and then conducted him to see the Earl of Bute.[26] We can be sure of the date since Johnson mentions it in a letter to his step-daughter, Lucy Porter, written the next Saturday.[27]

Happily, the meeting went off very well. Johnson expressed his sincere thanks for his Majesty's bounty, and insisted that he was highly honoured. Bute behaved in a handsome manner, and twice repeated the point that the pension was being given Johnson 'not for anything you are to do, but for what you have done'. According to Charles Burney, Johnson told him that this was said in answer to a question which he himself had put, before formally accepting the intended bounty: 'Pray, my lord, what am I expected to do for this pension?'[28] Another version of just what the Earl said comes from Murphy, who phrased it this way: 'No, Sir', said Lord Bute, 'it is not offered to you for having dipped your pen in faction, nor with a *design* that you ever should'.[29] From Johnson's point of view it was all very clear that the pension was given as a reward for past labours, and not future political support. And Johnson's close

[24] Ibid., I, 418.
[25] *Life*, I, 374.
[26] Murphy, in *Johnsonian Miscellanies*, I, 418, and n. 5.
[27] *The Letters of Samuel Johnson*, ed. R. W. Chapman, Oxford, 1952, No. 144 (24 July 1762).
[28] *Life*, I, 375, n. 1.
[29] Murphy, in *Johnsonian Miscellanies*, I, 418; also *Life*, I, 429.

friends all realised that this was true. But others, as we shall see, were not so sure.

On Monday evening, after the interview, Johnson regaled Reynolds and other friends with an account of what had happened. The next day he despatched a formal letter of thanks to Bute for His Majesty's generosity.

> Bounty always receives part of its value from the manner in which it is bestowed; your Lordship's kindness includes every circumstance that can gratify delicacy, or enforce obligation. You have conferred your favours on a man who has neither alliance nor interest, who has not merited them by services, nor courted them by officiousness; you have spared him the shame of solicitation, and the anxiety of suspense.
>
> What has been thus elegantly given, will, I hope, not be reproachfully enjoyed; I shall endeavour to give your Lordship the only recompense which generosity desires,—the gratification of finding that your benefits are not improperly bestowed.[30]

Public announcement in the newspapers came on Thursday, 22 July, when the *St James's Chronicle* carried the statement 'His Majesty has been graciously pleased to settle a Pension of 300 l per Annum, on Mr. Samuel Johnson, a Gentleman well known in the Literary World'. Other papers over the weekend repeated the announcement.[31]

As might have been expected, Johnson's personal friends and admirers naturally applauded the decision; those who were on the other side politically, or who disliked him personally, were shocked, and were quick to point out the inconsistency between his definitions of 'pension' in the *Dictionary* and his accepting one himself.

Evidence of this division may be easily found in the correspondences of the day, and in the local newspapers. Even among provincials who had never met Johnson one could find enthusiastic admirers. Witness William Bewley, a Norfolk surgeon, who wrote to his friend Charles Burney on 4 August:

> I rejoice at the prospect which the papers give us of Johnson's enjoying at last a decent independence in the eve of his days, in consequence of a pension from the Crown. Does this bounty flow immediately from the Throne?—*ex mero motu?* But I am arguing perhaps like the German Doctors about the Golden Tooth. Does such a pension really exist?[32]

And for clear evidence of the opposing reaction one has only to

---

[30] *Letters*, No. 143 (20 July 1762).
[31] *St James's Chronicle*, 20-22 July 1762; *Public Advertiser*, 23 July; *London Evening Post*, 22-24 July; *Gloucester Journal*, 26 July, etc.
[32] I owe this information to Roger Lonsdale of Balliol College, Oxford. The letter is owned by James M. Osborn of Yale.

look at the unpublished letters between Thomas Birch and his patron, Philip Yorke, 1st Earl of Hardwicke, a staunch Whig of the old dispensation.[33] While the Earl was in the country when parliament was not in session, Birch every Saturday sent him a long letter of London gossip and news. Thus on 24 July, after complaining about a recent Royal present of £50 to John Kennedy, a Derbyshire clergyman who had dedicated to the King 'an extravagant System of Astronomical Chronology deduc'd from the Old Testament, & which none but an Hutchinsonian can pretend to understand' (amusingly enough, Johnson had written the dedication for Kennedy!) Birch added: 'Sam. Johnson likewise, who would lately scarce have own'd the King's title, is now a Royal Pensioner with 300 £ a year. Monsr. Colbert was more delicate in his recommendations to Lewis XIV of Men of Genius & Learning than the Great Courtiers of more modern Times'.[34] Two weeks later Birch commented again to his patron:

> Sam. Johnson's becoming a pensioner has occasioned his Dictionary to be turn'd to in the Word *Pension* thus defined by him; 'An Allowance made to any one without an Equivalent. In England it is generally understood to mean Pay given to a State-hireling for Treason to his Country.' I do not know, whether the Acceptance of his pension obliges him to an Oath to the Government. If he now takes that Oath, I know what to determine about the Conscience of this *third Cato*.[35]

Others, too, hit upon the obvious discrepancy, but it was not until some weeks later that sharp attacks began to appear in print. The most vigorous came in the radical opposition weekly, the *North Briton*, edited by John Wilkes and Charles Churchill. At the end of No. XI, which appeared on 14 August, and which was largely given over to attacks on Bute and the periodical, *The Auditor*, which supported him, Wilkes added a paragraph stirred up by Johnson's pension.

> I hope *Johnson* is *a writer of reputation*, because as a writer he has just got a pension of 300 l *per ann.* . . . I hope too that he is become a friend to this constitution and the family on the throne, now he is thus nobly provided for: but I know he has much to *unwrite*, more to *unsay*, before he will be forgiven by the true friends of the present illustrious family, for what he has been *writing* and *saying* for many years.[36]

[33] B.M. Add. MS 35, 399.
[34] Ibid., f.307.
[35] Ibid., f.319—7 August 1762.
[36] Quoted by George Nobbe, *The North Briton: a Study in Political Propaganda*, New York, 1939, p. 74. If William Shaw is to be believed (*Memoirs*, pp. 116-17), Johnson did read this and remembered it years later.

Birch in his weekly letter to Lord Hardwicke refers to *The Auditor* and Arthur Murphy, its editor, and then adds: 'The *North Briton* of to day not only attacks him [Murphy], but likewise Sam. Johnson, the new pensioner, who has been lately seen at Lord Bute's Levee'.[37]

But Wilkes's most vigorous and penetrating attack came the next week, in No. XII of 21 August, which came out while Johnson was in Devonshire with Joshua Reynolds. (If Johnson ever read through this issue, one can understand his later reluctance to dine with Wilkes.) Because of his collaborator Charles Churchill's later better known attacks, many have assumed that he was the author of this number of the *North Briton*, but Wilkes later confessed that it was his.[38] Almost the entire number is centered on Johnson's pension, with numerous references to his *Dictionary* quotations, and an ironic suggestion as to Johnson's earlier position.

> Mr *Johnson's* many writings in the cause of liberty, his steady attachment to the present Royal Family, his gentleman-like compliments to his Majesty's grandfather, and his decent treatment of the parliament, intitle him to a share of the royal bounty. It is a matter of astonishment that *no notice* has till now been taken of him by government for some of the most *extraordinary* productions, which appeared with the name of *Samuel Johnson*: a name sacred to *George and Liberty*.[39]

Birch refers to this issue in his weekly letter the same day,[40] and it doubtless received much publicity.

It was stringent enough to draw strong protests from Johnson's defenders. The most detailed, as well as the most effective, came in an anonymous letter signed 'A South Briton' which appeared in the *St James's Chronicle* for 2 September.[41] The editor of the newspaper printed it all, as an example of how he was willing to give both sides of an argument, although at the same time testifying to his belief that the writer was too severe in his rebuttal. In many ways it is an interesting piece, which deserves more critical examination, even if the author has never been identified.

It has certain resemblances with the other anonymous letter of the autumn before. Both letters begin and end in much the same way—starting with regret over the lack of recognition in the past of Fine Arts, Literature, Science, Morality and Religion, and ending

---

[37] B.M. Add. MS 35,399, f.323—14 August 1762.
[38] See Nobbe, *North Briton*, p. 75.
[39] Ibid., pp. 83-4.
[40] B.M. Add MS 35,399, f.332.
[41] Issue of 31 August-2 September, p. 2. The *St James's Chronicle* had reprinted *The North Briton*, No. XII in its issue of 19-21 August, pp. 3-4.

with a disclaimer of any connection whatsoever with Johnson. Thus 'A South Briton' concludes: 'P.S. I solemnly declare I have not the least Connection with Mr. Johnson. The Indignation I conceived at seeing a Man of such Reputation and Abilities abused by a little barking Party-Cur, was the sole Cause of my troubling the Public with this Letter. Mr. Johnson himself knows nothing of it'. In the main body the two letters are quite different in content—the earlier concentrating on Johnson's failings and merits, and his need for financial help; the latter stressing the failings and corruption of the former administration. To be sure, Johnson's major works are mentioned—the *Dictionary*, *Rambler* and *Idler*—'Performances held universally in the greatest Esteem'—and the writer admits certain 'Disadvantages of Person' in Johnson, but insists that 'When I first heard . . . that a Gratuity was conferred on him, I could not help breaking out into a Rapture of Praise, and blessing the Royal Hand that shewed so worthy a Regard to real Learning and Merit'.

As to the definition of 'pension' and other matters stressed by Wilkes in his damning attack, the writer suggests that in the next edition of the *Dictionary* Johnson merely add

> N.B. The above Explanation was wrote in the R[eign] of G[eorge] the S[econd]; since the Acc[essio]n of G[eorge] the Th[ird], it bears an additional Meaning, *viz.* an annual Reward from the Prince, &c. as above; and a Reward given to learned Men for Merit, Worth, and Genius, &c. Qualities little regarded at the Time this Dictionary was first pub[lishe]d.

As a defence of Johnson and as a vigorous reply to the editors of the *North Briton*, the 'South Briton's' letter is very effective. Actually it contains one of the most devastating descriptions of ministerial chicanery and corruption under George II that one can find anywhere. With relentless vigour he piles up the descriptions of his opponent's qualifications—corruption, jobbing, venality, contracting, electioneering, avarice and ambition, ignorance, extravagance, rapacity, dulness, malevolence, subtle artifices, conceit, low cunning. These are the qualities which used to be rewarded. Now we hope all this is to be changed.

With such a savage political attack, I fear that there is little possibility of assigning the 'South Briton's' letter in the *St James's Chronicle* to the author writing from Cambridge who recommended Johnson in the first place. Instead, alas, we have two fascinating anonymous pieces connected with Johnson's pension to try to identify.

A few days after the *St James's Chronicle* defence, in the August *Gentleman's Magazine*, which came out early in September, Johnson's old friend and colleague John Hawkesworth, now acting as general editor of the periodical, in his usual section of excerpts from various other papers during the month, had only this to say about Wilkes's notorious piece: 'The *North Briton*, No. XII, has thought fit to insult and vilify the highest characters, for encouraging literary merit without regard to party principles'.[42] Birch in his letter to Hardwicke on 4 September commented:

> Hawkesworth, in the last Gentleman's Magazine, is angry, your Ldp sees, with the *North Briton* for animadverting upon the giving a pension to Sam. Johnson, which the candid & modest Superintendant of the Magazine stiles *encouraging literary Merit without regard to party principles*; a gentle Expression for furious Jacobitism. A Friend of Johnson's told me, that when he mention'd to him the Design of giving him a pension, he answer'd with a supercilious Air, 'If they offer me a small Matter, I will not accept of it.'[43]

To which Hardwicke answered from the country on 7 September:

> I took notice of Hawkesworth's most indecent Remark on the Pension given to his Fellow Labourer in Declamatory Impert'nence Johnson; & I presume from several symptoms in his *Collection*, that He flatters himself with the honor of standing next [? Oars in the] literary List. Both He & the others have changed their *Livery* lately & Let them Wear Whose they will, I shall have a most soverign Contempt for such Hackney Sycophants & Scriblers.[44]

The best known attack came in Churchill's third book of *The Ghost*, which appeared on Thursday, 23 September.[45] Johnson, as 'Pomposo', had been derided in earlier parts of the poem, for his supposed credulity in believing the Cock-Lane Ghost story, and other weaknesses. Now in the third part, which Birch in his letter of 25 September found inferior to the first two, Churchill lashed out at Pomposo for accepting a pension.

> How to all Principles untrue,
> Nor fix'd to *old* Friends, nor to *New*,
> He damns the *Pension*, which he takes,
> And loves the Stuart he forsakes.[46]

In other political caricatures and prints, Johnson is usually seen fawning on Bute, with '300L a year' attached to him somewhere.[47]

---

[42] *G.M.*, XXXII (August 1762), 379.
[43] B.M. Add. MS 35,399, f.344.
[44] Ibid., f.346 (the word 'Oars' and the two following are uncertain, but 'standing next oars' was a common expression at the time).
[45] See ibid., f.361.
[46] *The Poetical Works of Charles Churchill*, ed. Douglas Grant, Oxford, 1956, p. 127.
[47] See *Catalogue of Prints and Drawings*, esp. 'The Hungry Mob of Scriblers and Etchers' (IV, 3844) and 'John a Boot's Asses' (IV, 3979).

And in verse satires supporting the liberal Whig position 'Pensioner Johnson' is rarely omitted. As a sample I quote from an amusing later work entitled *The Theatres: a Poetical Dissection*, written supposedly by Sir Nicholas Nipclose, Baronet. After some hits at Johnson's *Irene*, 'a turgid, tasteless tragic' work, and his egotism, 'Who, in his own opinion, sits supreme, /Whatever stile he takes, whatever theme', the satirist continues:

> JOHNSON, who once, beneath a virtuous face,
> Gave venal pensioners to vile disgrace;
> JOHNSON, who since, more prudent grown, and old,
> Obeys the touch of all-converting gold;
> Of a court scribbler takes the paltry sphere,
> And damms his fame—for what?—three hundred pounds a year.⁴⁸

How did Johnson take such obloquy? Did he answer his attackers? Not really. He was away in Devonshire until late in September, and if any of his friends ever showed him the newspaper controversy, or some of the later satires, he never reacted publicly, or seemed emotionally affected. Some years later when Boswell mentioned 'the idle clamour' which had followed the announcement of his pension, Johnson, 'said, with a smile, "I wish my pension were twice as large, that they might make twice as much noise" '.⁴⁹

He would not answer such foolish lambasting. He had the Earl of Bute's definite assurance that the award had not been given him for future support, but solely for past writings, and he saw no reason to disbelieve him. In later editions of the *Dictionary* he never changed the definitions of 'Pension' and 'Pensioner'. He had meant what he said, and thought his own case an exception.

But what about his later political pamphlets in support of the King and his ministers? He wrote some of them in support of his friend Henry Thrale, a Member of Parliament with whom he was living a large part of the time, and all of them represented his own frank opinion at the time.⁵⁰ He never thought of them as being his response to royal generosity.

Did Bute and his ministers think they had bought a possible political supporter, or at least silenced a potential antagonist? It is

---

⁴⁸ London, 1772, p. 30 (perhaps by Francis Gentleman). In Edward Burnaby Greene's 'The Laureat' (1765), in *Poetical Essays*, London, 1772, p. 273, occur the lines:
> These the stern JOHNSON ey'd, and stalk'd along,
> The huge Colossus o'er an abject throng.
> This hand with conscious joy a PENSION bore,
> And grasp'd the idol, which it loath'd before.

⁴⁹ *Life*, I, 429, n. 2.

⁵⁰ See my *Hester Lynch Piozzi (Mrs. Thrale)*, 2nd edn rev., Oxford, 1968, p. 74; also Donald Greene's *The Politics of Samuel Johnson*, New Haven, 1960.

hard to say. They obviously had no illusions as to Johnson's immediate open support. But there is some evidence which leads one to wonder. Both Boswell and Johnson were probably unaware that the pension was paid out of a royal fund which was labelled 'Writers Political'. It was so labelled in a list made up at Pitt's request in August 1782 of 'Private Pensions, & Secret Service Money' paid out by one of the Secretaries of State or Chief Clerks of the Treasury. Johnson's name appears in this 'Private List' in the same column as a number of obvious cheap political writers.[51]

It is quite true that a little over a year later, probably in October 1763, Charles Jenkinson consulted Johnson about negotiations then in progress concerning the Peace, and left some important papers with him for his examination.[52] But Johnson did nothing about them, so that two years later Jenkinson had to write to get them back. If any of the ministers had any illusions of getting practical help from the new pensioner, this episode must have shown how vain was this false hope.

There can be no doubt as to Johnson's genuine gratitude to the King and to the Earl of Bute for their generosity, though it is not easy to document just how he showed it. Arthur Murphy told an amusing story of an argument which Johnson had with Dr William Rose, who had 'contended for the pre-eminence of the Scotch writers'. When Johnson exploded, Rose jokingly said he would name a Scottish writer, whom Johnson must acknowledge as the best in the kingdom. 'Who is that?' burst out Johnson. To which Rose replied, 'The Earl of Bute, when he wrote an order for your pension'. 'There, Sir', Johnson replied, 'you have me in the toil: to Lord Bute I must allow whatever praise you may claim for him'.[53] But whether or not Johnson ever said this is not clear. When Boswell asked him if the story were true, Johnson said he had never heard it.

Thus I end on a note of uncertainty. There is still so much we cannot settle. Who wrote the interesting anonymous letter suggesting the Pension? Who defended it so ably in the *St James's Chronicle*? Can we believe Arthur Murphy's stories? What did Johnson think about the whole affair? These are difficult questions to answer, but I still hope to be able to do so sometime. This is the way a literary biographer has to work. Nevertheless you must admit that it is all great fun.

[51] Public Record Office, 30/8/229, pt 1; in the Chatham Papers. Through the help of Donald Greene and Paul Korshin I have seen copies of the significant entries.
[52] See *The Jenkinson Papers 1760-1766*, ed. Ninetta S. Jucker, London, 1949, pp. 390-1, 203.
[53] Murphy, in *Johnsonian Miscellanies*, I, 419; see also *Life*, I, 429.

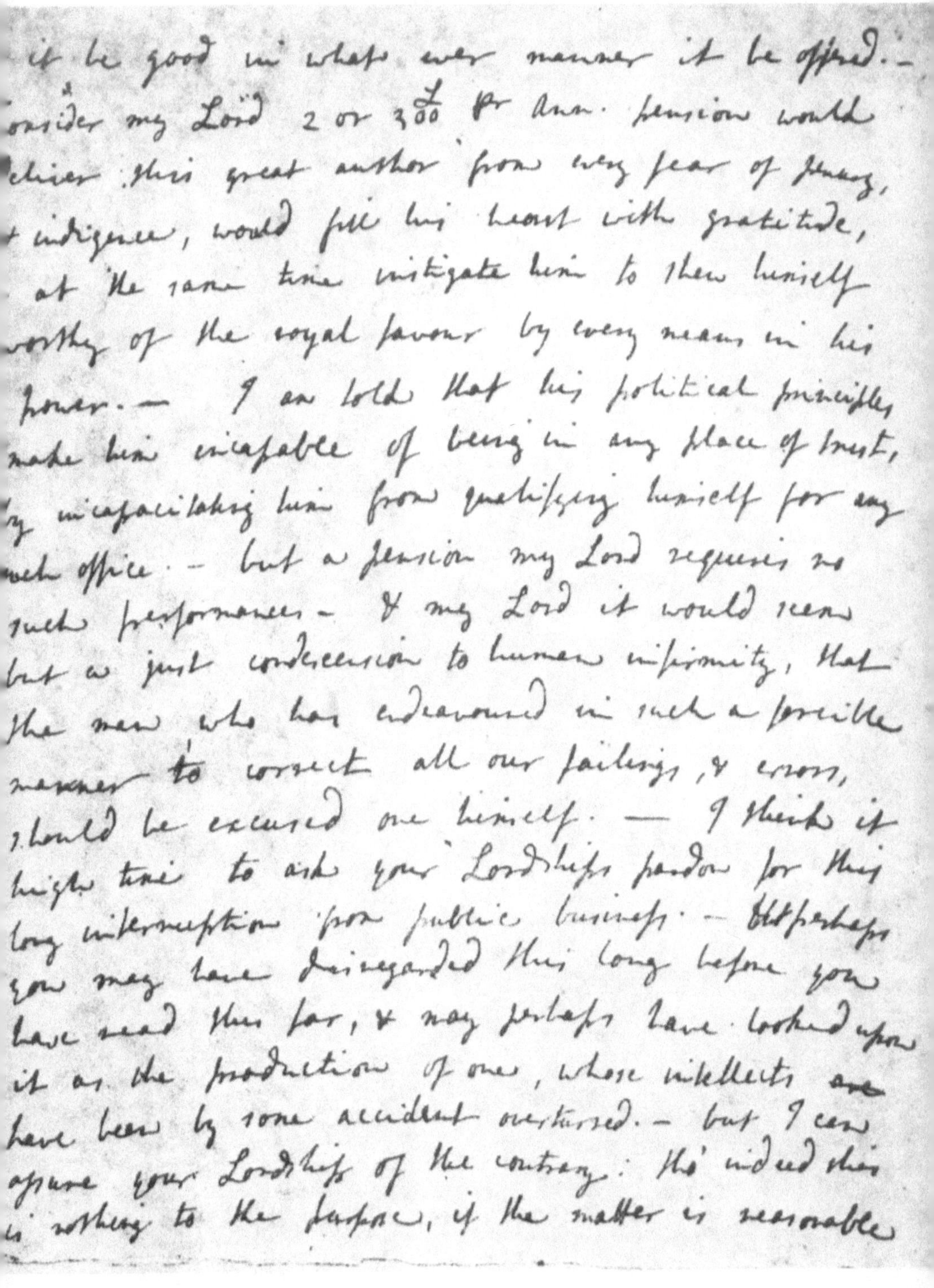

it be good in what ever manner it be offered. — Consider my Lord 2 or 300 £ pr Ann. pension would deliver this great author from every fear of penury, & indigence, would fill his heart with gratitude, at the same time instigate him to shew himself worthy of the royal favour by every means in his power. — I am told that his political principles make him incapable of being in any place of trust, by incapacitating him from qualifying himself for any such office. — but a pension my Lord requires no such performances — & my Lord it would seem but a just condescension to human infirmity, that the man who has endeavoured in such a forcible manner to correct all our failings, & errors, should be excused one himself. — I think it high time to ask your Lordship's pardon for this long interruption from public business. — but perhaps you may have disregarded this long before you have read thus far, & may perhaps have looked upon it as the production of one, whose intellects are have been by some accident overturned. — but I can assure your Lordship of the contrary: tho' indeed this is nothing to the purpose, if the matter is reasonable

Plate I Anonymous letter to the 3rd Earl of Bute. Reproduced by kind permission of the 6th Marquess of Bute.

Plate II. Boswell's Ebony Cabinet. Photograph by ... owner of [...]

Boswell's Ebony Cabinet

Mary Hyde

This cabinet is a famous piece of furniture in the literary world, an object of fascination to Boswellians, perhaps unwisely, because its importance has often been misinterpreted. The myth *will* persist that the ebony cabinet is synonymous with the 'papers of James Boswell', the biographer of Dr Samuel Johnson, and this is not so.

The ebony cabinet does *not* equate with Boswell's papers, and in the story I am going to tell, I want to differentiate between the two. It will be helpful to remember that no piece of furniture on earth could *ever* have held Boswell's enormous manuscript mass. Also, it is my opinion that much of the manuscript material was placed in the cabinet only a relatively short time before it was glimpsed by Professor Tinker and examined by Colonel Isham in the 1920s. But I am jumping ahead in the story.

Let us consider the ebony cabinet in Boswell's time. It was an heirloom which he valued greatly; indeed he usually referred to it in capital letters, as the 'Ebony Cabinet', repository of such family treasures as the collection of coins and medals, the 'rose diamonds', the fine 'lace-work' and other items of particular association and importance, including a few letters and papers.

The cabinet's appearance was—and is—impressive (Plate II). It rests on a frame of eight legs, some two and a half feet from the floor. The piece itself is almost five and a half feet in height, more than four and a half feet wide, and almost two feet deep, made of oak, veneered with ebony. At the base of the cabinet is a single locking drawer, the width of the piece. The central portion has two large doors, with lock. Inside, surrounding a small, square, central door, again with lock, are six rows of drawers, and behind the door are smaller, narrower drawers.

The cabinet originally belonged to James Boswell's great-grandmother, Veronica van Sommelsdyck, who married Alexander Bruce, second Earl of Kincardine, from whom Boswell claimed that the blood of Bruce flowed in his veins. The Earl of Kincardine, an ardent Royalist, had followed Charles II into exile in Holland. There, at The Hague, he met, courted, and won the Dutch heiress. They were married in 1659.

Two of the possessions which Veronica brought to her husband were the ebony cabinet and a fine set of dressing plate of silver gilt (most of the pieces made by Gerrit Vuystinck between 1653 and 1658). It is possible that both these splendid objects were wedding gifts, and some think that the cabinet originally housed the plate. The ebony veneer of the cabinet may well have come from Surinam, for the prime ebony area is not far away, and in Surinam the van Sommelsdyck family had large holdings. Veronica's father had been Governor there.

The cabinet and the plate descended to Veronica's third daughter, Elizabeth Bruce, who became the wife of James Boswell, grandfather of the Biographer. It was through 'Lady Betty' (as she was affectionately called) that these family heirlooms came to Auchinleck, and by that I mean the old house, which had been built about 1500. In time, Lady Betty bequeathed the cabinet and the plate to her son, Alexander, Boswell's father.

When Alexander Boswell built the present Auchinleck House, the dressing plate and the ebony cabinet were important objects of display in the new residence. Dr Johnson surely saw both when he was brought to visit by his young friend, James Boswell, in November 1773, after their tour of the Hebrides. Indeed, the historic collision between Boswell's father (proud Scot and strict judge of the Court of Session) and Dr Johnson (anti-Scot, anti-Whig, and anti-Presbyterian) must have taken place directly in front of the ebony cabinet, for in it Lord Auchinleck kept his collection of coins and medals[1]; and it was while Boswell's father was showing Johnson 'his collection of medals [that] Oliver Cromwell's coin unfortunately introduced Charles the First, and Toryism'. As Boswell reported:

> They became exceedingly warm, and violent, and I was very much distressed by being present at such an altercation between two men, both of whom I reverenced; yet I durst not interfere. It would certainly be very unbecoming in me to exhibit my honoured father, and my respected friend, as intellectual gladiators, for the entertainment of the publick; and therefore I

[1] The coins and medals are referred to as an appendage of the ebony cabinet being always kept in it—Answers and Claim for Alexander Boswell, Esq., of Auchinleck to the Memorial and Claim for the 'younger children', 15 February 1803. Copies of this document are in the legal office of Steedman, Ramage in Edinburgh and in the Isham Family Papers.

suppress what would, I dare say, make an interesting scene in this dramatic sketch. . . .²

So there was even a Johnsonian connection with the heirloom which meant so much to Boswell.

The ebony cabinet had stirred his romantic imagination as a young man, and even when it still belonged to his father, Boswell took a proprietary interest, envisioning the cabinet as a repository for special family mementoes; he eagerly collected such items. He had, for instance, several 'lively sallies' from his friend, John Wilkes —'curiosities of the first rate . . .', from 'a *Lord Mayor of London* . . . [which he] preserved in [his] cabinet'.³ He also had 'a good many' of David Garrick's gay and friendly letters 'fondly preserve[d] as brilliant gems in [his] literary cabinet'.⁴

When Boswell's father died in August 1782, many problems of estate and management confronted the new laird, but the collecting of significant items for his cabinet was not forgotten. A manuscript, now at Four Oaks Farm, which might well have qualified, is one of twelve folio pages containing genealogical notes on the Boswells of Auchinleck, a project which Boswell discussed with Johnson in the spring of 1783, on the first visit to London after his father's death. Boswell asked his mentor one day if he would write a history of the Boswell family and, to Boswell's pleasure, Johnson greeted the idea with enthusiasm, saying, 'Let me have all the materials you can collect, and I will do it both in Latin and English'.⁵ Unfortunately, as the manuscript pages show, Boswell did not finish his part of the assignment. He lamented the facts in the *Life* that he had missed so valuable an opportunity, for time ran out. Johnson died in the next year, on 13 December 1784.

Johnson's death was a shattering blow to Boswell. Not only did he suffer the loss of his firmest friend and adviser, but the sad event also caused a drastic change in his own life. His publishers immediately began to press for the manuscript of his long-planned biography of Johnson. He had talked openly about this project for twenty years, but had nothing to show, not even an outline; he had only a mass of unsorted material. To write a life worthy of Johnson, and worthy of himself, interminable work lay ahead.

For the moment, to satisfy his publishers, who were clamouring for a book about Johnson, Boswell decided to go to London, where

---

2 Boswell's *Life of Johnson*, ed. G. B. Hill, rev. L. F. Powell, 6 vols., Oxford, 1934-50, V, 382. (Hereafter cited as *Life*.)
3 James Boswell to John Wilkes, 26 May 1775, in *Letters of James Boswell*, ed. Chauncey B. Tinker, 2 vols., Oxford, 1924, I, 227. (Hereafter cited as *Boswell Letters*.)
4 James Boswell to Mrs Garrick, 16 April 1781; in *Boswell Letters*, II, 311.
5 *Life*, IV, 198.

he would prepare his manuscript journal of the tour to the Hebrides with Johnson for the press. When Boswell journeyed southward in March 1785, he took many of his papers, and possibly a few items from the ebony cabinet. Throughout April and May of 1785, he laboured on the *Tour*. As he recorded in his journal on 28 May: 'In all day in Nightgown and wrote "Hebrides" '.[6]

The same day he also wrote his will. One of the provisions of this stated:

> ... whereby the said Ebony Cabinet and dressing plate are now at my free disposal, I do by these presents dispone the same to the heir succeeding to the Barony of Auchinleck from generation to generation and I do declare that it shall not be in the power of any such heir to alienate or impignorate the same on any account whatever ... in case any of them shall alienate the said Ebony Cabinet and dressing plate, the person so alienating shall forfeit the sum of one thousand pounds sterling which shall be paid to the next heir succeeding by the Entail. ...[7]

The *Tour to the Hebrides* was published in October 1785, but the *Life of Johnson* was not published for another six years, not until May 1791. During this time Boswell's work on the biography necessitated his establishing himself in London, abandoning Auchinleck, except for occasional short visits.[8] This was a hard sacrifice: his property suffered from his absence, and his legal practice as well, for no business came to him in London. He was often tempted to go home, but he struggled on with his *'Magnum Opus'*, in low spirits amid financial difficulties and family tragedy.

When the date of publication grew nearer, the ebony cabinet was in his mind. Boswell asked his elder son, Alexander, for a copy of a poem he had written. Alexander, now sixteen and a schoolboy at Eton, had composed some verses to commemorate the 'Great Work' which would 'increase [his father's] great name'. Boswell told Sandie that: '... they are to me truly wonderful. You must revise them and improve them, so as they may be deposited in the *Ebony Cabinet*'.[9]

---

[6] *Private Papers of James Boswell from Malahide Castle*, ed. Geoffrey Scott and Frederick A. Pottle, 18 vols. [New York], 1928-34, XVI, 95. (Hereafter cited as *Boswell Papers*.)

[7] Holograph of James Boswell's will; Register House, Edinburgh.

[8] James Boswell's Book of Company at Auchinleck notes the duration of his visits; MS. at Four Oaks Farm.

[9] James Boswell to Alexander Boswell, 14 March 1791, in *Boswell Papers*, XVIII, 290. The verses, in Latin (English tr. by Boswell's younger son, James), were deposited in the cabinet. They are reproduced in *Boswell Papers*, XVIII, 341.

At Four Oaks Farm there is indication of another contribution, presumably from young James, an object wrapped in a piece of paper. Only the wrapper remains. This was once folded into a small rectangle 1″ x 1″ x 11/16″. It is docketed in Boswell's hand: 'From / Mr. Ja Boswell / to the / Ebony Cabinet'.

The month after publication, Boswell again approached his friend John Wilkes, this time for an appropriate tribute to his *Life of Johnson*: 'you said to me yesterday of my *Magnum Opus*, "it is a wonderful book". Do confirm this to me, so as I may have your *testimonium* in my archives at Auchinleck.'[10]

After publication of the *Life*, Boswell did not break away from London. He was exhausted from the long labour and deeply depressed, despite the popular success of his book. He stayed on in his house in Great Portland Street, the mass of working papers still there. During the last four years of his life, Boswell's stays at Auchinleck became so infrequent that he seemed only a visitor. His son, Sandie, was more often in residence. In London, Boswell was attempting to put his journals into some kind of publishable form which might help his family financially. His burdens were heavy and his health was failing. He died on 19 March 1795.

The question of whether Boswell's journals might be published was now considered by his three literary executors Edmond Malone, the Shakespeare critic, Sir William Forbes, an Edinburgh banker, and William Temple, a vicar in Cornwall. Malone examined many of Boswell's papers in London, as did Forbes in Scotland. Temple never saw the material (he died soon after Boswell, on 13 August 1796), but he did correspond upon the subject with the two other literary executors. All wished that some kind of publication might be possible for the benefit of 'the younger children' (meaning Boswell's children except Alexander, his elder son and heir). But Forbes and Malone agreed that the journals were not suitable for publication. They qualified this opinion, however, by saying that James Boswell junior, a representative of 'the younger children', then a bookish young man in his teens, should make the final decision in a few years, when his judgment would be mature.

When this time came, James gave the same opinion as his father's literary executors—that the journals were not suitable for publication. Thus, the papers should have been returned to Alexander at Auchinleck. Malone implied that they had been when he wrote to Boswell's daughter, Euphemia, in 1809, saying that they were 'now deposited at Auchinleck; in which repository, I trust, they will be suffered to remain in peace'.[11]

Alexander Boswell, the new Laird of Auchinleck, was twenty when he succeeded, a high-spirited, clever, and amiable young man. He was something of a poet, antiquary, and man of letters (in time he would establish a private press at Auchinleck). He had been

---

[10] James Boswell to John Wilkes, 25 June 1791; in *Boswell Letters*, II, 437.
[11] Edmond Malone to Euphemia Boswell, 4 May 1809; Pierpoint Morgan Library.

devoted to his father: he was proud of Auchinleck, proud of the family's history, and of the heirlooms.

His ownership of the ebony cabinet and the dressing plate was, for a time, in doubt. Interpretation of his father's will and financial pressures caused discord between Alexander and the 'younger children'. Veronica, Euphemia, James, and Elizabeth claimed that these treasured objects, as well as the collection of books, had been forfeited by Alexander's declining to take up the succession to the entire estate. After protracted arbitration proceedings, the decision was given in 1804 that 'Alexander Boswell will take as an Heir Loom (as the English call it) the Ebony Cabinet and Dressing Plate'.[12]

Alexander was a dedicated Laird of Auchinleck, and family affairs proceeded as well as could be expected until February 1822, when double tragedy struck. James junior died in London, aged forty-three and unmarried. Alexander left Scotland to attend the funeral and upon his return to Edinburgh, found waiting for him the challenge to a duel from one James Stuart of Dunearn, who, by bribery, had discovered during Alexander's absence that the laird was the writer of several anonymous newspaper attacks against him.

Three days later the duel took place. Alexander fired into the air and James Stuart (as he later claimed) closed his eyes and fired, alas, with fatal accuracy. Boswell's two sons thus died a little more than a month apart; both were in their forties.

Alexander had been married for some years to a Montgomerie cousin and by her had two daughters (Janet Theresa and Margaret Amelia) and one son, then a boy of 15. James, later Sir James, has been described by George Birkbeck Hill, that important and somewhat imperious Johnsonian editor, as 'a man of great natural ability, who, had he chosen, might have become distinguished'.[13] By this, Hill meant that Sir James was a fine English country gentleman, a sportsman, but not an intellectual.

Sir James had little interest in the family library or in the family papers. He was concerned with other matters: he built a large stable at Auchinleck, which still exists, and he constructed a practice track, a racing mile. His enthusiasm for art was confined to the paintings he commissioned of his favourite horses.

In 1830, Sir James Boswell married his cousin, Jessie Jane Cuninghame. They had two daughters—Julia and Emily—but no

---

[12] Interim Decreet in the Submission between Alexander Boswell and his Brothers and Sisters, dated and registered in the Books of Council and Session, 19 March 1804. Copies of this document are in the legal office of Steedman, Ramage in Edinburgh and in the Isham Family Papers.

[13] G. B. Hill, *Footsteps of Dr. Johnson, Scotland,* London, 1890, p. 284.

son. Understandably, when Sir James realised that he would have no son, he endeavoured to break the Auchinleck entail, and this he was able to accomplish in 1852. When he died five years later (aged fifty), Auchinleck House and the ebony cabinet and the dressing plate[14] passed to his widow, who continued to live at Auchinleck for over thirty years. After her death in 1884, the mansion house passed to her elder daughter, Julia, in 'liferent'. Julia, by this time, was married to George Mounsey, a Carlisle solicitor. The Mounseys' principal residence was in Carlisle, and they made only short visits to Auchinleck.

In 1873 Sir James Boswell's younger daughter, Emily, married the fifth Lord Talbot de Malahide, of Malahide Castle, Ireland. This fine castle, nine miles north of Dublin, has been in the family since 1174. Richard Wogan, the fifth Lord Talbot, and Emily had a son, their only child. They named him, with continuing sentiment, James Boswell. Emily died in 1893, when her son was twenty-four.

Three years later, in 1901, James's father married again. His second wife was Isabel Gurney, a widow, a strikingly handsome, forceful, public-spirited woman. Isabel became devoted to Malahide, both to the castle and to the garden. She also became interested in Auchinleck, when the house came to her stepson upon the death of his aunt, Julia Mounsey, in 1905. The contents of the house formed part of Mrs Mounsey's residual estate (bequeathed to the Cumberland Infirmary). The fifth Lord Talbot, however, purchased this residue and so the contents of Auchinleck, including the ebony cabinet and other papers, became his property.

After 1905 the Talbots paid annual visits to Auchinleck, and though the house belonged technically to James, he was glad to have things managed by his father and stepmother. He was not drawn to the ebony cabinet and the family papers, for rather than inheriting a literary flair, he had the enthusiasms of his grandfather, Sir James—horses and dogs, hunting and racing.

His father and Isabel, however, had pleasure in examining the contents of the ebony cabinet, also family papers which were elsewhere in the house. They sorted through manuscripts upon successive visits and, in time, decided to ship the material to Ireland. By 1908 Boswell's journals and much else were at Malahide. The

---

14 '. . . in the 1870's there was a big sale at Auchinleck and my Grandfather noticed the entire dressing set was offered . . .; the majority [of the pieces came to him, but a few that he did not purchase came up for sale many years later at Christies, 28 April 1965]. The entire service is however now in the possession of the Museum at the Hague.' The Earl of Elgin to Mrs Donald F. Hyde, 22 April 1969.

ebony cabinet, however, remained at Auchinleck, in the small morning room, at the left of the entrance to the house.[15]

Isabel and Lord Talbot became fascinated by the 'Diary of the Biographer', as did Lord Talbot's brother, Colonel Milo Talbot, a man with keen literary interests. The possibility of publication was often discussed among them. Indeed, in 1911, Lord Talbot asked the opinion of Sir John Murray, the publisher, for whom a typescript of almost the entire journal had been made. Sir John gave the text the same careful consideration that Boswell's literary executors and James junior had given it many years earlier. Murray's conclusion in 1911 was the same as theirs—that its candour made it unsuitable for publication.

In 1914, as war clouds gathered, the Talbots decided to ship the ebony cabinet to Ireland. Lady Talbot wrote from Malahide, in January 1915, that they now had 'Boswell's famous ebony cabinet, mentioned in his will. We thought [it] would be much safer here, in case [Auchinleck] is let'.[16]

They placed the ebony cabinet in a position of honour at Malahide, and often showed it to guests. Sometimes they brought out material to read for their entertainment, though never for long, delicacy prohibited Boswell's full flow.

Isabel said of the contents of the cabinet in her letter of January 1915:

> I will talk to Lord Talbot again about [the publication of] Boswell's Diary, but he is so sensitive about it that I hardly like to refer again to the subject. He thinks it is not fair on James or Boswell relations to see what horrors he wrote![17]

With the war, the Talbots made a full break from Auchinleck. They did not feel—no one feels—the dedication to a second house that one has for a principal residence. As Isabel wrote in October 1915:

> You know we are breaking away from Auchinleck, and I expect we shall have to sell the furniture. The mortgagees are demanding to have the debts of the late Sir James Boswell paid up through the estate, which must go. Personally I shall not regret the place, as I always thought it so melancholy.[18]

There were sales of furniture and books and Auchinleck House was leased in 1918 to Robert McCrone for five years. During this time,

---

[15] Samuel Gurney, *Isabel Mrs. Gurney, afterwards the Lady Talbot de Malahide 1851-1932*, Norwich and London, 1935, p. 140. (Hereafter cited as *Gurney*.)
[16] *Gurney*, p. 140.
[17] Ibid.
[18] Ibid., p. 141.

in 1920, Auchinleck was sold to Colonel John Douglas Boswell of Garallan, by descent a distant cousin of the biographer.[19]

In 1920, Professor Chauncey B. Tinker of Yale, who was preparing his edition of Boswell's *Letters*, wrote to *The Times Literary Supplement*, inquiring if any of James Boswell's letters survived in private hands. He received two affirmative replies; both advised him to try Malahide, and one specifically pointed out an 'escritoire', which the correspondent said was full of letters 'as yet uncatalogued'.[20]

In Boswell's time there were letters in the ebony cabinet (a few have been mentioned) as well as other items of family association, but the material which the Talbots considered all-important was the extensive series of journals, which they called the 'Biographer's Diary'. And because they thought the journals so important, I think, it was *they* who placed them in the ebony cabinet.

But to return to Professor Tinker: after receiving the clue about Malahide, he quickly sent a letter to the Hon. James Boswell Talbot, son of the fifth Lord Talbot, telling him that his edition of *Boswell Letters* for the Clarendon Press was in progress and asking if he might see Boswell's letters at Malahide. Professor Tinker received the following laconic reply: 'I am very sorry I am unable to give you any letters of James Boswell's for publication. I regret I cannot meet your views in this respect'.[21] This answer might seem to indicate that Boswell material did indeed exist at Malahide; however, Professor Tinker made no further move for a number of years. His edition of Boswell's *Letters* was published in 1924; his visit to Malahide was not until 1925.

Four years before this (a year after the Tinker letter) the fifth Lord Talbot had died, and his son had succeeded. James, at the time, had been forty-seven, unmarried, retiring, and extremely averse to any publicity. The sixth Lord Talbot was a man of taste and gentleness, also of gallantry and determination. After an interlude of profound thought, he would often make a cast-iron decision. And so, after one meeting, in March 1924, he determined with a fervour of which his ancestor would have been proud, that he would marry the young and beautiful Joyce Kerr, a member of the distinguished theatre family. The wedding took place in Stamford on 19 September 1924.

Joyce, Lady Talbot has written to me about her arrival in Ireland as a bride. She was welcomed to Malahide with the same

---

[19] Col. Boswell did not take over Auchinleck until 1923, at the termination of the McCrone lease.
[20] Elsie Mahaffy to C. B. Tinker, 21 July 1920; in the Tinker Papers.
[21] Hon. James B. Talbot to C. B. Tinker, 5 August 1920; in the Tinker Papers.

enthusiasm which had greeted Isabel over twenty years before.[22] The following quotation shows the climate at the castle a few months before Professor Tinker made his visit:

> Arriving in Ireland the entire village was on the platform. They had put some harmless explosive things which were to go off with loud bangs (of welcome) as the train drew in to the station. Thank goodness they failed to go off, the whole thing was hair-raising enough anyway. I was presented with a bouquet, and we were driven up to the castle in an open carriage—the village following. In the castle policemen were stationed all over the place, but James assured me they were only there *in case* of 'Trouble'. The villagers stayed around with barrels of beer emptying very fast. James made a speech, and finally everyone went away.
> Next day the Steward said 'A great evening m'Lord, a foine affair, all in bed by ten o'clock and not a head broken'.
> This beginning to my life in Ireland was all in character—can you altogether wonder I wasn't concentrating on Boswell's letters when Professor Tinker called?[23]

Professor Tinker approached the Talbots in a conventional and well-mannered way. He wrote to his friend, Charles Hathaway, the American consul in Dublin, asking for help in securing an introduction. Hathaway directed him to Archdeacon Lindsay, a close friend of the Talbots, and a book collector.

Through this chain of acquaintance, Professor Tinker was asked to come to Malahide Castle for tea. Lady Talbot says:

> When Professor Tinker came to Malahide my brain was being taxed by hundreds of problems it had never dealt with before, in connection with Malahide itself, and I was completely indifferent to the Biographer's papers at that time. Therefore it is *very* difficult to answer what I thought—or did—the day he came, over 40 years ago![24]

The impact of the visit was strongly felt by Professor Tinker. He wrote to a friend that, after tea:

> I was led into an adjoining room, where I found myself standing in front of the famous 'ebony cabinet'—a sort of highboy with many drawers. The drawers which I was permitted to pull open were crammed with papers in the wildest confusion. I felt like Sinbad in the valley of rubies. I glanced—panting the while—at a few sheets. One was a letter from Boswell to Alexander as a schoolboy. At once I realized that a new day had dawned for Boswellians, and that for C. B. Tinker there

---

[22] *Gurney*, p. 84.
[23] Joyce, Lady Talbot de Malahide to Mrs Donald F. Hyde, 22 March 1969.
[24] Ibid.

was a dreadful crisis, the resolution of which would alter the whole of his future life. (I did not sleep that night).[25]

The special asset which Professor Tinker could offer the Talbots, his authority as a scholar, was not an attraction. For them, the main result of his visit was the realisation that the 'Biographer's Diary' was indeed an important and valuable property. Substantial evidence of this fact came soon and as a direct result of Professor Tinker's visit, for upon return to America he had given a report of what he had seen at Malahide to a number of book friends, including A. Edward Newton, the Philadelphia book collector. Mr Newton was quick to inform Dr A. S. W. Rosenbach, the well known Philadelphia book dealer. The 'Doctor', with customary courage and intuition, at once cabled Lord Talbot that he would pay £50,000 sight unseen for the contents of the ebony cabinet.

The 'Doctor' received the following answer by letter: 'We regret that such Boswell papers as are in our possession are not for sale, nor can they be seen by anyone. Lord Talbot was very surprised and annoyed at the matter being opened by telegram'.[26]

The Talbots' annoyance is understandable, for the telegraph office in the small town of Malahide was a social meeting place, where news from cables was generally enjoyed before delivery was made by bicycle. After such a message, the problems at Malahide Castle of protection and insurance were greatly increased. The 'Doctor's' mention of large figures was thus vexing and disturbing, but it did, however, give specific reassurance on the point of value. Some day, it was not inconceivable, there might be a temptation to sell at least some of the papers, if the right person approached.

At this point in the story, as if by fate, a friend of Tinker, Newton, and the 'Doctor' appeared, a young book collector, greatly drawn to the eighteenth century, and to Johnson and Boswell in particular. He was Lt.-Col. Ralph Heyward Isham, a dashing American of thirty-five. His military title came from recent war service in the British Army, and he had been granted the additional distinction of a C.B.E. Ralph Isham was a handsome, attractive man, well-to-do, fired with imagination and ambition. He was seeking a cause commensurate with his powers. In the acquiring and publishing of Boswell's papers he saw a quest worthy of his talents. He viewed the project in large perspective, something to be undertaken with style and elegance, with zest and pleasure. He would publish beautiful as well as authoritative volumes. He would give Boswell to the world.

[25] C. B. Tinker to Alan G. Thomas, 17 August 1946.
[26] Lady Talbot de Malahide to Dr A. S. W. Rosenbach, 27 August 1925; in the Philip and A. S. W. Rosenbach Foundation.

Colonel Isham laid siege to the papers with the care of a military tactician and the finesse of a diplomat. He carefully gathered information about the Talbots, their interests and their friends. No routine introduction was sufficient for his purpose, he must have impressive credentials, and indeed he secured an introduction so impeccable that communication was launched without delay. But, though he answered, Lord Talbot was reserved; he made it clear that he had no thought of selling any papers. It would hardly be worth Colonel Isham's time to come to Malahide. There were only one or two specimens to be shown. Colonel Isham replied with enthusiasm: 'I should gladly go much further than Dublin to see even one letter of James Boswell. Perhaps in this I have something akin to the religious fervour that moves pilgrims to get out on their journeys to Mecca'.[27]

Another tea party took place at Malahide in mid-June, 1926. After tea, Colonel Isham was shown the ebony cabinet, but, as Lord Talbot had warned, there were only a few letters. Most of the 'rubies', which had dazzled Professor Tinker the year before, had now been removed to the Talbots' bank for safe keeping—a direct result of Dr Rosenbach's cable. But Colonel Isham was not daunted. He continued to manoeuvre with diplomacy and daring.

In a little over a year his efforts were crowned with considerable success, for in August 1927 he signed a contract which made him the possessor of all the Boswellian letters and miscellaneous papers then traced at Malahide. And indeed it was not long before he secured the journals as well, and the second phase of his project—publication—began. The first volume of the *Private Papers of James Boswell from Malahide Castle* was edited by Geoffrey Scott, and five more volumes came out under his supervision. After his untimely death in 1929, Professor Frederick A. Pottle of Yale University was chosen to succeed him as editor.

With the purchases he had made, Colonel Isham believed that he owned all of Boswell's papers in the Talbots' possession. In good faith, they believed the same. As Lady Talbot has written to me:

> So far as I can remember both James and I thought all Boswell MSS. were in the cabinet. *But* it must be remembered that at that time interest was always centered on his writings for publication and *the diary*. Family and personal letters would have been, to James, a family matter, and not of interest to people outside the family.[28]

[27] Isham to Lord Talbot de Malahide, 7 June 1926; in the Talbot Papers.
[28] Lady Talbot de Malahide to Mrs Donald F. Hyde, 22 March 1969. Certain letters from celebrated persons (Goldsmith, etc.) must be excepted from this statement. Lady Talbot had a number of such letters appraised in London, and, aware of their value, considered selling them.

Papers other than 'the Biographer's Diary' were, however, of considerable general interest, and to Colonel Isham's chagrin, as he proceeded with the publication of his handsome volumes of the Malahide Papers, more and more new material came to light. The major part of the manuscript of the *Life of Johnson*, for instance, appeared in a packing case, stored in the loft of a horse barn. This, together with many other items, was found when space was cleared for the emergency storage of grain during World War II.

Some years before, the manuscript of the *Tour to the Hebrides* had been found in a croquet box. There have been many romantic interpretations of the event.

Lady Talbot has the following comment:

> Croquet box. WE NEVER EVEN HAD A CROQUET LAWN. I was just 'tidying up', and found the box, opened it, and found papers. I have tried to kill all the frills to that story so often. No house-party, no footman, no game of croquet.
> The Box was in the tiny cupboard-cum-room behind the fireplace in our sitting-room (known as the small drawing-room). It was a very dry place, and I have so often repeated my idea that my father-in-law may have been going through these papers and kept them there, to hand, as it was close, dry, and locked. I wanted to tidy the place, so I found the box!
> . . . what did I do? I gave one horrified glance through the papers, and sat down and wrote to Colonel Isham.[29]

The seemingly endless finds at Malahide have puzzled scholars and the public as well. And the situation has not been helped by the lectures, press releases, and personal stories told by Colonel Isham, one of the great raconteurs of our time. Incidents have been embroidered with dramatic invention, and the truth, no less interesting, has been obscured. The facts, as stated, are that the fifth Lord Talbot and his wife supervised the moving of Boswell's papers from Auchinleck. They knew the full extent of the material —what was in the ebony cabinet and elsewhere. It was they who had the material shipped to Ireland and stored in various places at Malahide. Only after the death of the fifth Lord Talbot (and when his widow had moved away) did Professor Tinker see the ebony cabinet and did Colonel Isham purchase its contents. The persons then at Malahide had forgotten—or had not known—about the papers stored elsewhere.

The 'Biographer's Diary', as Lady Talbot stressed, was thought to have over-riding importance. When, however, the Talbots came to the surprising realisation that the scholarly world was interested in every recoverable scrap of Boswell's writing (which, in turn Colonel

[29] Ibid.

Isham felt obliged to acquire) they began to understand the problem. Time and again, new manuscripts surfaced and Colonel Isham was forced to make fresh purchases. The Talbots became sympathetic to his plight. For his part, Colonel Isham was generous in his payment, though the financial strain became in the end more than he could support. As for Colonel Isham's relationship to scholars, his kindness is well remembered: his hospitality on countless occasions, his granting of access to the papers, his constant desire to share the excitement.

One of the happiest seminars of the late 1940s was that held at Smith College, arranged by the college President, Herbert Davis, the Swift scholar. It was at this conference that Colonel Isham was introduced to the distinguished visiting lecturer, Professor David Nichol Smith, whom we are honouring here.

Stories of the Boswell Papers considerably enlivened the proceedings at Smith College, and they also strengthened the bond of friendship formed between Colonel Isham and Professor Nichol Smith. When the latter left America, he carried with him a Boswellian correction to Johnson's *Vanity of Human Wishes*, given by Colonel Isham, to present to the Bodleian Library—an intention of Boswell's which had not been carried out. As an incidental note, the two final pages of the manuscripts of the *Vanity of Human Wishes* were found in the ebony cabinet by the Hydes one afternoon at Malahide in 1955.

But to return to the great Isham collection of Boswell papers. This was sold to Yale University in 1949 and since that time the publication project of both the trade and scholarly editions of Boswell manuscripts has continued under the aegis of the Yale Editorial Committee and the McGraw-Hill Book Company.

The pattern of manuscript material unexpectedly coming to light in Ireland has also continued; but, as before, matters have been handled with understanding, generosity and good nature between Yale University and Lady Talbot and Milo, the seventh Lord Talbot, who succeeded to the title in 1948. Milo was a nephew of the fifth Lord Talbot, and hence no relation to the biographer. The Boswell line ended with the death of the sixth Lord Talbot. The seventh Lord Talbot's line was Shakespeare's Shrewsbury Talbots, 'a twig of the branch', as he expressed it. But despite his separation from James Boswell, Milo Talbot maintained a definite interest in the biographer. Lord Talbot was by profession a diplomat (Ambassador to Laos in 1955-6); his greatest outside interests were the maintenance of Malahide Castle, horticulture, and travel. And as many of you are aware, he had two important connections with Australia; his fine property, Malahide, Tasmania,[30] and his own publication project, the *Endemic Flora of Tasmania*, of which the first three volumes have appeared.

The sudden death of the seventh Lord Talbot this past April, while travelling in Greece, makes a sad note on which to end this account, in which, by the way, Lord Talbot took a friendly interest, answering questions and going to the trouble of having professional photographs made of the ebony cabinet. This monumental piece of furniture remains a firm fixture in the oak room at Malahide Castle, though much of what filled it, at various times, as well as much of the avalanche of so-called 'later-found' papers, are now, of course, well established in the Beinecke Library at Yale University.[31]

---

[30] A grant made to the Hon. William Talbot in 1824.

[31] I am indebted to David Buchanan for many facts in this paper. He is a Writer to the Signet in Edinburgh, the son of Colonel Isham's Scottish solicitor, and a captive of and expert on Boswell. His *Treasure of Auchinleck*, the authoritative and full history of the Boswell papers, is soon to appear, published by McGraw-Hill, New York and Heinemann, London.

Bath: Ideology and Utopia, 1700-1760

R. S. Neale

To talk about Bath is to talk about eighteenth-century England. But I am not prepared or able, like some historians, to talk about an England or a Bath that was objectively real or really there. I can only speak about Bath in the light of my own experience of its surviving buildings, mortgages, leases, newspapers, estate and corporation records, and a variety of other manuscripts, plans, prints, pamphlets, scraps of paper. I will do so with the aid of a conceptual apparatus in which the main parts are ideas about the relationships between society, men, and creativity and knowledge put forward by Karl Marx, Karl Mannheim, and Jean Duvignaud and insights derived from the art historians Erwin Panofsky and Rudolf Wittkower. I shall attempt to convey the results of my observation of this very small whole piece of the world through the inadequate metaphor of a language which forces me to speak and write seriatim however much I believe I can see, at one time, this small piece whole—a complex, dynamic and dialectical *gestalt*. What I would like to do is to write this piece of social history in the way Picasso painted Kahnweiler, whereas I can scarcely manage to do it as Hogarth painted Captain Thomas Coram.

It will probably be allowed that architecture is art and, therefore, that architecture in Bath is art. Certainly its architecture is as much a kaleidoscope of individual and collective acts of creation as the Book of Kells or St Peter's in Rome. Moreover, it could not have been built had not Brunelleschi created the Pazzi Chapel in Florence and Palladio published his *Quattro libri dell'architettura*. Art, however, is very rarely the mere representation of an order in society or of a style associated with it. Indeed, art continuously and anxiously opposes and questions order and Bath, I shall argue, was no mere reflection of an age, be it called Rational, Bourgeois, Georgian or Whiggish. Neither was it simply the Renaissance in

England. Rather, Bath consisted of personalised atypic responses to disorder and the anomie of a market economy, juxtaposed with collective and personal expressions which served and re-affirmed that newly-developing structure of society. Creative expression in Bath is, in Mannheim's sense, both ideological and utopian.[1]

Any answer to the question, What is the meaning of eighteenth-century Bath? is likely to be attempted at three levels. The objective level identifies historical Bath as an eighteenth-century watering-place and its buildings as lodging-houses. The expressive level looks to the purposes of its architects and builders and concentrates, on the one hand, on the expressed desire of John Wood, the city's leading architect, to re-create a Roman city complete with Forum, Gymnasium, and Circus and, on the other, on an imputed desire to reunite urban man with nature; Wood, it is argued, anticipated the Romantics and modern town planners. The third level is documentary or evidential, and it too points to something beyond the city itself, to the spirit of the age, to Whiggism and the Age of Reason.[2] There are elements of truth in all these answers, but those relating to the expressive and documentary levels are frequently stated with all the startling clarity of absolutes. Yet, if one pauses awhile to try to penetrate the form and structure of the city, to understand the historical space it occupies as well as the space in which it is situated, and to pass beyond the grey opaqueness of the buildings to men themselves, this startling clarity will be blurred, and brought into sharper focus only by a searching analysis of the beliefs, ideologies, and institutions of its time. I propose to attempt this by concentrating on the work of John Wood (1705-1754) and the first sixty years of the eighteenth century.

In the early eighteenth century Bath had a population of some seven hundred families or three thousand people. Most of them lived within the town walls which formed an irregular polygon with sides about four hundred yards long (Plate III). The town, situated in a loop of the Bristol Avon, had the river on two sides and the slopes of Lansdown and Beacon Hill to the north and west. It was an isolated urban enclave approachable in wet weather only from the London side. Its citizens worked to provide a rude accom-

---

[1] Karl Mannheim, *Ideology and Utopia: An Introduction to the Sociology of Knowledge*, London, 1972, pp. 49-87.

[2] Walter Ison, *The Georgian Buildings of Bath from 1700 to 1830*, London, 1948; John Summerson, *Architecture in Britain, 1530-1830*, ed. Nikolaus Pevsner, Harmondsworth, 1953, pp. 197-245; Nikolaus Pevsner, *An Outline of European Architecture*, Harmondsworth, 1960, p. 581; John Fleming, Hugh Honour, Nikolaus Pevsner, *The Penguin Dictionary of Architecture*, Harmondsworth, 1966, p. 242; Fritz Baumgart, *A History of Architectural Styles*, London, 1970, pp. 255-6; Colin and Rose Bell, *City Fathers: The Early History of Town Planning in Britain*, Harmondsworth, 1972.

modation for visitors to its baths and apprenticed their sons to the clothing, food, building and personal service trades. The wealthier among them held land outside the walls and kept inns and lodging houses, all built in the vernacular style—mostly three storied with casement and mullioned windows set in large decorated bays, attics, and high gables fronting the street. They were all architectural flourish and asymmetry. Lacking proportion and harmony, they were a collection of mere houses. According to report, they were inconvenient and uncomfortable.

As the century grew older so grew the nation's wealth. The two thousand families who possessed the land and governed it, protected by law against the claims of the Crown and the common man, increased their grip on power and sought social occasions for harmless sensual pleasures. Bath became a resort for gambling, horse racing, drinking, eating, revelling, dancing, and whoring; or at least it did so twice a year, in the spring and the autumn. As the author of *A Step to the Bath* described it in 1700,

> 'tis neither Town nor City, yet goes by the Name of both; five Months in the Year 'tis as Populous as *London*, the other seven as desolate as a Wilderness. it's [sic] chiefest Inhabitants are Turn-Spit-Dogs; and it looks like Lombard-street on a Saints-day. During the Season it hath as many Families in a House as *Edenborough*; and Bills are as thick for Lodgings to be Let, as there was for Houses in the *Fryars* on the Late Act of Parliament for the Dissolution of Priviledges; but when the *Baths* are useless, so are their Houses, and as empty as the new Buildings by St. *Giles* in the Fields; the *Baths* I can compare to nothing but the *Boylers* in *Fleet-lane* or *Old-Bedlam*, for they have a reeking steem all the year. In a word, 'tis a Valley of Pleasure, yet a sink of Iniquity; Nor is there any Intrigues or Debauch Acted at *London*, but is mimick'd there.[3]

As well as catering to the sensuous needs of men and women Bath also benefited from the pre-scientific state of medicine and the continuing belief in magic this encouraged. Dr Oliver, the inventor of the Bath Oliver biscuit, was an astute businessman quite clear about the profitability of magic. He sought to attract customers to Bath by persuading them that a healthy life could be theirs if only they would take the waters inside and out. In his *Practical Dissertation on Bath Waters* Dr Oliver told potential patients that the waters would cure gout, rheumatism, palsies, convulsions, lameness, colic, consumption, asthma, jaundice, scurvy, the itch, scab, leprosy, scrofula, gravel, as well as coldness and pain in the head, epilepsies,

---

[3] Anon., *A Step to the Bath: with a Character of the Place*, London, 1700, p. 16.

most diseases of the eyes, deafness and noise in the ears, running of the ears, palpitation of the heart, sharpness of urine, wounds, ulcers, piles, numbness in any part, and all the special diseases of women including infertility. For good and crucial measure, the waters would also cure the pox—'If they can't be cured by drinking and bathing here', wrote Dr Oliver, 'they will never be cured any where'.[4] Yet, according to other reports, the converse was more likely to be true, a visit to 'The Bath' was as like to bring on the pox as cure it!

Sensuous self-indulgence and a desire for magical cures to ease its worst effects were the reasons that people flocked to Bath. This influx of visitors caused the first building booms of the century and created in Bath what the eighteenth century and John Wood knew as 'Civil Society', a state of incessant self-regarding and socially disruptive competition.

Although, in these early years, the need to build houses fit for gentlemen in the 'new' Palladian style produced a number of elegant houses and one or two courts designed as wholes, builders were generally more concerned with supplying comfort at a price than with aesthetics. Therefore, local landowners and builders built a house here and another there, added a scatter of public buildings, such as a pumproom, a theatre, and an assembly room, and, in the occasional new street, built according to individual designs. The result was that, in the first quarter of the century, Bath showed every sign of growing piecemeal like any other Cotswold town. And there were good reasons why this should be so. Demand for the services Bath could provide was uncertain, subject to the vagaries of harvest and war. Consequently capital and land were not yet moving freely into real estate development. Moreover, as far as land was concerned, there was another impediment, the problem of tenure. Within the town itself and immediately on its northern, eastern, and southern boundaries land was only available in quite small parcels whether of freehold, copyhold or leasehold land. Where land was potentially available in large blocks controlled by one owner, either corporate or private, the existence of long leases for three lives meant that any potential for development on a grand scale would be frustrated unless those life-hold leases could be brought into the ambit of a market economy and turned into leases for terms of years. Only on the western side of the town was there real development potential. There lay three large blocks of land. First, ninety acres of common land held in trust by the Corporation for the benefit of the freemen of the city and, therefore,

---

[4] William Oliver, *A Practical Dissertation on Bath Waters*, London, 1707, p. 70.

undeveloped for the whole of the eighteenth century. Second, a large area of low-lying meadow, Great Kingsmead and Little Kingsmead, parts of which were thought suitable for development. And, third, the eighty-five acre Barton estate owned by a commercially-minded absentee landlord Robert Gay, a successful barber-surgeon in London. On this estate the problem of life-hold leases had been long since settled. Since it was to be the main site for development there can be little doubt that the first creative acts transforming Bath were constrained and shaped by the uneven penetration of capitalist agriculture into this part of Somerset.[5]

All I have said about the function of tenure in setting the boundaries for action illustrates the importance for the eighteenth century of private property and of the Lockeian notion of absolute property which gave agrarian capitalist practice ideological sanction.[6] This notion, absolute property, meaning freedom to use to the extent of destroying, was a philosophic bludgeon used with almost equal effect against the Crown as against copyholders, life-holders, customary tenants, and all foolish communitarians. It was the kingpin in the ideological scaffolding within which Bath was built. It, too, had west country origins.

But, there was more to property law than that and more than one pin in the scaffolding. In the three-quarters of a century preceding the development of Bath, property owners, secure in law against the Crown and the common man, had employed their lawyers and the Court of Chancery to good effect to develop a system of land law that was flexible and functional rather than absolute and categorical. They produced the settled estate in which, in its classic form, the nominal possessor was in fact only a life tenant. Seisin, or, for the want of a better word, ownership, was vested in trustees. With the development of the principle of equity of redemption as applied to mortgages, those with seisin who were also mortgagors were deemed merely to have an estate in land, while mortgagees had a right to an income from it. Some major consequences of these developments were: settled estates encumbered with all kinds of legal commitments were almost certain to remain intact for several generations; titles to property were more certain and unalienable; the rights of mortgagees were protected by law. Therefore, settled estates and conveyances by way of lease flowing from them were good mortgage investments—a 4 per cent

[5] See my 'Society, Belief, and the Building of Bath, 1700-1793', in *Landscape and Society, 1500-1800*, ed. C. W. Chalkin and M. Havinden, London, 1973.

[6] See John Locke, *Two Treatises of Government*, I, 39; also C. B. MacPherson, *The Political Theory of Possessive Individualism: Hobbes to Locke*, Oxford, 1962; Harold Perkin, *The Origins of Modern English Society, 1780-1880*, London, 1969, pp. 51-3.

mortgage on Pulteney's estate in Bathwick was as safe as holding government stock. It also offered a better return. The significance of these legal developments for building in Bath arises from the fact that it was a city of small fortunes. As even piecemeal development at £300 to £500 per house was expensive, widespread mortgage facilities and institutions and people with experience in mortgages were essential. Moreover, since most surrounding estates were settled, little land could be bought for building purposes and almost all building was on land let on leases for ninety-nine years. These leasehold titles, secure in law, could be re-let by developers in the form of building sub-leases into which were written building controls and conditions. All leases and sub-leases could be used as mortgage security. The combination of settled estate, building leases and sub-leases, and widespread mortgaging also made it possible to plan and carry through capital-intensive development projects like the Circus and the Royal Crescent, which cost at least £100,000 to complete.[7] In fact, whatever else it might be, Bath is a monument to the credit-raising ingenuity of the eighteenth century, for a very high proportion of the two million pounds invested in its construction, an amount almost equal to that invested in fixed capital in the cotton industry, was raised on mortgages secured by leases of land from settled estates.

Therefore, the initial decision of a landowner either to build himself or to grant building leases was crucial. He not only provided the site but, through the development of the concept of absolute property and with the assistance of developments in property law, he also supplied first class collateral for raising finance from hundreds of cautious small investors. In this way the market economy of agrarian capitalism, as well as determining the strength of demand for the good things Bath supplied and the site and sequence of development, also made it possible to tap reservoirs of capital in such a way as to enable a creative developer like John Wood to translate his image of man and nature into architectural forms. Thus Bath was both product and symbol of the achievement of agrarian and commercial capitalism, an existential expression of the social and economic structure of society and its dominant ideology. It was also, by mid-century, one of the principal resorts in England, providing opportunities for respectable social emulation and containing, as it were, the social forces which alone gave it its being. However, every expansion of the physical facilities necessary

[7] R. S. Neale, 'The Bourgeoisie, Historically, has played a Most Revolutionary Part', in *Feudalism, Capitalism, and Beyond*, ed. Eugene Kamenka, Canberra, 1974; A. W. B. Simpson, *An Introduction to the History of the Land Law*, Oxford, 1961.

for this purpose widened the area, physically and socially, into which capitalist practice penetrated. In the end Bath was doomed by the very success of its capitalist citizens and the expansion of civil society.

So to the work of John Wood. I realise that to concentrate on his work and, therefore, on the thirty year period after 1727, is to simplify the milieu into which Wood entered and to do injustice to other early eighteenth-century architect-builders like Killigrew, Strahan, and Greenway. My justification is that Wood *was* a giant among provincial architects and *did* give a new dimension and meaning to Bath. As well, he and his son, also John Wood, were responsible for planning and supervising the building of property with a capital value of some £400,000[8] or about one-fifth of the domestic building carried out in Bath in the eighteenth century.

John Wood was born the son of a mason in 1705. Whether he was born in Bath or Yorkshire is still uncertain. As a young man he worked as a surveyor in London and Yorkshire where, in 1725, he drew up plans for rebuilding Bath as a Roman city. Having unsuccessfully sought the assistance of several landowners in implementing his projected schemes, he entered in 1726 into a contract for digging dirt in the cut at Twerton, which was part of the improvement of the Avon between Bath and Bristol. In 1727 he was contracting surveyor for the development of Chandos Court for the Duke of Chandos. In 1728, and without capital, he began building Queen Square as an independent undertaker or architect-developer.

As an architect-developer Wood had to reconcile two contrasting parts of his being; capitalist and member of civil society, and creative artist. His books suggest that he understood perfectly that without success as a capitalist he would be unable to create. There was an additional problem. He was a deeply religious man, but as a struggling capitalist and artist he catered for the high consumption demands of a self-indulgent clientele 'in a sink of iniquity'. Thus he could neither succeed as a capitalist nor create anything unless he continued to produce what satisfied this market in the context of and according to the conditions of agrarian capitalism already described. Indeed, this seemed the only market that would enable him to do anything at all. Consequently his career is marked by one compromise after another; Queen Square, North Parade, and the Exchange building in Bristol are only three of them. Wood was also fully conscious of the socially disruptive nature of this 'civil society' in which he so actively participated. Writing in and of an

[8] Particulars of Fee Farm Rents, 1787; A Particular of Perpetual Fee Farm Rents, 1771, Guildhall Archives, Bath; Wood Box.

age yet to be blessed by Adam Smith's invention of the hidden hand, he wrote, 'Reason as well as Experience sufficiently demonstrates that without Law there can be no Government; and without Government, mankind cannot long subsist in Civil Society with one another'.[9] I shall attempt to argue that the tensions produced by the contradictions of this state of 'disorder' in the milieu of Bath are evident in his work and I shall suggest that they were the source of the prodigious energy he displayed in designing and carrying through his projects in the face of opposition, legal difficulties, capital shortage, labour deficiency, and economic depression. They may also account for the fact that he was a prickly sort of man. In any case, his were certainly atypical responses to the 'disorder' of civil society in early eighteenth-century Bath and to the anomie of a developing market economy. Fortunately for him and for posterity, they brought him recognition as a valued participator in the new society. A study of his work, which was both a protest against that society as well as a way of adjusting to it, may take us nearer to the expressive or documentary meaning of Bath.

John Wood, astronomer, antiquarian, and mythologist, as well as architect and capitalist, was what learned men have described as 'self taught' by which they mean he was untutored within the rigid bounds of formal subject learning. His contribution to building apart, he is thought unworthy of serious consideration. Consequently architectural historians and the myriad popularisers of their work have largely ignored or dismissed Wood's writings as a farrago of nonsense. They seem either to contemporise Wood's Bath by making it relevant to twentieth-century town planning or to place it neatly within the context of a linear history of building or architectural styles. The notion that they might try writing history rather than histories scarcely touches their work. The social historian, however, *must* look at Wood's writings as well as his buildings, for his books, *The Origin of Building; or, The Plagiarism of the Heathens Detected* (1741), *An Essay towards a Description of Bath* (1742 and 1749), and *A Dissertation upon the Orders of Columns* (1750), show how Wood, whose work shaped Bath so much in his own image, saw the world and his own place and the place of his buildings in it. If we wish to try to 'read' the early eighteenth century as Wood 'read' it and as he tried to write it in stone, and not as we see it now through the clutter and destruction of the last two hundred and fifty years, we must read these works to learn the language of his polemic signs—those signs which, in Duvignaud's terminology, are a group of activities with a double

---

[9] John Wood, *An Essay towards a Description of Bath*, 1765, repr. Bath, 1969, p. 353.

function: recognising that there is an obstacle (either of participation or expression) to be overcome; and the real or imagined attempt to overcome the obstacle. These functions endow the work of art with a dynamic value of which perhaps even the artist himself is unaware.[10]

We begin this part of our inquiry by taking a look at the landscape in and around Bath. We shall try our best to see it as Wood saw it and from that try to understand his perception of nature, towns and buildings, and, thereby, to comprehend the origins of the polemic signs used by him in his work as architect.

As Wood saw it Bath was but the core of an earlier city the size of Babylon built originally by Bladud, descendant of a Trojan prince, about 480 B.C. Bladud, under the name of Abaris, High Priest of Apollo, had spent eleven years in Greece as 'a Disciple, a Colleague, and even the Master of Pythagoras'.[11] He was, as might be expected, a devotee of a heliocentric system of the planets from which the Pythagorean system was probably derived. This Bladud/Pythagorean system was the reason for the great size of Wood's antique Bath; for, by enlarging it to a triangle with sides fifteen miles by ten by eight he incorporated Stanton Drew. At Stanton Drew there was an impressive circle of standing stones which Wood carefully measured and showed to be a model of the Pythagorean planetary system built by Bladud for use in the Stanton Drew university for British Druids. Wood drew attention to the use of circles in this work and pointed out that the chief ensign of Druidism was a ring. Moreover, the Temple of the Moon at Stanton Drew was identical with the Temple Cyrus ordered the Jews to build in Jerusalem.

Nearer to the surviving core of the city Wood noted the existence of five hills with characteristics of small mountains. Their names meant: Mars' Hill, the Moon's Hill, the Sun's Hill, the King's Hill. the Holy Hill. Hills the elevation of which was such, 'that their Summits command a Country so exceedingly beautiful, and of such vast Extent, that the Eye that views it, and the Mind that considers it with Attention, can never be enough satisfied'.[12] From the tops of these hills Wood reported seeing no sign of the impact of agrarian capitalism, no glimpse of the Bristol slave trade, and no sound of manufacture from the thickening cluster of woollen towns which had crept like Triffids to the boundaries of the city— Wood was no Defoe. Instead, he set his *Essay towards a Description of Bath*, his account of his own contribution to the city, against a

---

[10] See Jean Duvignaud, *The Sociology of Art*, London, 1972, p. 51.
[11] Wood, *Essay*, p. 40.
[12] Ibid., p. 54.

portrayal of a fantastic historic landscape peopled with Druids, Greeks, and cultivated Britons engaged in building temples, altars, castles, palaces, and forums, all in the antique style. Their forums had a particular fascination for Wood for they applied them to the most noble purposes and in them 'convened the People, held their solemn Assemblies, sacrificed to their Gods, delivered their Orations, and proclaimed their Kings'.[13] The city was also a place where the Britons, 'placed all their other Idols about the hot Fountains, so as to make the City appear as the grand Place of Assembly for the Gods of the Pagan World'.[14] It was a city dedicated by a Pythagorean to Apollo, a God whose chief quality, 'was Divination; whose Musick was the Harmony of the Spheres; and to whom the *Britons* . . . paid the highest Honours'.[15]

Even as Wood looked at what was really there he saw through the eyes of a Greek. Hippocrates had said that cities 'that face the East, and are sheltered from the westerly Winds, RESEMBLE the SPRING; . . . the Inhabitants have good Complexions; and the Women, besides being very fruitful, have easy Times'. As Wood observed, Bath faced east, was sheltered from the westerlies, and, receiving the beams of the rising sun must be admitted to be, 'in a SITUATION that RESEMBLES the SPRING; ever Youthful, ever Gay'.[16]

In short, Wood looked at the Bath landscape with the eyes of a man steeped in the antique style of the Renaissance in which verisimilitude had little part. Consequently, in his eyes, Nature itself was antique. Therefore Man, as Nature, was antique. But antique with a difference. Wood enlarged classical antiquity to include pre-Roman Britain and the pre-Hellenic Holy Land. The point of this was to establish connection and continuity between Jewish, Hellenic, and British culture in order to anglicise and puritanise the antique as part of his attempt to overcome his fear of paganism. Wood, as a young, inexperienced and largely self-taught architect building in a new style for a sensual, albeit puritanically developing society, felt threatened by the pagan origins of the Palladian style. Whereas the artists and architects of the High Renaissance, influenced by Ficino, had achieved a relaxed synthesis of antique form and Christian content, Wood was an architectural late starter, a provincial and puritanical Briton, who continued to be plagued by Christian doubts about pagan forms similar to those of the proto-Renaissance. It was the observation of attempts to resolve these doubts which led Panofsky to formulate the 'principle

[13] Ibid., p. 48.
[14] Ibid., p. 57.
[15] Ibid., p. 53.
[16] Ibid., pp. 56-7.

of disjunction'. This principle claims that, 'wherever in the high and later Middle Ages a work of art borrows its form from a classical model, this form is almost invariably invested with a non-classical, normally Christian, significance'.[17] The principle is equally true for Wood in the eighteenth century. It is my contention that, in consciously seeking to reconcile paganism and puritanism, Wood opened up to his secular art emotional spheres which had hitherto been the preserve of religious worship and transformed his buildings in a secular 'sink of iniquity' into symbols of religious and social harmony. His building projects are polemic signs adapted from the antique to indicate a social and religious utopia at odds with the society in which he lived and worked. Unfortunately for Wood it was a utopia unlikely to be achieved because the increasing strength and diversification of the agrarian and commercial capitalism (in which he was such an active and activating agent) was destroying, in its ideal form, what he set out to build.

Evidence for this assertion about the polemic nature of Wood's architecture is set out in his first book published in 1741. It was entitled, *The Origin of Building: or, the Plagiarism of the Heathens Detected* and contained,

> An ACCOUNT *of the* RISE *and* PROGRESS *of* ARCHITECTURE, *from the Creation of the World to the Death of King* Solomon; *and of its Advancement in* Asia, Egypt, Greece, Italy, *and* Britain, *'till it arriv'd to its highest Perfection.* WHEREIN *the Principles of* Architecture, *the proper* Orders *of* Columns, *the Forms and Proportions of* Temples, Basilicas, Churches, *and other celebrated* Edifices, *as well Antient as Modern, are Explained, and Demonstrated to have their Rise from the Works of the* Jews, *and not* Greecians, *as suggested by* Pagan Writers, *and their* Followers.[18]

In the body of the book Wood argued that beauty in building and classical architecture were brought into the world at God's command with the building of the Tabernacle. God *was* the Divine Architect. He worked only with 'perfect harmony, and the most delightful proportion'. Above all others he preferred and expressed himself in the circular form. Since, in his *Essay on Bath*, Wood also emphasised the importance of circles and circular movement in the Bladud/Pythagorean heliocentric system and in the construction of the Druidical university at Stanton Drew, the threefold and unify-

---

[17] Erwin Panofsky, *Renaissance and Renascences in Western Art*, London, 1970, p. 84.
[18] Advertisement for *The Origin of Building: or, The Plagiarism of the Heathens Detected*, London and Bath, 1741, in *A Description of the Exchange at Bristol*, Bath, 1745, p. 37.

ing symbolism of the circle should be plain. It was Jewish and, thereby, Christian first, then British and Greek; the polemic sign of God, and, therefore, of absolute beauty; of absolute beauty, and, therefore, of God. In this manner Wood re-synthesised for himself antique form and Christian content and freed himself from threatening pagan associations. In doing so he released his creative genius to incorporate religious polemic signs in every building he designed.

God as absolute beauty was unknowable except through Man as made by God in his own image. But this was sufficient for Wood, who considered Man a good starting-point from which to move towards a comprehension of God. He wrote,

> In the works of the Divine Architect of all things, we find nothing but perfect figures, consisting of the utmost *Regularity*, the sweetest *Harmony*, and the most delightful *Proportion*: And as his works universally tend to a circular form, and are as universally constituted of three different principal parts, so those three parts generally carry with them, in the whole, and severally, the properties of *Use, Strength, and Beauty*; to illustrate which, the figure of a Man, created in the image of GOD, is the most notable example.
>
> The parts of Man are mostly circular; and of the infinite number with which he is composed, there is not one superfluous, or that do not answer some particular use, conducive to his existence.
>
> Man consists of three principal parts, namely, the head, the trunk, and the limbs; all the parts, in their utmost extent, are comprehended in a square, or in a circle; and so exact is the mechanism of his whole structure, that all the parts mutually assist each other, and contribute to the *Strength* of the whole.
>
> Man is a complete figure, and the perfection of order.[19]

Man so comprehended was God. Thus Wood's architecture, which can be thought of as a re-creative imitation of nature and of Man, was also a re-creative imitation of God. The symbolic representation of this idea of the omniscience, essence, and beauty of God, and of his unity with Man as his most perfect work embodying order, proportion and harmony, is the Vitruvian figure referred to by Wood in the previous extract. This is a naked man, arms and legs diagonally outstretched with the points of his feet and hands touching the circumference of a circle and the perimeter of a square. Palladio's religious architecture derived from this concept and he employed abstracted versions of the Vitruvian figure in their construction. Wood, a disciple of Palladio, also worked with

[19] *Origin*, p. 71.

the concept and used versions of the Vitruvian figure as polemic signs in his secular architecture. (cf. Plates IVa with IVb and Va with Vb for Wood's uses of the figure).

Before we explore Wood's use of the circle and of the Vitruvian figure as polemic signs in his building, two other aspects of the Judaeo-Christian content he gave to antique forms must be described. They concern windows and the principal orders of columns. Windows were Tabernacles. For example, Wood described the windows in Belcomb Brook Villa as a model of the 'Octostyle Monopterick Temple of *Delphos*', and those in Titanbarrow Logia as 'dressed so as to become compleat Tabernacles'.[20] We are already acquainted with the significance of the Jewish Tabernacle in his account of the origin of building. It appears likely that Tabernacle windows acted as polemic signs pointing to God as the Divine Architect and served to remind Wood himself of his denial of the pagan origins of antique forms. Such necessarily repeated reminders suggest a continuing uncertainty and tension. Wood's views about the orders of columns are more fully documented. The evidence shows the complexity of their symbolism, while the fact that he published a third book solely on columns indicates the importance he attached to it. The principal orders, Doric, Ionic, and Corinthian, had a threefold symbolism. First, they represented Nature in general and trees in particular; all pillars were imitation trees. Thus, when describing the Corinthian order at Titanbarrow Logia, Wood wrote,

> And all the mouldings and sofits in the whole front, proper to be carved, are to be fully enriched, that nothing may be wanted to decorate the order, which, as it represents nature in all her bloom, requires the greatest profusion of ornament to embellish it that can be put together with propriety and elegance.[21]

Secondly, the three orders were, 'the most lively Symbols of the Robust Man, of the Grave Matron, and of the Sprightly young Girl'.[22] Consequently, the north side of Queen Square, built in the Corinthian order and symbolising a sprightly young girl as well as Nature in all her springlike glory, is described by Wood as soaring above the other buildings with a sprightliness which gives it the elegance and grandeur of a palace. And this in a city itself likened by Wood to spring, youthfulness and gaiety. So to the third symbolic meaning of the orders of columns which flows only from

20 Wood, *Essay*, p. 238.
21 Ibid., p. 240.
22 John Wood, *A Dissertation Upon the Orders of Columns*, London, 1750, p. 27.

the fusion of all three orders considered as a total re-creative imitation of Man made in God's image. When the three orders are placed upon one another, Wood wrote, 'a Harmony will, in many Cases attend the Composition beyond any Thing that can be produced by Columns of unequal Altitudes sustaining one another'. However, by making the shafts of the columns of each order of one and the same diameter at bottom

> the Delicacy and Stateliness of one entire Column above the other becomes still more Conspicuous. For as the Orders advance towards Virginal Beauty and Elegance, the Columns increase in their Altitude, and thereby one Order receives a Majesty above the other, even in Miniature upon Paper, which words can scarcely describe.[23]

One could almost imagine the impossible and believe that Wood had not only seen Botticelli's *The Birth of Venus* and equated Venus with the Corinthian order, but also understood Botticelli's portrayal of divine or transcendent love. Certainly no one who looks at Wood's Bath knowing what Wood tried so desperately to say can ever again look at the orders of columns and see merely pillars —he should at least see Venus or the Three Graces, and pretend he can see God.

So, what are we to make of Wood as he worked to assemble his contribution to Bath as a total polemic sign consisting of circles, squares, Vitruvian figures, Tabernacle windows, the orders of columns, all expressed harmoniously according to the idea of unity in diversity, of three in one, and built in and for a market economy? Principally, Wood contrived to put a frame rather like a proscenium arch around the urban environment of civil society with the purpose of enhancing Man's awareness of himself as made in God's image, and, thereby, his awareness of God.

Look first at the plan for Queen Square (Plate IVb). This square was a novelty in Bath; it let far more light and air into its surrounding houses than reached those in Chandos Court or Beaufort Square, or those in the courts of early eighteenth-century Edinburgh. But the enlargement of the space enclosed does not alter the fact that what Wood planned was an enclosure and not a street or an isolated block of houses. Further, all the surrounding houses were to face into the central area of this enclosure which was designed as a perfect square and intended to be perfectly level. At the centre of the square was to be a perfect circle radiating four diagonals, each ending in smaller circles. The whole geometrical design looks like an abstract Vitruvian figure. This visual impression should be

[23] Ibid.

borne in mind when one reads what Wood wrote about the purpose of the enclosure, which he persisted with in spite of the heavy expense involved. He wrote,

> I preferred an inclosed Square to an open one, to make this as useful as possible: For the Intention of a Square in a City is for People to assemble together; and the Spot whereon they meet, ought to be separated from the Ground common to Men and Beasts, and even to Mankind in General, if Decency and good order are necessary to be observed in such Places of Assembly; of which, I think, there can be no doubt.[24]

Clearly, Wood intended the enclosure as an environmental determinant of good order. It was to be a place in which a chosen few would be able to assemble apart from the bustle of every day things, the animal kingdom, and the generality of men—apart, that is, from civil society. As these few contemplated the north side of the square their spirits would soar in the manner already described. Nature, except in the shape of a green turf and formal shrubs, was expressly excluded. There were to be no forest trees in the square, only low stone walls and espaliers of elm and lime. The fact that the exquisite chapel dedicated to the Virgin Mary and built in the Doric order as part of the whole development scheme attracted a very high demand for building sites in the neighbourhood, suggests that many of his customers, even in the midst of iniquity, fancied the form, if not the substance of his own social and religious beliefs.

When Wood began his next development in the Parades in 1739 he turned the square inside out, and thus the houses of the Grand and South Parades and of the South Parade parallel with it (Plate Vb) became the central square form, while the associated places of assembly were opened up to the surrounding countryside. Nevertheless, his main concern was to create paved open areas for the practice of public walking and talking, activities which distinguish men from beasts. He hoped to render these activities more congenial in the South Parade by letting in the winter sunshine and developing the open space as a forum. For St James' Triangle, the open space in front of the Grand Parade, he designed a formal garden in the shape of a Vitruvian figure. As in Queen Square this open space was important since, while he thought of the houses on the Grand Parade as outward looking, he also intended that they should be viewed from *across* that formal garden. In this way Nature, except in its antique and formal shape, was still kept at a safe distance and provided only a subdued background to his man-centred buildings. Moreover, whatever aesthetic appeal Nature had

[24] Wood, *Essay*, p. 345.

was derived from its antique and religious associations. The principal natural feature to be seen from the Grand Parade was Solsbury Hill. In Wood's mythology this had been the site of the Temple of Apollo. He wrote, 'If those Works had still existed; their Tremendous Look, from the *Grand Parade*, must have inspired Mankind with a Religious Awe as often as they should consider that the Great God of Heaven and Earth was Adored by them'.[25]

It is in the design of his third great work, the Circus, that Wood gave fullest expression to the ideas he published in 1741 (Plate VI). He planned the Circus as two perfect circles, one inside the other. The outer circle of buildings is 318 feet in diameter, which is virtually identical with the present circumference of the chalk wall at Stonehenge, which measures 320 feet from crest to crest, and with the north-south dimension of Queen Square which is 316 feet. Wood's design also incorporated a threefold expression of his idea of the trinity and of unity in diversity; he cut the outer of the two circles into three equal segments, made three approaches to the centre circle, and piled the three principal orders of columns one on top of the other. This piling of the orders had the further symbolic meaning already described. Combining virginal beauty, elegance, and altitude they generated a majesty beyond words. Since a circle of buildings throws the eye more towards the centre and seems to enclose the space within more effectively than a square of buildings, so the Circus, enclosing a smaller area than Queen Square, was even more inward looking than it. Moreover, the Circus was built without any incline on a level ledge cut into the hillside. It was also designed to be totally devoid of natural vegetation. Only its southernmost entrance let in the sun and a distant view of Beechen Cliff. It was designed as pure space enclosed by three equal segments of a perfect circle. Since, as I have argued, Wood's architecture sprang from tension involving a sense of the awfulness and omniscience of God, which he infused into the antique forms with which he worked, this austerity of the Circus and the deliberate exclusion of forest trees and of all nature is an integral part of the Circus as a total polemic sign (Plate VII). In designing the Circus Wood was not concerned to unite town and country or to plan towns; rather, in the midst of the corruption of civil society and in its interest, he worked to glorify God by writing *The Whole Duty of Man* in stone. Subsequently his son financed it with the help of loans from local Quakers who had close ties with the West Indian slave and sugar trades.[26] Thus, Wood's utopia, like Marx's capital,

---

[25] Ibid., p. 351.
[26] See mortgages in Wood Box, Guildhall Archives, Bath, especially Indentures, 10 October 1771 and 11 January 1779.

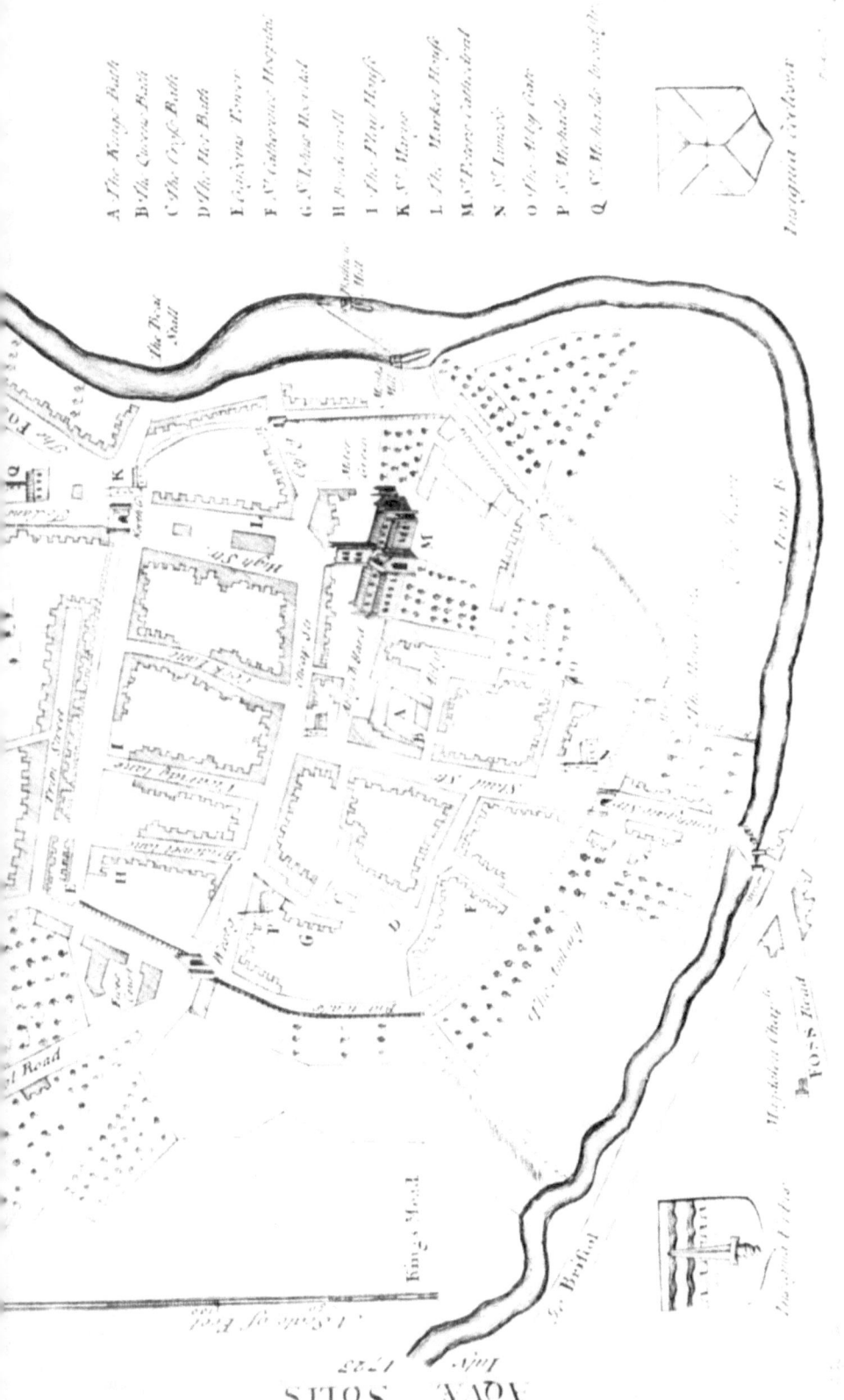

Plate III Map of Bath, 1723; from William Stukeley, *Itinerarium Curiosum* (1724). Reproduced by permission of Bath Reference Library.

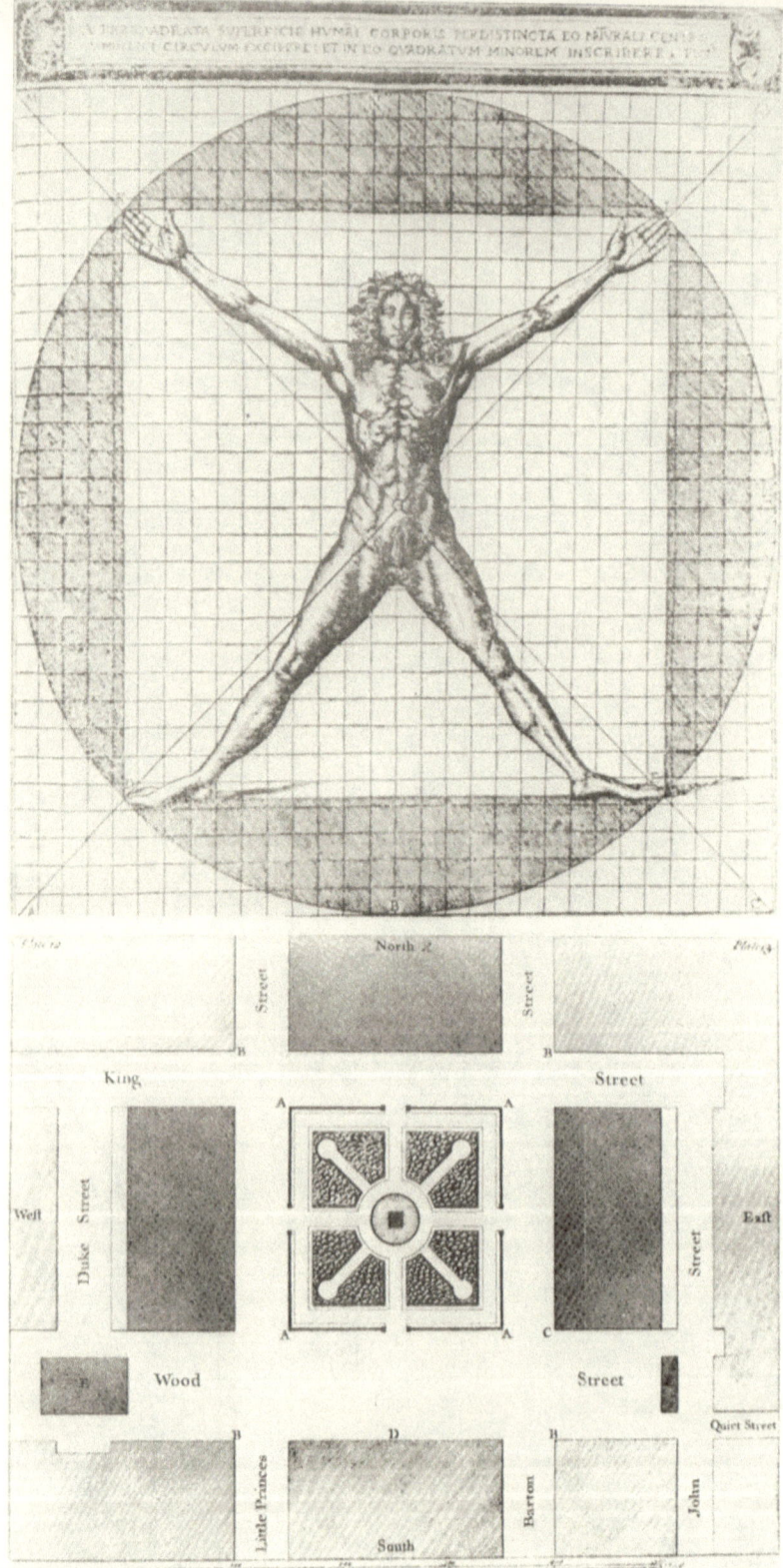

Plate IV (a) Vitruvian Figure, from Cesariano's edition of Vitruvius (Como, 1521).
(b) Queen Square, Bath; from Wood's *Essay towards a Description of Bath* (1765).

came into the world, 'soiled with mire from top to toe, and oozing blood from every pore'.[27]

Other historians have offered different explanations of Wood's Bath; for, with the aid of a rather naïve deterministic biographical approach to history, which emphasises simple causal relationships between environment and action, it is possible to explain Wood's achievement in terms of the existence and influence of a style. Such 'stylistic' explanations are generally made with one eye firmly on the linear history of architecture and town planning. They are sometimes adequate for their purpose. However, I have emphasised that Wood's creative responses to his circumstances were atypical. Atypical responses cannot be explained by general causes. Objective conditions such as the existence and character of agrarian capitalism and its ideology, the demands of a wealthy clientele, the nature of land law and the structure of landownership, the developing puritanism of society, the existence of a style and the availability of technology, the enduring character of Whig patronage, and the circumstances of personal biography can set the boundaries of objective responsibilities and shape conditions for creativity. They can neither determine nor explain its form; there were at least ten architect/builders in early eighteenth-century Bath, but only one John Wood. And therein lies a deal of the difficulty we have in attempting to see Bath as Wood saw it and meant it. His finished works do not obviously spring, soar, or uplift; indeed, one might well question whether strictly classical architectural forms could ever do so. Furthermore, few of Wood's customers in civil society, then or since, had enough grasp of the language of his polemic signs to enable them to read these appearances into his buildings and to grasp his message. Writing in 1749 Wood seemed to have understood this himself. Following a devoted and detailed description of the three country houses he had built he wrote,

> These modern Instances shewing us in Miniature how happily *Bath* is situated for the execution of beautiful Works in Architecture; let the contiguous Building of the City now Demonstrate the Great Regard that hath been lately shewn to display the Free Stone of the Country to as much Advantage as can be well expected in a Place where the Houses, in general, are applied to such Uses as Bring them down almost to the Rank of common Inns.[28]

If this was the view of the author of many of them it is little wonder that while many people could see a generalised beauty in

[27] Karl Marx, *Capital*, 2 vols., London, 1962, II, 843.
[28] Wood, *Essay*, p. 240.

Bath, particularly when the city sparkled white on a clear spring morning, most missed the point of Wood's Bath. Smollet, himself a moralist, nevertheless made his Matthew Bramble dismiss the Circus as 'a pretty bauble; contrived for shew' and let his Lydia Melford, a lovesick modern miss, delight in it as a sumptuous palace in an earthly paradise,[29] a view endorsed in the twentieth century by the doyen of English architectural historians, Sir John Summerson, who finds it, 'quaintly beautiful—as if some simple-minded community had taken over an antique monument and neatly adapted it as a residence'.[30]

But something of Wood's utopian vision forces itself upon us, for, although we may look at Wood's Bath without a knowledge of his polemic signs, the dynamic aesthetic quality they imparted to his works gives them strength to speak for themselves. Naturally the context in which they speak is different. Wood's building influenced the designs of his contemporaries and successors, Palladians all. Since, however, they were less tortured than he about the pagan origins of their style and were more in tune with the vagaries of the market, they built in a lighter vein. Their buildings act as foils to his. Then they appear to us scarred by our own and Victorian vandalism, distorted by the filter of romantic nature, and encroached upon by forest trees and motor cars. Nevertheless, the effect of his polemic signs is to force us to consider seriously his views about the way in which urban men ought to live—views which Burley Griffin's successors have ignored to Canberra's cost. And views which Bath itself is fast forgetting. The polemic signs of Wood's twentieth-century successors in Bath, Bath City Council, city architects, development companies, and city planners point only to the anomie of sub-urban living and the wasteland of the market. Concern for absolute property, whether corporate or private, whether of the retail grocer or of the car owner dominates decision making. John Locke, too, is still with us, as, indeed, he was with John Wood. The difference is that John Wood created the Circus; his twentieth-century successors merely build. Even the dream of utopia eludes them.

---

[29] Tobias Smollet, *The Expedition of Humphry Clinker*, ed. L. M. Knapp, London, 1972, pp. 35, 39.
[30] Summerson, *Architecture*, p. 235.

Social Stratification and the Obsequious Curve: Goldsmith and Rowlandson

Robert H. Hopkins

1974 marks the bicentennial of Oliver Goldsmith's death, and *The Vicar of Wakefield* continues to be, in the words of the *Johnsonian News Letter*, 'one of the best—and most baffling—of 18th-century novels'.[1] By far the most baffling aspect of *The Vicar* has been its tonality, Goldsmith's attitudes towards his materials. Is *The Vicar* a sentimental romance which begins comically, turns melodramatic, and concludes happily? In 1768 Fanny Burney testified in her diary that she was tempted at first to throw the book aside but then was '*surprised into tears*—and in the second volume . . . really sobb'd'. But for her the best part of the book was that it turned 'one's grief out of doors, to open them [sic] to laughter'.[2] The singularly humourless illustrations after Thomas Stothard in the 1792 edition of the novel must have conditioned many readers to respond in the manner of Fanny Burney (Plate VIII). But if *The Vicar* is seen instead as an ironically sustained comedy which satirises false benevolence and parodies the style of sensibility, then Rowlandson's illustrations provide a much more apt commentary on the book than Stothard's.[3]

All illustrations in this essay are reproduced with the permission of The Henry E. Huntington Library and Art Gallery, San Marino, California.
    [1] XXXIII (1973), No. 1, p. 12.
    [2] *The Early Diary of Frances Burney, 1768-1778*, ed. Annie Raine Ellis, 2 vols., London, 1889, I, 12-13. Critics never seem to add that sixteen-year-old Fanny Burney deprecates *The Vicar*, preferring to it Griffith's *Henry and Frances*, and that she is known to Arthur Young, an old family friend, as 'feeling Fanny'.
    [3] The illustrations appeared in the 1817 edition, published by R. Ackermann. Re-issued in 1823. Austin Dobson referred to Rowlandson's illustrations as a 'pictorial outrage' (*Side-Walk Studies*, London, 1902, p. 139). George Saintsbury replied two decades later that if his old friend had said such a thing when they were together at the Athenæum, he would have retorted, 'Fudge!' (*The*

In recent years critical discussions of *The Vicar* have tended to favour a critically comic, if not satiric, interpretation; and Ricardo Quintana has been the most distinguished advocate of trusting Goldsmith's artistry and seeing the writer as a superb Georgian ironist. But, as one reviewer has complained, it seems hardly worth while justifying Goldsmith's irony as an adequate aesthetic end in itself when very few twentieth-century readers may be reading Goldsmith at all.[4]

In the critical debate over Goldsmith's sense and sensibility we have failed to consider adequately why—other than for money—Goldsmith wrote *The Vicar of Wakefield* in the first place, or how Goldsmith's imagination transcends his era so that his novel is still worth reading. I should like to avoid as much as possible the problem of sentimentality and focus on social stratification in the novel and the treatment of obsequiousness which is posed in Rowlandson's frontispiece (Plate IX). Rather than dismiss Rowlandson's caricature as a 'pictorial outrage', I should like to explore the possibility that Rowlandson, both here and in a number of other illustrations to *The Vicar*, responded intuitively to Goldsmith's deep concern with the changing relationships between classes in a society increasingly dominated by extremes of wealth and poverty.

Nathan Bailey had defined 'obsequious' as 'very ready to obey or to assist; diligent to please, complaisant, dutiful'. Johnson defined the word as 'obedient; compliant; not resisting'. When we turn to the *Oxford English Dictionary*, the first definition of 'obsequious' reads,

> Compliant with the will or wishes of another, esp. of a superior; prompt to serve, please, or follow directions; obedient; dutiful. Now *rare*.

The second definition is what we are accustomed to,

> Unduly or servilely compliant; ignobly submissive; manifesting

---

Vicar of Wakefield, intr. George Saintsbury, London and Boston, 1926, p. xxx. This edition contains the twenty-four Rowlandson illustrations). For a non-interpretive analysis of Rowlandson's illustrations, see Edward C. J. Wolf, *Rowlandson and his Illustrations of Eighteenth-Century English Literature*, Copenhagen, 1945.

[4] Review essay by George Rousseau (*Eighteenth-Century Studies*, V (1971-2), 629-36), discussing Ricardo Quintana's 'Oliver Goldsmith, Ironist to the Georgians', in *Eighteenth-Century Studies in Honor of Donald F. Hyde*, ed. W. H. Bond, New York, 1970, pp. 297-310. Rousseau's objection is that to praise *The Vicar of Wakefield* for its ironic technique is too limited when one fails to confront the content of the work. Rousseau asks, 'When *will* the "entire novel" concern us and who will judge it if not the leader of Goldsmith studies?' (p. 631). My essay is intended to answer in part Rousseau's query.

or characterized by servile complaisance; fawning, cringing, sycophantic.⁵

Between Bailey's and Johnson's honorific definitions of 'obsequious' and its modern pejorative sense there is, I would suggest, a significant shift in class consciousness. Dorothy George has recognised such a shift in her magnificent *Hogarth to Cruikshank: Social Change in Graphic Satire*. Her introduction outlines a social stratification of early eighteenth-century England characterised by considerable fluidity and easy intercourse between the classes. Foreign visitors marvelled at how readily and unselfconsciously the labouring classes and the aristocracy mingled in taverns and parks. George believes that with minor exceptions class antagonism in England did not surface to any great extent before the French Revolution, that it developed after 1815, and that only in the later Regency did it make a 'belated impact on social satire', with the 'decline of subordination' and the 'stirrings of democracy'.⁶ Peter Laslett had earlier arrived at a similar conclusion with his thesis that traditional English society was essentially a one-class society highly subordinated in structure but in which mobility both upwards and downwards was 'normal rather than exceptional'. Unlike Dorothy George, however, Laslett sees the rise in class consciousness as being heralded in the Wilkesite radicalism of the 1760s which was a 'sign of an altered relationship between the common man and his gentleman superior, in which quiescent political ignorance had begun to give way to demands for a share in the national political life'. To understate how the 'élite, the ruling segment, was related to the rest' is for Laslett a study of the greatest importance; he warns that historians will have to show 'imaginative sensitivity to all those subtle influences which enable a minority to live for all the rest' and that it is 'the symbolic life of our ancestors which will be the most difficult to handle', 'especially their symbols of status'.⁷

There is one Hogarth print that has always seemed to me to be a remarkably apt illustration of a subordinated English society along the lines that Laslett describes and in which there is a symbol of status whereby one performs a role vicariously for all the rest. It is, of course, Plate 12 of Hogarth's *Industry and Idleness*: 'The

⁵ Nathan Bailey, *Dictionarium Britannicum*, London, 1730, s.v. 'obsequious'. Samuel Johnson, *A Dictionary of the English Language*, London, 1755, s.v. 'obsequious'. *OED*, s.v. 'obsequious'. See 'servile' in the above for the qualities associated with the modern senses of 'obsequious'.
⁶ New York, 1967, p. 15. See also Jean Hecht's review essay, 'Eighteenth-Century Graphic Satire as Historical Evidence', *Studies in Burke and His Time*, X (1969), 1257-66.
⁷ *The World We Have Lost: England Before the Industrial Age*, 2nd edn, New York, 1971, pp. 195, 211, and 54.

Industrious 'Prentice Lord-Mayor of London' (Plate X). Francis Goodchild, the successful apprentice, becomes the epitome of middle-class success even as the attendants of Frederick Prince of Wales and his consort seem to be indifferent to the spectacle below. The ambivalence of this print for Hogarth has been subtly analysed by Ronald Paulson: even as the print in the morality sequence 'hails the industrious hero', it casts 'doubt upon the value of his reward, and perhaps even his kind of success'. And, as Paulson also shows, the close parallel between the crowd and the procession in this print, and the crowd and the procession of Tom Idle to the gallows at Tyburn creates an ironic statement directed 'at society itself'.[8] If one also sees that both the Lord Mayor and the Prince of Wales are prisoners of their official roles, Hogarth's print becomes comically subversive.

The significance of obsequiousness as an organising motif for this essay is that it focuses on the integrity, or lack of integrity, of relationships between classes. If Dorothy George is correct, by 1817 when Thomas Rowlandson illustrated *The Vicar of Wakefield*, society was highly conscious of the uneasy relationships between classes. His repertoire included, as we shall see, a stock line or posture which I shall term the 'obsequious curve' and which is used in three important illustrations to *The Vicar*. If Laslett is correct in placing the rise of class consciousness in the 1760s, Goldsmith's many artistic statements on this topic must be taken into account.

It has long been recognised that *The Deserted Village* is not directed against the enclosure system in agriculture *per se*, but rather against the rural depopulation caused by the newly-rich commercial classes moving to the country and building pleasure gardens. As such, the poem represents a conservative reaction to the earlier Whig panegyric verse of Thomson and others, which eulogised an expanding mercantile economy founded on a growing empire.[9] The last four lines of *The Deserted Village*, generally attributed to Samuel Johnson, argue for a small country's prospering through internal industry rather than by means of external commerce:

> That trade's proud empire hastes to swift decay,
> As ocean sweeps the labour'd mole away;
> While self-dependent power can time defy,
> As rocks resist the billows and the sky.
>
> (lines 427-30)

[8] *Hogarth: His Life, Art, and Times*, 2 vols., New Haven and London, 1971, II, 71-4.

[9] Howard J. Bell Jr, 'The Deserted Village and Goldsmith's Social Doctrines', *PMLA*, LIX (1944), 747-72. For a very sound explication of the poem, see Roger Lonsdale's commentary in *The Poems of Thomas Gray, William Collins, Oliver Goldsmith*, London, 1969, pp. 669-94.

This was a favourite thesis not only of Johnson but of Goldsmith as early as 1759 in *The Bee*:

> The true interest of every government is to cultivate the necessaries, by which is always meant every happiness our own country can produce; and suppress all the luxuries, by which is meant, on the other hand, every happiness imported from abroad. Commerce has therefore its bounds. . . .[10]

What Goldsmith feared most from the wealth accumulated by foreign commerce was the creation of a new class of nabobs. Such a class could tend towards an aristocracy, a form of government which Johnson had defined as placing 'the supreme power in the nobles, without a king, and exclusively of the people'.[11] For Goldsmith the best protection against such a plutocracy would be a strong independent middle class and a strong monarch to keep men equal within a society subordinated on the basis of merit:

> For just experience tells in every soil,
> That those who think must govern those that toil,
> And all that freedom's highest aims can reach,
> Is but to lay proportion'd loads on each.
> (*The Traveller*, lines 371-4)

When this political balance is disturbed, the middle class and the lower classes are endangered: 'Hence, should one order disproportion'd grow,/Its double weight must ruin all below'. When the monarchy is weakened, justice itself is in jeopardy:

> But when contending chiefs blockade the throne,
> Contracting regal power to stretch their own,
> When I behold a factious band agree
> To call it freedom, when themselves are free,
> Each wanton judge new penal statutes draw,
> Laws grind the poor, and rich men rule the law.
> (lines 381-6)

This political philosophy is identical with Dr Primrose's in his political 'harangue' (*The Vicar*, Chapter XIX: 'The description of a person discontented with the present government, and apprehensive of the loss of our liberties.'). Primrose complains that it is 'in the interest of the great . . . to diminish kingly power', that because 'more riches flow in from external commerce, than arise from internal industry', 'wealth in all commercial states is found to accumulate' until the states 'become aristocratical'. 'Again, the very laws also of this country may contribute to the accumulation of wealth; as when by their means the *natural ties that bind the rich*

---

[10] *Collected Works of Oliver Goldsmith*, ed. Arthur Friedman, 5 vols., Oxford, 1966, I, 442. (Hereafter cited as *Collected Works*.)
[11] *Dictionary*, s.v. 'aristocracy'.

and poor together are broken . . .'¹² (italics mine). How these 'natural ties' are broken is described in 'The Revolution in Low Life' (*Lloyd's Evening Post*, 14-16 June 1762), the essay which R. S. Crane once described as the '*Deserted Village* in Prose' and which seems equally seminal for *The Vicar*.¹³ Written in the form of a letter to the editor, the essay describes the writer's stay in a country village the inhabitants of which are forced to leave because the estate on which they live has been purchased by a 'Merchant of immense fortune in London' who 'intended to lay the whole out in a seat of pleasure for himself'. These villagers will be forced 'to toil as hirelings under some rigid Master, to flatter the opulent for a precarious meal . . .'. Throughout the country, the writer asserts, one 'sees one part of the inhabitants of the country becoming immensely rich' while 'the other' is 'growing miserably poor, and the happy equality of condition now entirely removed'. In a country 'divided into the very rich and very poor', the writer observes, 'the Great' are 'not so bad as they are generally represented', but the 'dependents and favourites of the Great' are 'strangers to every sentiment of honour and generosity', 'Wretches, who, by giving up their own dignity to those above them, insolently exact the same tribute from those below'.¹⁴

Economic disparities between classes increase so that 'natural ties' are destroyed and human relationships become insincere. It is easy to see how the honorific sense of 'obsequious' applied to traditional subordinated relationships takes on pejorative colourings. In Letter C: 'A life of independance praised', The Citizens of the World, Goldsmith through his mouthpiece Lien Chi Altangi, reverses the usual treatment of charity, focusing not on giving but on 'the ignominy of receiving'. He who 'thrives upon the unmerited bounty of another, if he has any sensibility, suffers the worst of servitude', 'the humble dependant is taxed with ingratitude upon every symptom of discontent', 'every new obligation but adds to the former load' which keeps 'the vigorous mind from rising; till at last, elastic no longer, it shapes itself to constraint, and puts on habitual servility'. (Lien Chi Altangi excludes from the 'meanness of a life of continued dependance' those 'natural or political subordinations which subsist in every society'.) Such servility destroys authentic relationships between classes based on mutual obligations: 'It is perhaps one of the severest misfortunes of the great, that they are, in general, obliged to live among men whose real value is lessened

---

12 *Collected Works*, IV, 100-1.
13 *Times Literary Supplement*, 8 September 1927, p. 607.
14 *Collected Works*, III, 195-8. Notice Friedman's footnote 2 (III, 195-6), which states that most of *The Vicar* was 'probably in great part written by the summer of 1762'.

by dependance, and whose minds are enslaved by obligation'. Altangi concludes that 'a life of independance is generally a life of virtue' and that the 'sturdy gloom of laborious indigence' is 'far more lovely' than the 'fawning simper of thriving adulation'.[15]

Given this summary of Goldsmith's political philosophy and his concern with authenticity in relationships between the classes, we may return to Rowlandson's frontispiece and to the vexing problem as to what might have motivated Goldsmith to write *The Vicar*. Primrose, accompanied by his two daughters one of whom is dropping a penny into the hat of a robust, mendacious beggar, is depicted as comically self-satisfied. Rowlandson's frontispiece satirises not a benevolence directed to ameliorating the plight of the genuinely suffering poor, but the kind of patronising that symbolises a falsely-subordinated relationship between the gentry and the lower classes. We may dismiss this frontispiece as a travesty of the real essence of Goldsmith's novel. We may want to interpret Rowlandson's view as possibly depicting a social tension characteristic of 1817. But Rowlandson may also provide a genuine insight into *The Vicar*.

Why does Goldsmith continually stress reversal of social role throughout *The Vicar*? Primrose is reduced to one of the lowest rungs of the Church of England; Sir William Thornhill disguises himself as Mr Burchell, a gentleman 'of broken fortune'; George Primrose, an Oxford alumnus, tries to make his fortune in London starting at the bottom. Is it not to illustrate the turmoil resulting from a commercial society in which a mixed constitution is diminished, by an erosion of the power of the monarchy, to the extent that greatness is dependent solely on wealth and on the power which comes from wealth? When much later in the novel Dr Primrose delivers his political speech to his host (who turns out to be the butler), he argues that the 'very laws ... of this country' so contribute to 'the accumulation of wealth' that the 'natural ties that bind the rich and poor together are broken'. When the very wealthy man purchases power for power's sake 'in making dependants, by purchasing the liberty of the needy or the venal', or by gathering around him 'a circle of the poorest of the people', those who are 'willing to move' in such a 'great man's vortex, are only such as must be slaves'. They become the 'rabble of mankind, whose souls and whose education are adapted to servitude, and who know nothing of liberty except the name'. For Dr Primrose—and for Goldsmith as well—only the middle class subsisting 'between the very rich and the very rabble' is 'the true preserver of freedom'.[16]

[15] Ibid., II, 396-9.
[16] Ibid., IV, 101-2.

At the very beginning of *The Vicar* the Primroses are settled in a genteel situation which is described adjectivally as 'an elegant house, . . . a fine country, . . . a good neighbourhood'. In the pecking order of subordination, the Primrose family is visited very frequently by poorer cousins who are treated generously, while occasionally the family is made uneasy because the Squire would 'sometimes fall asleep in the most pathetic parts' of Primrose's sermon or 'his lady' would 'return' Mrs Primrose's 'civilities at church with a mutilated curtesy'. Because of his having 'a sufficient fortune' of his own, Dr Primrose is 'careless of temporalities' and has made over the 'profits' of his living to 'the orphans and widows of the clergy' of the diocese. He keeps no curate and knows every man in his parish.[17]

This idyllic state of being is shattered when George Primrose, having just left Oxford, fixes his affections upon Miss Arabella Wilmot, 'the daughter of a neighbouring clergyman, who was a dignitary in the church, and in circumstances to give her a large fortune'. In exchange Mr Wilmot knows that Dr Primrose 'could make a very handsome settlement' on his son. The courtship period is lengthened and includes a round of being 'awaked in the morning by music, and on fine days' by hunting. 'Walking out, drinking tea, country dances, and forfeits, shortened the rest of the day'. Unfortunately, Dr Primrose's tract in favour of monogamy for clergymen runs counter to Mr Wilmot's violent attachment to the opposite opinion—he is courting a fourth wife—and during the debate with Mr Wilmot on this topic, Primrose learns that his fortune is lost to an absconding merchant. The match is broken off, and Dr Primrose moves to 'a small Cure of fifteen pounds a year' offered him 'in a distant neighbourhood'. Normally, in a traditional society, authority and hierarchy are founded upon the sanctions of law and religion, but G. F. A. Best has shown how in the eighteenth century the ecclesiastical authority of the Church of England's own courts was superseded by the authority of the temporal courts.[18] If, as Peter Laslett notes, the 'squire and sometimes the parson were the links between the village and the nation', the authority of the parson would be lessened, particularly with over half of the benefices in England, according to Best, under the patronage of laymen.[19] The smugness of Primrose's earlier situation is grounded in part on his material wealth. By removing that wealth and reducing Primrose to the lower role of an 'inferior clergyman' Gold-

---

[17] Ibid., IV, 18-22.
[18] *Temporal Pillars: Queen Anne's Bounty, the Ecclesiastical Commissioners, and the Church of England*, Cambridge, 1964.
[19] Laslett, *The World We Have Lost*, p. 193; Best, *Temporal Pillars*, p. 46.

smith is better able to nighlight the tension between an ideal social structure based on moral worth and a social structure increasingly based on power and wealth.

I believe that Rowlandson has captured some of the nuances of this tension when he depicts the Primroses' departure from Wakefield (Plate XI) and their arrival at the new parish (Plate XII). In Plate XI I refer specifically to the man fourth from the right of the picture, dejectedly bent over. The same kind of posture occurs in Plate XIII on the left side of the picture in the figure of the man slouching over his gaping family. I have entitled this motif 'the obsequious curve'. Neither figure is described in Goldsmith's text, but certain of Goldsmith's phrases may appropriately be called to mind. When the Primroses leave Wakefield, for example, how many of us have noticed the subtle implications of this passage?

> The leaving a neighbourhood in which we had enjoyed so many hours of tranquility, was not without a tear. . . . Besides, a journey of seventy miles to a family that had hitherto never been above ten from home, filled us with apprehension, *and the cries of the poor, who followed us for some miles*, contributed to encrease it.[20] (my italics)

When Primrose arrives at his new parish, however, the neighbourhood is described as 'consisting of farmers, who tilled their own grounds, and were equal strangers to opulence and poverty'.[21] In view of a similar passage in 'The Revolution in Low Life' (noted by Arthur Friedman)[22] it seems clear that Goldsmith intended to depict in Wakefield extremes of opulence and poverty. In the new parish, more agrarian and more traditional, the farmers are self-sufficient, like Mr Williams who, because he 'owed his landlord no rent', 'little regarded' Mr Thornhill's indignation when both were courting Olivia Primrose.[23] What Rowlandson has done is to convey through the obsequious curve in Plate XI an attitude of respectful obedience, and in Plate XII a slouch more probably the effect of farm-labour. Thanks to Rowlandson we are suddenly made conscious of Goldsmith's treatment of social stratification in the novel.

Such close attention to one motif is not a distortion of Rowlandson's artistry. A. P. Oppé has observed that it is 'in the character of the line' that Rowlandson's 'whole humour, or it may be horror, resides'.[24] Bernard Falk maintains that a typical Rowlandson group is 'not a mere maze of squiggles meant to represent human beings,

[20] *Collected Works*, IV, 27.
[21] Ibid., IV, 31.
[22] Ibid., IV, 32, note.
[23] Ibid., IV, 86.
[24] *Thomas Rowlandson: His Drawings and Water-Colours*, ed. Geoffrey Holmes, London, 1923, p. 22.

but cunningly formed figures bending this way and that in obedience to a central motif'.[25] Finally, Robert Wark notes that 'Rowlandson's concern is precisely with those minor circumstances of day-to-day living that are too trivial for the historian but invaluable for revitalizing a particular segment of the past in our imaginations'.[26] While Rowlandson assimilates *The Vicar* to his own plastic medium, he did produce twenty-four illustrations—a substantial artistic commitment which, I believe, has a kind of unity of its own and which offers subtle insights into Goldsmith's verbal medium. Although this essay focuses on only one motif and several of Rowlandson's illustrations dealing with this motif, it should be recognised that many of the illustrations to *The Vicar* are not caricatures and that Rowlandson also captured the pastoral nostalgia of an agrarian world that has captivated so many readers and that was essential to Goldsmith's purpose.[27]

To attempt to force verbal meaning onto Rowlandson's art, which like all great plastic art exists on its own visual terms, does raise a question of methodology. If Laslett's phrase 'symbolic life of our ancestors' is to have any significance, however, the plastic and the verbal arts should both be studied, particularly when the plastic arts still have mimetic orientation. Rowlandson shows enormous sensitivity to the inhumanity of a society in which people are so conditioned by their class status that their relationships with one another are limited by that status. Rowlandson's obsequious curve, which seems to depict not merely an individual but the class of which that individual is a type, is almost unique to him. It should have turned up, but does not, in Hogarth's *The Gate of Calais; or, O the Roast Beef of Old England*; Hogarth had recounted the 'poverty, slavery and Insolence with an *affectation of politeness*' (italics mine) which he had found in Calais. Hogarth's labouring poor do not slouch or have stooped postures from years of back-grinding work; rather, they bend rigidly from the waist at a forty-five degree angle. Rowlandson has a number of drawings and engravings dealing with obsequious situations but none more corrosive than the drawing entitled 'The Lord of the Manor Receiving his Rents' from the Huntington Art Gallery (Plate XIII). One

---

[25] *Thomas Rowlandson: His Life and Art*, London [1949], p. 54.
[26] *Rowlandson's Drawings for a Tour in a Post Chaise*, ed. Robert R. Wark, San Marino, California, 1963, p. 13.
[27] The full range of Rowlandson's art has been happily analysed by John Hayes, *Rowlandson: Watercolours and Drawings*, London, 1972; and Ronald Paulson, *Rowlandson: A New Interpretation*, New York, 1972. As these two critics show, it is simply not true that Rowlandson is merely a caricaturist. Perhaps the most poignant pastoral design to *The Vicar* is Plate 8: 'The Dance', which reminds me of line 398 from *The Deserted Village*: 'I see the rural virtues leave the land'.

cannot but wonder if Rowlandson subtly influenced Charles Dickens's visual imagination.

Part of the baffling nature of *The Vicar of Wakefield* is that it confronts us with a not totally reliable narrator who is both spectator and participant. As with *Moll Flanders* critical discussion tends to focus on such a narrator to the exclusion of the total fictional world of the narrative. Once Primrose has left Wakefield and has been demoted on the social scale he must not only correct his family's pretensions to gentility but rid himself of his own false biases. On the one hand Primrose cautions his family to keep to their own rank—referring to Ned Thornhill's interest in Olivia—while on the other he judges Mr Burchell to be a 'man of broken fortune'. Earlier, Primrose first meets Mr Burchell by spontaneously lending him money and then shortly after is surprised because although Burchell 'was a money-borrower' he 'defended his opinions with as much obstinacy as if he had been [his] patron'. Blinded by his own pride and by his earlier gentility, Primrose accepts Lady Blarney and Miss Carolina Wilelmina Amelia Skeggs not as 'ladies of the town' but as 'ladies of ... high breeding'. He is swindled out of his horse by the confidence-man Ephraim Jenkinson. Finally, when Primrose confronts Mr Burchell with his lost pocket-book, which the family had found, and with a letter, the seal of which Primrose had broken so that the letter could be read, he addresses him, 'Nay, never falter man; but look me full in the face ...'. When Burchell does, Primrose describes his action as 'unparallelled effrontery'. It is essential to Goldsmith's purpose that Primrose himself through a series of misfortunes be purged of his tendency to evaluate other human beings in terms of status and money.

It is our knowing very early in the novel that Mr Burchell is really Sir William Thornhill which enables us to see how Dr Primrose's gentility is an obstacle to his seeing reality. But it also is a necessity for Sir William Thornhill to free himself from his Squire Allworthyian circle of 'dependents and favourites' in order to know the truth about human nature. Johnson had written in the *Rambler*, No. 96, that in 'order that all men may be taught to speak truth, it is necessary that all likewise should learn to hear it; for no species of falsehood is more frequent than flattery ...'. In Letter C from *The Citizen of the World* previously quoted, Lien Chi Altangi, after deploring the 'misfortunes of the great' obliged 'to live among men whose real value is lessened by dependance', advises his son that one remedy often used by the great is to 'dismiss their old dependants, and take new'.[28] We are told that

---

[28] *Collected Works*, II, 398.

Sir William Thornhill 'surrounded with crowds, who shewed him only one side of their character' began to 'lose a regard for private interest in universal sympathy' and became so philanthropic that he lost his money and his sycophantic friends. He laid down 'a plan of restoring his falling fortune', then 'travelled through Europe on foot'. No critic has explained satisfactorily why Goldsmith found it necessary to split one character into two except as a *deus ex machina* to resolve the fairy-tale conclusion. Surely it is clear now that the vision of the great, who are prisoners of their fortune, their power, and their circle, needs to be supplemented by the moral vision of the kind that Burchell provides Thornhill.[29]

Even as Burchell is the necessary alter ego of Sir William Thornhill, so his nephew demonstrates the tyranny of the great who betray their natural obligations. Using law as a weapon first to threaten, then to throw Primrose into prison, Ned Thornhill from the very beginning demonstrates an insolence the exact opposite of obsequiousness. On first encountering the Primrose family, he attempts to salute the daughters without a proper introduction and approaches them with a 'careless superior air'. Much later in the narrative he is described as addressing Dr Primrose 'with his usual air of familiarity'. Ned is the portent of a new order of the great, of 'The pride which fools so oft reveal; /Who think it a fine state decorum, /When humble merit stands before 'em'.[30] What has not been recognised in the Dr Primrose-Ned Thornhill relationship is Primrose's own genteel snobbishness in disapproving of Thornhill's interest in Olivia, not so much on grounds of bad character, but because Primrose is against 'disproportioned friendships'. For Goldsmith, intermarriage between classes was easier in a society cemented by natural ties than in a society in which class was defined by wealth. Two essays from *The Citizen of the World* attacked the parliamentary act of 1753 which sought to prevent clandestine marriages but which seemed to Goldsmith so to inhibit marriages between the classes that only the rich could 'marry among the rich'.[31] Because Primrose is against fortune hunters and does not want his daughters to be seen as such, Goldsmith's major point has

---

[29] *Collected Works*, IV, 29. I am greatly indebted to Paul Privateer for discussions on this point; he has a paper in progress on the full significance of the Burchell-Sir William relationship.
[30] William Combe, *The Tour of Doctor Syntax in Search of the Picturesque*, London, 1812, pp. 99-100.
[31] Letters LXXII and CXIV, in *Collected Works*, II, 298-303, 440-5. Lien Chi Altangi writes in the latter that the 'laws of this country are finely calculated to promote all commerce, but the commerce between the sexes' (II, 440). Incidentally, Friedman's comment (II, 299, n. 2) that Goldsmith in the former essay 'gives an exaggerated statement of some of the provisions of "An act for the better preventing clandestine marriages" of 1753 (26 Geo. II, c. 33)'

been missed. The rich do marry the poor in this novel despite the act of 1753, despite Thornhill's villainy which backfires, and despite Primrose's own reverse snobbery.

Another insight is given into the social stratification of London after George Primrose is discovered on the stage by his father and returns home to tell his story. In a social hierarchy based on tradition and natural ties, most members of this hierarchy would possess a fairly secure sense of social identity. In a chaotic urban society or one in which status depends on wealth or the appearance of wealth, dissimulation replaces authenticity. George's first scheme on arriving in London is to become an usher at a boarding school until his cousin, who has been one, talks him out of it. Finding that 'there was no great degree of gentility affixed to the character of an usher', George sets out to be an author. He meets one would-be writer who for twelve years has maintained himself not on writings but on proposals for writings. He seeks subscriptions from a nobleman returning from his travels, a 'Creolian' arriving from Jamaica, or 'a dowager from her country seat', and besieges his prospective subscribers 'with flattery'. George continues to try to write well, only to discover that his 'efforts after excellence' are buried among 'the diffusive productions of fruitful mediocrity'. It is then that George encounters in St James's Park an old 'intimate acquaintance at the university', Ned Thornhill. He is given a fine suit and admitted to Thornhill's table 'upon the footing of *half-friend, half-underling*' (italics mine). He begins to assume the function of a servant but has as his rival a 'captain of marines, who was formed for the place by nature', whose 'mother had been laundress to a man of quality' and 'thus early acquired a taste for pimping and pedigree'. This captain made it the

> study of his life to be acquainted with lords, though he was dismissed from several for his stupidity; yet he found many of them who were as dull as himself that permitted his assiduities. As *flattery was his trade*, he practised it with the easiest address imaginable; but it came aukward and stiff from me; and as every day my patron's desire of flattery encreased, so every hour being better acquainted with his defects, I became more unwilling to give it.[32] (italics mine)

George is about to give the field to the captain when Thornhill asks him to fight a duel for him with a 'gentleman whose sister it

---

can now be understood in the light of Best's *Temporal Pillars*. The Act took considerable power away from the ecclesiastical courts and gave it to civil authority. Goldsmith resented the Act on the one hand because it seemed to place more emphasis on marriage for money, and on the other because it seemed to *secularise* the marriage ceremony.

[32] *Collected Works*, IV, 112.

was pretended he had used ill'. George disarms his antagonist, only to learn that the 'lady' was a woman of the town and the fellow her 'bully and a sharper'. Thornhill leaves town after giving George recommendatory letters and a suggestion that he sees his uncle Sir William Thornhill and 'another nobleman of great distinction, who enjoyed a post under the government'. Sir William, distressed at the duel, turns down George's application; and George turns to the other 'great man'. He gains admittance only 'after bribing the servants with half [his] worldly fortune'. Just as 'his lordship' is about to speak with George, he is called away to his coach; George hastens after him with 'three or four more, who came, like me, to petition for favours';

> His lordship, however, went too fast for us, and was gaining his Chariot door with large strides, when I hallowed out to know if I was to have any reply. He was by this time got in, and muttered an answer, half of which only I heard, the other half was lost in the rattling of his chariot wheels. I stood for some time with my neck stretched out, in the posture of one that was listening to catch the glorious sounds, till looking round me, I found myself alone at his lordship's gate.[33]

Rowlandson's eighteenth illustration, 'ATTENDANCE ON A NOBLEMAN' (Plate XIV), captures magnificently the overall point of George's narrative—obsequiousness is the way of the world. The lesson is extended to the continent where, among other things, George learns the sham of being a connoisseur.

The sequence of misfortunes leading to Dr Primrose's imprisonment and to Olivia's earlier abduction, both orchestrated by Ned Thornhill, is intended to demonstrate the truth of one of Goldsmith's favourite maxims, uttered by Dr Primrose after he is in prison: 'it is among the citizens of a refined community that penal laws, which are in the hands of the rich, are laid upon the poor'.[34] It is precisely in the prison scene, therefore, that we would expect Rowlandson to draw obsequious curves as signs of oppression. Dr Primrose on first entering the prison and expecting 'nothing but lamentations, and various sounds of misery' finds instead that it is filled with the 'riot, laughter, and prophaneness' of prisoners 'forgetting thought in merriment or clamour'.[35] Rowlandson draws the scene where the Vicar reads a 'portion of the service' to the prisoners who are 'perfectly merry' and where 'Lewd whispers, groans of contrition burlesqued, winking and coughing, alternately excited laughter'.[36] That there are no obsequious curves seems true to

[33] Ibid., IV, 114.
[34] Ibid., IV, 150.
[35] Ibid., IV, 141.
[36] Ibid., IV, 145.

Goldsmith's description, but Rowlandson has created a masterstroke in the cocky woman sitting on the left side of the illustration ('THE VICAR PREACHING TO THE PRISONERS'; Plate XV). Her arched back is the very reverse of the obsequious curve. If Rowlandson's imagination were twentieth-century, the design might suggest a kind of existential thesis that only in prison can there be freedom in the kind of world that Goldsmith describes; but this would seem totally alien to Goldsmith's intention. I have elsewhere interpreted Dr Primrose as being an object of Goldsmith's 'amiable satire', but here in prison Primrose has his finest hour.[37] Here, he too is free to be most authentically human, to be radically *Christian*. When Primrose first announces to his family his plan of reforming the prisoners, they react with 'universal disapprobation, alledging the impossibility and impropriety of it' and warning that he 'might probably disgrace' his 'calling'.[38] Does not Goldsmith thereby suggest the shallowness of a genteel Christianity wherein religious experience is diminished by middle-class consciousness?

If my interpretation of Goldsmith's treatment of obsequiousness in both its honorific and pejorative senses is valid, all the characters in the novel are stripped of their genteel pretensions while Primrose is in prison and brought back to moral reality. Even as the wheel of fortune turns, however, and injustice rectified, corruption returns in the form of gentility and affluence. The fairy-tale is complete, and we return to the beginning with Rowlandson's final illustration: 'THE WEDDINGS' (Plate XVI). The obsequious curve returns also in the figure of the parish clerk and so does the Vicar's priggishness. Rowlandson has caught effectively the nuances of Goldsmith's stylistically modulated conclusion which suggest that while the plot resolution of the novel may satisfy our need for a sense of happy ending, it may very probably be also a parody of such a need—particularly, I might add, when the conclusion is predicated on a *return* to the genteel existence which was so comically undermined at the very beginning. We cannot return to this primeval state, however, for as readers we are wiser and more reflective than we began. *The Vicar of Wakefield* is an extra-ordinarily sophisticated narrative with all the craft behind it of *The Citizen of the World* and with Goldsmith's deep moral and political convictions. *The Vicar of Wakefield* rewards critical intelligence because it reflects Goldsmith's maxim that 'True learning and true morality are

[37] Robert H. Hopkins, *The True Genius of Oliver Goldsmith*, Baltimore, 1969, pp. 166-230. See Sven Backman, *This Singular Tale: A Study of The Vicar of Wakefield*, Lund, 1971, for a sharply differing interpretation.
[38] *Collected Works*, IV, 148.

closely connected; to improve the head will insensibly influence the heart'.[39]

What I have tried to do in this paper is to focus on a neglected dimension of *The Vicar of Wakefield* and to show what there was for writers like Jane Austen and Charles Dickens to learn from Goldsmith. How men relate to other men in a world of change characterised by urbanisation, growing commerce, and a loss of 'natural ties' has surely been one of the major concerns of the English novel from its very beginning. There is a need for more study of obsequiousness as a literary theme. The uneasiness of the subordinated relationship between an élite minority living vicariously for all the rest, and those others (hinted at in Hogarth's print of the Lord Mayor's procession, and graphically caricatured in Rowlandson's designs) comes to the very foreground in the Victorian novel. One encounters characters such as Dickens's Uriah Heep and George Eliot's Mr Bulstrode who are orphans or offspring of the urban poor, who attend charity schools where they are trained for literacy and bookkeeping, who begin as clerks deferring obsequiously to their betters as they go about making their fortune, who are almost always religious hypocrites, who turn treacherously against their befrienders, and who get their comeuppance only because of the poetic justice of the author. In Dickens's *Hard Times* there is Mr Bounderby, a 'self-made' man who is 'always proclaiming' his 'old ignorance and his old poverty' and 'who was the Bully of humility' (an ideal candidate for Rowlandson).[40] Then there is tragic Stephen Blackpool, forty, a 'good power-loom weaver', 'of perfect integrity', a 'rather stooping man, with a knitted brow' and a 'pondering expression of face', who at work is 'bent over his loom, quiet, watchful, and steady'.[41] When Stephen feels compelled to seek counsel from Mr Bounderby, his 'principal employer', the imaginative possibilities are endless. Stephen steps into the parlour where Bounderby is at his lunch supervised by Mrs Sparsit. Dickens writes:

> Stephen made a bow. Not a servile one—these Hands will never do that! Lord bless you, Sir, you'll never catch them at that, if they have been with you twenty years!—and, as a complimentary toilet for Mrs Sparsit, tucked his neckerchief ends into his waistcoat.[42]

Stephen, who has not read Goldsmith—'Each wanton judge new

[39] 'An Enquiry into the Present State of Polite Learning in Europe', Ibid., I, 259.
[40] *Hard Times*, I, iv.
[41] Ibid., I, x, xi.
[42] Ibid., I, xi.

penal statutes draw, /Laws grind the poor, and rich men rule the law'—comes to ask Mr Bounderby why, if 'great fok' can be 'set free fro' *their* misfortnet marriages, an' marry ower agen', he cannot also be set free from his wife who is alcoholic and a slut. Dickens writes:

> In the strength of his misfortune, and the energy of his distress, he fired for the moment like a proud man. In another moment, he stood as he had stood all the time—his usual stoop upon him. . . .[43]

But this is another essay.

---

[43] Ibid. I am greatly indebted to Jean Gandesberry for reminding me of just how pertinent *Hard Times* might be to my concern with obsequiousness as a literary theme.

Rousseau and the Common People

L. G. Crocker

Rousseau's attitude toward 'le peuple', like many aspects of his life and thought, suffers from any attempt to reduce it to simple and unitary terms. On the contrary, it is bifocal. The lens through which he peers changes, as it was his wont, according to polemical circumstance, truly in chameleon-like fashion. It changes also with the substance of his considerations; and I shall endeavour to distinguish his personal or affective attitudes from his political reflections. Even though the former permeate the latter, *la distinction s'impose*. However, the deepest roots of Rousseau's bifocality lie in neither of these two factors. His attitudes towards the common people manifest that ambivalence which suffuses his life, character and writings, and which in itself constitutes the true 'unity' of Rousseau that has been so often debated. The basic form of this ambivalence is the unresolved tension between the craving for dependency, which assumes multiple guises in his behaviour, including the extreme form of sexual masochism, and the strident assertions of independence, which are ego-protective. This is not the place to discuss the origins of Rousseau's peculiarities of character, but I believe his ambivalence to be paradigmatic of what is known as the obsessional neurosis.[1]

First, let us define who constitutes the common people, or 'le peuple'. The basic definition, in the minds of all writers of the *ancien régime*, included all those who worked with their hands.[2] The word thus often refers to a 'class', in the post-Marxian or economic sense, rather than to hierarchical order, the Tiers Etat; though it is sometimes also used that way, or again, in the meaning of a nation. It is the first acceptation that interests us mainly, and

---

[1] See L. G. Crocker, *Jean-Jacques Rousseau: The Quest*, New York, 1968, pp. 14-15.
[2] See Denis Richet, 'Autour des origines idéologiques lointaines de la Révolution française', *Annales; Economies, Sociétés, Civilisations*, XXIV (1969), 5-7.

the connotation is one of exclusion.³ A second, negative characteristic is always present in Rousseau's mind: the absence of literate culture and the sophistication that accompanies it.

Second, as an indirect approach to our subject, let us note an equivalent ambivalence in Rousseau's attitude towards the great, one which is the counterpart of his attitude toward the people. 'C'est dans un de ces transports d'attendrissement que je dis une fois à M. de Luxembourg en l'embrassant: Ah, M. le Maréchal, je haïssois les Grands avant de vous connoître, et je les hais davantage encore, depuis que vous me faites si bien sentir combien il leur seroit aisé de se faire adorer.'⁴ Analysing this spontaneous and revealing exclamation, we observe the following elements: (1) Rousseau's affection for the Duke, part of which derives from the feelings inspired by the way the nobleman treats him; (2) the semi-jocular expression of hatred for the Duke's class, which pierces through the turn of the compliment; (3) the implied adoration of the Duke, and the implied wish that it might be extended to all of his class. No less revealing is the apology (the *Confessions*, an *apologia pro vita sua*, encloses many apologies within the whole) that immediately follows the emotional outburst. Rousseau's guilt-feelings are easily aroused, never more easily than when his chosen image is threatened. Since it is dependent on the 'look' of the 'other', or the image he wants others to have of the real Jean-Jacques, he steadfastly announces his independence from 'opinion', and his scorn for it. All these elements are present in his next sentence:

> Au reste j'interpelle tous ceux qui m'ont vu durant cette époque, s'ils se sont jamais apperçus que cet éclat m'ait un instant ébloui, que la vapeur de cet encens m'ait porté à la tête; s'ils m'ont vû moins uni dans mon maintien, . . . *moins liant avec le peuple*, moins familier avec mes voisins, moins prompt à rendre service à tout le monde. . . . Si mon cœur m'attiroit au Château de Montmorency par mon sincère attachement pour les maitres, il me ramenoit de même à mon voisinage goûter les douceurs de cette vie égale et simple, hors de laquelle il n'est point de bonheur pour moi. (italics mine)

This passage is but one of many illustrations of Rousseau's failure to achieve identity (as Ronald Grimsley demonstrated in

---

³ For further analysis, see Werner Bahner, 'Le Mot et la notion de "peuple" dans l'œuvre de Rousseau', *Studies on Voltaire and the Eighteenth Century*, LV (1967), 113-27. It will be seen that my views on the subject differ in many respects from Professor Bahner's.

⁴ *Confessions*, in *Œuvres complètes*, ed. Bernard Gagnebin and Marcel Raymond, Vol. I, Paris, 1959, p. 527. (This Pléiade edition henceforth cited as *Œuvres*.)

his notable book *Jean-Jacques Rousseau: A Study in Self-Awareness*), and of his searching for an anchor in two opposing camps. By affirming his affiliation with the common people, he maintains the credibility of his elected image, and denies the dependency on the great that he also needed. Both the *Confessions* and the correspondence offer repeated recurrences of Rousseau's vacillating attitude toward those of high birth and high place. As with the Prince de Conti, he is both shy and proud, almost arrogant, at the first approach. Then, when he believes his claim to independence adequately established, he is eager to have both association and a dependent relation with the elect of the *haut monde*. His letters to Conti contain such expressions of dependency, even of fawning. Other examples could of course be cited, including the unconsummated relationships with Frederick the Great and George III.

Rousseau's own origins were humble. This was enough for him to feel inferiority or unconscious shame in the *haut monde*, and to seek in some way to rise above his origins, partly by frequenting the *haut monde*. His family were watchmakers, and often tottered on the edge of respectability. In his dedication of the *Discours sur l'origine de l'inégalité* to the 'Magnifiques, très honorés et souverains Seigneurs' of Geneva's Petit Conseil, he tried very hard to confer respectability on his father, who had run foul of the law.[5] A statement in the *Confessions* is much to the point: 'Né dans une famille que ses mœurs *distinguaient du peuple* je n'avois receu que des leçons de sagesse et des exemples d'honneur de tous mes parents'[6] (italics mine).

From childhood, and partly from his readings, he bore with him the dream of a romantic destiny. It was a princess in her tower that he looked for when he trudged back from Italy to Annecy. The women he fell in love with were high-born. He tried unsuccessfully to make his way in the Parisian *salons*, and later turned the whiplash of his scorn on the emptiness and vices of a milieu he rejected because it had not accepted him as he thought he deserved to be accepted. Yet his friendships and associations continued to be, to a considerable extent, with the literary men, the sophisticates, the aristocrats whom he did not cease to condemn. Magnetically attracted to the great, he longed to be recognised by the best spheres of society, which he despised, hated and envied.

> To be an aristocrat, *un grand*, was to belong to a *magic* category of beings, since their greatness seemed to come from something outside the individual himself. Rousseau's dreams, as well

[5] *Discours sur l'origine et les fondements de l'inégalité parmi les hommes*, ed. J.-L. Lecercle, Paris, 1965, pp. 54-5.
[6] *Œuvres*, I, 61.

as his acts, were oriented to the aristocracy. The same orientation subtly infuses his writings and theories, for he really divides his ideal society, quite consistently, into a directing élite and the masses. . . . Rank, family, inherited wealth and power, 'connections'—these were incontrovertible and 'magic' qualities, and those who possessed them were the chosen ones. . . . How could he be certain of his worth if they denied it? Their acceptance, on the other hand, would be a reassurance, a confirmation.[7]

Rousseau's unconscious snobbery served, then, when he was not humiliated or rebuffed, to produce a false sense of identity, as some of the 'magic' rubbed off on him. It served to satisfy his need for dependency on a man or woman who was protective and powerful. Being sought after and adulated by select circles of men and women who had the magic of power, of possessing everything without doing anything, gave him a satisfaction that he heightened by playing the role of the unwilling and sometimes rude bear. This kind of association was a way of identifying himself with their power and transcendence of ordinary life. The dividing line was his *réforme* and the new image, the new role, into which he cast himself and which he tried to thrust upon the world. After that time, the protectiveness, and the dependency had to *seem* not destructive of the image. When his friends and protectors were unable to satisfy his peculiar requirements, as was most often the case, he asserted his independence by quarrelling with them.

Rousseau's acerb condemnation of the sophisticates and the aristocracy was thus both a sincere conviction and a defensive reaction. His connection with *le peuple* could not be broken, and he often exalted them, again out of the same motives. He could not abolish another fact. He felt at ease with the commoners, most often ill at ease with the others. Association with them had peculiar advantages. With the former there was no need to strive and strain to make them acknowledge his equal or superior worth. Unfortunately, this acknowledgment was what he craved, and the 'look' of the elect alone could satisfy it.

We shall now turn from Rousseau's life and behaviour to what he says. Jean-Jacques did not really like peasants, I think, but he nourished his illusions about them, attributing to them a simple, virtuous, carefree life. 'Le peuple ne s'ennuie guère', he says in *Emile*.[8] And again, 'C'est le peuple qui compose le genre humain'.[9] This judgment was based on his belief that the common people are

---

[7] Crocker, *Rousseau: The Quest*, pp. 150-1.
[8] *Emile*, ed. François and Pierre Richard, Paris [1951], p. 438.
[9] Ibid., p. 265.

the carriers of true moral values—respect for work, family, self-sacrifice, honesty. The fact that his family and he himself were far from being exemplars of all these values is another matter. We may set side by side Julie's statement, 'car il vaut mieux déroger à la noblesse qu'à la vertu, et la femme d'un charbonnier est plus respectable que la maîtresse d'un prince',[10] with one in the *Confessions*: 'Parmi le peuple où les grandes passions ne parlent que par intervalles les sentiments de la nature se font plus souvent entendre'.[11] Comparisons such as this one, implied or expressed, with *les grands*, recur frequently. They are almost always favourable to *le peuple*. Saint-Preux contrasts the ideal of a 'peuple heureux et simple' with one that is 'aimable et galant', a people 'qui vit pour vivre, non pour gagner ni pour briller'.[12] In his famous portrait of 'ces aimables Parisiennes', Saint-Preux explains their styles in this way: 'Elles savent que des idées de pudeur et de modestie sont profondément gravées dans l'esprit du peuple. C'est là ce qui leur a suggéré des modes inimitables'.[13] The populace would cover immodestly dressed women with coarse insults: 'et, dans cette occasion, comme en beaucoup d'autres, la brutalité du peuple, plus honnête que la bienséance des gens polis, retient peut-être ici cent mille femmes dans les bornes de la modestie'.[14] Saint-Preux, who has achieved, *vis-à-vis* Wolmar, the state of infantile dependency and docile submissiveness for which Rousseau himself longed, and which is reflected in all his educational and political writings, quotes that godlike figure:

> Croiriez-vous que l'entretien même des paysans a des charmes pour ces âmes élevées avec qui le sage aimerait à s'instruire? Le judicieux Wolmar trouve dans la naïveté villageoise des caractères plus marqués, plus d'hommes pensant par eux-mêmes, que sous le masque uniforme des habitants des villes, où chacun se montre comme sont les autres plutôt que comme il est lui-même.[15]

Condescension and the smugness of superiority surface through the *bonhomie* of Wolmar's *sagesse*.

There is no question about Rousseau's genuine sympathy for the plight of the French peasant and other commoners. He can be acidly sardonic. 'Pourvu que les grands soient contens, qu'importe que le peuple vive?'[16] He can be indignant. The tale of the peasant who

---

10 *La Nouvelle Héloïse*, ed. R. Pomeau, Paris, 1960, p. 620.
11 *Œuvres*, I, 147.
12 *La Nouvelle Héloïse* (ed. Pomeau), pp. 48, 54.
13 Ibid., p. 245.
14 Ibid., p. 246.
15 Ibid., p. 540.
16 *Lettre à d'Alembert*, ed. M. Fuchs, Lille and Geneva, 1948, p. 153, n. 2.

hid his food to deceive rapacious tax-collectors, which Rousseau recounts in the *Confessions,* is well known. It leads to a flat declaration of his allegiance. 'Ce fut là le germe de cette haine inextinguible qui se developpa depuis dans mon cœur contre les vexations qu'éprouve le malheureux peuple et contre ses oppresseurs.'[17] His cry of outrage at the close of the *Discours sur l'inégalité* is too well known to bear repetition. Nowhere is his sympathy more outspoken than in this work. Easy to dupe, the people were, at the very beginnings of social organisation, the victims of a conspiracy by the rich and powerful. Once entrapped, they are helpless. 'Les peuples une fois accoutumés à des maîtres ne sont plus en état de s'en passer.'[18] They become fascinated by their leaders and their propaganda, despite the fact that the happiness of the powerful is built on their own deprivation, and this not only in an economic, but more importantly in a psychological sense.[19] At the end of his disquisition, Rousseau returns to his idea of the people as the moral element of society: 'le peuple est le véritable juge des mœurs: juge intègre et même éclairé sur ce point, qu'on abuse quelquefois, mais qu'on ne corrompt jamais'.[20] He could scarcely have been more wrong; but he returns occasionally, in varying forms, to the same notion. In the *Lettres écrites de la montagne* he asserts that the people never favour fraud or injustice: 'C'est en ceci que la voix du peuple est la voix de Dieu'. Only, he continues, it is a weak voice when raised 'contre le cri de la puissance; et la plainte de l'innocence opprimée s'exhale en murmures méprisés par la tyrannie'.[21]

Rousseau's indignation is sincere. Its origin rests largely on his own experiences and humiliations. There is a bitter sentence in *La Nouvelle Héloïse:* 'Ceux qui vont à pied ne sont pas du monde; ce sont des Bourgeois, des hommes, du peuple, des gens de l'autre monde'. Bernard Guyon comments: 'On sent ici passer une fois encore l'indignation du roturier humilié, de l'homme à pied'.[22]

He wanted to be loved by the people, and several times said that he was. The manoeuvres of the Petit Conseil to turn the 'populace' against him were disturbing, but the open hostility of the people of Môtiers upset him deeply. 'Je devois, j'ose le dire, être aimé du peuple dans ce pays-là, comme je l'ai été dans tous ceux où j'ai vécu, versant les aumones à pleines mains, ne laissant sans assistance

---

[17] *Œuvres,* I, 164.
[18] (Ed. Lecercle), p. 49 (see also *Rousseau juge de Jean-Jacques,* in *Œuvres,* I, 920-1).
[19] *Discours,* pp. 139-40.
[20] Ibid., p. 187.
[21] Rousseau, *Political Writings,* ed. C. E. Vaughan, 2 vols., Cambridge, 1915, II, 256.
[22] In *Œuvres,* II, Paris, 1961, 1489. Rousseau's sentence is at p. 252.

aucun indigent autour de moi, . . . me familiarisant, trop peutêtre avec tout le monde, en me dérobant de tout mon pouvoir à toute distinction qui put exciter la jalousie'.[23] The feelings of separateness and superiority are again evident in the condescending *bonhomie*. And, once more, the common people were duped, and became the helpless tools of Montmollin.

Rousseau's wrath toward those who dupe the people for their own pleasure and profit has its counterpart in a feeling of vexation toward those who allow themselves to be exploited.

> Je vois des peuples infortunés gémissant sous un joug de fer, le genre humain écrasé par une poignée d'oppresseurs, une foule affamée, accablée de peine et de faim, dont le riche boit en paix le sang et les larmes, et partout le fort armé contre le faible du redoutable pouvoir des lois. Tout cela se fait paisiblement et sans resistance. C'est la tranquillité des compagnons d'Ulysse enfermés dans la caverne du Cyclope, en attendant qu'ils soient dévorés.[24]

This statement may be taken as revolutionary, even as pre-Marxist. It is comparable to another, in which he affirms that 'tous ces grands mots de société, de justice, de lois, de défense mutuelle, d'assistance des faibles . . . ne sont que des leurres inventés par des politiques adroits ou par de lâches flatteurs, pour en imposer aux simples'.[25] That is why he was convinced that the call for reforms was only a trap, one that would perpetuate the same system, the same basic evils.

The common people may be the bearers of morality, but they are obviously susceptible to being aroused to a pitch of unreasoning passion and of being directed into committing foolish, wicked and brutal acts. Rousseau's vocabulary calls for a commentary. The word 'peuple' is amorphous in value—favourable, pejorative or neutral. 'Canaille' usually denotes that portion of 'le peuple' that falls short of his ideal image. Montaigu's house 'se remplissoit de canaille'.[26] At Môtiers he calmly continued his usual walks 'sans m'émouvoir des clameurs de toute cette canaille'.[27] The spies sent by 'vos Messieurs' to hound him are also 'canaille'. The same enemies conspire to make 'cet infortuné [himself] le jouet du public, la risée de la canaille'.[28] A special use occurs in the *Discours sur l'inégalité*, where he says that in street brawls, 'c'est la canaille, ce sont les femmes des halles qui séparent les combattants et qui empêchent les

---

[23] See *Confessions*, in *Œuvres*, I, 624.
[24] 'Fragments politiques', in *Political Writings* (ed. Vaughan), I, 302.
[25] *Œuvres*, III, Paris, 1964, 475 ('Fragments politiques', II).
[26] Ibid., I, 307. See a similar remark about Mme de Warens, I, 47.
[27] Ibid., I, 631.
[28] *Rousseau juge de Jean-Jacques*, in *Œuvres*, I, 725, 743. Also I, 716, 653.

honnêtes gens de s'entr'égorger'.[29] Here the word 'canaille' is used more favourably because it is the *philosophes* who would call them by that derisive term. But the Romans who sold their votes were also 'canaille'.[30] The words 'multitude' and 'populace' are sometimes used in a neutral sense. 'Tandis que la multitude affamée manque du nécessaire'.[31] But in a note in the *Discours* he writes: 'Laissons donc parler des gens à qui l'on n'a point fait un crime d'oser prendre quelquefois le parti de la raison contre l'avis de la multitude'.[32] And in *Emile*, 'qu'il méprise la multitude', is a basic precept.[33] 'Populace' generally, but not always, is given a marked pejorative sense.[34]

Rousseau's uncertainties—one might say difficulties—with vocabulary reflect his ambivalent attitudes. Thus he explains that if he did not become a professional writer (of course he was that), it was because his proud and lofty genius would have been stifled by having to say 'moins des choses utiles et vraies, que des choses qui plussent à la multitude'.[35] This statement is comparable to an earlier one, written during the polemics over the first *Discours*. In the 'Préface d'une seconde lettre à Bordes' (1753) he declares: 'Je vais vaincre enfin mon dégout et écrire une fois pour le Peuple'.[36] It may also be compared with one in his *Dernière réponse* in which he justifies his taking up his pen again: 'afin que mon silence ne soit pas pris par la multitude pour un aveu'; and with another in the 'Préface d'une seconde lettre à Bordes', in which he scolds his critic for clever sophistries that are 'doublement dangereux pour la multitude'.[37] Clearly he holds himself both apart from and above the herd. D'Alembert, in his reply to Rousseau, shrewdly noted this: 'Vous avez encore su plaire à la multitude par le mépris même que vous témoignez pour elle, et que vous eussiez peut-être marqué davantage en affectant moins de le montrer'.[38]

The common people are, above all, stupid. They do not know what is good and what is bad. 'Plus les capitales frappent d'admiration les yeux stupides du peuple, plus il faudrait gémir de voir les campagnes abandonnées, les terres en friche, et les grands chemins inondés de malheureux citoyens devenus mendiants ou voleurs, et

---

[29] (Ed. Lecercle), p. 98.
[30] *Du Contrat social*, IV, iv; in *Œuvres*, III, 447.
[31] *Discours sur l'inégalité* (ed. Lecercle), p. 145.
[32] Ibid., p. 180.
[33] (Ed. Richard), p. 281.
[34] See *Confessions* in *Œuvres*, I, 590, 609, 624-31.
[35] Ibid., p. 402.
[36] *Œuvres*, III, 107.
[37] Ibid., p. 71.
[38] *Lettre à Jean-Jacques Rousseau, citoyen de Genève*, in *Œuvres de d'Alembert*, 5 vols., Paris, 1822, IV, 432; again on p. 436.

destinés à finir un jour leur misère sur la roue ou sur un fumier'.[39] 'Je reconnus bientôt', writes Wolmar, 'qu'il était impossible de faire entendre raison à la multitude'.[40] 'Les paysans', we are told in *Emile*, '. . . sont rustres, grossiers, maladroits'.[41] Speaking of Grimm's malicious play-acting, Rousseau comments: 'Je n'y pense jamais sans sentir combien sont trompeurs les jugements fondés sur l'apparence auxquels le vulgaire donne tant de poids'.[42] That is one reason why the theatre is so bad for them: 'le peuple, toujours singe et imitateur des riches, va moins au théâtre pour rire de leurs folies que pour les étudier, et devenir encore plus fous qu'eux en les imitant'.[43]

The untrustworthiness of the common people in regard to religion is sometimes emphasised by Rousseau. There is nothing but scorn for them in his lines to Christophe de Beaumont, in which he speaks first of the order of the universe:

> Le peuple y fait peu d'attention, manquant des connoissances qui rendent cet ordre sensible, et n'y ayant point appris à réfléchir sur ce qu'il apperçoit . . .; c'est ignorance, engourdissement d'esprit. La moindre agitation fatigue ces gens-là. . . . Ils répètent les mêmes mots sans y joindre les mêmes idées. . . . Le peuple, à portée de tant d'instructions [in the churches], est encore si stupide.
> Les préjugés du peuple n'ayant aucune base fixe sont plus variables; ils peuvent être altérés, changés, augmentés ou diminués.[44]

The important elements in this passage are the people's stupidity, their changeableness and, most important, their malleability; and finally the attitude of distantiation taken by Rousseau.

The attitude of distantiation is obvious in many of his writings. Replying to Bordes's refutation of his first *Discours*, he acknowledges the work of thinkers and legislators in ancient Greece. 'J'ai déja dit cent fois qu'il est bon qu'il y ait des Philosophes, pourvû que le Peuple ne se mêle pas de l'être'.[45] In *La Nouvelle Héloïse*, Julie asks: 'si le philosophe et le sage se règlent dans les plus grandes affaires de la vie sur les discours insensés de la multitude, que sert tout cet appareil d'études, pour n'être au fond qu'un homme vulgaire?'[46] And in *Rousseau juge de Jean-Jacques* he expresses his

---

39 *Discours sur l'inégalité* (ed. Lecercle), p. 162.
40 *La Nouvelle Héloïse* (ed. Pomeau), p. 230.
41 (Ed. Richard), p. 118.
42 *Confessions*, in *Œuvres*, I, 473.
43 *La Nouvelle Héloïse* (ed. Pomeau), p. 230.
44 *Lettre à Christophe de Beaumont*, in *Œuvres*, IV, Paris, 1969, 951-2, 968.
45 In *Œuvres*, III, 78.
46 (Ed. Pomeau), p. 131.

pride in never following 'les opinions de la multitude'.[47]

The extension to politics is an easy transition. Distrust, first and above all. He is writing about public happiness: 'Le vulgaire s'y trompe sans doute mais à quoi ne se trompe-t-il pas?'[48] This opinion takes on a wider focus in the first version of the *Contrat social*, where he argues that men cannot dissociate themselves from their egocentricity. 'De plus; comme l'art de généraliser ainsi ses idées est un des exercices les plus difficiles et les plus tardifs de l'entendement humain, le commun des hommes sera-t-il jamais en état de tirer de cette maniére de raisonner les régles de sa conduite . . .?'[49] No, indeed; instead, he will mistake his own self-interest for the general will and the moral law: 'Mais les notions sublimes du Dieu des sages, les douces loix de la fraternité qu'il nous impose, les vertus sociales des ames pures, qui sont le vrai culte qu'il veut de nous, echaperont toujours à la multitude'.[50]

This weakness is emphasised in the published *Contrat social*. The people cannot understand, Rousseau explains:

> Les sages qui veulent parler au vulgaire leur langage au lieu du sien s'en sauraient être entendus. Or, il y a mille sortes d'idées qu'il est impossible de traduire dans la langue du peuple. Les vues trop générales et les objets trop éloignés sont également hors de sa portée: chaque individu ne goûtant d'autre plan de gouvernement que celui qui se rapporte à son intérêt particulier, aperçoit difficilement les avantages qu'il doit retirer des privations continuelles qu'imposent les bonnes lois
> (Livre II, ch. vii)

It is obvious that 'popular sovereignty' does not mean to Rousseau what it means to us, and that there is to be no popular rule. We shall see that there will be the appearance of popular rule, a 'beneficent illusion', and a necessary one. The following chapter is entitled, 'Du Peuple'. It discusses the limits to what can be done with a *peuple*, which is here taken in a generic rather than a class sense, although when he compares the people to 'ces malades stupides' the sense seems to change abruptly in his mind. This chapter would not pertain to our subject, were it not that the central idea restates one of Rousseau's main contentions: 'La plupart des Peuples, ainsi que des hommes, ne sont dociles que dans leur jeunesse'.[51] In other writings I have tried to show the critical importance of the notion of docility in Rousseau's political

---

[47] In *Œuvres*, I, 844.
[48] Ibid., III, 510 ('Fragments politiques', VI, 3).
[49] Ibid., pp. 286-7.
[50] Ibid., p. 285.
[51] *Du Contrat social*, II, viii; in *Œuvres*, III, 385.

and educational theories (these two being inseparable). A person, or a people hardened in corrupt habits, cannot be reformed; a revolution is the only desperate remedy, and then effective only in special circumstances.

It is well known that the relation of the people to their rulers ('the Prince') is radically changed in Rousseau's conception of the social contract. Although 'people' was often used to refer to the body of a nation, it was he who (as Bahner points out)[52] gave the word the specific content of inalienable sovereignty and excluded the notion of privileged orders. The equality of political and civil rights which ensues does not refer, however, to status, wealth, prestige or position, nor to actual power. Moreover, such theoretical notions of equality seem to me less important than what actually happens to the people in the good society, or the true society, as Rousseau conceived of it.

Another essential point is made in Book II, chapter iii, when Rousseau begins by stating that the deliberations of the people are untrustworthy. 'On veut toujours son bien, mais on ne le voit pas toujours.' He maintains the moral qualities attributed to the people: 'Jamais on ne corrompt le peuple'.[53] However, they are easily deceived. This is a major factor. Rousseau's strategy will be to take advantage of it, but for their own good.

He reaffirms the same idea, in a confused and contradictory way, in the last paragraph of Chapter VI. It is the judgment of the 'multitude aveugle', not their will, that is deficient. The consequence is logical and of the utmost significance:

> Il faut lui faire voir les objets tels qu'ils sont, quelquefois *tels qu'ils doivent lui paroître*, lui montrer le bon chemin qu'elle cherche, la garantir de la séduction des volontés particulieres. . . . Tous ont également besoin de guides: Il faut obliger les uns à conformer leurs volontés à leur raison; il faut apprendre à l'autre à connoitre ce qu'il veut'.[54] (my italics)

We may comment parenthetically that if the people are to made to think and to will according to a leader's previous decision, there is really nothing left for them to decide. They are called on only to assent, they are asked for a commitment. The genius and the charisma of a great leader, or (in the beginning) lawgiver, is central to Rousseau's scheme of things. Thus he calls on Emile to 's'élever au-dessus du vulgaire; car on ne connaît point les préjugés quand on les adopte, et l'on ne mène point le peuple quand on lui

[52] In *Studies on Voltaire*, LV, 119.
[53] *Du Contrat social*, II, iii; in *Œuvres*, III, 371.
[54] II, vi; ibid., p. 380.

ressemble'.⁵⁵ And he several times regrets the disappearance of demagoguery, which he terms 'eloquence' or 'persuasiveness'. We need only refer to the last chapter of the *Essai sur l'origine des langues*, 'Rapports des langues aux gouvernemens', where, *inter alia*, he asks: 'A quoi serviroit-elle [l'éloquence] aujourdui que la force publique supplée à la persuasion? . . . Quels discours restent donc à faire au public assemblé?'⁵⁶

It is Rousseau's firm conviction that, given the appropriate circumstances and the right leader, individuals can be 'dénaturés', and citizens 'formés'. A people, too, can be moulded into the desired shape:

> . . . c'est beaucoup que l'état soit tranquille et la loi respectée: mais si l'on ne fait rien de plus, il y aura dans tout cela plus d'apparence que de réalité, et le gouvernement se fera difficilement obéir s'il se borne à l'obéissance. S'il est bon de savoir employer les hommes tels qu'ils sont, il vaut beaucoup mieux encore les rendre tels qu'on a besoin qu'ils soient; l'autorité la plus absolue est celle qui pénétre jusqu'à l'intérieur de l'homme, et ne s'exerce pas moins sur la volonté que sur les actions. Il est certain que les peuples sont à la longue ce que le gouvernement les fait être. Guerriers, citoyens, hommes, quand il le veut; populace et canaille quand il lui plaît. . . . Formez donc des hommes si vous voulez commander à des hommes: si vous voulez qu'on obéisse aux lois, faites qu'on les aime, et que pour faire ce qu'on doit, il suffise de songer qu'on le doit faire. . . . Mais nos gouvernemens modernes . . . n'imaginent pas même qu'il soit nécessaire ou possible d'aller jusque-là.⁵⁷

This statement in the article 'Economie politique' is one of the most precise formulations of a theme that infuses and directs all of Rousseau's writings touching on the social and political problem, or on education. One of the things that separates Rousseau from his contemporaries except, to some extent, Helvétius, is his refusal to accept their naïve belief that with good laws and an honest administration we should have the good society.⁵⁸ 'Si quelquefois les lois influent sur les mœurs, c'est quand elles en tirent leur force.'⁵⁹ Men, not being naturally social, that is, naturally putting the general

---

⁵⁵ *Emile* (ed. Richard), p. 214. Rousseau is, to be sure, sometimes pessimistic, as in this 'Fragment': 'Il n'y a aucun gouvernement qui puisse forcer les Citoyens de vivre heureux, le meilleur est celui qui les met et état de l'être s'ils sont raisonnables. Et ce bonheur n'appartiendra jamais à la multitude' (*Œuvres*, III, 153—'Fragments politiques', VI, 8).
⁵⁶ *Essai sur l'origine des langues*, ed. Charles Porset, Paris, 1968, p. 197.
⁵⁷ 'Economie politique', in *Political Writings* (ed. Vaughan), I, 248.
⁵⁸ See the chapter on education in *De l'Esprit*, Disc. IV, ch. xvii. However, Helvétius only sketches what Rousseau develops fully in theory and detail.
⁵⁹ *Lettre à d'Alembert* (ed. Fuchs), p. 89. This idea is frequently repeated.

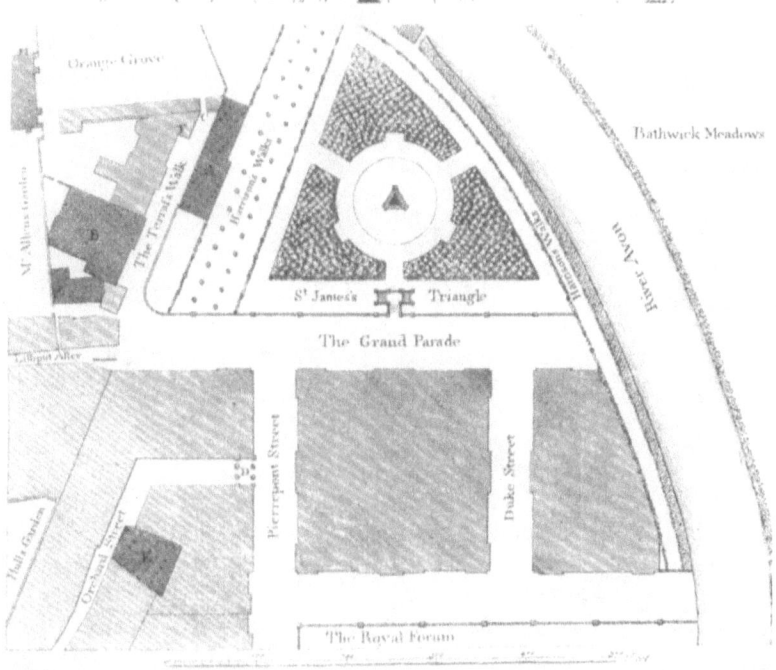

Plate V (a) Vitruvian Figure; Leonardo's version.
(b) The Parades, Bath; from Wood's *Essay towards a Description of Bath* (1765).

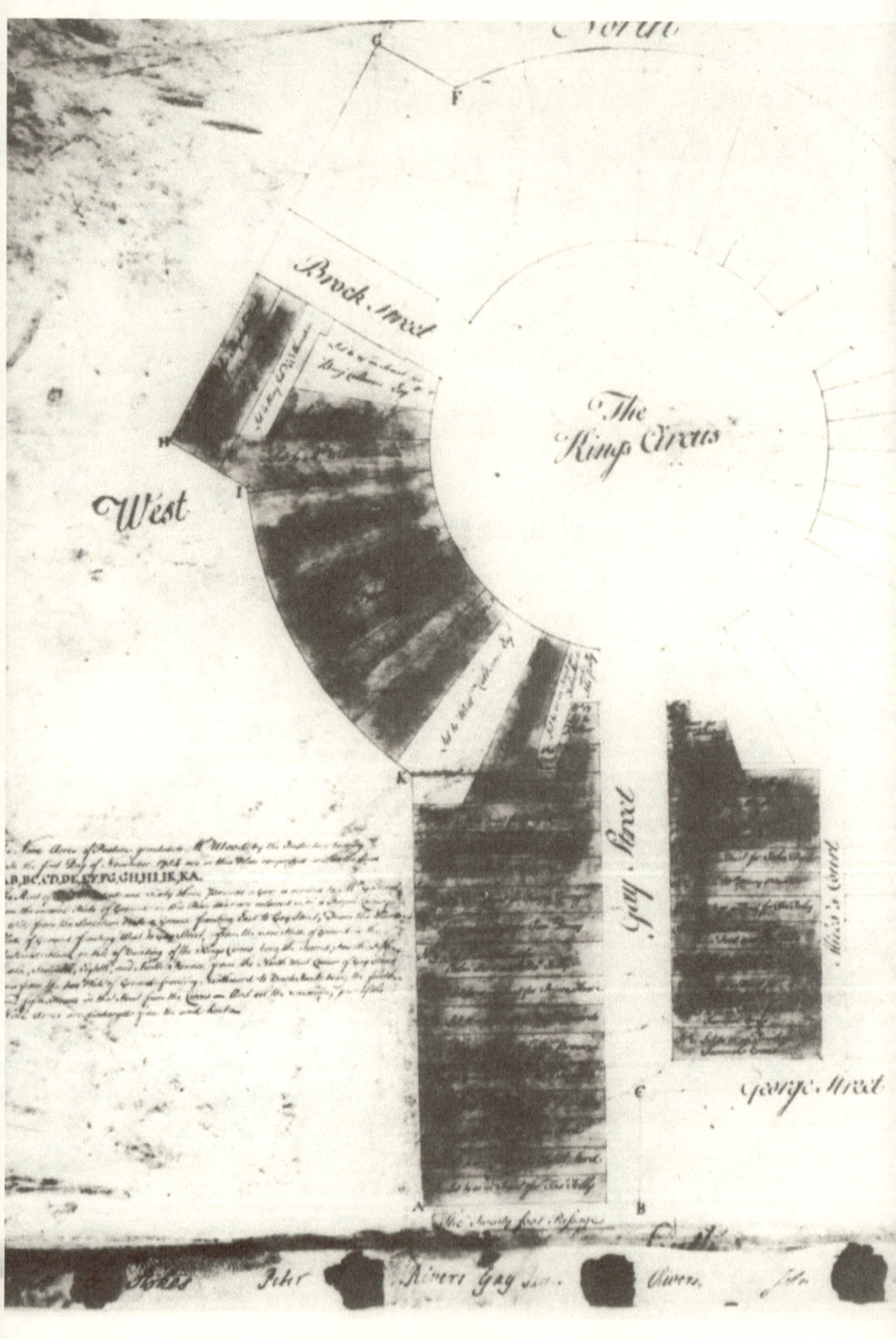

Plate VI The Circus, Bath. Drawing by John Wood. Reproduced by permission of Bath City Council.

interest above self-interest, must be remade by a total process of behavioural engineering. Rousseau's ingenious program in many ways lays out the techniques that Mao Tse-tung and Fidel Castro are following in our own time. I have analysed it elsewhere.[60] Here we need concern ourselves mainly with the role of the common people in Rousseau's new order.

The components of a true society include reflexive action or response in favour of the general will rather than the private will, the reduction of the independent or private sphere (and of privacy) in favour of the organic concept of the social body with total dependence of the parts; consequently unanimity, order and stability. I shall refrain from quoting the texts, and turn to a statement in *Emile* in which Rousseau demands a fixed society: 'Dans l'ordre social, où toutes les places sont marquées, chacun doit être élevé pour la sienne. Si un particulier formé pour sa place en sort, il n'est plus propre à rien'. 'Assigner à chacun sa place et l'y fixer.'[61] To leave one's place is destructive of order.

In this hierarchical scheme, the common people are assigned a place apart, one that befits their social role. Education is harmful, except for the chosen few. 'Le pauvre n'a pas besoin d'éducation'.[62] The widening of the worker's mental horizons and the increase in his education do not improve but rather worsen his attitude to work. Rousseau's phrase 'douce et précieuse ignorance'[63] applies here, and a model is furnished in the treatment of workers in *La Nouvelle Héloïse*. They are ruthlessly exploited, their thoughts, emotions and sex life repressed and regimented. The overt benevolent paternalism is only a method of incentives, reassurance and self-protection (often easily eluded), to carry out better the exploitation that is unknown to the workers but revealed to Saint-Preux, the intended novitiate of the small élite. Like the drones in Huxley's *Brave New World*, the plebs are designed or engineered for a role from which there can be no escape. 'Sur ce principe on s'attache ici . . . à contribuer autant qu'on peut à rendre aux paysans leur condition douce, sans jamais leur aider à en sortir.'[64] One of countless examples of Rousseau's sophistry is his defence of beggary as a useful social role, inasmuch as beggars arouse feelings of pity.[65]

While Rousseau could not conceive of Huxley's biological engineering, he did invent behavioural and social engineering, and

---

[60] See my *Rousseau's 'Social Contract'. An Interpretive Essay*, Cleveland, 1968.
[61] (Ed. Richard), pp. 11-12, 63.
[62] *Emile*, p. 27.
[63] *Œuvres*, III, 54 ('Observations . . . sur la Réponse qui a été faite à son Discours').
[64] *La Nouvelle Héloïse* (ed. Pomeau), p. 519.
[65] Ibid., pp. 523-4.

this is, in my opinion, the most remarkable product of his genius, though many refuse to recognise it. The common people are simply not to be treated as people. In addition to being 'dénaturés' and conditioned for their role, they are to be ruthlessly denied the development of their potentialities. 'Ceux qui sont destinés à vivre dans la simplicité champêtre n'ont pas besoin, pour être heureux, du développement de leurs facultés, et leurs talents enfouis sont comme les mines d'or du Valais que le bien public ne permet pas qu'on exploite.... N'instruisez point l'enfant du villageois, car il ne lui convient pas d'être instruit.'[66] Rousseau, to be sure, affirms self-protectively: 'L'homme est un être trop noble pour devoir servir simplement d'instrument à d'autres',[67] but this is followed by a long and sophistical justification for doing just that. 'J'ai peine à croire', Julie concludes for Rousseau, 'que tant de talents doivent être tous développés; car il faudrait pour cela que le nombre de ceux qui les possèdent fût exactement proportionné au besoin de la société'. Rousseau is therefore not in disagreement with Voltaire's belief[68] that there has to be a vast group of uneducated people (using that adjective in our sense); but all the people must be 'educated' in *his* sense of the word, one that is closely analogous to the sense it has in China today, as contrasted with Western liberal societies.

This attitude is not confined to *La Nouvelle Héloïse*. It is contained in Rousseau's detailed scheme for a regimented, organic society for Corsica. In his very first social work, the *Discours sur les sciences et les arts*, what he attacked, as he later claimed in his replies to critics, was less knowledge in itself than its popular dissemination and its effect on morals. We have seen that he would allow it for an élite; but for the populace 'l'ignorance, l'innocence & la pauvreté' are 'les seuls biens'.[69]

Rousseau's ambivalence, unrecognised by himself, is most striking on this point. The common people's ignorance, which, as we have seen, so frequently provoked his scorn, is politically desirable, necessary to their virtue—this word being taken in both the moral and political sense. They must be kept in that happy ignorance, to perform their allotted role. The power of the State must be used to preserve them from contagions, such as that of the theatre, which would expose them to 'des horreurs qu'il ne devroit pas même connoître'.[70] This policy of deliberately limiting horizons, of controlling the knowledge that reaches the people, is carried out con-

[66] Ibid., p. 553.
[67] Ibid., p. 521.
[68] So Bahner, in *Studies on Voltaire*, LV, 125.
[69] *Discours sur les sciences et les arts*, ed. G. R. Havens, New York, 1946, pp. 157-9. See also *Œuvres*, III, 76 ('Dernière Réponse').
[70] *Lettre à d'Alembert* (ed. Fuchs), p. 43.

sistently in Rousseau's planned societies. It is part of a total process of thought control, which includes invasion of privacy (its abolition, as far as possible), universal spying and denunciation, and censorship in its broadest possible scope. There is no other way of overcoming the radical vice of human society, which he had uncovered so powerfully in the second *Discours* and the *Préface de Narcisse*, its atomistic egocentricity, the pitiless, anti-social competition for wealth, power and place. As he puts it in a Fragment:

> Sitôt qu'un homme se compare aux autres il devient necessairement leur ennemi, car chacun voulant en son cœur être le plus puissant, le plus heureux, le plus riche, ne peut regarder que comme un ennemi secret quiconque ayant le même projet en soi-même lui devient un obstacle à l'exécuter. Voilà la contradiction primitive et radicale qui fait que les affections sociales ne sont qu'apparence. . . .[71]

We can touch only briefly on the role of the people in government. The first essential, as Rousseau states in other Fragments, is to keep the people involved in public affairs, and constantly studying the laws as a kind of catechism.[72] The goal, he says in *Emile*,[73] is for each to see himself and think of himself, to feel himself and to be felt only in the whole—a policy that is being successfully carried out in China today. Both the dedication of the second *Discours* and the *Contrat social* make it clear that if the ending of exploitation and the abuse of personal and class power is an essential reason for the people's sovereign privilege of consenting to laws, an equally urgent motive is the desire for total participation, for total commitment to the general will as expressed in law. The voting is described as a solemn, ceremonial event of commitment necessary to the desired organic quality, to the spirit of unanimity and the surpassing of the detested 'moi humain', or 'private will'. 'Mieux l'Etat est constitué, plus les affaires publiques l'emportent sur les privées dans l'esprit des Citoyens. Il y a même beaucoup moins d'affaires privées, parce que la somme du bonheur commun fournissant une portion plus considérable à celui de chaque individu, il lui en reste moins à chercher dans les soins particuliers.'[74]

Of course the people are incapable of formulating laws; and they need 'guides' to enlighten them before they say 'yes' or 'no' without being allowed to enter into any kind of association or even discussion. The famous phrase, 'la voix du peuple est en effet la voix de Dieu', is immediately followed by reservations of just this kind—

[71] *Œuvres*, III, 478 ('Fragments politiques', II, 10).
[72] Ibid., pp. 489, 492 ('Fragments politiques', III, 25, IV, 6).
[73] (Ed. Richard), p. 9.
[74] *Du Contrat social*, III, xv; in *Œuvres*, III, 429.

but they are less strikingly quotable than that phrase.[75] These guides are apparently the same people who formulate the laws and who, as we are told, know the general will before the people decide what it is. 'Qui est-ce qui a proposé que le peuple exerçât sans règle la puissance législative?', Rousseau asks in the *Lettres écrites de la montagne*.[76]

The people are best qualified to choose those who perform the functions of government, and may boot them out at will, but at the same time, 'c'est l'ordre le meilleur et le plus naturel que les plus sages gouvernent la multitude'.[77] Indeed the power of those who govern is immense, checked only by the assembled citizenry who act under the 'guidance' of those who govern them. During the interval between assemblies, decrees and other acts of government are not acts inhering in the sovereign, that is, the people. As in foreign affairs, for example, 'les grandes maximes d'Etat ne sont pas à sa portée; il doit s'en rapporter là-dessus à ses chefs'.[78] This separation between government and sovereign is one of Rousseau's cleverest and most subtle points. I confess that in my little book on the *Social Contract* I did not give it its full due. The inalienable sovereignty of the people (which, unaided, they are unable to exercise wisely) is expressed in laws, not in acts of government. Laws, Rousseau stipulates, must have generality, cannot be directed against individuals. This protection does not extend to acts of government. Now, the whole apparatus of thought and behavioural control falls within the jurisdiction of the government. Censorship, surveillance, education and all the mechanisms of regimentation are such acts, not laws. It is essential to note also that there is no accountability for specific acts of government, only the periodic, general accountability, under controlled conditions, of a vote of confidence. Rousseau believes that this can easily be managed. 'Le peuple, convaincu que ses chefs ne travaillent qu'á faire son bonheur, les dispense par sa déférence de travailler à affermir leur pouvoir'.[79] We can readily imagine with what delight Rousseau's leaders would welcome radio, television, the mass media, all the modern means of swinging elections.

Ever-present suspicion of the people implies a separation of rulers and ruled into 'we' and 'they'. Essentially, it is the government that acts on the people. It must continuously do so, to maintain the remedy of 'art' against the seductions of nature, that is, devotion to

---

[75] 'Economie politique', in *Political Writings* (ed. Vaughan), I, 243.
[76] In *Political Writings* (ed. Vaughan), II, 266.
[77] *Du Contrat social*, III, v; in *Œuvres*, III, 407.
[78] *Lettres écrites de la montagne*, in *Political Writings* (ed. Vaughan), II, 220.
[79] 'Economie politique'; ibid., I, 250.

the *moi commun* instead of the *moi humain*. 'Un imbécille obéï peut comme un autre punir les forfaits . . .; c'est sur les volontés encore plus que sur les actions qu'il [le chef ou l'homme d'état] étend son respectable empire.'[80] Capture wills! This is Rousseau's cry in all his writings. Capture minds, he also said, or meant when he wrote time and again of the need to learn the art of changing opinions, forming opinions, governing opinions. How can wills be captured, unless minds are captured? It is for the government to mould people: 'J'avois vu que tout tenoit radicalement à la politique, et que, de quelque façon qu'on s'y prit, aucun peuple ne seroit jamais ce que la nature de son Gouvernement le feroit être'.[81] If we correlate this basic point with another, that laws themselves cannot control behaviour or change men, the extent of the role of government, and of its power, becomes clear.

If laws are useless by themselves, how will the government go about its task? 'Par où le gouvernement peut-il donc avoir prise sur les mœurs? Je réponds que c'est par l'opinion publique. . . . Quand on ne vit pas en soi, mais dans les autres, ce sont leurs jugements qui règlent tout. . . . Ainsi l'on a beau faire; ni la raison, ni la vertu, ni les lois ne vaincront l'opinion publique, tant qu'on ne trouvera pas l'art de la changer.'[82] Public opinion, so dangerous and corrupting in existing societies, can become, when properly directed and manipulated, a powerful force in remaking man. We know that Rousseau was right.

The emotions of the common people must also be controlled and utilised. Puritanism and the damping of the fires of sexuality is a necessary check on aggressive egocentricity and the turning in toward the *volontés particulières* (China has carefully taken this precept into account). However, the proletariat, and only they, are required to marry, to re-supply the corps of workers.[83] They will be required to have a simple life and simple tastes, being thus more manageable. They will be prevented from knowing other possibilities.[84] But more positive action is needed to make the sheep-like people identify themselves with the nation. In the *Lettre à d'Alembert*, Rousseau repeatedly drives home the importance of public spectacles and games in creating a spirit of unanimity, of belonging less to oneself than to the common whole, and in whipping up a patriotic and martial spirit. 'Faites que chacun se voie et s'aime

---

[80] Ibid., p. 250.
[81] *Confessions*, in *Œuvres*, I, 404.
[82] *Lettre à d'Alembert* (ed. Fuchs), pp. 89-90, 93.
[83] *La Nouvelle Héloïse* (ed. Pomeau), p. 642 (also *Projet de constitution pour la Corse*, Part II).
[84] Ibid. (also 'Economie politique', and *Lettre à d'Alembert* (ed. Fuchs), p. 169 note).

dans les autres, afin que tous en soient mieux unis.'[85] Where spontaneity fails, clever art—in which, Rousseau has said, lies the remedy for both human and natural failures—will create spontaneity.

If the common people can be incited to bad actions, as in Geneva and Môtiers, skilful leaders can also arouse their emotions for good purposes. The whipping up of patriotic fervour, of what Rousseau calls 'zeal', and the adroit use of the competitive and emulative instincts, deviated, like the irrigation stream in Pastor Lambercier's garden, from nature's law of self-interest to the social goal, are essential means of capturing wills. These ideas are developed throughout Rousseau's writings. To them he adds religion, which must be remade to contain a powerful nationalistic core.[86]

Most of all, the leaders must take advantage of the facility with which the common people can be duped. Rousseau has pointed out that in present societies the powerful (what we now call 'the Establishment') use this weapon for their own profit. In the good society, it will be used for the benefit of the people themselves. The common people are only children, he tells us, and we know how he treats Emile: 'Il n'y a point d'assujetissement si parfait que celui qui garde l'apparence de la liberté; on captive ainsi la volonté même. . . . Sans doute il ne doit faire que ce qu'il veut; mais il ne doit vouloir que ce que vous voulez qu'il fasse'.[87] We see the same system of 'beneficent illusion' in all the writings. 'On y reconnaît toujours la main du maître et l'on ne la sent jamais.'[88] It permeates the plans written for Corsica and Poland. It is the controlling power behind the stage play of popular sovereignty, in the *Contrat social*, as is clear in the chapter on censorship and in Chapter xii of Book II, where Rousseau writes that the really important law is written in the hearts of the citizens:

> Je parle des mœurs, des coutumes, et sur-tout de l'opinion; partie inconnue à nos politiques, mais de laquelle dépend le succès de toutes les autres: partie dont le grand Législateur s'occupe en secret, tandis qu'il paroit se borner à des réglemens particuliers.[89]

Or, as he puts it in *La Nouvelle Héloïse*, 'sans paraître y songer, on établit des usages plus puissants que l'autorité même'.[90] In *Emile*

---

[85] (Ed. Fuchs), pp. 168-9.
[86] *Œuvres*, III, 958 ('Considerations sur le gouvernement de Pologne'), and *Contrat social*, IV, viii *passim*.
[87] (Ed. Richard), p. 121.
[88] *La Nouvelle Héloïse* (ed. Pomeau), p. 351.
[89] In *Œuvres*, III, 394.
[90] (Ed. Pomeau), p. 432.

he speaks of rules 'que je lui dicte en secret'[91] and what is *Emile*, if not a manual of hidden behavioural control?

In the role assigned to Legislators and guides lies the answer to Rousseau's apparent contradiction: the people are to judge whether the formulation of a law corresponds to the general will, while at the same time, it is precisely because they cannot do so (for the reasons we have noted) that they need guides. I have no doubt that Rousseau felt men needed a little benevolent conspiracy (a form of 'art') to create the beneficent illusions.

How thoroughly Rousseau would have the people manipulated, conditioned and regimented can best be seen in his practical applications, in several pages of the *Projet pour la Corse*,[92] for instance, and especially in the astounding second part. Here, too, only the people may pass the laws, but real power is all in the hands of the leaders, in a frankly absolute government.[93] Again the essential point is that their task is not only to regulate (that is, to rule), but to mould.[94] 'Les arbitres de l'opinion d'un peuple le sont de ses actions.' 'Je les mettrai dans une position telle qu'ils auront ces vertus, sans en connaître le mot; et qu'ils seront bons et justes, sans trop savoir ce que c'est que justice et bonté.'[95] All of this is matched, in *Considérations sur le gouvernement de Pologne*, by a remarkable totalitarian theory of education; and still more, perhaps, by the constant drumroll of propaganda or other kinds of pressures with which the minds of children and adults are to be continually assailed.[96] In these pages, which must be reread, Rousseau belongs to the twentieth century, not to his own.

From this investigation we may conclude that Rousseau's attitude toward the common people was a typical manifestation of his psychological outlook. He was attracted and repelled by them, and fascinated by the problem they represented. They were the material that had to be shaped if the war within men and among men were to be surpassed in an organic society. In his mind they were always a separate category of beings, from which the élite, like himself, were distinguished, even when on occasion they mingled. In his treatise for Poland, he would not touch the power and wealth of the aristocracy and the church, or ameliorate the miserable condition of the serfs. If he was outraged by their exploitation by individuals or vested interests, he planned for their benevolent but still more

---

[91] Ibid., p. 554.
[92] *Political Writings* (ed. Vaughan), II, 331-5, will do for an example.
[93] Ibid., p. 342.
[94] See, for example, ibid., pp. 344-5, 351.
[95] Ibid., pp. 344, 354.
[96] Ibid., pp. 427, 433-4, 491-3, among others.

absolute exploitation by the State, for the good of all, after having created a relationship of complete dependency.

We have observed two main consequences. The 'new man' was to arise from a complex process of thought control and will control. Rousseau initiates the techniques of operant conditioning and pressure propaganda, including use of the arts and the media. 'Governments should try to make a new kind of man by integrating culture to the total system of politics.' The statement, by a Soviet minister, might have been written by Rousseau. The reply of a Chinese to a visitor's question, 'We consider it a very happy life to live and work with our friends and comrades of the great proletarian People's Liberation Army', is precisely the kind of programmed response we find time and again in the mouth of Emile, the kind of reflexive response Rousseau admittedly seeks to cultivate, one that brings into the social sphere the necessity of physical laws (as he urges in that work). That is why it is the leader's task to persuade without convincing.

The second consequence is the political process of total, democratic involvement, together with the 'guidance', partly open, mostly hidden. During the French Revolution a book appeared, entitled *Jean-Jacques Rousseau, aristocrate*.[97] Both in his own feelings and in his ideal society, the élitist element, however concealed from others or from himself, is dominant. In the *Contrat social*, he proclaims his preference for aristocratic government. Rousseau was the hero worshipper, and he calls for strong, magnetic, godlike leaders. As in Marxist theory, the élitist potentiality shines through. Both Rousseau and Marx tend to transform the people or proletariat into the political raw material of a utopia, to be reprocessed by leaders, guides or party, who justify their leadership on their possession of the theory itself (precisely as Rousseau does with Emile), and on their accurate consciousness of the general will.

Consequently, I do not think it adequate to say that the 'peuple' have become 'populace' because they have been subjected and corrupted by despotism; and that Rousseau hoped for their regeneration through the restoration of natural 'mœurs'.[98] The heart of his theory is that men are inevitably corrupted in society, unless they are subjected (as they were by Moses and Lycurgus) to what he time and again calls an iron yoke; and that (as in the parable of Julie's garden) it takes much 'art' to restore and to maintain 'nature'. However, both the character of the yoke and the completeness of the subjection are radically different in Rousseau from what obtained in the aristocratic society of the Old Régime or in the

[97] By C. F. Le Normant, Paris, 1790.
[98] So Bahner, in *Studies on Voltaire*, LV, 123-4.

liberal and constitutional bourgeois societies that superseded it. The closest analogues (despite many differences resulting in part from history and practice versus abstract rationalism) are the present societies of China and Cuba.

Nonetheless, when the French Revolution reached Geneva, Rousseau was worshipped as its prophet and its moral authority. Although he was an aristocrat in most of his aspirations and theorising, the Genevans remembered his *Lettres écrites de la montagne*, his attacks on the French nobility and on tyranny. 'Popular sovereignty' and the 'general will' had become magical phrases and *idées-force*. They remembered, too, the pull of his plebian class origins, which he had not hesitated to display. Most of all they felt ennobled by his putting moral rectitude above the privilege of birth, and by his devotion to virtue. They probably did not understand what he meant by that word.

We return, finally, to Rousseau's fundamental ambivalence. Professor Maurice Cranston recently wrote: 'He regarded appearance as the domain of deception and therefore as bad; and reality as the province of truth, and therefore as good. . . . Appearance and reality he conceived to be antithetical; so he could never fully understand the life of politics, where appearance is almost as important as reality: is even indeed a part of it'.[99] Although we can find in Rousseau ample evidence of this attitude toward appearance and reality, his attitude toward them in politics is precisely the contrary of Professor Cranston's statement. We have seen that truth and illusion, reality and appearance are changeable values for him, according to who uses them and how. To him the province of truth was often very bad. He consistently praises and uses calculated techniques of deception. He advises them as necessary in politics—which is the management of people in a society. And it was by using 'appearance' that reality could be changed. One ignores these ambivalences, and the unity that subtends them, at one's peril.

---

[99] *New York Times*, 13 August 1972.

Jacques le Fataliste: *un problème de cohérence structurelle*

François Van Laere

Introduction: Le problème sous l'angle historique.
Il existe peu d'écrivains dont le style soit aussi limpide que celui de Diderot. Pourtant des querelles d'interprétation ont surgi à propos de maints de ses textes. On peut naturellement concevoir que des ouvrages où la philosophie privilégie la méthode heuristique puissent conserver un caractère d'indétermination qui ne favorise guère les exégèses tranchées. Il est plus singulier que des œuvres de fiction (des œuvres où la fiction du moins prend la place prépondérante, comme dans *Le Neveu de Rameau* ou *Jacques le Fataliste*), c'est-à-dire des narrations où la relative gratuité pourrait s'allier à une grande force d'évidence pour imposer un sens clair, entraînant l'unanimité, continuent en fait à susciter des controverses parmi les critiques, qui ne parviennent pas à s'entendre non seulement sur la signification globale qu'il convient de donner à ces récits, mais aussi —on pourrait dire: mais déjà et surtout—sur la structure et l'organisation méthodique que l'on peut, éventuellement, y distinguer.

En particulier *Jacques le Fataliste et son Maître* a été considéré très longtemps comme une œuvre de pure improvisation, dépourvue de structure, d'organisation—voire de signification, au sens univoque et didactique du terme. Diderot n'aurait cherché qu'à se divertir (ce qui n'est pas un défaut) et il n'aurait pas hésité à s'amuser aux dépens, en partie, du lecteur. On n'a pas manqué de rappeler le goût qu'avait pour la mystification l'auteur de *La Religieuse*.[1] Un Thibaudet pouvait encore se figurer que *Jacques le Fataliste* avait été écrit au hasard, sans plan arrêté ni intention

---

[1] Citons, dans les dernières années, Roger Kempf, *Diderot et le roman ou le démon de la présence*, Paris, 1964; et Jean Catrysse, *Diderot et la mystification*, Paris, 1970.

définie. Tel était bien le point de vue de la critique traditionnelle, qui réduisait l'originalité du récit à un plaisant et total décousu, parfaitement inorganique, rebelle par conséquent à toute mise en ordre.

Toutefois, depuis 1950 environ, une originalité d'un type nouveau, structurale celle-ci, est devenue visible dans le texte. Progressivement, la conviction qui l'a emporté fut que l'œuvre était, en vérité, le fruit d'une composition surveillée, dominée, et qu'elle possédait une ferme architecture. Mais, par réaction aux attitudes critiques antérieures, on est allé jusqu'à soumettre le texte à des grilles interprétatives d'une grande rigidité, qui décelaient de la préméditation jusque dans le moindre détail et supposaient chez l'auteur une impressionnante rigueur consciente.[2]

On s'étonnera, en passant, qu'il ait fallu attendre longtemps pour que soit posé en termes clairs le problème de l'homogénéité narrative de *Jacques le Fataliste* et celui des lois internes au texte qui président à sa structuration. Ce retard peut s'attribuer à deux raisons. La première, c'est l'habileté même de Diderot artiste qui s'est ingénié à masquer les mécanismes qui opéraient dans sa fiction, et il a trop bien réussi, pour ainsi dire, à 'gommer' les procédés qui agençaient et articulaient les éléments du récit; la seconde raison tient aux progrès qui se sont accomplis, durant des deux dernières décennies, dans l'analyse sémiologique et structurale du discours narratif et qui nous ont rendus plus attentifs à la production textuelle du récit, à ses lois rigoureuses, à ce que A. J. Greimas nomme sa 'grammaire'.

Un bel indice des perplexités que l'ouvrage de Diderot a provoquées se marque dans la difficulté, qui se rencontre dès l'origine, à le désigner, à le classer dans un genre déterminé, même s'il est de tradition de le ranger parmi les *Œuvres romanesques* de l'auteur (aux côtés du *Neveu de Rameau*, qui soulève le même type de difficulté). L'on sait que Diderot a expressément refusé à son texte l'appellation de 'roman'; et, de fait, le roman, en tant que genre, a été de tout temps une notion difficile à définir et à circonscrire; mais faut-il pour autant se laisser séduire par l'idée que *Jacques le Fataliste* serait un 'Anti-Roman', au sens que prend cette formule dans le sous-titre (ou plutôt dans le titre alternatif) donné par Charles Sorel à son *Berger extravagant* ou dans la préface rédigée

---

[2] V. par exemple, J. Robert Loy, *Diderot's Determined Fatalist. A Critical Appreciation of Jacques le Fataliste*, New York, 1950; Francis Pruner, *L'Unité secrète de 'Jacques le Fataliste'*, Paris, 1970; et Roger Laufer, 'La structure et la signification de *Jacques le Fataliste*', *Revue des sciences humaines*, no 112, (oct.-déc. 1963), 517-35. Dans l'article présent nous utiliserons l'édition procurée par H. Bénac, *Diderot: Œuvres romanesques*, Paris, 1962, qui sera citée par numéro de page.

par Jean-Paul Sartre pour le *Portrait d'un inconnu* de Nathalie Sarraute? Globalement juste à première vue, cette désignation strictement négative ne nous avance guère, dans la mesure où elle ne renseigne que sur un seul aspect du texte; par ailleurs, une théorie générale de l'anti-roman reste à faire; enfin, un anti-roman, qu'il s'agisse du *Don Quichotte* ou de *Ulysses*, n'en reste pas moins une expression du genre romanesque, puisque le roman vise, par essence, à enfreindre sans cesse les règles qu'il s'assigne de façon toujours provisoire; ainsi, l'anti-roman nous reconduisant au roman, nous tournons dans un cercle vicieux.

Quant à nous, pour désigner *Jacques le Fataliste*, nous reprendrions volontiers à Diderot lui-même le terme de *satire* qu'il a appliqué à deux de ses textes, d'une part la *Satire I sur les caractères et les mots de caractère, de profession, etc.*, où s'énonce une thèse—'autant d'hommes, autant de cris divers'[3]—et d'autre part *Le Neveu de Rameau*, la satire II, qui fournit une illustration pratique de la thèse; mais on peut considérer que la démonstration se poursuit dans *Jacques le Fataliste*, chaque locuteur y étant caractérisé par son langage, de sorte que ce récit se groupe fort bien, au moins sous cet angle, avec les deux autres textes. Diderot prête au mot 'satire' la double acception qu'il reçoit dans l'Antiquité—chez Horace, Juvénal, Perse—celle tout à la fois de 'mélange' et d'ouvrage caustique, socialement critique. Il faut accorder un intérêt particulier au sens, d'ailleurs étymologique, qui signale la satire comme un 'pot-pourri', un ensemble hétéroclite, une combinaison à dessein explosive de pièces détachées pouvant relever de genres différents. C'est en effet, comme nous le verrons, le sens qui correspond de la façon la plus adéquate à la forme de la narration de Diderot—et nous entendons le terme de 'forme' dans sa pleine valeur technique.

Méthodologie de la lecture

Toute lecture procède d'une attitude qui, orientant le sens, se révèle nécessairement déterminante: cette attitude ou prise de position face au texte, il convient de l' 'avouer', de la déclarer comme un préalable méthodologique. Or, le plus souvent, le lecteur professionnel qu'est le critique cherche à dissimuler, ou en tout cas passe sous silence, le fait qu'il a trouvé le sens dans un discours extérieur au texte. Nombreuses sont ainsi les lectures de *Jacques le Fataliste* qui, sous prétexte d'en éclairer la signification, ont recouru à des lumières extérieures en surimposant à l'œuvre une hypothèse interprétative qui brouillait à coup sûr l'organisation technique-

---

[3] Diderot, *Œuvres*, ed. A. Billy, Paris, 1951, p. 1217.

ment formelle parce que l'hypothèse privilégiée escamotait le problème de cohérence, supposé *ipso facto* résolu.

Pour citer quelques exemples: on a connu une exégèse hégélienne qui subordonne la fiction aux relations d'autorité entre maître et esclave (dès le début du récit on voit le Maître 'tombant à grands coups de fouet sur son valet')[4] et qui estime que le Maître est le lieu de l'aliénation de Jacques et, corrélativement, Jacques le lieu de l'aliénation du Maître; la lecture existentialiste, elle, a montré que les personnages existent par leurs actes plutôt qu'ils n'accomplissent une essence, et cela à travers la problématique d'une liberté, morale avant tout; n'oublions pas la lecture marxiste qui voit dans le récit une interrogation sur la réification de l'homme; une des dernières lectures en date, envisage *Jacques le Fataliste* comme un ancêtre du Nouveau Roman français actuel et rattache l'ouvrage à une esthétique délibérément d'avant-garde.

Notre propre intention est de tenter une lecture aussi 'neutre' que possible, qui relègue la question de la signification à un stade dernier pour donner la priorité au texte lui-même, pris comme un système où se produisent des relations internes régies par des structures génétiquement primordiales. Avant de risquer une hypothèse quant à la signification du tout, il importe de recenser les unités élémentaires de signification constitutives de cet ensemble et d'étudier comment elles engendrent, en la tissant, l'étoffe narrative.

Dans ce but, il convient de considérer avec attention la manière ordinaire qu'avait Diderot d'élaborer un texte et qui le singularise comme un véritable 'compositeur' (nous désignons par là le technicien chez qui prédomine la faculté de 'composer', au sens plein du terme). Car il faut tenir compte de manière précise des prédilections techniques, dans la mesure où, comme le rappelait autrefois Sartre, une technique renvoie toujours à une métaphysique. Et quel est le procédé d'assemblage que nous voyons fonctionner dans des œuvres aussi dissemblables que les *Pensées philosophiques* (dès le début de la carrière donc), *De l'interprétation de la nature*, le triptyque du *Rêve de d'Alembert*, le *Neveu de Rameau* et, tout à la fin, l' *Essai sur les règnes de Claude et de Néron*? Il consiste curieusement en une pratique qui n'est pas sans rappeler le stade qui, dans la réalisation d'un film cinématographique, s'appelle le 'montage', lequel implique un 'découpage' préalable de la matière filmée et le réassemblage des fragments et séquences en fonction d'une économie réfléchie, opérant des rapprochements ou des disjonctions intentionnels. On prouverait sans peine que ce procédé répond aux

---

[4] p. 495.

principes de l' 'œuvre ouverte', telle qu'elle a été définie par l'esthéticien italien Umberto Eco,[5] c'est-à-dire une œuvre qui ne trouve l'achèvement de sa signification que grâce à une collaboration active du lecteur, auquel il incombe de participer lui aussi à la construction—pour ainsi dire littérale—du texte. Dans un même ordre d'idées, on songe tout naturellement au dispositif privilégié du dialogue, omniprésent chez Diderot et dont les virtualités complexes lui permettent aussi bien de scinder sa réflexion personnelle en pôles dialectiquement antagonistes et, sur un mode ambigu souvent retors, d'en appeler au lecteur: belle conjonction de l'introversion et de l'extraversion!

Nous avons indiqué comment nous comptions garantir l'asepsie de nos instruments critiques afin de ne pas contaminer notre lecture d'une exégèse prématurée. Il s'agit de se livrer, pour commencer, à un déchiffrement aussi constatif que possible, en déconnectant l'innervation d'une signification globale, enveloppant le texte entier. Et, une fois la cohérence établie, peut-être assisterons-nous à l'assomption d'une lecture performative accomplissant, achevant le sens, lequel a chance en vérité de s'être produit chemin faisant, pour peu que notre lecture ait été un acte, un mode de collaboration textuelle.[6] Il nous sera toutefois permis—sans que nous préjugions de la signification totale du récit—de nous fier à deux données objectivement observables, que nous garderons en mémoire, points de repère et guides fixes, tout au long de notre itinéraire méthodique.

Première donnée: Diderot a choisi une orientation qui peut surprendre dans le champ de l'imaginaire: sa fiction prétend atteindre à la vérité! 'Mon projet', dit-il, 'est d'être vrai';[7] et il met le lecteur en garde: 'Celui qui prendrait ce que j'écris pour la vérité, serait peut-être moins dans l'erreur que celui qui le prendrait pour une fable'.[8] Le voyage de ses personnages rejoint ainsi une quête du vrai—mais un vrai de quelle sorte sinon celui qui, plus sûrement, se moule en creux au sein rêveur où le réel et le fictif se mirent l'un dans l'autre.

La deuxième donnée à observer est plus singulière. Davantage qu'une simple donnée, c'est—pourrait-on dire—la véritable 'donne' dans cette partie fictive, puisqu'elle y intervient d'entrée de jeu: 'Jacques disait que son capitaine disait que tout ce qui nous arrive de bien et de mal ici-bas était écrit là-haut'.[9] On note tout de suite

---

[5] Cf. *Opera aperta*, Milan, 1962.
[6] Nous adaptons aux besoins de notre propre argumentation les concepts et le vocabulaire de J. L. Austin, *How to do Things with Words*, London, 1962.
[7] p. 731.
[8] p. 505.
[9] p. 493.

la réduplication, le dire qui se redit. Nous voulons y voir une métaphore de l'écriture même, et non pas une allusion, si ordinaire au XVIIIe siècle, à ce Grand Livre de la Nature cher au Vicaire Savoyard.[10] Nous avons affaire à un double registre, d'une part le registre de ce qui est manifeste, signifiant, littéral, et d'autre part un registre moins saisissable où ce qui est manifesté, rappelle les évanescences d'un ordre symbolique ou herméneutique. Quand Jacques assure qu'il lit avec assiduité 'dans le grand livre' ('Ah! mon maître, on a beau réfléchir, méditer, étudier dans tous les livres du monde, on n'est jamais qu'un petit clerc quand on n'a pas lu dans le grand livre . . .'[11]), il nous renvoie en fait à une sorte de comptabilité en partie double: il y a 'le calcul qui se fait dans nos têtes' et 'celui qui est arrêté sur le registre d'en haut'.[12] Le partage vertical est aussi essentiel que radical; à l'ici-bas contingent, capricieux, imprévisible, que narre un texte vagabond, s'oppose un 'là-haut' qui sera le lieu, cette fois, du Texte (ici encore nous distinguerons par la majuscule l'immanence conceptuelle de sa réalité signifiante). Cette confrontation de 'l'écriture d'en haut'[13] avec sa trace dans l'ici-bas se répercute à tous les niveaux textuels, depuis le récit dans son cours le plus simple jusqu'au débat éthique ou philosophique, en passant par la poétique narrative. Le Texte, c'est 'le grand rouleau', 'qui contient toute vérité', sans la moindre 'ligne fausse'; mais 'le doigt qui a tracé toute l'écriture qui est là-haut' n'en a pas moins, du même geste, signé l'ici-bas: 'Tous les deux étaient écrits l'un à côté de l'autre. Tout a été écrit à la fois. C'est comme un grand rouleau qui se déploie petit à petit . . .'.[14]

Métaphore de l'écriture, disions-nous, parce que l'aventureux permanent du texte, où à chaque instant, à chaque mot, tout semble de nouveau possible, restitué à la relance, instable, gratuit, fortuit, demeure néanmoins constamment référé à l'exigence de nécessité du Texte; et le Texte, à son tour, pour fonder sa propre et (finalement) singulière nécessité (puisque le texte et le Texte s'écrivent du même trait), n'a pas d'autre issue que de distribuer et d'ordonner la substance signifiante.

Cette interprétation se confirme jusque dans de menus détails, qui désignent cette métaphore élue du texte et de l'écriture. Par exemple, 'le décousu dans la conversation' est comparé à 'la lecture

[10] 'On eût dit que la nature étalait à nos yeux toute sa magnificence pour en offrir le texte à nos entretiens. Ce fut là, qu'apres avoir quelque temps contemplé ces objets en silence, l'homme de paix me parla ainsi' (J.-J. Rousseau, *Emile*, Livre IV; dans *Œuvres complètes*, ed. Bernard Gagnebin et Marcel Raymond, IV, Paris, 1969, 565).
[11] p. 666.
[12] p. 504.
[13] p. 736.
[14] pp. 503, 656, 499.

d'un livre dont on aurait sauté quelques feuillets', ou bien ailleurs il est signalé que: 'le texte de notre conversation n'était pas triste'.[15]

On ne s'étonnera pas, après tout cela, que, dans ce jeu (ou système) textuel, Jacques finisse par se voir attribuer un 'texte' justement—et, pour bien faire, il faudrait écrire le mot avec une initiale qui serait *à la fois* minuscule et majuscule; un texte qui, quoique purement imaginaire,[16] serait à situer *entre*, d'une part, le signifiant manifeste où se récitent les aléas de l'aventure itinérante, et, d'autre part, le signifié problématique de l' 'écriture d'en haut': en effet, le livre qu'aurait écrit Jacques ne serait autre qu'un traité de divination, où la méthode préconisée substitue à la dive Bacbuc une gourde de vin fournissant une inspiration qui se reçoit de haut en bas[17] pour deux raisons très logiques: d'abord parce que c'est bien ainsi que l'on boit; ensuite parce qu'il s'agit d'établir la liaison entre le Texte et le texte, le 'là-haut' et l' 'ici-bas'.

Par cette insistance à se désigner elle-même, la substance textuelle entend, évidemment, assurer sur soi une clôture, au sein da laquelle, préfigurés par les deux registres de l'écriture, des discours multiples, proliférants, divergents, vont s'entrelacer et se tresser; des fils, interrompus puis renoués, vont s'emmêler comme des ondes d'amplitude variable. Mais le propos aura beau se diversifier, favoriser la dispersion et la dissémination, les facteurs centrifuges, l'hétérogénéité, il n'empêche que dans le même temps une espèce de norme informulée—très précisément la cohérence, dans sa vertu active, structurante—travaillera à homogénéiser progressivement la parole, à diffuser une énergie centripète, amalgamant les composants épars. Si bien qu'il reste, malgré tout, essentiel de respecter l'intrication du tissu textuel, car c'est elle qui lui donne son moiré vivant. En aucun cas nous ne pourrons la perdre de vue: principe méthodologique dont il y aura lieu de nous souvenir surtout quand nous en viendrons à dissoudre le texte en ses unités fonctionnelles de base, c'est-à-dire à démêler et isoler ses composants narratifs. (Nous nommerons ceux-ci 'récits tiroirs' et définirons cette notion en son temps.)

Les grandes structures de fonctionnement.

Le pré-texte. Avant de décomposer—et nous insistons sur les constituants du mot: 'dé-composer'—le texte en ses unités, lesquelles se révéleront relativement mobiles, il est utile de fixer, parmi les

---

[15] pp. 547, 746.
[16] C'est le discours de l'Auteur qui assume (pp. 716-17), dans une tonalité d'ironie et de fantaisie, l'attribution à Jacques d' 'un petit traité de toutes sortes de divinations'.
[17] p. 716.

conditions qui rendent cette narration-ci, très précisément, possible, les grandes structures invariantes, dont la validité effective se vérifie en droit pour tous les points de la surface textuelle, à la façon de lois générales (mais dans la clôture particulière de ce récit singulier).

Paradoxalement, la première de ces structures amples est celle qui constitue l' 'en dedans' du texte à partir d'un 'en dehors', sans que l'on puisse parler proprement d'emprunt. On peut, en effet, considérer comme tranchée la question, longtemps controversée, de la dette que Diderot aurait contractée à l'égard de Sterne; en pratique, ce dont il est redevable à celui-ci ressemble, par le traitement qu'il fait subir à la source, au thème inaugural d'un morceau de musique.[18] On a démontré de façon décisive l'originalité de Diderot, qui ne doit guère à Sterne, et il n'est plus possible de tomber dans l'erreur d'un Balzac qui voyait dans *Jacques le Fataliste* un plat démarquage de *Tristram Shandy*.

Dyade itinérante. Très vite, cependant, Diderot installe un décalage entre son propre texte et celui de Sterne. Ainsi, la relation qui unit l'Oncle Toby et l'humble caporal Trim n'est rien comparable au contrat narratif qui lie au Maître l'insolent Jacques.[19] A celui-ci revient une sorte de prééminence: il précède son Maître dans le titre (on voit même l'intitulé se réduire au seul nom de Jacques),[20] procure un support véhiculaire au refrain 'fataliste', mais surtout fait figure de locuteur fondamental, de 'diseur' par excellence; il n'est 'actant'[21] que parce qu'il se définit comme 'parlant'—et, bien plus que le dire, sa fonction, c'est le 'redire'. En tant que disant—et disant l'écho[22]—il prend la parole le premier dans le récit, avant son Maître, juste après le Lecteur et l'Auteur. Il n'est pas indifférent que cette structure d'écho surgisse comme une dédicace, au seuil d'un texte où foisonneront les récits rapportés ('un tel dit qu'un tel a dit . . .').[23]

Toutefois, Jacques ne peut, sans absurdité, se concevoir autonome; il n'existe textuellement que parce qu'il forme avec son Maître une parfaite dyade; cette structure, bien connue pour sa

---

[18] Nous renvoyons à Alice Green Fredman, *Diderot and Sterne*, New York, 1955.

[19] Ce n'est pas par hasard que le thème du contrat est directement attesté dans le texte même—notamment dans la scène de jugement parodique, où le contrat se dénoue pour se renouer (p. 663). Le contrat peut être qualifié de 'narratif' en ce que c'est l'acte de conter qui, entre Jacques et le Maître, scelle le pacte sur le plan signifiant et, de ce fait, engendre le récit entier.

[20] p. 714.

[21] Nous empruntons ce terme—et le concept qu'il désigne—au système du sémanticien A. J. Greimas (*Sémantique structurale*, Paris, 1966).

[22] 'Jacques disait que son capitaine disait que . . .'.

[23] Concurremment, Jacques a, tout autant que son grand-père Jason, les redites en horreur: pour rien au monde il ne consentirait à raconter deux fois un même récit.

valeur opératoire—par exemple, depuis le *Don Quichotte* jusqu'au *Godot* de Beckett, en passant par *Bouvard et Pécuchet*—permet à tout moment de projeter sur un fait, un événement, une péripétie, l'éclairage contrasté qu'allument les foyers d'une réaction duelle.

Au départ, ce qui importe à Diderot, c'est le schéma purement structural de la relation dyadique (accessoirement sa modalité dialogique); c'est pourquoi Jacques et son Maître sont essentiellement 'abstraits', celui-ci l'étant davantage encore du fait que, voué à l'anonymat, il s'identifie à son statut apparent. Taillés dans une étoffe universelle, ils sont bien faits pour illustrer un proverbe.[24] Aussi bien leur voyage ne peut-il être que spirituel, comme la quête du *Quichotte*, la navigation rabelaisienne, ou la chasse au Snark.

On objectera que, chemin faisant, nos deux protagonistes—quoiqu'ils disposent à peine d'un physique—perdent pourtant une partie de leur caractère abstrait. Jacques fait l'objet d'informations biographiques diverses (le frère Jean, le grand-père Jason, la kyrielle des maisons où il a servi . . .), tandis que le Maître prend de la consistance dans le bain révélateur de ses amours. Néanmoins la volonté d'abstraction persiste, et Diderot la manifeste quand, plutôt que d'enrichir le registre des notations et nuances caractérielles, il choisit de doter les pôles dyadiques de stéréotypes fonctionnels—respectivement: le prurit de dire, le plaisir d'écouter—et surtout d'objets tenant lieu de quasi-emblèmes: la gourde de Jacques (réservoir d'inspiration irrationnelle), la tabatière et la montre du Maître (symboles de l'ennui). Il en résulte que si l'on cherche à prêter à nos voyageurs une 'psychologie', on se heurte à des inconséquences apparentes: par exemple, la dévotion de Jacques pour son capitaine exigerait qu'il eût été au service de celui-ci bien plus longtemps que le texte ne le permet; et pour ce qui est du Maître, on peut estimer que son comportement final (le duel à mort avec le chevalier de Saint-Ouin, suivi de sa fuite) détonne dans la série entière de ses réactions.[25] Mais les incohérences et contradictions de ce genre sont négligeables en regard d'un facteur primordial, qui est la vertu transitive[26] de la dyade, laquelle, par fonction, propage le goût de conter, assure la mobilité et la circulation des divers récits ou unités de base.

---

24 'Jacques mène son maître' (p. 665).
25 Il est superflu de recourir à une prétendue explication 'psychologique', comme le fait Francis Pruner (*L'Unité*, p. 314) quand il prétend que le Maître, en abandonnant son valet, obéit à la fois à un réflexe de caste et à une rancune accumulée contre Jacques.
26 Par 'vertu transitive', nous voulons dire que l'action essentielle qui fonde la dyade—l'action de conter—peut se transférer; de la sorte, le sens grammatical du mot 'transitif' ne se perd pas, mais nous renvoyons surtout à l'acception logique ('propagation' d'une relation).

La référence de Diderot à Rabelais est plus qu'une simple coquetterie culturelle. Le cheminement spirituel de la dyade finit par entrer en concordance de phase avec la quête de Pantagruel et de ses compagnons escortant Panurge vers la Dive Bacbuc—rapprochement textuel que catalyse l'attirance marquée de Jacques pour le vin (il prend le départ, s'engage comme soldat, parce qu'il s'est enivré au lieu de conduire les chevaux à l'abreuvoir). Panurge, quant à lui, s'en allait consulter l'oracle pour savoir s'il serait ou non cocu. Or, le point final où aboutit *Jacques*, c'est l'indifférence du personnage à l'égard de son éventuel cocuage. Au long du récit, l'allégeance à Bacchus s'affirme de plus en plus clairement (les libations culminent à l'Auberge du Grand-Cerf, mais, à peine reparti, Jacques se saoule de nouveau en compagnie de Richard[27]) et, en même temps, on voit le thème de Diderot (le 'fatalisme') converger avec celui de Rabelais (le cocuage). Non que l'infidélité amoureuse soit absente du registre thématique de Diderot, mais elle expliquerait mal, à elle seule, l'image ultime d'un Jacques en posture de Panurge.

Une temporalité fallacieuse. S'il était vain de vouloir tracer l'itinéraire du voyage d'après un référent géographique réel, on aboutit à un résultat non moins décevant lorsque l'on tente de vérifier l'hypothèse d'une temporalité agencée de manière à régir par ses structures le déroulement textuel, et organisant ou distribuant les données narratives selon des vecteurs chronologiques.

Assurément, on distingue deux points fixes permettant d'équilibrer la durée dans son relief diachronique, mais de façon très sommaire car il s'agit de chiffres ronds: Jacques boite depuis vingt ans, les amours du Maître remontent à dix ans (âge du bâtard). Il est clair que Diderot ne se soucie point de pourvoir sa fiction d'une temporalité fine, comme le confirme la désinvolture avec laquelle il se réfère à des événements historiques—bataille de Fontenoy, prise de Port-Mahon, prise de Berg-op-Zoom, tremblement de terre de Lisbonne—en les désignant à la fois avec vague et précision (si l'on ose dire), sans se préoccuper de disposer ces allusions en un réseau cohérent et signifiant. Un exemple caractéristique de cette désinvolture, c'est le sort de cette brave Denise, qui double le record de patience de Pénélope puisqu'elle aura attendu son Jacques vingt ans! Et que Desglands, lui, ait attendu ce tardif mariage pour s'éprendre de Denise ne respecte plus—volontairement—aucune vraisemblance. Dans le même contexte, l'on sent bien que lorsqu'une seconde fois le charitable commissaire tire le Maître d'embarras, il

---

[27] p. 715: 'Aussi tu t'en es donné du vin de l'hôtesse jusqu'au nœud de la gorge. Hier au soir, avec le secrétaire, tu ne t'es pas ménagé davantage'.

n'y a pas lieu de s'apercevoir que dix années séparent les deux interventions.

Il est d'autant plus difficile de dégager une temporalité unitaire que celle-ci—pour peu qu'elle existe—apparaît brouillée, stratifiée, du fait que chaque récit partiel qui vient s'intercaler introduit, de droit, sa durée propre, qu'il s'agisse des amours de Jacques, de la vengeance de Mme de La Pommeraye, ou même simplement de l'histoire jumelée du Frère Jean et du Père Ange. La ligne du temps, continuellement fractionnée, ne cesse de s'ouvrir pour accueillir quantité de durées hétérogènes, que nous n'appellerons pas secondaires parce qu'elles ont valeur égale, à ceci près que le cadre temporel général du récit—le temps du voyage—est, lui, nécessairement englobant.[28] Cette disparate chronologique provient de la multiplication des récits, qui, comme unités pures, ne sont que des multiplicandes; souverain, le principe multiplicateur impose son effet structurant à la temporalité qui, loin d'être subordonnante, s'avère tributaire.

Il s'ensuit qu'il importe peu que le voyage puisse se découper en journées (et il importe encore moins qu'il faille en compter huit ou neuf), car il est visible que Diderot n'a pas songé à tirer parti de ce découpage qui ne s'est inscrit dans le texte que par voie de conséquence et non comme une cause déterminante. Nous ne voulons pas dire, bien entendu, que l'ordre dans lequel se disposent les récits partiels (et leurs éventuelles fractions) soit indifférent; au contraire, la relation d'antériorité et de postériorité régit en partie le déroulement, l'apparition de certains récits obéissant à un 'avant' et un 'après': Jacques, par exemple, doit séjourner chez les paysans, puis chez le chirurgien, avant d'arriver au château, ou bien encore il convient à l'harmonie narrative que l'histoire de Mme de La Pommeraye précède celle du Père Hudson. Mais, en revanche, il n'existe aucun rapport nécessaire. Il est sans intérêt de savoir que l'histoire du Père Ange, celle de M. Le Pelletier et, mettons, celle du capitaine et de son ami se racontent durant la cinquième journée, que l'histoire du Père Hudson prend place dans la huitième journée, que le récit du pucelage de Jacques appartient à la neuvième, et ainsi de suite. Le facteur essentiel, c'est qu'il se noue entre les récits partiels (ou fractions de récits) des liens subtils qui justifient l'emplacement qui leur est ménagé dans le texte, et l'action de ce dispositif de mise en place transcende la chronologie linéaire du voyage; comment, d'ailleurs, localiser au sein des journées les récits 'hors chronologie', ceux, par exemple, que l'Auteur raconte en son

---

[28] Le procédé pourrait, ici de nouveau, suggérer un parallèle technique entre *Tristram Shandy* et *Jacques le Fataliste*; mais Diderot n'opère jamais sur la durée les étirements et condensations qui caractérisent Sterne.

propre nom (l'histoire du poète de Pondichéry, les aventures de Gousse . . .)?

Tout au plus concédera-t-on que les nuitées—les 'couchées', comme dit le texte—installent des lieux (la demeure du lieutenant général de Conches, la maison du bourreau, l'auberge du Grand-Cerf, etc.) qui forment des nœuds dans le tissu narratif; et le Grand-Cerf constitue même un nœud multiple, complexe. Nous aurions de la sorte une opposition pertinente entre l'allure pérégrine (la route et ses incidents) et les arrêts d'étape: le découpage de la narration se réaliserait mieux par *nuits* que par *jours*. Mais parfois les lieux qui fournissent le décor sont évoqués indépendamment de toute relation avec les nuitées du voyage.[29]

Quoi qu'il en soit, à la différence des indices de temps, les lieux contribuent à structurer le texte. Pour n'en citer que deux: le château de Desglands mérite une mention particulière pour sa fonction polarisante,[30] et l'auberge du Grand-Cerf se situe au centre précis de l'espace textuel.[31]

Si la temporalité ne propose pas un support approprié pour dresser l'architecture de la narration, cela tient sans doute à la valeur exceptionnelle que revêt, dans le cadre d'ensemble, l'acte de 'donner' un conte—car il y a 'donation', 'dédicace' (ou encore: 'donne', au sens ludique) en même temps que production ('faire' le récit). Et la prise en considération de cet acte fondateur nous renvoie à une question première: quelle est l'apparence textuelle du 'donateur'?—autrement dit: *qui parle?*

L'éclatemen du 'je' narratif. Curieusement, le premier à prendre la parole, c'est le Lecteur, dont la curiosité ne peut encore être motivée que par le seul titre. Il est, bien sûr, exceptionnel qu'un récit feigne de laisser son destinataire fictif s'exprimer alors que rien n'est encore narré, que vient tout juste de s'énoncer l'amorce germinative de l'intitulé dyadique. L'Auteur consent à répondre aux cinq questions prêtées au Lecteur, toutes déterminantes (et l'une des réponses est elle-même une question . . .); il a donc choisi pour aspect initial

---

[29] Orléans, pour l'histoire de M. Le Pelletier; Paris, lieu-carrefour puisqu'il faut l'associer à Mme de La Pommeraye, aux amours du Maître, au premier récit concernant le Père Hudson (comment il déjoue le piège qu'on lui tend); un deuxième récit situe le Père Hudson dans un lieu d'une précision rare, inutile dans le système du texte, mais peut-être motivée par le référent de l'anecdote (sa source dans le réel: 'un château situé entre Châlons et Saint-Dizier, mais plus près de Saint-Dizier que de Châlons, et à une portée de fusil de l'abbaye d'Hudson'; p. 681). Sur cette question de référent, consulter F. Pruner, *Clés pour le Père Hudson*, Paris, 1966.

[30] Ce château—dont l'invention dérive probablement du château allégorique des pp. 513-14—sert d'écrin à Denise, le Maître et Jacques s'y sont croisés il y a vingt ans sans se connaître, il prépare l'aboutissement de la narration, etc.

[31] Dans l'édition que nous utilisons, la séquence complète de l'auberge représente 89 pp., est précédée de 84 pp., et suivie de 113 pp.

celui d'un Conteur qu'il faut prier: ce n'est que si on le sollicite qu'il trouvera moyen d'accroître les virtualités de l'imaginaire.[32]

Cet Auteur, on le sait, va revêtir au fil du texte d'autres aspects, dont la diversité a été souvent commentée. Par exemple, Robert Mauzi[33] lui reconnaît trois hypostases principales: l'acteur, qui se raconte lui-même; l'auteur proprement dit, qui dialogue avec ses personnages ou se substitue à eux; l'agent provocateur enfin, qui interpelle le lecteur et 'joue' avec lui. Michel Butor distingue des hypostases plus subtiles encore,[34] et il faudrait entrer dans le détail des modes, divers, d'intervention dont dispose l'Auteur[35] et qui multiplient encore les figures de ce personnage. Ce que nous avons à en retenir d'essentiel, quant à nous, c'est que, par son apparence ainsi 'éclatée', le *je* de l'Auteur va pouvoir servir de modèle pour la multiplication des donateurs de récits. Comme il est techniquement impossible que le Lecteur entre dans cette catégorie, il n'aura, lui, qu'un seul visage et ses réactions, singulièrement pauvres, se réduiront à la curiosité, l'impatience, la frustration.

Le couple du paragraphe d'ouverture—fonction textuelle dont l'Auteur est donc la variable—a pour dérivées premières (il est banal de le rappeler) les voix du Maître et de Jacques, d'emblée transcrites comme dans le livret d'une pièce de théâtre (une présentation de dialogue que Diderot affectionne). Il n'est pas indifférent d'observer que le tout premier emploi d'un *je* dans le texte revient à Jacques, qui inaugure *en fait* le réseau concret, signifiant, des narrations.

L'identité psychologique de nos deux voyageurs est elle-même relativement variable; peu importe qu'ils ne ressemblent pas toujours à eux-mêmes—par exemple lorsque le Maître et Jacques transforment la mésaventure du Père Hudson en tableau de Fragonard, c'est l'Auteur qui réintègre à soi ses créatures. L'Auteur s'en amuse —et s'amuse aux dépens du Lecteur épris de cohérence. Car ce qui prime, c'est que Jacques et son Maître remplissent l'office fonctionnel d'embrayeurs, de *shifters* diraient les linguistes:[36] ils doivent avant tout rendre possible l'articulation d'un récit partiel sur un

---

[32] L'étymologie nous rappelle que l' 'auteur' est précisément celui qui ne crée que parce qu'il vient 'augmenter', 'accroître' ce qui existe.

[33] 'La parodie romanesque dans *Jacques le Fataliste*', *Diderot Studies* (1964), pp. 89-132.

[34] Cf. le chap.: 'Diderot le Fataliste et ses Maîtres' dans *Répertoire III*, Paris, 1968, pp. 103-58 (mais typiques sont les pp. 147-9).

[35] Pour Robert Mauzi ('Parodie romanesque'), les interventions du je-Auteur renvoient à une gamme d'attitudes: le personnage peut être respectueux, poli, sournois, effronté, injurieux; selon Francis Pruner (*L'Unité*), il y a deux ordres d'intrusion: le commentaire (ou glose) et la digression pure et simple.

[36] Cette notion de *shifter*—le terme vient de Roman Jakobson—est entrée dans la critique française, surtout grâce à Roland Barthes.

autre, le passage d'un plan narratif à un autre, c'est-à-dire l'enclenchement dans le texte d'autres *je*, secondaires. Et secondaires même si, en tant que donateurs de récit(s), ils prennent de l'importance par l'espace textuel que couvre leur parole. C'est le cas, par exemple, de l'Hôtesse du Grand-Cerf, qui, elle non plus, n'a pas une identité clairement assurée. Et de même, on pourrait soutenir que le nom du marquis des Arcis unifie trois hypostases qui eussent pu accéder à l'autonomie.[37] Tant il est vrai que ces personnages comptent moins par ce qu'ils *sont* que par ce qu'ils *disent*. A ce niveau également, en effet, nous vérifions que la psychologie des donateurs narratifs doit s'effacer pour que joue la loi de multiplication, en cascade, des *je*.

Mais cette loi, qui vise à accroître autant que possible le nombre des narrations, a encore paru insuffisante. Aussi Diderot conjugue-t-il la division du *je* avec le fractionnement des récits qu'il impute à ces *je* explosées. Le résultat le plus typique (et le plus notoire) de cette loi d'appoint, c'est, bien sûr, que les Amours de Jacques se racontent distribués sur une bonne dizaine de volets.[38] Le principe de disruption[39] ne s'applique pas à tous les récits partiels, mais en théorie il le pourrait. Virtuellement, les narrateurs successifs sont en droit de s'interrompre mutuellement, et le texte s'engendre comme le produit de ces discours qui se contrarient, s'empêchent, empiètent les uns sur les autres.

Le texte marque d'ailleurs d'un accent d'insistance ses propres vertus génératives, en mettant à profit le lien fictif qui lie Lecteur et Auteur.[40] Ces moments périodiques de faux dialogue sont l'occasion de présenter sous la forme, frustrante, d'un étagement paradigmatique une série de possibles narratifs, qui soi-disant s'équiva-

---

[37] Négligeons le fait qu'il nous soit d'abord présenté comme plus jeune que son secrétaire (p. 582). Mais le 'bourreau' de la pauvre Nicole, le protagoniste de la Vengeance de Mme de La Pommeraye et le donateur du récit relatif à Richard et au Père Hudson auraient fort bien pu porter des noms différents. Ce problème est bien connu de la critique balzacienne, qui, par exemple, distingue trois Rastignac; cf. Jean Pommier, 'Naissance d'un héros: Rastignac', *Revue d'histoire littéraire de la France*, L (1950) 192-209. Et dans *Splendeurs et misères des courtisanes*, Asie est au moins double. . . .

[38] On peut adopter des critères variables pour dénombrer les volets que comporte cette narration de Jacques, à tous égards axiale, et aboutir à des totaux différents. Mais qu'il y ait 10, 16 ou 21 fractions narratives ne change rien au raisonnement. Nous aurons à reprendre cet argument à propos du décompte des 'récits-tiroirs'.

[39] L'ancienne chirurgie désignait par ce terme 'la rupture', 'la fracture'; il nous paraît utile de l'emprunter en ce que son préfixe souligne l'idée de séparation: ce n'est pas la solution de continuité (l'interruption) qui compte, mais bien le sort divergent des parties de l'unité rompue.

[40] Pour en revenir aux *shifters*: la linguistique française parle plutôt de 'déictiques',—et, dans le cas présent, au sein du couple Lecteur-Auteur, c'est naturellement l'Auteur qui est le véritable déictique (c'est grâce à lui que le Lecteur remplit, dans le texte, sa fonction). Sur cette question, on consultera Emile Benveniste, *Problèmes de linguistique générale*, Paris, 1966, chap. V.

lent. 'Vous allez croire que . . .'—et l'Auteur ouvre un éventail d'hypothèses. Ou bien il envisage tout un choix pour les lieux de couchée.[41] Le procédé travaille volontiers aussi par 'piles' de questions; 'Qu'est-ce qui m'empêcherait de . . .?'[42]—suit un paradigme de possibilités, pour finir exclues: 'Mais il n'y eut rien de tout cela'; ou encore l'Auteur passe interrogativement en revue les personnages qu'il pourrait faire rentrer en scène.[43]

Ces dispositifs paradigmatiques, quoiqu'ils s'associent, de façon paradoxale, tout ensemble à l'exclamation: 'Qu'il est facile de faire des contes', 'de filer un roman', et à l'assurance que le 'projet est d'être vrai',[44] ne doivent pas nous masquer que l'axe essentiel demeure celui, syntagmatique, du fractionnement horizontal, qui régit la discontinuité textuelle, la constitue et l'entretient. C'est sur ce plan-là que se pose le problème technique majeur: l'emboîtage des composants narratifs. Quand, à l'intérieur d'une parenthèse, on en ouvre une seconde, voire une troisième (et ainsi de suite): il arrive un moment où il convient de songer à l'ordre de fermeture. De même les unités fragmentaires obtenues par disruption—récits partiels et fractions de récits partiels—qu'elles soient englobantes ou qu'elles soient encloses, appellent un montage qui régularise l'accueil et la clôture.

Cordes vibrantes sensibles. Mais tandis qu'il s'occupe d'emboîter des fragments, Diderot peut voir entre ceux-ci se multiplier[45] des relations inattendues, qui échappent à la stricte régularisation. De la mise en ordre naissent d'heureuses surprises. Le calcul vient se revivifier à quelque foyer originel qui ressemble au hasard; à moins que le hasard ne se laisse captiver aux mailles de l'élaboration. On sait en tout cas que, volontiers, Diderot commençait par jeter ses idées sur le papier au hasard justement, afin de leur conserver la saveur imprévue et le caprice du vivant même. Que l'on se souvienne de telle attaque musicale: 'C'est de la nature que je vais écrire. Je laisserai les pensées se succéder sous ma plume, dans l'ordre même selon lequel les objets se sont offerts à ma réflexion; parce qu'elles n'en représenteront que mieux les mouvements et la marche de mon esprit'.[46] Ecriture et nature, vie et pensée n'auront chance

---

[41] pp. 504-5, 513-14.
[42] pp. 495-6. Et par exemple encore p. 746. Un comble: c'est l'Auteur qui accuse le Lecteur d'être abusivement questionneur (cf. p. 497).
[43] pp. 746, 731.
[44] pp. 495, 731.
[45] Nous dirons que l'éclatement du *je* n'a été provoqué que parce qu'il favorisait cette multiplication-ci, à coup sûr capitale.
[46] *De l'interprétation de la nature*, lignes initiales. Tout aussi typique, ce début de l'*Addition à la lettre sur les aveugles*: 'Je vais jeter sans ordre, sur le papier, des phénomènes qui ne m'étaient pas connus, et qui serviront de preuves ou de réfutation à quelques paragraphes de ma *Lettre sur les aveugles*';

d'entrer en composition que si respire dans l'entreprise ordinatrice un fécond désordre.

Mieux encore. Comparons 'les fibres de nos organes à des cordes vibrantes sensibles';[47] la métaphore ne prépare-t-elle pas, déjà, la rencontre illustre, sur la table de dissection du récit, 'd'une machine à coudre et d'un parapluie'? Aussi bien, relisons cette page de l'*Entretien entre d'Alembert et Diderot*—mais en prenant soin de substituer partout au mot 'idée' l'expression 'fragment narratif':

> La corde vibrante sensible oscille, résonne longtemps encore après qu'on l'a pincée. C'est cette oscillation, cette espèce de résonance nécessaire qui tient l'objet présent, tandis que l'entendement s'occupe de la qualité qui lui convient. Mais les cordes vibrantes ont encore une autre propriété, c'est d'en faire frémir d'autres; et c'est ainsi qu'une première idée en rappelle une seconde, ces deux-là une troisième, toutes les trois une quatrième, et ainsi de suite, sans qu'on puisse fixer la limite des idées réveillées, enchaînées (. . .). Cet instrument a des sauts étonnants, et une idée réveillée va faire quelquefois frémir une harmonique qui en est à un intervalle incompréhensible.[48]

Ce que Diderot énonce là, nous voulons y voir l'analogue du dynamisme narratif qui a produit *Jacques le Fataliste*.

La fragmentation proliférante et la recherche d'harmoniques obéissent cependant à un principe de liberté surveillée. Il est certain que, comme l'a montré Georges May,[49] l'image de la gourmette dont tous les chaînons se tiennent[50] a une valeur symbolique: en dehors du contexte 'fataliste', elle se prête[51] a désigner l'effet du montage précisément. Si bien que, en fin de compte, il sera difficile de décider (incertitude probablement voulue, entretenue par Diderot) si tel emboîtage—par exemple: l'insertion entre le diptyque du Père Hudson et le premier volet des Amours du Maître des épisodes narrant la perte de pucelage renouvelée de Jacques—a été prémédité ou bien s'il s'est négocié entre fragments narratifs.

Il est aisé de constater que la stabilité et l'équilibre du montage

---

on voit ici Diderot, de surcroît, adopter une attitude d'ambiguïté indifférenciée (preuve/réfutation) que l'on retrouve au cœur de *Jacques le Fataliste*: dans la fiction également, des contraires essentiels (vérité/imaginaire), forment un 'tourniquet', au sens sartrien.

[47] *Entretien entre d'Alembert et Diderot*; dans les *Œuvres philosophiques*, Paris, 1961, p. 271.

[48] Ibid.

[49] Dans *Quatre visages de Diderot*, Paris, 1951.

[50] Proposée dès le début par Jacques (p. 494), elle est reprise plus tard en écho par le Maître (p. 563).

[51] Qu'il y ait eu ou non intention de la part de Diderot. Observons toutefois que ce sont bien des 'aventures' (bonnes et mauvaises) que Jacques compare aux 'chaînons'.

se trouvent garantis par des jeux simples de symétries, qui harmonisent le texte entier—aux deux extrémités le Maître subit une chute, l'opération chirurgicale de la fin répond à celle du début;[52] au centre Mme de la Pommeraye et le Père Hudson se font pendants; les Amours de Jacques et celles du Maître entretiennent, quant aux thèmes, des rapports de symétrie inverse, etc. (nous n'aurions aucune peine à dresser une liste fort longue d'exemples). Mais en dehors des cadres de ce dispositif régulateur, le Voyage en territoire textuel regagne tous ses droits, l'Auteur pas plus que ses personnages ne sait où il va et de plein gré abandonne l'initiative aux composants narratifs.

On mesure dès lors la distance qui sépare *Jacques le Fataliste* d'un recueil traditionnel de récits tel que *le Décaméron*, mais aussi d'un assemblage plus sensiblement ordonné comme *l'Heptaméron* avec lequel, pourtant, le texte de Diderot présente au moins pour caractéristique commune de ne proposer aucun récit sans lui adjoindre une 'moralité', même lorsque cela semble une gageure comme dans l'histoire du pucelage de Jacques.[53]

L'originalité technique de Diderot ne peut se comparer, en son temps, qu'à l'ingénieuse construction des *Illustres Françoises*. Dans les deux cas, la multiplication et, pour ainsi dire, la 'propagation' des récits est suscitée par les structures principales de fonctionnement. Chez Robert Challe, c'est la combinatoire des 'devisants', tantôt narrateurs et tantôt acteurs, qui produit l'ouverture.[54] Chez Diderot, le texte lui-même peut s'amplifier indéfiniment—et, néanmoins, à la différence des *Illustres Françoises*, réussit à donner l'illusion d'un achèvement.

Les composants narratifs ou 'récits-tiroirs'
Consistance définitoire. Voici donc venu le moment de nous transporter sur le plan concret et d'examiner de plus près la consistance textuelle des unités de fonctionnement que nous avons, jusqu'ici, appelées composants narratifs. En un point crucial—exactement *entre* les Amours de Jacques et celles du Maître, si on ose ainsi s'exprimer—l'œuvre elle-même se définit comme 'une insipide rapsodie de faits, les uns réels, les autres imaginés, écrits sans grâce

[52] Après avoir annoncé au Lecteur (p. 507) qu'il lui épargnerait la classique opération chirurgicale, l'Auteur lui en inflige deux.
[53] Une fois de plus, Diderot tourne en plaisanterie ses propres règles du jeu (en l'occurrence l'obligation de toujours tirer une morale); ainsi Jacques met-il son Maître au défi de trouver un 'but moral' à 'cette impertinente histoire', et le Maître réussit à imaginer trois moralités! (pp. 700-1).
[54] L'éditeur des *Illustres Françoises*, Frédéric Deloffre, après avoir d'abord misé sur l'orthographe 'Chasles', a des raisons pour préférer désormais la graphie 'Chalee'. Quoique archaïque, le terme 'devisants' de Marguerite de Navarre fournirait un synonyme avantageux pour notre formule 'donateur de récit'.

et distribués sans ordre', citation que nous aurons bientôt à reconsidérer lorsqu'il conviendra d'interroger le référent socio-idéologique.[55] L'étymologie, opportune, rappelle que le 'rhapsode' a pour tâche de 'coudre et ajuster des chants'; ainsi, nous mesurons mieux la portée de cette 'distribution sans ordre' (et 'distribution' est précisément le terme que la linguistique utilise pour désigner l'ensemble des environnements, ou contextes, que reçoit une unité de sens). Ces 'chants' (très évidemment pour nous des 'récits'), ces unités—nécessairement mobiles puisque les environnements, pour chacune, sont susceptibles de varier (et ont dû varier, en pratique, durant l'élaboration de l'œuvre)—nous choisirons de les baptiser 'récits-tiroirs'. Ce concept, simplement élu pour son efficace opérante, a valeur définitoire: de même que le tiroir est bien ce compartiment coulissant emboîté dans un meuble, les récits auxquels nous avons affaire se caractérisent, à la fois, par leur emboîtement et par leur virtuelle mobilité. Circonscrit de cette manière, le concept se différencie des notions de 'pièce—ou roman—*à tiroirs*' qui rendent compte de scènes ou récits intérieurs à une action principale. Dans *Jacques le Fataliste*, aucune notion ne se peut qualifier de principale—au sein de cette nébuleuse en expansion de récits mobiles, tous égaux en droit.

L'on commettrait, en effet, une erreur de conséquence à prendre pour l' 'action' principale le Voyage parabolique. Nous dirons que, d'une certaine façon, fait défaut le récit qui remplirait l'office du meuble où viendraient se loger les autres récits à des emplacements réservés, fixés. Nous serions en présence d'un meuble vacant qui ne se constituerait que par la grâce des 'tiroirs' mêmes.

Un classement possible. A première vue, l'hétérogénéité des récits-tiroirs, dans leur désordre volontaire et entretenu, semble défier tout classement rationnel. La complexité et la variété des articulations imbricatives apparaîtraient à l'évidence si nous avions le loisir (il nous manque ici) de procéder à une analyse minutieuse des emboîtages. Il suffira néanmoins de disposer les récits-tiroirs fondamentaux en un tableau (on se reportera à notre Appendice)—dont, pour la clarté, se trouve exclu le narré des incidents du Voyage[56]—pour que se dégagent quelques principes ordinateurs.

Le classement le plus commode consisterait à polariser le champ en fonction des donateurs de narration[57] afin de regrouper, selon ces centres émetteurs, les divers récits-tiroirs—dont les dimensions

---

[55] p. 714.

[56] Qu'il faut, cependant, regarder comme un seul et même récit-tiroir 'donné' par l'Auteur (lequel, *in fine*, se mue en Editeur).

[57] Ce classement—insistons-y—ne rejoint, en soi, aucune réalité structurale: il aide à saisir les effets d'articulation, l'entrelacs des récits et les harmoniques suscitées.

sont elles-mêmes des plus variables: quelques lignes (Esope allant au bain), quelques paragraphes (M. Le Pelletier), des pages entières (Mme de La Pommeraye). Et le nombre de récits-tiroirs, doit, lui aussi, varier suivant que l'observateur envisage telle séquence narrative—mettons: la perte de pucelage de Jacques—comme un seul récit-tiroir ou comme un collectif de 'volets' plus ou moins indépendants (on peut estimer par exemple, que l'épisode du vicaire bègue[58] a droit à l'autonomie). Quel que soit, en vérité, le critère choisi pour dénombrer les récits-tiroirs, le jeu relationnel qui les anime demeure intact.

Le récit-tiroir très particulier, véritable tissu conjonctif, qui rapporte les incidents du Voyage n'est pas le seul qui appartienne à l'Auteur; il faut également imputer à celui-ci une série d'autres composants narratifs en général courts.[59] Au donateur le plus généreux, notre bavard de Jacques, reviennent la fameuse narration disruptive de ses Amours[60] et une dizaine de récits-tiroirs d'un impact souvent très sûr. Le Maître lui-même ne se borne pas à raconter ses propres Amours, puisqu'on doit lui attribuer au moins les deux histoires relatives à Desglands.[61] On notera le mécanisme ingénieux qui transmue tel protagoniste d'un récit en narrateur à son tour (le Marquis des Arcis raconte l'histoire de Richard, Gousse celle de l'intendant); cependant Diderot n'emploie que de façon exceptionnelle ce procédé, générateur de base chez Challe.

Par un phénomène remarquable, certains récits-tiroirs 'riment' entre eux—au sens où Raymond Queneau a défini cette notion de 'rime' appliquée à la fiction:[62] citons pour exemples typiques les histoires, nombreuses, de duellistes[63] ou les volets relatifs à la perte

---

[58] Cet épisode, qui prend sens isolément, peut également s'inscrire dans des rapports de dépendance: il apparaît alors comme une 'suite' à l'histoire de Dame Suzanne ou comme un 'post-scriptum' à la perte de pucelage de Jacques (de même, le 'Fragonard' de Jacques serait un post-scriptum à l'histoire du Père Hudson).

[59] On se risquerait même à considérer comme un mini-récit-tiroir (revenant à l'Auteur) la célèbre exclamation: 'Le premier serment que se firent deux êtres de chair, ce fut au pied d'un rocher . . .' (p. 604).

[60] Dont le perpétuel suspens entretient le texte/Texte entier.

[61] Mais aussi, par exemple, l'histoire de l'octogénaire atteint de la pierre. Et on pourrait même dire qu'il tire de la fable de Garo (p. 756) un parti qui équivaut à la raconter (on sait qu'il s'agit du *Gland et la Citrouille* de La Fontaine).

[62] Dans *Bâtons, chiffres et lettres*, Paris, 1965, p. 42: 'J'ai écrit d'autres romans avec cette idée de rythme, cette intention de faire du roman une sorte de poème. On peut faire rimer des situations ou des personnages comme on fait rimer des mots, on peut même se contenter d'allitérations'.

[63] Le Capitaine et son camarade, M. de Guerchy, Desglands, le Maître lui-même . . . Observons que, si ailleurs (*Encyclopédie*, article 'Héroïsme'), Diderot juge très sévèrement le duel, dans *Jacques le Fataliste* il lui prête une valeur strictement narrative (nulle appréciation éthique): ainsi les deux officiers sont-ils comparés, flatteusement, à des paladins (p. 557).

de pucelage de Jacques. Ce recours à des 'doublets'[64] vaut aussi pour des personnages (Frère Jean et le Père Ange) on pour des situations (Jacques et les chirurgiens), et, dans son principe, permettrait à l'étoffe textuelle de s'étendre à l'infini. Autre indice que le texte a pour vocation de se dilater: telles pièces d'attente demeurées sans conséquence (le Maître assure qu'il a eu à se plaindre des moines et qu'il s'en expliquera,[65] le fils naturel de Desglands, éveillant tout le château, finit par exiger on ne sait quoi d'exorbitant).[66]

L'art de clore en préservant l'ouverture. Nous avons eu l'occasion d'indiquer que, même si, de façon intrinsèque, tous les récits-tiroirs ont valeur égale, il en est deux qui assument une fonction spéciale, et qui ont déjà en commun de comporter un nombre exceptionnel de volets disruptifs: les Amours de Jacques et les Amours du Maître, celles-ci s'articulant d'ailleurs sur celles-là. Nous avons pu dire que, à bien des égards, ces deux récits se répondent. On relève même telles harmoniques singulièrement précises: Jacques contraint Justine à lui céder et le Maître, de son côté, se figure posséder Agathe malgré elle.

En dépit de leur discontinuité, les deux narrations tendent vers la clôture du texte: nous arriverons au bout du (grand) rouleau lorsque 's'achèveront', sous le signe paradoxal de l'"inachèvement', les Amours et de Jacques et du Maître, dont les destins, qui se croisèrent jadis au château de Desglands, sont appelés a se rejoindre de nouveau en ce même lieu.

Par ailleurs, axialement, les deux récits conduisent aux trois 'fins' postiches. Nous négligerons la fin 'ouverte'—cela en ferait une quatrième—qui laisse au Lecteur le soin de continuer la narration à sa fantaisie. Mais, contrairement à Francis Pruner qui écarte avec mépris ces trois fins,[67] nous pensons que les trois 'paragraphes' proposés par l'éditeur prétendu ne sont pas une pirouette.

Nous avons justifié précédemment la prééminence que mérite l'issue sternienne. Mais—encore un paradoxe!— c'est le finale des Mandrins qui, parce que, d'une part, il amène (comme dans *Candide*) les retrouvailles des personnages axiaux, et, d'autre part, forme un ultime nœud des thèmes,[68] doit permettre à Jacques de

---

[64] Doublets qui peuvent donner lieu à effet de symétrie inverse: par exemple, l'histoire de l'emplâtre de Desglands est un doublet inversé de l'histoire du duelliste cloueur (et toujours vaincu).
[65] p. 536.
[66] 'Mais c'est le reste qui est incroyable . . .' (p. 751): seulement, le reste ne sera pas dit.
[67] *L'Unité*, pp. 317 et seq.
[68] Fatalisme, 'pantagruélisme', spinozisme—et le vin même: 'Desglands criait: Qu'on apporte des verres et du vin' (p. 780).

s'endormir en paix,⁶⁹—et cela d'autant mieux que, sur le plan référentiel (nous y viendrons dans un moment), les brigands équilibrent tout l'appareil de justice déployé dans la narration. Finale des finales, ce troisième 'paragraphe', qui semble le plus assurer l'ouverture, favorise subtilement la clôture textuelle.

Défi à l'érudition. Quel intérêt peut encore présenter, après tout cela, le relevé des incohérences et failles de toutes sortes qui se marquent dans le champ narratif? Nous croyons avoir démontré que ces prétendues 'défaillances' étaient non seulement rendues possibles mais quasiment sollicitées par les mécanismes structuraux. Et pas uniquement parce que certains de ces mécanismes produisent dans les récits des phénomènes a-psychologiques. Mais—pour aller au plus profond—le dispositif d'ensemble aurait perdu sa nature foncièrement mobile, dynamique, son pouvoir d'amplifier et d'accroître l'imaginaire, si Diderot avait poussé trop loin une conciliation avec les principes de la rigeur ou de la logique ordinaire.

L'histoire du texte, au sens philologique, et surtout son établissement ne s'en trouvent guère facilités, naturellement.⁷⁰ Mais cela aussi fait partie de la 'règle du jeu'. Aussi bien, ce n'est plus seulement du Lecteur que l'Auteur-Editeur se moque, mais de tous les érudits présents et à venir, quand il ironise: 'Il y a ici une lacune vraiment déplorable dans la conversation de Jacques et de son maître. Quelque jour un descendant de Nodot, du président de Brosses, de Freinshémius, ou du père Brottier la remplira peut-être; et les descendants de Jacques ou de son maître, propriétaires du manuscrit, en riront beaucoup'.⁷¹

Ne sont certes pas à dédaigner les travaux de tous ceux qui tâchent, louablement, de résoudre ces problèmes textuels, et il faut rendre spécialement hommage au Professeur Yvon Belaval pour sa remarquable édition critique.⁷² Mais nous croyons que tel savoir— par exemple la certitude que les récits-tiroirs grivois de la dernière partie ont été introduits tardivement⁷³—ou que telle découverte

---

⁶⁹ Les deux derniers mots du texte sont: 'il s'endormait'. C'est alors, en effet, que peut se vérifier ce que Jacques annonçait p. 752: 'Pardon, mon maître, la machine était montée, et il fallait qu'elle allât jusqu'à la fin'.

⁷⁰ A propos de ces problèmes (trés complexes) d'établissement du texte, on consultera notamment Jean Varloot, 'Jaacques le Fataliste et La Correspondance littéraire', *Revue d'histoire littéraire de la France*, LXV (1965), 629-36.

⁷¹ pp. 717-18.

⁷² Paris, 1953.

⁷³ C'est un point que Francis Pruner commente longuement (*L'Unité*) pp. 227 et seq.). Nous observerons, quant à nous, que le principe structural de symétrie installé comme régulateur textuel autorise la mise en rapport de ces épisodes finaux avec, au début, la paysanne à l'oreille qui démange, et au centre, la Fable de la Gaîne et du Coutelet.

matérielle (une copie jusqu'ici inconnue), n'apporteront aucune lumière supplémentaire sur la nature profonde de la cohérence structurelle de *Jacques le Fataliste*. Car de telles informations seront à porter au crédit des principes ordinateurs. Alors que la cohérence dont nous parlons tient aux ambiguités d'un désordre provoqué.

On débouche sur un problème du même genre—la conciliation des contraires—lorsqu'on se livre à un examen, même rapide, des éléments référentiels mis en jeu.

Conclusion: Risquer un sens pour l'œuvre?

Resteraient à explorer bien des domaines purement techniques. On a souvent commenté les modes si divers du dialogue.[74] Mais, à notre connaisance, personne n'a encore étudié Diderot comme un précurseur de la très moderne technique du 'collage', qui, littérairement, consiste à introduire dans le texte des 'corps étrangers' (on favorise ainsi son ouverture). C'est le cas lorsque, pour consoler Jaques de la mort supposée de son Capitaine, le Maître lui fait lecture d'une oraison funèbre,[75] ou lorsque l'Hôtesse du Grand-Cerf, arbitre du différend entre nos deux voyageurs, leur dit un 'prononcé qu'elle avait pillé dans quelque ouvrage du temps'.[76] Relèveraient aussi du 'collage' telles citations ou allusions, voire même le 'plagiat' sternien, etc.[77] Jusque dans sa substance lexicale, le texte s'avère sollicité de manière génératrice, puisque l'on voit entrer en fermentation[78] certains sémantèmes: bigre, foutre, engastrimute, hydrophobe, etc.

Nous avons dit que, comme Sartre, nous pensions que toute technique renvoie à une métaphysique. Or, il nous a fallu, néanmoins, dénier toute primauté à un quelconque message philosophique. C'est que la véritable métaphysique qui vient innerver une technicité dont on ne peut négliger l'importance (mais qui n'est jamais ostentatoire) débouche sur un jeu, éminemment philosophique;[79] de narrativité, où se préserve indéfiniment la relance du récit. Dans sa mobilité intrinsèque, le texte est conçu pour

---

[74] Mais il manque encore une analyse rigoureuse, validée par le système d'ensemble des techniques du texte.

[75] pp. 538-9. Il est difficile d'admettre que le Maître récite cette tirade de mémoire.

[76] p. 663.

[77] Par exemple, 'la fable de Garo' (p. 756), laquelle a peut-être 'induit' le nom de Desglands, puisque le titre réel de cette fable de La Fontaine est *Le Gland et la Citrouille*.

[78] La critique joycienne emploi l'expression 'fermented words' à propos de la langue de *Finnegans Wake*.

[79] On sait que tout un courant philosophique se fonde sur une conception ludique de l'existence. Nous renvoyons, par exemple, à Eugen Fink, *Spiels als Weltsymbol*, Stuttgart, 1960.

Plate VII The Circus, Bath. Etching by J. R. Cozens. Reproduced by permission of Bath Victoria Art Gallery.

Plate VIII Thomas Stothard, 'Rescue of Sophia from Drowning', *The Vicar of Wakefield*, London 1792 edition, Plate 2 (Plates VIII-XVI reproduced by permission of the Henry E. Huntington Library and Art Gallery).

s'amplifier de façon vivante, naturelle. Mieux qu'un Anti-Roman (comme on le dit souvent à la légère), *Jacques le Fataliste* est un instrument de musique narrative qui, pour accroître ses harmoniques, se serait mis à rêver d'une infinité de cordes.

Sans doute, en avouant à ce point l'imaginaire, Diderot semble-t-il viser à quelque 'réalisme' au second degré. Mais il est peut-être de l'essence du réalisme d'échouer toujours, en versant précisément dans l'ambiguïté.

Aussi bien, lorsque l'on tente, en présence d'un pareil texte, de surmonter les termes des contradictions multipliées—Anti-Roman ou roman traditionnel, fiction avouée ou réalisme supérieur, fatalisme ou libre-arbitre, etc.—on achoppe très vite sur une impuissance à opter. Les polarités duelles ont pour fonction de maintenir en vigueur dans le tissu textuel la loi d'antagonisme, principe universel du mouvement. C'est la vie même qui, au lieu fictif de l'écriture, vient nous frustrer dans notre dérisoire aspiration à l'univocité du sens.

Ambiguë, la signification des récits-tiroirs l'est fréquemment; et pourtant elle n'est jamais indifférente. De nulle part venue et sans autre fin possible que la commune issue mortelle, la longue route signifiante où pérégrine la très loquace dyade mime la pensée dans sa danse épuisante—la pensée toujours contrainte de prêter du sens, mais qui voit le sens lui être rendu légion, divisé, contredit, questionneur: sans cesse il faut repartir. Jusqu'au jour où il ne reste plus, dans la gourde, la moindre goutte de vin à consulter.

Appendice

Esquisse d'un TABLEAU des 'récits-tiroirs'

Remarque: Les données suivantes ont été négligées (parce que leur prise en considération eût exigé un tableau beaucoup plus complexe et rigoureux):

1. certaines informations biographiques relatives à Jacques (l'histoire du grand-père Jason, par exemple)
2. le récit—qui a pour 'donateur' l'Auteur lui-même—des incidents du Voyage
3. le fait que des récits-tiroirs, fragments disruptifs, volets, épisodes, etc. soient annoncés—amorcés—avant, et parfois bien avant, d'être en fait donnés.

Ordre adopté: la succession au sein du tissu textuel.

Les Amours de Jacques (Donateur: bien sûr Jacques lui-même)	Autres récits-tiroirs	Donateurs
La chaumière: 1ᵉʳ volet: Jacques est recueilli 2ᵉ volet: les trois chirurgiens 3ᵉ volet: l'oreille démange à la paysanne		
	Allégorie du château au frontispice	Auteur
N.B.: Il est très tôt annoncé que les Amours du Maître vont s'enclencher dans celles de Jacques: cf. p. 522, et comparer p. 536) La chaumière (suite): 4ᵉ volet: le chirurgien opère		
	Histoire du poète de Pondichéry	Auteur
	Frère Jean et Père Ange (deux volets, en fait)	Jacques
	Mini-récit: Esope va au bain	Auteur
5ᵉ volet: Jacques marchande avec le chirurgien		
	Histoire de M. Le Pelletier	Jacques
	Le Capitaine et son camarade	Jacques
	Histoire de Gousse 1ᵉʳ volet: présentation 2ᵉ volet: Gousse et Prémontval 3ᵉ volet: les livres du docteur de Sorbonne	Auteur
	Le mari octogénaire soigné par le Frère Cosme	Maître
Jacques chez le chirurgien: plusieurs volets et sous-volets		

Les Amours de Jacques	Autres récits-tiroirs	Donateurs
	Histoire de Gousse (suite): la prison	Auteur
	L'homme qui raclait de la basse	1er Donateur: Gousse 2e Donateur: l'Auteur
	Version 'améliorée' du *Bourru bienfaisant*	Auteur
	L' 'amoureux' de Nicole	Hôtesse du Grand-Cerf
	Histoire de la Vengeance de Mme de La Pommeraye. A l'intérieur de ce récit-tiroir viennent s'articuler:	Hôtesse
	La fable de la Gaîne et du Coutelet	Jacques
	Histoire de M. de Guerchy ou du camarade du Capitaine: plusieurs volets	Jacques
Jacques au château de Desglands		
	Première histoire relative à Desglands	Maître
	Histoire de Richard et du Père Hudson: plusieurs volets	Marquis d'Arcis
	Histoire du mari incroyant de 'la jolie femme au cabriolet'	1er Donateur Richard 2e Donateur: Jacques
Jacques perd son pucelage 1er volet: Bigre et Justine 2e volet: Dame Suzanne 3e volet: Dame Marguerite		
	L'enfant qui refuse de dire A	Jacques
	Le vicaire bègue	Jacques

Les Amours de Jacques	Autres récits-tiroirs	Donateurs
	Les Amours du Maître 1er volet: des intermédiaires louches	Maître
	Mini-récit du pauvre limonadier qui laisse deux orphelins	Auteur
	Les Amours du Maître (suite) 2e volet: Agathe est nommée: 'elle a pleuré' 3e volet: lettre d'Agathe 4e volet: 'aveux' du Chevalier 5e volet: 'vengeance' du Maître	Maître
	Deuxième histoire relative à Desglands (l'emplâtre). S'y intercale:	Maître
	L'histoire (inachevée) de l'insupportable enfant de Desglands	Jacques
	Les Amours du Maître: 6e volet: le Maître est 'surpris' dans le lit d'Agathe	
Jacques au château de Desglands (on notera le grand écart qui sépare le volet précédent de celui-ci): seconde opération chirurgicale, les jarretières		
Finale triple: les trois 'paragraphes' 1. Jacques aux pieds de Denise 2. le 'paragraphe' sternien 3. les Mandrins		L'Auteur sous le masque de l'Editeur

The Fortunes of Voltaire's Foppington

Colin Duckworth

The story I wish to unfold goes from 1659 to 1888, and moves back and forth across the English Channel. Disregarding Lewis Caroll's advice to begin at the beginning, I shall start at the end. In the mid-1860s, one Dr Doran, F.S.A., wrote a bitter complaint in his *Annals of the English Stage*.[1] It was to the effect that the French had had the cheek to stage Vanbrugh's *The Relapse* at the Odéon in the spring of 1862 calling it a posthumous work by Voltaire. He says:

> All the French theatrical world in the capital flocked to the Faubourg St. Germain to witness a new play by Voltaire. Critics examined the plot, philosophised on its humour, applauded its absurdities, enjoyed its wit, and congratulated themselves on the circumstance that the Voltairean wit especially was as enjoyable then as in the preceding century! Of the authorship they had no doubt whatever; for, said they, if Voltaire did not write this piece, who *could* have written it? The reply was given at once from this country; but when the mystification was exposed, the French critics gave no sign of awarding honour where honour was due, and probably this translation of the 'Relapse' may figure in future French editions as an undoubted work by Voltaire!

That prophecy has come true, and there is some justification for it, since Voltaire's play, variously known as *L'Echange*, or *Le Comte de Boursoufle*, or *Quand est-ce qu'on me marie?*, is not so much a translation as a free adaptation bearing Voltaire's own stamp. However, that is not how it was viewed either in Paris or in London in 1862.

[1] See *'Their Majesties' Servants': Annals of the English Stage*, ed. and rev. by Robert W. Lowe, 3 vols., London, 1888, I, 231-2.

The first to react from the London end was *The Athenæum*, dated 8 February 1862. 'After more than a century has elapsed', writes the author of the article entitled 'Voltaire's Newly-Discovered Comedy',

> it has been reproduced at the Odéon, in Paris, and it is a 'success'. . . . Thus the French are witnessing Vanbrugh, and calling it listening to Voltaire!
>
> They pay the former a compliment, for they aver that the fine and racy Voltairian humour pervades the whole. . . . It was a hazardous game to play, for detection was *almost* inevitable.[2]

The writer claims he is not surprised at the French deception (or ignorance), considering that French provincial editor who maintained, in all seriousness, that the author of *Candide* had a part in the writing of the *Waverley Novels*: they had been written, he said, by Voltaire-Scott.

The riposte was made swiftly in Paris, by *La Revue britannique*.[3] This writer, we find, has taken the trouble to look at what he calls throughout *Le Comte de Boursouflé*, and at *The Relapse*, and concludes: 'Quant au dialogue, ce ne sont pas les mêmes phrases, mais c'est le même esprit, plus grossier chez Vanbrugh que chez Voltaire'. He sensibly points out what London critics would have remembered had they not been so filled with indignation: Vanbrugh had borrowed from Cibber, and Sheridan from Vanbrugh. As we shall see, when it comes to the question of who took what from whom, the situation is rather more complicated than that.

On 23 February 1862 we find Philarète Chasles complaining bitterly in the *Journal des débats* that the public should be applauding the play as a French work, but his objection is diametrically opposed to that of *The Athenæum* and of Dr Doran. This gives us some insight into the differences between French and English attitudes to comedy. His arguments are based on a considerable knowledge of English theatre (although it is not clear that he knows about Etherege's debt to Molière's Mascarille in *Les Précieuses ridicules*), but his prejudices have their roots deeply embedded in the classical view that the French know what theatre should be, whereas the English most certainly do not. They are too vulgar for words. 'Ce n'est pas un théâtre, c'est la terrible caricature de Hogarth jetée sur la scène'. More precisely, he claims, the whole purpose behind the creation of Foppington was to ridicule the court of Louis XIV. On this point one must admit that both dramatists put French into the fop's mouth as a feature of his snobbery. This is as true of *The Careless Husband* as it is of *The Relapse*. It also

[2] January-June 1862, p. 192.
[3] In the 'Correspondence de Londres' section, Année 1862, I, 491.

goes without saying that Vanbrugh had every reason to be anti-French after his unjustified incarceration in the Bastille. Looked at in this light, the way Vanbrugh has Foppington unceremoniously locked up by the rural English knight could be interpreted as a subconscious revenge. However, Philarète Chasles did not think of that; not that he would have wished to admit that Vanbrugh had been given cause for complaint against the French. Chasles is particularly hard on the gentle Etherege, 'le premier maître de ce théâtre effronté' who, in *The Man of Mode*, had 'livré au sarcasme du parterre [anglais] le beau et l'aimable *"sir* Fopling Flutter" *(M. Fat du Papillon)'*. It was because of his anti-French satire that Etherege was so successful, he says; and he goes on to broaden his attack to cover not only Etherege but Wycherley, Congreve and Vanbrugh—all of them inspired by hatred of French ways. 'Ils pursuivent d'une satire acharnée . . . l'air français, le ton de Louis XIV, ou l'air de la cour.' He piles up the scandalised epithets: 'incroyable licence . . . dévergondage effréné . . . ordure'. And yet, he complains, in Paris, in this year 1862, actors, directors and spectators at the Odéon, writers, artists, students, servants, ignoramuses; young and old; friends and enemies of Voltaire; lovers of Racine and Corneille as well as those whose taste goes back no further than 1830; clerics and anti-clerics, all races, sects and parties, 'écoutent, admirent et applaudissent depuis un mois comme nouvelle et française une comédie vieille d'un siècle et demi'. 'How dare they!' cries Philarète Chasles, 'it's treason!' 'How dare they!' cries Dr Doran, 'it's piracy!'

On the day following Chasles's diatribe, the matter was pursued further in the pages of the *Journal des débats* by the weighty Jules Janin: this has been a sad week for Voltaire and for French criticism, he begins; on the other hand, they are dancing with joy 'en la superbe Albion', since the English have discovered that Voltaire was a frightful plagiarist, and that our critics are very ignorant—'ignorantissimes'. With mock seriousness he says he now sees that although Voltaire went to England ostensibly to appreciate English life and customs, his real dastardly purpose was to filch from the English their comic masterpiece, *The Relapse*, and secretly place it at the charming feet of Mme la marquise du Châtelet!

The indignation of English critics is rather frivolous in view of the fact that from the middle of the nineteenth century French plays were being used to provide plots for the London stage with great regularity. Indeed, in 1881 Percy Fitzgerald wrote: 'At this moment it may be said that the English stage is virtually subsisting on the French'.[4]

---

[4] *The World behind the Scenes*, London, 1881, p. 289.

Here, then, we have an interesting example of cultural cross-fertilisation. Interesting, because it was regarded as double-crossing —double-dealing in fops: Moliere—Etherege—Cibber—Voltaire. *A bon fat, bon rat,* as it were. As we shall see, the exchange did not stop here.

Voltaire himself would have been surprised and delighted by this furore in the 1860s and by the success of his play. He never intended it for professional performance, and repeatedly denied authorship of it, as he did of so many of his works in order to protect his reputation or his safety. As the play has three versions and three titles, and as there is no contemporary manuscript to be found, the problems of establishing text and authorship are not simple. How can we be sure he was sufficiently interested in Vanbrugh's play to adapt it?

During his exile in England from 1726 to 1728, Voltaire was an almost nightly spectator at Drury Lane and took the trouble to borrow and read each play before the performance. We know that he was able to make close acquaintance with three, and possibly four, incarnations of Fopling Flutter (or Foppington): in Cibber's *Love's Last Shift* (variously translated into French as *L'Amour aux abois* and *La Dernière Chemise d'amour*), Etherege's *Man of Mode,* and *The Relapse.* These were all regularly performed during his stay in London. By the time he brought out the 1748 edition of the *Lettres philosophiques* he also knew Cibber's *The Careless Husband* (but by that time his own play was written).[5]

Voltaire's own copy of Vanbrugh's plays is now in the Voltaire library in Leningrad. It is the 1719 Tonson and Wellington two-volume edition, of which the first contains *The Relapse.* Unfortunately there are no marginal notes in it, such as would have thrown more light on his methods of translation and adaptation.[6]

According to Fanshaw, writing in the early 1730s, Voltaire remarked that 'English plays are like their English puddings: nobody has any taste for them but themselves'.[7] His opinion of Vanbrugh's comedies, expressed in the nineteenth 'Lettre sur les Anglais', was that they were 'encore plus plaisantes, mais moins ingénieuses' than Wycherley's. Apart from that, there is a curious self-contradiction in his judgment of Vanbrugh. In the Jore edition of the *Lettres philosophiques* he seems to endorse the view that Vanbrugh wrote

---

[5] See Henning Fenger, 'Voltaire et le Théâtre anglais', *Orbis Litterarum* (Copenhagen), Vol. VII, 3-4 (1949), pp. 161-287.
[6] *Bibliothèque de Voltaire,* Moscow and Leningrad, 1961, item 3390. I am grateful to Mme Ljublinskaya for examining the book for me.
[7] Quoted in Joseph Spence, *Observations, Anecdotes and Characters of Books and Men,* ed. J. M. Osborn, 2 vols., Oxford, 1966, I, 398.

as he built—'un peu grossièrement'.⁸ But the original English version reads thus: '[Vanbrugh] is as sprightly in his writings as he is heavy in his Buildings'. This is a close enough rendering of the Thieriot edition: 'il écrivait avec autant de délicatesse et d'élegance, qu'il bâtissait grossièrement'.⁹ Voltaire maintains that if one goes to Congreve for wit and exact observation, and to Wycherley for strength and boldness, it is to Vanbrugh that one goes for gaiety. This is the quality that would have attracted Voltaire sufficiently to *The Relapse* to warrant making two plays out of it himself during the mid-1730s.

It is during this same period that we find Voltaire concerning himself particularly with the French originator of Foppington: Molière. It should be borne in mind that in the 1730s Molière's plays were disapproved of as being in low taste. In the 1733 edition of *Le Temple du goût* Voltaire joins in the prevailing tendency to criticise Molière for having 'donné dans le bas Comique',¹⁰ but he nevertheless wrote his *Vie de Molière* with the intention—abortive as it turned out—of using it as an introduction to the 1734 grand quarto edition of Molière. My reason for wishing to stress Voltaire's interest in Molière with reference to the genesis of *Le Comte de Boursoufle* is this: the influence of Molière on Vanbrugh was minimal and indirect. It came through previous English comedy, especially Etherege and Wycherley. However, *The Relapse* contains a double dose of Molière, which may have been among the factors that made it appeal to Voltaire. Not only does Act I, sc. iii (the fop's dressing scene) stem from *Le Bourgeois Gentilhomme*, II.v, but the originals of Sir Tunbelly Clumsey and his daughter, Hoyden, are to be found in the Sganarelle and Isabelle of *L'Ecole des maris*.¹¹ These characters become, in Voltaire's comedy, the Baron de la Cochonnière and Thérèse, but we must bear in mind that *L'Ecole des maris* was the basis of Wycherley's *Country Wife*, which was played regularly at Drury Lane and Lincoln's Inn Fields during Voltaire's stay in London. Hence, the comic possibilities of the main characters who became Boursoufle, the Baron and Thérèse were doubly reinforced in Voltaire's mind on both sides of the channel.

Yet another link between *L'Ecole des maris* and Voltaire during the mid-1730s is to be found in *L'Enfant prodigue*, in which Vol-

---

⁸ *Lettres philosophiques* (à Rouen chez Jore, 1734), p. 109.
⁹ See *Lettres philosophiques*, ed. Gustave Lanson, 2 vols., Paris, 1924, II, 107 and textual notes.
¹⁰ See *Le Temple du goût*, ed. Ely Carcassonne, 2nd edn, Geneva and Lille, 1953, p. 169. And W. H. Barber, 'Voltaire and Moliere', in *Essays in Honour of W. G. Moore*, ed. W. D. Howarth and Merlin Thomas, Oxford, 1973, pp. 201-17.
¹¹ See D. H. Miles, *The Influence of Molière on Restoration Comedy*, New York, 1910, p. 236.

taire made the central theme the rivalry between elder and younger sons, as in *Le Comte de Boursoufle*. Considering the importance of the Molière element in all these plays, Philarète Chasles's charge that hostility for the French is at the bottom of the social criticism levelled by Vanbrugh loses some weight. But who could deny that Voltaire saw in the character of Foppington a chance of satirising the useless type of French aristocrat he attacked in the *Lettres philosophiques*?

Contrary to what Dr Doran believed, Voltaire did not translate *The Relapse*. He used just a part of it as the basis of a dialogue and structure largely of his own making. The principal difference lies in his concentration on the rivalry between the two brothers for the girl with the dowry. Why did he omit the rest of *The Relapse*—namely, the main plot concerning the relapse of the erring husband into adulterous ways?

For the first reason, we must go to the attack made in 1698 by Jeremy Collier on *The Relapse* in his *Short View of the Immorality and Profaneness of the English Stage*. Collier, defending the Unity of Action, points out that '*Lovelace* [sic], *Amanda*, and *Berinthia*, have no share in the main Business'[12]—that is, Young Fashion's triumph over Foppington.

There is evidence that Voltaire knew this work of Collier's, which is hardly surprising in view of his passionate interest in English theatre and dramatic theory.[13] And too, in the same classical spirit, Voltaire restores the Unity of Action, reduces Vanbrugh's week-long action to about twenty-four hours, and has only one change of scene. He achieves this by cutting Vanbrugh's diamond in two, giving us but one half in *Le Comte de Boursoufle*. As for the other half, he had already put it to good use some four years previously, in another comedy written for private performance. This was *Les Originaux* (1732), in which the main character was the same Comte de Boursoufle. Here, however, we find him in a situation identical with that of Foppington in Cibber's sequel to *The Relapse*, the 'genteel' sentimental comedy of 1704, *The Careless Husband*. Both dandified lords have married for the sake of the dowry, and both are regretting the ties of the marital state. In *Les Originaux*, then, Voltaire had already dealt with the Loveless-Amanda type of problem. It should be noted that he had chosen to give it a sentimental solution of repentance *à la* Cibber, rather than a cynical one *à la*

---

[12] London, 1698; repr. Menston, 1971, p. 230.
[13] See *Lettres philosophiques* (ed. Lanson), II, 111. The sentence which occurs in Lettre XIX ('Une femme fâchée contre son Amant lui souhaite la vérole'—II, 103n.) is attributed by Lanson to Collier, either directly, or else indirectly through Charles Wilson's refutation of Collier in his *Memoirs of the Life of William Congreve*.

Vanbrugh.[14] We can understand, therefore, why he had no wish to cover the same ground again. He felt free to turn his attention to the more entertaining subject of the humiliation of the rich and powerful by the young and impoverished.

Although there remain many mysteries surrounding Voltaire's play *Le Comte de Boursoufle*, it has a fairly well documented history. It is first mentioned in the *Correspondence* on 3 January 1736—at least, it is assumed that it is about this play Mme du Châtelet is writing when she says: 'Nous allons jouer dans notre petite république de Cirey une comédie qu'il a faite pour nous et qui ne le sera que par nous'.[15] This gives the impression it had recently been written. It is stated by Beuchot[16] (and all critics since) that the play dates from 1734, but I can find no evidence for this. On 22 January 1736 this 'très mauvaise comédie de ma façon' was still in rehearsal.[17] Emilie, said Voltaire, was 'une actrice admirable' in the role of Thérèse. By 25 January it had been successfully performed: 'Emilie a joué son rôle comme elle fait tout le reste'.[18] They acted it on the small but delightful stage set up at the end of a gallery, resting on empty barrels.

In 1738 Mme de Graffigny, whose sharpness of observation equalled that of her tongue, went to stay at Cirey. She frequently mentions performances of the comedy. By then the part of Thérèse had been taken over by Mme du Châtelet's daughter, Françoise Gabrielle, aged 12. Mme de Graffigny also took part; no doubt she played the Nurse, since this is the only other female role.[19] It was part of the regular dramatic repertoire at Cirey, which sometimes began at mid-day and went on until seven the next morning.

We then lose sight of the play until 1747, when it was played (in private again) at the Château d'Anet, the summer home of the duchesse du Maine. Fortunately for posterity, the duchess had in her service Mlle de Launay, Baronne de Staal, whose lively letters to Mme du Deffand provide us with a record of the performance.[20] Mme du Châtelet, as Thérèse, 'a si parfaitement exécuté l'extravagance de son rôle, que j'y ai pris un vrai plaisir', she writes,

[14] *Les Originaux* is excellent source-hunting country: Cibber's *Love's Last Shift*, Farquhar's *The Beaux' Stratagem*, Destouches' *Le Glorieux*, Congreve's *Love for Love*, have all left their mark. See Fenger, 'Voltaire', pp. 226-8.
[15] *Correspondence and Related Documents*, definitive edn, by Theodore Besterman, in *The Complete Works of Voltaire*, Vols. 85- (Institut et Musée Voltaire, Geneva; University of Toronto Press; and The Voltaire Foundation, Thorpe Mandeville, 1968-), letter D.958. Hereafter cited as *Correspondence*.
[16] A. J. Q. Beuchot, *Œuvres complètes de Voltaire*, nouvelle éd., 52 vv., Paris, 1877-83, Vol. III: *Théâtre*, vol. ii (1877), p. 251.
[17] *Correspondence*, D.995.
[18] Ibid., D.996.
[19] Ibid., D.1704 (22 December 1738).
[20] Ibid., D.3562 (15 August 1747) and D.3567 (27 August 1747).

despite the fact that Emilie was not the right shape for Thérèse, 'qui devrait être grosse et courte'. Voltaire 'ennobled' the play with a new prologue, which he and Mme Du Tour spoke. In it, we see Voltaire's diffidence regarding the quality of the comedy, in view of the fact that it was to be acted on an important occasion, 'Pour le jour de Louis, pour cette auguste fête' of the Duchesse du Maine, before an invited audience of a hundred. Mme Du Tour, speaking Voltaire's words, starts in a rage, complaining that the 'belle farce' is not good enough. 'Mais que voulez-vous donc pour vos amusements?' asks Voltaire. Horrible copies of English tragedies? He was thinking of Otway's *Venice Preserv'd*, which La Place had just adapted, but we can assume that he had his tongue in his cheek, since he was at that moment presenting—unbeknown to anyone but himself—what he regarded as a horrible copy of an English comedy! Madame Du Tour replies to Voltaire's question in terms that we must regard as Voltaire's statement of the formula for the ideal comedy:

> De la simple nature,
> Un ridicule fin, des portraits délicats,
>   De la noblesse sans enflure;
> Point de moralités; une morale pure
> Qui naisse du sujet, et ne se montre pas.
> Je veux qu'on soit plaisant sans vouloir faire rire;
> Qu'on ait un style aisé, gai, vif et gracieux;
> Je veux enfin que vous sachiez écrire
> Comme on parle en ces lieux.[21]

Voltaire agrees to withdraw the comedy. With inconsequential femininity she refuses to let him: she wants to see him ridiculed:

> On amuse souvent plus par son ridicule (she says)
>   Que l'on ne plaît par ses talents.

Le Comte de Boursoufle was performed on the evening of 24 August 1747—the eve of the departure of Voltaire and Mme du Châtelet from Anet. Emilie came on to the stage highly over-dressed for the part of Thérèse. She and Voltaire had a row about it, but she won: 'c'est la souveraine et lui l'esclave', Mme de Staal commented.[22]

The day after Voltaire and Mme du Châtelet left Anet, Mme de Staal received a letter from him saying he had lost the manuscript

---

[21] Renouard (see n. 31) does not publish the prologue, which apparently became separated from the manuscript of *Le Comte de Boursoufle*. The Kehl edition uses it as a preface to *La Prude*, quite indefensibly and ignoring the reference in it to 'Thérèse', a character in *Le Comte de Boursoufle*. Beuchot prints it at the head of *L'Echange* (*Œuvres complètes*, Vol. III: *Théâtre*, vol. ii). It is his edition I have followed for the prologue.

[22] *Correspondence*, D.3567 (27 August 1747).

of the play and of the prologue. He asked her to find them and to send them to him, not by post, '*parce qu'on le copierait*, de garder les rôles crainte du même accident, et d'enfermer la pièce *sous cent clefs*.' She remarks sarcastically, 'J'aurais cru un loquet suffisant pour garder ce trésor!'[23] His orders, she says, were duly executed, but the fact remains that the manuscript seems to have been lost sight of until, in 1761, it surfaced again in two places at once: Paris and Vienna. But it had undergone a few changes. The Comédie Italienne announced it under the title of *Quand est-ce qu'on me marie*, and called it an anonymous work. The Vienna version, called *L'Echange*, went further, reducing the three acts to two, and changing the names of the characters (Boursoufle becomes a close cousin of his ancestor Foppington—Fatenville).[24] The Vienna version, most important of all, turned the dénouement into a gala of virtuous sensibility. Vanbrugh would surely have turned in his grave to see his anti-sentimental *Relapse* turned back again into a sentimental comedy that would have delighted Cibber. Although this Vienna version has no Voltairean authenticity, it is interesting as an example of the dictates of mid-century sentimentality. In all the three-act versions extant, the elder brother (the Comte), when released from his smelly incarceration tied up to the manger in the stable, admits to his younger brother (the Chevalier) that he has been unjust and mean, offering him 20,000 francs if he will let him marry the girl. The Chevalier refuses (just as Young Fashion refuses Foppington's offer of £5000). But the Chevalier then suggests going halves by which he means: 'Je prendrai la dot, et [je] vous laisserai la fille'. Of course, the Comte thinks this is a poor bargain and turns it down. The Chevalier is quite implacable: he says he will have his revenge for his brother's lack of charity by taking the girl *and* the dowry.

Now, in the Vienna version (also performed at The Hague in 1771)[25] the Chevalier goes through a sentimental *crise de conscience*. He returns the marriage contract to the girl's father, proclaiming that he cannot rob a brother whom he loves. The Comte returns these generous sentiments and gives the Chevalier 10,000 francs. Not

[23] Ibid., D.3569 (30 August 1747).
[24] Beuchot (*Œuvres complètes*, III, ii, 252) maintains that these names (Fatenville, Canardière, Trigaudin, Gotton, etc.) were used at the Comédie Italienne for the production in 1761. However, Fréron, in his review (n. 27 below), refers to them as 'Boursoufle', etc., as they appeared in the manuscript in his possession. Had the names in performance differed from the names in writing, it is to be assumed he would have called them by the former, since it was the performance he was reviewing.
[25] The edition of *L'Echange* published by H. Constapel at The Hague in 1771 has on the title-page: 'Représenté pour la première fois au Théâtre de la Haye, le 22 Avril 1771'.

only that, but the Baron gives the young brother both daughter and dowry, saying these immortal words, in the style of Diderot: 'Les belles actions valent mieux que des richesses. Vive l'honneur!' The moral seems to be: Honesty is the best policy, especially when you have been caught out anyway.

When Voltaire heard that the Comédie Italienne was going to put on the piece in 1761, he became somewhat heated: 'Est-il vrai qu'on joue aux italiens une parade intitulée le comte de Boursoufle sous mon nom?' he asked d'Argental—unwittingly admitting authorship, since the play was billed under a quite different title. 'Justice, justice. Puissances célestes, empéchez cette profanation . . .', he appealed.[26] His main concern was that his name should not be prostituted (as he put it) by appearing on the posters of the Comédie Italienne. In the end the play was billed without an author's name, but with an innocently ironic subterfuge: the play, read the poster, had been 'traduite de l'Anglais'.

It opened on 26 January 1761 and—of course—Voltaire's arch-enemy, Fréron, was there. He reported in his *Année litteraire*:[27] 'Dès la première Scène, je me trouvai en pays de connoissance'. No, he had not spotted *The Relapse* in disguise. He had simply remembered once having a manuscript. He turned out a cupboard, and there, at the bottom, was *Le Comte de Boursoufle*, with Voltaire's name upon it. Certain of its authorship, Fréron went into the attack with his customary ferocity.

This was the last time the play was heard of in eighteenth-century France. In 1819 Renouard published it from a manuscript communicated to him by M. de Soleinne out of the Pont-de-Veyle (or Vesle) library. Beuchot, in his edition, for reasons that escape me, published it under the title given to it in Vienna, *L'Echange*, and also changed the characters' names from those we know were used by Voltaire to those adopted in the Vienna edition.[28]

However, those are details of editorial interest. Let us look a little more closely at what Voltaire made of *The Relapse*. Bonamy Dobrée points out in his introduction to *The Complete Works of Sir John Vanbrugh*,[29] how inferior Sheridan is in every alteration he made to *The Relapse* in turning it into *A Trip to Scarborough*: 'Not only is the gusto gone, as much of the phrasing as he could destroy, and the tang of English that is really felt, but the life-blood of the artist'. Can we say that Voltaire managed to retain any of

---

[26] *Correspondence*, D.9575.
[27] 1761, IV, 73-85 ('Lettre à M. Fréron sur une Comédie donnée au Théâtre Italien'). The description of the review as a letter to Fréron was a subterfuge.
[28] See Beuchot, *Œuvres complètes*, Vol. III/ii, p. 258.
[29] *Complete Works*, ed. Bonamy Dobrée and Geoffrey Webb, 4 vols., Bloomsbury, 1927, I, xxvii.

these qualities in his version? There are times when he keeps very close to his original. For example, Hoyden goes up to inspect Foppington, bound hand and foot, and asks: 'Is this he that would have run away with me? Fough, how he stinks of sweets! Pray, father, let him be dragged through the horse-pond'. Foppington says to himself, 'This must be my wife by her natural inclination to her husband'.

> HOYDEN: Pray, father, what do you intend to do with him, hang him?
> SIR TUNBELLY: That at least, child. . . .
> FOPPINGTON: Hitherto this appears to me to be one of the most extraordinary families that ever man of quality matched into. (IV.vi, 48-54, 56-8)[30]

Voltaire renders this with the daughter, Thérèse, demanding:
> Que je voie donc comment sont faits les gens qui voulent m'enlever. Ah! papa, il m'empuantit d'odeur de fleur d'orange; j'en aurai des vapeurs pour quinze jours. Ah! le vilain homme!

(So, for her English cousin's horse-pond, she has genteeley substituted the vapours.) The Comte goes on:

> Beau-père, au goût que cette personne me témoigne, il y a apparence que c'est là ma femme . . .
> LE BARON:—. . . il sera pendu comme ravisseur et comme faussaire.
> LE COMTE:—Ce baron est une espèce de beau-père bien étrange. (II.vii)

Occasionally Voltaire expands Vanbrugh's text. When, for example, Hoyden, in the same scene, realises that Foppington is one of those strange creatures, a beau:

> O gemini! Is this a beau? Let me see him again. Ha, I find a beau's no such an ugly thing neither.
> [YOUNG] FASHION (aside):—I'gad, she'll be in love with him presently. (IV.vii, 69-71)

Voltaire works on the subtext here, sees that more can be made of the girl's feelings:

> THERESE: Pardi, plus je regarde ce drôle-là, et plus il me paraît, malgré tout ça, avoir la mine assez revenante. Il est bien mieux mis que mon mari: ma foi, il est au moins tout aussi joli. Oh! vive les gens de Paris! je le dirai toujours. Mais de quoi t'avisais-tu de prendre si mal ton temps pour m'enlever? Ecoute, je te

---

[30] Quotations are taken from *The Relapse*, ed. Curt A. Zimansky, London, 1970.

pardonne de tout mon cœur; puisque tu voulais m'avoir, c'est que tu me trouvais belle; j'en suis assez charmée, et je te promets de pleurer quand on te prendra. (II.viii)[31]

This outburst of sympathy does not prevent her saying shortly after that she does not mind whom she marries, so long as she gets away to Paris.

One can begin to see why this scene was chosen by the actress Yvonne Lifraud for her first examination at the Conservatoire. Victorien Sardou was delighted, got up from his place in the jury, and walked over beaming with pleasure to Jules Truffier, saying: 'Vous avez déniché là une scène excellente pour cette enfant. Il faut engager tout de suite cette petite-là! Elle est prodigieuse de malice et, en même temps, de vraie ingénuité.'[32] Voltaire must be given his due for writing a script that brought out her qualities.

Let us compare the fop's dressing scene with the scenes from Molière, Etherege and Vanbrugh, from which it evolved. Both in *Le Bourgeois Gentilhomme* (Act II, sc. v) and *The Relapse* (Act I, sc. iii), we have the complaint about the tight shoes falling on the shoemaker's deaf—or unbelieving—ears. Voltaire avoids using this *jeu de scene* again, for he would have been seen as plagiarising not from Vanbrugh, but Molière. Instead, he concentrates all the various fittings into one item: the periwig. Foppington complains that his wig is too far off his face: 'a periwig to a man should be like a mask to a woman' (I.iii. 136-7). Boursoufle complains just as bitterly—but in the opposite direction: he has told his wigmaker a thousand times that his periwigs do not fly back enough, away from the face. He will be a laughing-stock with his face buried in hair. So much for changes in fashion, London 1696 and France 1736. In Voltaire's play, the wig-fitting is reduced to its barest essential. Indeed, the whole scene goes at breakneck speed, with its two conflicting elements (Boursoufle's egocentricity and his young brother's criticism of it) weaving in and out of each other in counterpoint. In the Molière and Etherege scenes there is no critical element except as formulated by the spectator). (*The Man of Mode*, III, ii.)

In *The Relapse*, Young Fashion greets his brother in Act I scene iii, after rejecting Lory's advice to show some respect for the newly-created lord:

> FASHION: Respect! Damn him for a coxcomb! . . . But let's accost him. . . . Brother, I'm your humble servant.
> LORD FOPPINGTON:—O Lard, Tam, I did not expect you in Eng-

---

[31] Quotations from *Le Comte de Boursoufle* are taken from the Renouard edition in *Œuvres complètes*, Vol. VII, Paris, 1819.

[32] See Jules Truffier, ' "Le Comte de Boursoufle" de Voltaire', *Conferencia: Journal de l'Université des Annales*, XXIe Année, I, 12 (5 June 1927), 591.

land. Brother, I am glad to see you.—(Turning to his Tailor) Look you, sir, I shall never be reconciled to this nauseous packet. (I.iii.59-65)

Fashion does not speak again until line 111, aside to his servant:

> FASHION: Well, Lory, what dost think on't? A very friendly reception from a brother after three years absence!
> LORY: Why sir, it's your own fault. We seldom care for those that don't love what we love. If you would creep into his heart, you must enter into his pleasures. Here have you stood ever since you came in and have not commended any one thing that belongs to him.
> FASHION: Nor never shall, whilst they belong to a coxcomb. (I.iii. 111-18)

Turning now to Voltaire's scene (I.iii), we see that Boursoufle's self-engrossment is so concentrated that he fails to register the presence of the Chevalier and Maraudin (an innocuous re-incarnation of Vanbrugh's Old Coupler) even after they have addressed him three times. His greeting to Maraudin ('Hé! bonjour, monsieur Maraudin, bonjour') is positively effusive in comparison with the one to his brother: 'Oh! vous voilà, Chonchon'.

Voltaire continues almost immediately with the asides between younger brother and servant. In his transposition Voltaire makes the speech more direct and concrete than the exchange in *The Relapse*. This will show better if I put it into English:

> THE CHEVALIER: A plague on the coxcomb! He will not lower himself even to look at me.
> PASQUIN: Ah! But why do you address him, his person? Why do you not speak to his wig, to his embroidery, to his retinue. Flatter his vanity instead of bothering about touching his heart.
> THE CHEVALIER: No. I'd rather snuff it than pay court to his impertinence. (I.iii)

Pasqun picks out the items whereby Boursoufle's vanity may best be tickled, giving the Chevalier advice which Lory had given Young Fashion in Act I sc. iii: 'Apply yourself to his favorites, speak to his periwig, his cravat, his feather, his snuff box . . .'.

Vanbrugh's dressing scene ends with Foppington going off in his coach to the House of Lords, but Voltaire follows this scene immediately with the scene in which the elder brother refuses to give financial aid to the younger. This scene does not take place until Act III scene i of *The Relapse*.

These examples of adroit telescoping are characteristic of Voltaire's handling of *The Relapse*. It is not simply a question of shortening the dialogue, but rather of a radical re-structuring, especially at the end. In this respect it is interesting to compare Voltaire's adaptation with a later English one. Not Sheridan's *Trip to Scarborough*, which keeps to the Vanbrugh original, but with John Lee's *Man of Quality* (1771), which was staged at Covent Garden on 27 April 1773 (nine years before Sheridan honoured the memory of Vanbrugh with his bowdlerised version). Lee, like Jeremy Collier and Voltaire before him, saw that the rivalry of the two brothers for the girl with the dowry was the main plot, and therefore cut out all the Loveless-Amanda intrigue. In a manner that makes one think he may have set eyes on Voltaire's version, Lee also splices together the dressing scene and the interview at which money is requested and refused by the brothers. Like Voltaire, Lee also reduces the play to three acts. He begins his second act at the gate of the country-house, and has the two young people married in the interval between Acts II and III. All of this Voltaire had done before him. Again, as in *Le Comte de Boursoufle, the* young brother is brought back immediately after the elder one's release and recognition, so that the whole affair can be rounded off there and then in Act III. None of these ways of shortening *The Relapse* and of avoiding Vanbrugh's double dénouement is the obvious only way. The coincidences are quite striking. If, as I strongly suspect, Lee knew of the Paris performances of Voltaire's three-act version, then the cross-channel trade in Foppingtons was even freer than was thought by those who complained about it exactly a century later.

How do the social and moral attitudes of *Le Comte de Boursoufle* compare with those of *The Relapse*? By isolating the Foppington-Fashion plot and concentrating on it, Voltaire appears to be attacking primogeniture, and in very strong terms. Indeed, in 1826, when the French government introduced a bill to re-establish the *droit d'aînesse*, Voltaire's play was re-published with the sub-title *Les Agréments du droit d'aînesse*. However, let us keep this in perspective. Voltaire was clearly aware of the injustice of primogeniture, but he did not have an obsession about being a younger brother. His Chevalier is a less sympathetic person than Young Fashion, and, furthermore, in *L'Enfant prodigue*, it is the younger son, Fierenfat, who is satirised and beaten to the altar by the elder brother, who is a rogue with a heart of gold.

If we look at Voltaire's play in the light of the accusations of moral cynicism levelled by Collier at Vanbrugh's *Relapse*, we observe that two sources of Collier's displeasure are absent from Voltaire's play. Namely, the bawdy, and the adultery. However, when Collier objects that Young Fashion is given 'a second fortune, only for debauching away his first', and that the moral 'puts the

Prize into the wrong Hand',[33] we are forced to the conclusion that his objections would apply even more strongly to Voltaire's version. Whereas Hoyden and Young Fashion are made for each other, with Hoyden obviously preferring him to Foppington, Thérèse is quite indifferent as to which of the two brothers she marries: 'Ça ne me fait rien, pourvu que j'aille à Paris, et que je sois grande dame', she says (III.v). The deception carried out by the Chevalier on his brother is rewarded, as in *The Relapse*, but he deserves it even less than Young Fashion does, for though he asserts 'J'ai mangé mon bien au service du roi', Pasquin corrects him: 'Dites en service de vos maîtresses, de vos fantaisies, de vos folies' (I.i.) Thus, although Voltaire's play results, like Vanbrugh's, in a wider distribution of wealth, it is not certain that the money goes to the more deserving.

The Relapse ends with an amusing but churlish comment by Foppington on Hoyden: 'You have married a woman beautiful in her person, charming in her airs, prudent in her canduct, canstant in her inclinations, and of a nice marality, split my windpipe' (V.v. 257-60). Boursoufle ends on the same resigned note that Foppington adopted just before the outburst of spite I have just quoted: 'On pourrait bien de tout ceci me tourner en ridicule à la cour; mais quand on est fait comme je suis, on est au-dessus de tout, foi de seigneur' (III.v.). He is untouched by the outcome, whereas Foppington tries to cover his indignation with forced serenity.

Vanbrugh's norms are characterised by the affirmation of *some* higher values in the society he depicts. Voltaire's picture, on the other hand, is of a society of unrelieved self-interest and cynicism. There is little to choose between the three main characters of his play—the two brothers and the girl.

Perhaps it is this materialism that made Voltaire's play so popular to audiences in Second Empire Paris—a society that had thrown over the sentimentality and heroic deeds of Romanticism. Be that as it may, it is only because of the play made for private performance at Cirey in 1736 that one of the finest of English Restoration plays became known in France, for there is to this day no published French translation of Vanbrugh's *Relapse*.

---

[33] *Short View*, p. 210.

Nerves, Spirits, and Fibres: Towards Defining the Origins of Sensibility

G. S. Rousseau

We have all heard a great deal in the last decade about Kuhn's 'paradigms'. His definition in *The Structure of Scientific Revolutions* has itself become something of a classic:

> Aristotle's *Physica*, Ptolemy's *Almagest*, Newton's *Principia* and *Opticks*, Franklin's *Electricity*, Lavoisier's *Chemistry*, and Lyell's *Geology*—these and many other works served for a time implicitly to define the legitimate problems and methods of a research field for succeeding generations of practitioners. They were able to do so because they shared two essential characteristics. Their achievement was sufficiently unprecedented to attract an enduring group of adherents away from competing modes of scientific activity. Simultaneously, it was sufficiently open-ended to leave all sorts of problems for the redefined group of practitioners to resolve.
>
> Achievements that share these two characteristics I shall henceforth refer to as 'paradigms', a term that relates closely to 'normal science'.[1]

During the last decade we have also read and heard that large segments of the scientific community are not happy with Kuhn's definition. They argue that the deflection of human energy by unprecedented, open-ended theories is inadequate to describe the origin of scientific revolutions.[2] Nevertheless, Kuhn's paradigms

---

[1] Thomas S. Kuhn, *The Structure of Scientific Revolutions*, Chicago, 1962, p. 10.

[2] The literature of Kuhnian criticism is enormous and cannot be reduced to a few bibliographical references. Perhaps the single best criticism is one not directly attacking Kuhn but substituting for his 'paradigm' a different but not unrelated theory of the 'episteme'; see Michel Foucault, *Les Mots et les Choses*, Paris, 1966; English version, *The Order of Things: An Archaeology of the*

have considerable worth; if nothing else, Kuhn's definition typifies and describes his own achievement. No other single concept in the last ten years has deflected serious thinkers so much from their own pursuits, nor is any other in the recent history and philosophy of science so open-ended as to have caused students of every background to scrutinise it and even to imitate it, as does Michel Foucaut's theory of the *episteme* in *Les Mots et les Choses*, first published in 1966.[3] Even today, in this post-Popperian age, and at the risk of labouring a now well-known theory, it is worth repeating that Kuhn's 'paradigm' refers to books, and that his concept of paradigms was formulated by examining the way that science textbooks charted the route to 'normal science'.[4]

What does such a theory do for us, students of the eighteenth century? We might extend Kuhn's list by adding many works, for example Locke's *Essay Concerning Human Understanding*, clearly an 'open-ended' work that deflected many men through its use as a scientific textbook. But would we add Hume's *Treatise of Human Nature* or Adam Smith's *Theory of Moral Sentiments*? It all depends on the level at which we decode, and on our understanding of Kuhn's original definition. Application of the theory, as we can see, has already presented a slight problem; but in fairness to Kuhn we ought to remember that he reserved the term 'paradigm' for unprecedented works demonstrating open-ended theories and deflection in the highest possible degree. Thus, while it probably can be shown (and I say probably because it has not yet been shown) that Locke's *Essay* deflected all sorts of men in addition to ethical philosophers and soon established itself as a scientific textbook leading to understanding of the 'new science', the science of man— the same (and here I want to be somewhat the loose Humean) perhaps cannot be said of the treatises by Hume and Smith. If

---

Human Sciences, New York, 1970. Although I vigorously disagree with Foucault about the simple facts of European scientific history 1600-1800, I have been enormously influenced by his way of doing intellectual history, i.e. decoding beneath visible surfaces, as I have by Robert K. Merton's theory 'that in each age there is a system of science which rests upon a set of assumptions, usually implicit and seldom questioned by the scientists of the time'; in *The Sociology of Science*, ed. Bernard Barber and Walker Hirsch, New York, 1962, p. 41. Kuhn's own revaluation of his concept of the 'paradigm' is of considerable interest; see his 'Postscript—1969', in *The Structure*, 2nd edn, enlarged, Chicago, 1970, pp. 174-210.

[3] I have attempted to show some of the differences between Kuhn and Foucault in 'Whose Enlightenment? Not Man's: The Case of Michael Foucault', *Eighteenth-Century Studies*, VI (1972-3), 238-56.

[4] Kuhn, *Scientific Revolutions*, p. 10: 'In this essay, "normal science" means research firmly based upon one or more past scientific achievements that some particular scientific community acknowledges for a time as supplying the foundation for its further practice'.

nothing else, we can probably prove beyond a shadow of doubt that these later works were far less tentative than Locke's; and furthermore, that in the case of Hume the point made was too precise to leave ensuing practitioners in open-ended doubt; and that in Smith's case the contents summarised the theories of others and made them available to everyone in a new form rather than put forward a radically new and open-ended theory itself. A similar case can be made for certain works by Diderot, Rousseau and other *philosophes*, for La Mettrie, Le Cat, Marat. In paradigmatic terms then, and if I may take the liberty of expanding on Kuhn's original term, the Rousseauistic doctrine *je sens, donc je suis*, is the end rather than the beginning of a revolution in knowledge.

We are therefore left with John Locke, a condition that will surprise or horrify some and that others will call reductionist or even patently foolish. But if we accept Kuhn's theory (and despite its difficulties it is still the best available) and follow it to its logical conclusion, Locke's *Essay* alone among textbooks about the 'new science' of man satisfies Kuhn's two extraordinary conditions. Is this in itself not extraordinary? Not at all extraordinary in the fact that Locke's is a seventeenth-century work (published in 1690), nor in the further fact that no scientific works other than Newton's, Franklin's, and Lavoisier's are mentioned by Kuhn for the eighteenth century, but rather in the fact that Locke's *Essay* is the first to deal with a science that had not as yet developed: the *science* of man. Here Kuhn's theory about Franklin and electricity is equally instructive. 'Only through the work of Franklin and his immediate successors did a theory [of electricity] arise that could account with something like equal facility for very nearly all these effects and that therefore could and did provide a subsequent generation of "electricians" with a common paradigm for its research.' Likewise, by the time Locke published his *Essay* in 1690, a *theory* of the new science of man had evolved that was sufficiently unprecedented and open-ended to deflect at least three subsequent generations of moral scientists: Mandeville, Shaftesbury, Hume, Adam Smith, La Mettrie, the *philosophes*, and dozens of others. Call this science what you will: social science, the science of morals, or, as Peter Gay has called it, the 'Science of Man',[5] and give it any label you fancy—a crisis, an ethical dilemma, a revolution, an epoch of transition. One thing, however, is clear: without Locke and his immediate successors, the theory could not have developed.

What then precisely was it about Locke's *Essay* that allowed for, indeed insisted on, this paradigmatic treatment? Surely it was his

[5] See *The Enlightenment: An Interpretation*, Vol. II: *The Science of Freedom*, New York, 1969, pp. 167-215.

application of crucial aspects of the physical sciences to a realm—ethics and politics—that was not previously imagined to yield to scientific types of explanation. Locke's integration of ethics and physiology has little, if anything, to do with the fact that he himself was a physician. For every physician in 1690 who was integrating seemingly non-allied terrains, there were dozens, perhaps hundreds, who saw no connection at all. And even among the integrationists only one thinker's genius inclined him, for whatever mysterious reason now lost to time, to grasp at the one realm—ethics—most requiring an unprecedented theory to be arrived at by radical integration of disparate areas of study. Physico-theologists like the Boyle lecturers, like Ray and Derham, annually were integrating the physical sciences into the study of religion. The difference between their endeavours, which certainly led to no revolution in knowledge, and Newton's is evident: if there is one thing the *Principia* and *Opticks* are not it is physico-theologies. Newton, the man whose open-ended theories deflected men for over a century by replacing the old textbooks with his new ones, also kept science and religion apart when it came to writing books. We all know his protestation that he could not tell anyone 'why is gravity, only what is gravity'.[6] Paradigmatic achievement, therefore, does not depend upon integration as an efficient cause. In Locke's case it happens to function as such, but this is partly owing to the rapid acceleration of scientific research immediately after the Restoration, and partly to Locke's own monumental genius in recognising that integration working below the surface statement of these disparate realms—ethics and physiology—would result in the open-ended effect about which Kuhn speaks. Locke intuitively realised, as Descartes had not, that the whole argument about knowledge pivots upon the concept and definition of 'sensation'.

Now our isolation of Locke's *Essay* as paradigmatic is in itself of no great interest except that we have tended to think of 'sensation', and hence of the ensuing cults of 'sensibility' and 'sentiment', as mid eighteenth-century phenomena. We speak of a 'sensibility movement' commencing with Richardson in the 1740s, transforming itself until the 1790s, and persisting until something called 'romanticism' eclipsed it. Here I wish to make clear my temporary suspension of belief in nominalism; for the moment, I am not interested in semantic labels and tags; it is paradigms and paradigmatic works, that is books, related to sensibility, that I wish to consider. Everyone knows that Northrop Frye has called English

[6] See Alexander Koyre, *Newtonian Studies*, Cambridge, Mass., 1965, pp. 63-7, and *From the Closed World to the Infinite Universe*, Baltimore, 1957, pp. 131-4, for analysis and discussion of Newton's reasons.

literature between Richardson and Wordsworth the product of an 'Age of Sensibility',[7] and those still hovering in doubt will be convinced by R. F. Brissenden's book, *Virtue in Distress: Studies in the Novel of Sentiment from Richardson to Sade*. And yet the half-century between 1690 and 1740, between the appearance of Locke's *Essay* and Richardson's *Pamela*, an epoch separating men two generations apart, has continued to elude us. If we follow Kuhn's argument and my subsequent reasoning to its apodictic end, should Frye's 'Age of Sensibility' not have occurred fifty years earlier? Have we been dangerously promoting an historical fallacy by alleging that its appearance was a mid, even a late, eighteenth-century phenomenon?

Not really. For such reasoning dangerously and erroneously assumes that imaginative literature—and by this I mean poetry, fiction, the drama—is influenced by science at once, and we know this is not true of the eighteenth century merely by noticing that it took Newtonian science at least one generation to 'demand the muse'. It is no less dangerous at this point and no less consequential for the future of eighteenth-century studies, for us to confuse *imaginative literature* and *speculative science*.

What I am therefore suggesting is that the eighteenth-century revolution in intellectual thinking regarding the 'science of man' owes its superlative debt to John Locke. Secondly—and this is the more important of the two points—that sensibility, not merely sentimentalism,[8] is at the very heart of this revolution (precisely for the two reasons given in Kuhn's definition of paradigms) and of subsequent revolutions. But sensibility was not a mid eighteenth-century phenomenon, certainly not in philosophy or the natural sciences. It was a late seventeenth-century development, owing its superlative paradigmatic debt to books—and here, again, I adopt Kuhn's emphasis—books like Thomas Willis's *Pathology of the*

---

[7] 'Towards Defining an Age of Sensibility', *ELH*, XXIII (1956), pp. 144-52.

[8] I do not consider the two identical, although they are obviously related in dozens of aspects. Historically and generally speaking sensibility was the larger of the two, touching almost every aspect of life; sentimentalism came later, especially in imaginative literature, and was the more religious, moral, literary, and far less aristocratic of the two; it was also the one that lent itself more readily to radical modifications and variations from an already blurred original. In every case the distinction is grey, never black or white. Some excellent philological explorations into these labels have already been undertaken: see E. Erametsa, *A Study of the Word 'Sentimental'*, Helsinki, 1951, and R. F. Brissenden, ' "Sentiment": Some Uses of the Word in the Writings of David Hume', in *Studies in the Eighteenth Century: Papers Presented at the David Nicol Smith Memorial Seminar Canberra 1966*, ed. R. F. Brissenden, Canberra, 1968, pp. 89-106 and *Virtue in Distress*, London, 1974, Part I, chap. ii: ' "Sentimentalism": An Attempt at Definition'.

Brain,[9] and also to one unprecedented, integrative work, Locke's *Essay*. The mid eighteenth-century neurological treatises of Haller and Whytt and the many others who entered the arenas of debate were not paradigmatic works that led to a revolution in the scientific approach to the study of man, or to the sensibility movement in literature. They were the deflections, not the deflectors. These were not the works that paved the way for *Clarissa*, *A Sentimental Journey*, and *Justine*: nor were the earlier treatises of Dr George Cheyne, with whom Richardson for example corresponded so prolifically. At the deepest level of decoding, the level at which I believe Kuhn has decoded, the revolution in sentiment occurred in the last quarter of the seventeenth century. It took imaginative writers like Richardson and Sterne a half century to 'catch up', as it were; and more importantly, it also took most scientific thinkers like Cheyne, Haller and Whytt almost as long to understand what had transpired in the interim.

This observation should not surprise us. Almost fifty years ago, R. S. Crane warned that if we wish to understand the origins of sensibility 'we must look to a period considerably earlier than that in which Shaftesbury wrote'.[10] And I am suggesting now that it

[9] *Pathologiae Cerebri* (1667), tr. Samuel Pordage as *An Essay of the Pathology of the Brain*, in *The Remaining Medical Works of Dr Thomas Willis* (1681); Willis's two other most important works are *Cerebri Anatome* (1664) and *De Anima Brutorum* (1672), the last also tr. by Pordage as *Two Discourses concerning the Soul of Brutes, which is that of the Vital and Sensitive Soul of Man* (1683).

[10] 'Suggestions Toward a Genealogy of the "Man of Feeling"', in *The Idea of the Humanities*, 2 vols., Chicago, 1967, I, 188-213, originally published in *ELH*, I (1934), 205-30. Crane's exact words are (I, 190): 'If we wish to understand the origins and the widespread diffusion in the eighteenth century of the ideas which issued in the cult of sensibility, we must look, I believe, to a period considerably earlier than that in which Shaftesbury wrote and take into account the propaganda of a group of persons whose opportunities for moulding the thoughts of ordinary Englishmen were much greater than those of even the most aristocratic of deists'. Crane's intuition about a chronology 'earlier than that in which Shaftesbury wrote' is sound but his reasons are altogether unacceptable. He maintains that sensibility was 'not a philosophy which the eighteenth century *could have* derived full fledged from ancient or Renaissance tradition. It was something new in the world—a doctrine, or rather a complex of doctrines, which a hundred years before 1750 would have been frowned upon, had it ever been presented to them, by representatives of every school of ethical or religious thought' (I, 189-90, italics mine). Benevolence and related ideas of 'doing good' almost certainly *could* have developed before 1750, or 1660, or (for that matter) 1640, for they are everywhere present in the Bible, and in medieval and Renaissance Christian ethical teaching. But a theory to explain the self-conscious personality could not have derived from earlier times (earlier, that is, than the Restoration) because there was no scientific model for it. '*Sensibility*' used more narrowly, as a term to connote self-consciousness and self-awareness, has a history different from Crane's umbrella term (although my usage is not altogether unrelated to his). This is the sense in which many eighteenth-century writers, especially scientists, employed it, and it is the sense in which I use it.

is equally dangerous to think that the revolution in sensibility was a mid or late eighteenth-century phenomenon. To trace its origin to Shaftesbury, or even solely to Locke, is to indulge in sheer mysticism and to have no philosophy of the influence of history on literature. I realise that I have been partly responsible for some of the confusion in my essay on science and the imagination in eighteenth-century England, but I am not so culpable as Mr Frye, who was satisfied to repeat what every Victorian and Edwardian school-teacher knew, and to garnish his main point with consolation to the effect that English literature between Gray and the Romantics is not altogether dull.[11]

I must now demonstrate that at least in scientific thought the revolution in sensibility was *not* an eighteenth-century phenomenon; in other words show that unless one decodes at Kuhn's level one does not possess a meaningful, let alone cogent, model of literary change so far as contents are concerned, and moreover that decoding at the level Kuhn's paradigms imply is essential for students of the eighteenth century today. If this is done and accepted, one significant consequence is that propositions of the form 'the social sciences were born in the eighteenth century' must be thrown out of court on grounds of false aetiology. They may have matured and flowered then; they were not born then. The social sciences of man, about which mid eighteenth-century Frenchmen had much to say, may not have had an influence on the manifold aspects of routine daily life until the mid eighteenth century, but it is absurd to suggest 'birth' at that time if we decode at the level of Kuhn, Michel Foucault, Levi-Strauss, some of the literary phenomenologists and other recent powerful analytical minds.

What then were the 'paradigms' of sensibility, and was a revolution in knowledge about man created by them? Crudely speaking they were sets of physiological texts published shortly after the Restoration that were sufficiently 'open-ended' (like Willis's *Anatomy of the Brain* and *Pathology of the Brain*) to deflect all types of scientists, not merely other anatomists and physiologists. (This is not to suggest that the physiological dimension of these texts is the

---

[11] Frye writes: 'I do not care about terminology, only about appreciation for an extraordinarily interesting period of English literature, and the first stage in renewing that appreciation seems to me the gaining of a clear sense of what it is in itself'; and 'Contemporary poetry is still deeply concerned with the problems and techniques of the age of sensibility, and while the latter's resemblance to our time is not a merit itself, it is a logical enough reason for re-examining it with fresh eyes'. These two sentences appear in *ELH*, XXIII (1956), pp. 145, 152. As Frye indicates, he is uninterested in the label—as I am—but concerned with literary techniques and strategies, especially the sense of time held by authors 1750-1800 and their Longinian view of literature as 'a process' culminating in various calculated, emotional responses.

crucial aspect. It is not: physiology text books were being written certainly by the second century A.D., when Galen published his paradigmatic physiological work, *On the Natural Faculties*.)[12] After 1660 their numbers increased owing to regental and internal university support of scientific research. It is essential to note that these books (however cognisant or not their authors) were ultimately attempts to answer Cartesian science. That is—and here again I follow certain of Kuhn's philosophical theories, especially his notion that the precise nature of scientific works is never accidental—the history of science is best conceived of as a continuum in which paradigmatic works periodically deflect 'groups of practitioners'.[13] Until we discover which are the paradigms and which the deflected responses, we cannot understand revolutions in intellectual thought: the rise of sensibility is a good case in point, especially as regards the continuum in which it takes place.

Before the Restoration Descartes's *Discourses* and his *Passions of the Soul* were paradigmatic works, especially for anatomy, and deflected all types of natural scientists, directing them almost compulsively to the study of physiology. But for various political reasons, the Interregnum among them, their influence in England was temporarily abortive. The next such paradigmatic works in the biological and medical sciences were Thomas Willis's texts on the brain published in the 1660s and 1670s and translated in the early 1680s. Although there were other paradigmatic texts before the nineteenth century (e.g. Whytt, Haller, Cullen), these were not of the same class as Willis's. His special genius, like Descartes's before him, lay not in the scientific veracity of his theory but in his ability to deflect men. The theory itself was of course unprecedented: he was the first scientist clearly and loudly to posit that the seat of the soul is strictly limited to the brain, nowhere else. Shadows and

---

[12] Galen's enormous influence on the history of medicine is a subject in itself, especially the manner by which some (but not all) of his physiological doctrines remained virtually intact during the seventeenth and eighteenth centuries. Of unusual interest to my thesis are the following: R. B. Onians, *The Origins of European Thought about the Body*, 2nd edn, Cambridge, 1954; Erich Voegelin, *Anamnesis*, Munich, 1966; K. E. Rothschuh, *Physiologie: der Wandel ihrer Konzepte*, Munich, 1968; Peter H. Niebyl, 'Galen, Van Helmont, and Blood Letting', in *Science, Medicine and Society in the Renaissance*, ed. Allen G. Debus, 2 vols., New York, 1972, II, 13-23; *The History and Philosophy of Knowledge of the Brain and its Functions: An Anglo-American Symposium*, ed. F. N. L. Poynter, Oxford, 1958; rev. edn, 1972. F. Solmsen's study of physiological theories prevalent in the time of Plato makes it evident at least by implication that Galenic concepts would have been sufficiently 'open-ended' to create interest; but whether they deflected enough men to be 'paradigmatic' in Kuhn's sense I cannot say. See 'Tissues and the Soul', *Philosophical Review*, LIX (1950), 435-68.

[13] Kuhn's phrase for the scientific community that becomes deflected after a paradigmatic work (p. 10).

anticipations of this revolutionary theory can be found before 1660, but nothing loud and plain.[14] In the sense of cause and effect, it was this theory that inspired a revolution in intellectual thought concerning the nature of man and that greatly enhanced the doctrines of anti-Stoic and anti-Puritan divines of the Latitudinarian school about which R. S. Crane has written so brilliantly.[15] Every competent physiologist of the late seventeenth century knew that nerves, morphologically speaking, carry out the tasks set by the brain. But not every physiologist or anatomist suspected—(or if he did know Willis's work, would have agreed), that the soul is located in the brain. Without this knowledge, an imaginative leap of the first order, it is impossible to account for the intense interest after the Restoration (but not before) in nerve research, and consequently for the emergence of diverse cults of sensibility.

Here it is delightful and amusing, but no more, to recount that Willis was Locke's teacher at Oxford, that Locke is known to have voluntarily copied into notebooks everything he (Locke) thought he might later use in his own work. It is no exaggeration to say that Willis's brain theories had a profound influence on Locke in some of his most formative years. It would be nothing less than treacherous, however, to argue that it was Willis's theory of the brain that 'deflected' Locke into writing the *Essay*. In rehearsing the influence of Willis on Locke my intention is not to minimise other factors (especially religious and political) in the development of Locke's imagination, but to question whether the deepest substratum of the *Essay*, especially its unspoken assumptions, is not more intelligible when viewed in the light of Locke's education at Oxford.

If we continue this line of inquiry regarding the revolution in physiology, it becomes evident why nerves, and their subsidiaries, fibres and animal spirits, could not be accounted the basis of knowledge, and consequently of human behaviour, until the seat of the soul was limited (not merely moved) to the brain. For this organ alone depends upon the nerves for all its functions. Once the soul was limited to the brain, scientists could debate precisely how the nerves carry out its voluntary and involuntary intentions, and what the relation between nerves and other systems, especially blood and lymph, is. The history of science reveals that they did this: no topic in physiology between the Restoration and the turn

---

[14] See *The History and Philosophy of Knowledge of the Brain*, especially three papers in the Third Session: Walter Pagel, 'Medieval and Renaissance Contributions to Knowledge of the Brain and its Functions', pp. 95-114; Walther Riese, 'Descartes's Ideas of Brain Function', pp. 115-34; W. P. D. Wightman, 'Wars of Ideas in Neurological Science—from Willis to Bichat and from Locke to Condillac', pp. 135-48.

[15] In *ELH*, I, 205-30.

of the nineteenth century was more important than the precise workings of the nerves, their intricate morphology and histological arrangement, their anatomic function. It is true, this collective scientific endeavour could not have been undertaken without Harvey's discovery in the 1620s of the circulation of the blood, expounded in another paradigmatic work, *De Motu Cordis*. Nor would it have been possible without Willis's revolutionary theory of the brain.

These admittedly sweeping abstractions about a chapter in the history of science have now been minutely documented by Edwin Clarke, our most distinguished historian of physiology. In an important article entitled 'The Doctrine of the Hollow Nerve in the Seventeenth and Eighteenth Centuries', he concludes: 'Despite the welter of speculation and observation concerning the supposed hollow or porous nerve which had accumulated in the seventeenth and eighteenth centuries, little advance beyond Galen's original suppositions had in fact been made'.[16] Why did this 'welter' exist in the first place, and what difference does it make to a history of sensibility? If indeed the soul is limited to the brain, as Willis and his followers in the 1670s contended, then nerves alone can be held responsible for sensory impressions, and consequently for knowledge; it also follows that the nerves must necessarily be hollow tubes rather than solid fibres, so that the brain's unique secretion, animal spirits, can freely flow through them to the body's vital organs. It was essential to the deepest and probably most unconscious assumption of these physiologists that the old model of nerves as hollow tubes be sustained. But the rapid and marked acceleration of the 'welter of speculation' after Willis's paradigmatic books on the brain is equally notable. Once Willis's paradigms are understood by us, a context for physiology manifests itself, and we can begin to perceive how the war between mechanists and vitalists, a war about which we have heard so much, developed at the end of the seventeenth century.

[16] In *Medicine, Science, and Culture*, ed. L. G. Stevenson and R. P. Multhauf, Baltimore, 1968, p. 135. Clarke rightly notes two exceptions: 'But there were two investigations in the eighteenth century, the results of which were readily available to all, which pointed to the future. In 1717 Leeuwenhoek saw and illustrated the single myelinated nerve fiber, the center of which (the axis cylinder or axon) he took to be hollow. . . . Of greater significance, however, was the second discovery, made by Fontana in 1779. . . . Again, this was the myelinated axon of today, but Fontana's work seems to have had little immediate effect, probably because of the suspicion engendered by most eighteenth-century microscopic investigations'. My own research on nerves and animal spirits corroborates Clarke's findings: I have found no evidence that the discoveries of Leeuwenhoek and Fontana were acknowledged, understood, or digested. This development is not surprising in view of the fact that Leeuwenhoek himself never realised what he had observed.

The mechanists, like their vitalist or animist opponents, were dualists. Followers of Descartes, they accepted his mechanistic explanation of all bodily functions except that of the soul, which, again like Descartes, they located everywhere in the body but whose activities, they asserted, do not act in any known mechanistic fashion. When asked by vitalists how the soul does act, mechanists from the time of Descartes to that of La Mettrie and Haller more than a century later, answered that in essence it does not matter how, because the soul has little power in and of itself—virtually everything depends on the clockwork movements of the body, a perfectly constructed machine whose basic motions would be enacted whether or not the soul willed them voluntarily. After Willis brilliantly limited the soul to the immediate area of the cerebrum and cerebellum and its surrounding network of nerves, the mechanists avidly set about to prove, although they did not succeed, that all nerves were in fact hollow tubes through which the quasi-magical fluid secreted by the brain flowed. Unless they could prove that nerves were porous, cavity-like structures, they would need to surrender their most fundamental assumption about the dualism of body and soul (or mind).

But precisely this fierce attempt to prove that nerves are porous cavities gave animists like Stahl and his many followers in the eighteenth century their biggest impetus. Monists of varying degree, the Stahlians—Stahl, Whytt, Cullen, to mention just the most celebrated—had never accepted Descartes's dualism of body and soul, although they had been deflected by his theories from the very start. Instead they preferred to adhere to an animate, functioning soul whose mechanical operations throughout the body were maximised to the greatest possible degree. In other words, every part of the body was chemically and physically governed by this soul, which did not function predictably, rationally, or mechanistically, but was influenced by non-mechanical, unconscious phenomena. It is hard not to notice how the whole dispute between Cartesian mechanists and Stahlian animists was radically displaced (altered would falsify the facts) by Willis's limitation of the soul to the brain. After 1680 mechanists and animists alike, dualists as well as monists, had no choice but to refute Willis's unprecedented contention by demonstrating unequivocally that nerves are in fact solid, or to agree with him. For if the nerves were solid fibres rather than porous hollow tubes, no avenue existed by which to explain the brain's control over the rest of the body—not, at least, before the discovery of electricity in the mid eighteenth century. That is, no means existed otherwise by which to account for knowledge gained by experience, for non-innate knowledge. But no one in the eighteenth century could prove the solidity of the nerves; i.e. no one could disprove Willis's theory by adducing concrete microscopic evidence.[17] The only remaining alternative was to work away at proving the one condition that would in turn prove Willis's theory, the hollowness of the nerves.

If we stop at this point, surely we scatter to the wind the most essential thread and consequences of the argument: the manner in which the idea that nerves control human consciousness gradually took hold. We also lose sight of the fundamental concept of 'sensation' upon which the entire debate had centered.

If Willis had not appeared on the scientific scene with his striking theory about the autonomous brain, the question of nerves could never have held the dominant sway it did. For by the 1660s the study of anatomy was sufficiently well developed, especially with regard to circulatory and respiratory systems in the body, for scientists to insist that the nerves are the slaves of the brain and, conversely, that the brain is thoroughly enslaved to the nerves and unable to function without them. This had been unequivocally demonstrated by Vesalius, Van Helmont, and their contemporaries. Without Willis physiologists and other scientists would have continued to debate the problem of how to prove the hollowness of nerves, the precise morphology of their fibres (which no one had seen microscopically), and the chemical composition of animal spirits. But other organs than the brain, such as the heart, stomach, bowels, would then have commanded superior positions as subjects for investigation by philosophers as well as anatomists.

Willis's paradigmatic leap, if we continue in this line of decoding, was to locate the brain in the soul in a series of experiments and books possessing just the right balance between observed fact and un-

---

[17] Clarke, *Medicine, Science, and Culture*, pp. 123-41, has performed the research and settled the matter once and for all. His statement (p. 124) about scientific models in physiology is revealing and germane to the rise of 'sensibility' as a serious subject for scientific concern: 'In general, the customary sequence of events during the accumulation of knowledge regarding a part of the animal or human body is that its morphology is established first of all: *thereafter its physiology can be investigated*. This has been true with structures like the heart, but in the case of nerves the advancement has been more complicated because of the greater complexity of nervous tissue and organs. Here, during the seventeenth and eighteenth centuries speculation predominated in respect to both form and function. It is probable that the ancients, having accepted the suggestion that the nerve acted by means of a substance passing through it, *also had to postulate a hollowness or porosity so that this would be possible*. Structure was therefore *determined* by the demands of function' (italics mine). But Willis's paradigmatic works created a revolution in science in that he made it *possible*—in Clarke's sense—to explore the physiology of nerves in the first place. Until the seat of voluntary and involuntary motion was limited to the cerebrum and cerebellum and their network of surrounding nerves, speculation about Clarke's 'form' (i.e. morphology) was necessarily erratic and uncontrollable.

Plate IX Thomas Rowlandson, Frontispiece to *The Vicar of Wakefield*, London 1817 edition (Huntington Library and Art Gallery).

Plate X William Hogarth, 'The Industrious 'Prentice Lord-Mayor of London', *Industry and Idleness*, Plate 12 (Huntington Library and Art Gallery).

precedented hypothesis to deflect bewildered scientists for over a century, to the time of Haller, Whytt and Cullen—that is to say to the very end of the eighteenth century.[18] Unless the consequences of this imaginative leap are fully understood we can never comprehend the origins of those ideas resulting in the diverse cults of sensibility so clearly visible by the middle of the eighteenth century. A new assumption about the fundamental anatomy of man arose

[18] Especially in *Pathologiae Cerebri* and *De Anima Brutorum*. Almost every modern historian of physiology has spoken about Willis with wonder and awe, e.g. Sir Michael Foster, *Lectures on the History of Physiology during the Sixteenth, Seventeenth and Eighteenth Centuries*, Cambridge, 1901; repr. with an intro. by C. D. O'Malley, New York, 1970, p. 269; 'Though Malpighi . . . devoted much attention to the histology of the nervous system, we find in his writings very little concerning its functions. . . . One man alone perhaps during this century stands out prominently for his labours on the structure and functions of the brain, namely Thomas Willis'. One of Willis's most thorough biographers, Dr Hansruedi Isler (*Thomas Willis*, Stuttgart, 1965; tr. by the author, 1968, New York and London), maintains that 'Willis' achievements in neuroanatomy and neurophysiology comprise the first useful theory of brain localization of psychic and vegetative functions as well as the first interpretation of nerve action as an energetic process. His new concept of nerve action led him to the idea—and the term—of reflex action, whereas his localization theory gave rise to the development of experimental physiology of the central nervous system. In order to complete his account of the nervous system Willis described the bulk of the nervous and psychic diseases: the three books he published from 1667 to 1672 contain *the most complete text of neuropsychiatry since Greek antiquity*. Most later interpretations of psychophysical relationships have been influenced by his ideas, either directly or indirectly' (p. x; italics mine). John F. Fulton, surely the most distinguished twentieth-century historian of neurophysiology, considers the cornerstones of modern neurology to be based on six books by Willis (1664), Whytt (1751), Magendie (1822), Hitzig (1874), Ferrier (1876), and Sherrington (1906) (*Physiology of the Nervous System*, 2nd edn, London, 1943, p. 163). Fulton, while recognising some of the important discoveries of Robert Whytt, considers him relatively unimportant in the line of revolutionary theories about brain localisation like those of Willis: 'In his memorable *Cerebri anatome*, published in 1664, Thomas Willis, suggested that the cerebrum presided over voluntary motions and that the cerebellum governed involuntary movements'. Willis had noted that 'when the cerebellum was manipulated in a living animal the heart stopped, and if the cerebellum was removed the animal died. Suggestive indeed was the idea that the cerebellum facilitated involuntary action. . . . There was little further advance until 1809 . . .' (*Physiology of the Nervous System*, p. 463). Kenneth Dewhurst, another biographer of Willis, has also stressed Willis's revolutionary role in the development of modern science: see *Thomas Willis as a Physician*, Los Angeles, 1964. In two other important works, he demonstrates Willis's profound influence on Locke: *John Locke, 1632-1704, Physician and Philosopher: A Medical Biography*, London, 1963, and 'An Oxford Medical Quartet—Sydenham, Willis, Locke, and Lower', *British Medical Journal*, II (1963), 857-80. R. K. French (*Robert Whytt, The Soul, and Medicine*, London, 1969, p. 134) is right to note that 'Towards the end of the century opinion inclined away from placing mental functions in structures within the brain, and many, agreeing with Steno that Willis had been too speculative, favoured a more general placing of the soul in the substance of the brain'. Nicolaus Steno's *Discours . . . sur l'anatomie du cerveau*, Paris, 1669 and Humphrey Ridley's *The Anatomy of the Brain*, London, 1695 were among these works. But *all* these books were answers to Willis and merely attest to his 'paradigmatic' ability to deflect, as Kuhn says, 'succeeding generations of practitioners'.

through Willis's deflection of several generations of scientists, including mechanists, vitalists and animists of every variety and persuasion. The unspoken assumption was hardly a 'paradigm' in Kuhn's sense; but a radically new assumption arose about man's essentially nervous nature. From pure anatomy, it was one step to an integrated physiology of man and just another to a theory of sensory perception, learning, and the further association of ideas. Locke, in the course of time Willis's best student, took these steps perhaps not visibly in the written *Essay* but in the stages that may be construed as the preformation of the *Essay*; and the schools of moral thinkers he in turn deflected—Shaftesbury, Hutcheson, Hume, Adam Smith, and many others—carried his brilliant act of integration to its fullest possible conclusion.[19] Collectively they developed a scientific approach to every aspect of the study of man by means of a theory of sensory perception and a theory of knowledge that directly followed from their understanding of the physiology of perception. Today, we are still the heirs of the revolution. Witness our specialised scientific approaches to the study of man: psychology, sociology, anthropology, psycho-history, psycholinguistics, and so forth. If we understand the revolution set in motion by Willis and Locke, and the theories of the former without the latter would not have had an impact as quickly as they did, then we can at last begin to come to terms with sensibility. We still require narration of the whole story of this development; for I have outlined the crudest sketch and essential features only. Even so, the outline demonstrates some salient facts about European intellectual history in the seventeenth and eighteenth centuries: first that no adequate theory of perception arose, or could arise, until physiological questions pertaining to anatomy were at least partially solved, not by actually *answering* the deepest questions— we know they were not answered—but by endowing the answers with enough authority to permit men seriously to study them, i.e.

[19] While there is a great deal of evidence pointing to Willis's influence on Locke in the *Essay* (see, e.g., Isler, *Thomas Willis*, pp. 176-81, in which Isler traces many Lockean passages to Willis), there is less known about his influence on later physiologists. To propound that Whytt and Haller were perfectly well aware of his theories about voluntary and involuntary motions, and all the replies, rebuttals and disagreements regarding his all-important 'intercostal' nerve, is to indulge in simplicity about the history of science: one might as well set out to prove that Pope had heard of Milton (see R. K. French, *Robert Whytt*, pp. 32ff.). The response of vitalists and animists equally demonstrates clear knowledge (even if it is not always unequivocally stated) of every aspect of Willis's brain theory. See H. Driesch, 'Georg Ernest Stahl (1660-1734)', in *The History and Theory of Vitalism*, tr. C. K. Ogden, London, 1914, pp. 30-6; George Canguilhem, *La Formation du Concept de Reflexe*, Paris, 1955; L. J. Rather, 'Stahl's Psychological Physiology', *Bulletin of the History of Medicine*, XXXV (1961), 37-49.

to permit the serious study of physiology. Second, that a scientific approach to the study of man, such as the one we see flourishing in the eighteenth-century schools of Scottish morality, English empirical philosophy, and even French ethical thought (persuasively presented by Lester Crocker in his books on the subject), required as a prerequisite a developed science of physiology. Call this science anatomy or morphology of the nervous system if you will; in either case it was new. Speculation about it had existed for centuries as a marginal aspect of more general science, but at the end of the seventeenth century it came into its own and permitted, as it were, the new science of man to begin to practise. To decode further at this level, the 'revolution' in anatomical thinking was not an eighteenth-century phenomenon but a late seventeenth. Mechanism, animism and vitalism were responses to previous radical ideas and not radical new ideas themselves. All three depended for their lifeblood on the institutionalisation of physiology as a serious endeavour in itself, and there is good reason that all three philosophical positions were not hotly debated before the end of the seventeenth century. While Willis and his contemporaries can hardly be credited with making the study of physiology respectable by their own teaching, studying and restudying it, texts like his *Anatomy* and *Pathology of the Brain* and those of his student John Locke directly contributed to the 'revolution' we now call the scientific study of man. Whether these men also made it possible in the first place depends almost exclusively on one's theory of cause and effect.

We can now begin to understand all sorts of connections not evident earlier. By comprehending precisely how 'sensation' was at the heart of the revolution in physiology, we can observe how it was also the parent of a child called the science of man. We can, furthermore, see why theological systems, even dissenting theological systems, based on a theory of the soul that was more or less anatomically grounded, were ultimately asked to account for the phenomenon of sensation. But we can do much more. We can now understand realms that hitherto have seemed disparate: the cults of melancholy, hypochondria as a national institution, the 'English Malady', as Cheyne called it, Richardson's novel of sentiment, later on the well-formed and mature 'man of feeling', Sterne's bizarre variations and subtle alterations on this theme, the eighteenth-century's eventual attack on all forms of sentiment as fake; throughout the century the insistence, indeed obsession, with the relation of mind (soul) to body, and, still later, Romanticism with a capital R. We can begin to understand why Mrs Donnellan, no scientist or learned lady, could directly link (in the sense of outright cause and effect) Richardson's wretched health with his far more than usual sensibility as a writer:

> Misfortune is, those who are fit to write delicately, must think so; those who can form a distress must be able to feel it; and as the mind and body are so united as to influence one another, the delicacy is communicated, and one too often finds softness and tenderness of mind in a body equally remarkable for those qualities. Tom Jones could get drunk, and do all sorts of bad things, in the height of his joy for his uncle's recovery. I dare say Fielding is a robust, strong man.[20]

That is, unlike Richardson! This is no 'attempt to console Richardson for his perpetual ill-health', as Ian Watt has suggested;[21] rather than consolation this is the clearest possible indication, at the deepest and most unconscious level, of a revolution in thinking that had been set in motion in the late seventeenth century. All Mrs Donnellan's unstated premises had been scientifically worked out for her by Willis, Locke, and many others. Crudely stated in the form of a syllogism: (a) the soul is limited to the brain; (b) the brain performs the entirety of its work through the nerves; (c) the more 'exquisite' and 'delicate' one's nerves are, morphologically speaking, the greater the ensuing degree of sensibility and imagination; (d) refined people and other persons of fashion are usually born with more 'exquisite' anatomies, the tone and texture of their nervous systems more 'delicate' than those of the lower classes; (e) the greater one's nervous sensibility, the more one is capable of delicate writing. The ordering of the unspoken assumptions here could not be clearer if it tried. They—the assumptions—may conceal a mythology only partly grounded in physiological research; this notwithstanding, they doubtless thrive on an innate and steadfast distinction between persons of different social origins and economic backgrounds. But these assumptions nevertheless formed part of the substratum of thought of an epoch extending over several generations until the early nineteenth century and are not easy to reconstruct at this removal of time. Richardson represented to contemporaries like Mrs Donnellan the man *par excellence* of exquisite and truly delicate sensibility, and other women as well knew why he was able to write so delicately, even if we do not today.

We can now begin to understand that the novel of sentiment in all its multitudinous forms, especially as it developed in the 1740s under Richardson's influence, ultimately owed nothing to the notorious neurological debates between Haller and Whytt, or even

---

[20] *The Correspondence of Samuel Richardson*, ed. Anna L. Barbauld, 6 vols., London, 1804, IV, 30.
[21] *The Rise of The Novel*, Berkeley, 1957, p. 184.

to Richardson's earlier debt to Dr George Cheyne with whom he was on intimate terms and from whom he learned so much about his perverse bodily constitution. Nor did it owe much to Hutcheson's *Passions and Affections* published in 1728, or to his *Ideas of Beauty and Virtue* published in 1725, or to Shaftesbury's *Characteristics* published in 1711. The debate between Haller and Whytt did not erupt until 1751,[22] four years after *Clarissa Harlowe* was published. Even if it had broken earlier, even if it had erupted before Richardson composed *Clarissa*, and even if it could be proved beyond a shadow of all doubt that Richardson absorbed every detail of the Haller-Whytt controversy; even if Richardson himself had revealed to us in the preface to *Clarissa* or elsewhere that his knowledge about sensibility and science, sentiment and the heart, derived from his intensive reading about the controversy—that would prove nothing more than token influence.

For we, like Kuhn early in the 1960s, have not been decoding at a level of mere surface and linear relation or of necessarily one-to-one and direct influence. And it is consequently of no more concern to us whether Richardson read Haller and Whytt, or Haller *or* Whytt, for example, than whether he read Dr Cheyne or Hutcheson or Shaftesbury before them. His reading is of immense concern to Richardsonians only as Sterne's is to Sterneans. What counts to those among us who would understand the deepest levels, the most original ideas, which made the many cults of sensibility possible in the first place—whether in the novel or elsewhere in imaginative literature—is the simple fact (and it is so simple that we have never bothered to notice it) that no novel of sensibility could appear until a revolution in knowledge concerning the brain, and consequently its slaves, the nerves, had occurred. If Sterne or Smollett, or even Jane Austen with *Sense and Sensibility,* had chronologically pre-empted Richardson by writing for the first time about the delights of moral sentiments or charitable sensibility, it would make no substantive or even impressionable difference to the historian of ideas. For Mrs Donnellan has already told us *why* Richardson could perform so well in this species of writing, and presumably she would have found similar explanations for an ailing Sterne or Smollett or Austen, or for that matter a suitable Hogarth, Reynolds, or Gainsborough, a Handel or Boyce. Her explanation for exquisite refinement in painting or music would not have substantially differed from the one she gives for the physiologically sensible Richardson; and her testimony is valid because, like dozens of other similar passages in eighteenth-century letters, it was uttered without

[22] For the most exhaustive survey of the controversy, see R. K. French, 'The Controversy with Haller: Sense and Sensibility', in *Robert Whytt*, pp. 63-76.

any degree of forethought or premeditation and in a moment of total sincerity. She is obliged to give *no* elaborate reasoning, because her unstated assumptions are precisely those of the age. Nor does it matter in the least whether she was right in any absolute sense: each age is entitled to believe what it wishes, to create the revolutions in knowledge it desires; and even if we profoundly wish it otherwise, generations of men in the future will continue to fabricate their own mythologies despite subsequent protestations.

It is our task—and I hope I will be forgiven for such heavy-handed moralising—neither to falsify the unspoken and unwritten ideas of previous ages, nor to give emphasis or credit where it is not due. But an even greater task for contemporary intellectual historians is a steadfast refusal to reduce highly complex contents to embarrassingly simple structures that neither do justice to reality nor ask or answer the 'big' questions. The simple fact of literary history, for example, that it took almost thirty or forty years for English writers to grasp the full extent of the brain-nerve revolution, is of no greater interest, except to literary specialists, than what Richardson actually read. Recent imaginative writers in this century have taken that long, if not longer, to understand at the level of unspoken assumption paradigmatic works by Darwin, Einstein, Freud, Heisenberg, and others—and some still have not. The exact chronological distance in years between writers of sensibility (such as Richardson, Sterne, Mackenzie, Sade) and the intellectual revolutionaries themselves—in this case Willis and his pioneering Oxford and London colleagues—must remain an academic sport to engage the attention of highly specialised scholars of the interrelations of science and literature. So, also, must the precise manner in which the brain-nerve revolution influenced the totality of medical research from 1680 onwards. That must concern a small group of medical historians primarily.

Our task is to chart the blurry interconnections of seemingly non-related realms. In doing so for sensibility, we can also understand why it is virtually unnecessary for us to demonstrate the influence of particular thinkers on these writers of sensibility when we decode at this substratum of uttered thought. It would indeed almost be improper. For given that a physiological theory of perception was a necessary condition to explain feelings of every sort (whether genuine or otherwise) and especially the diversity of simple and complex passions, it is of little concern to us, and certainly no cause for celebration, if we discover an identical passage or perfectly clear analogue in a scientific work known to have influenced the writer in question. We must consider as arbitrary which scientific author wrote the following: 'Feeling is nothing but the Impulse,

Motion or Action of Bodies, gently or violently impressing the Extremities or Sides of the Nerves, of the Skin, or other parts of the Body, which . . . convey Motion to the Sentient Principle in the Brain'.[23] It is immaterial to us, who would understand the truest origins of sensibility, if the author of this passage is Haller, Whytt, Hartley, La Mettrie, Hume, Cheyne, William Hunter, Nicholas Robinson, Ephraim Chambers, Hermann Boerhaave, Hutcheson, Shaftesbury, or any one of a dozen other scientific thinkers. It happens to be Dr Cheyne, Richardson's confidante, but any of these men could have written it. Only if it appeared in a work written before the paradigmatic books of Willis, Locke and their colleagues would we be concerned.[24] My contention all along is that it could not have appeared earlier; that it was impossible before the revolution in brain theory to expect the totality of human feeling to be nothing but motion in the nerves. Considered in the broadest sense, this implies that every response to a moral crisis is physiologically grounded, fated, and determined in the *a priori* sense.

Even more important, we can now begin to understand why all diseases, not merely those considered hysterical and hypochondriacal, were eventually classified as 'nervous' and after a reasonable amount of time were internalised by persons of fashion as visible emblems of refinement and delicacy—thereby functioning as tangible proof of distinct upper-crust difference from the lower and middle classes. Slowly but surely, it becomes painfully clear that Richardson, Sterne, Diderot, Rousseau, Mackenzie, and even the Marquis de Sade were the posterity of two generations of thinkers who had increasingly 'internalised'—and that is the important word—the new science of man, directing thought about man from his visible eyes and expressive face to his unseen nerves and controlling brain, from what he looks like to what he feels, and from what he feels to what he knows. Internalisation as a process means that man is no longer satisfied to understand himself as a doer of deeds and a thinker of thoughts. He—man—wants to know precisely how his feelings have shaped his knowledge; and for the first time in European history he is unable to keep them separate, unable not to relate his emotions to his percipience. Richardson penetrates his own fictive creation Clarissa, as Sade does his Justine, by turning inwards and internalising the relation between Clarissa's anatomy, feelings, actions, and finally knowledge. Clarissa must die, as many heroines before her

[23] The passage is found in George Cheyne, M.D., *The English Malady*, 2 vols., London, 1733, I, 71.
[24] One can test the hypothesis by consulting scientific works written in the 1650s, especially by Hobbes and some of the early Cambridge Platonists; nowhere is the brain invoked in this manner before 1664, the date of publication of Willis's *Cerebri Anatome*.

must die, but in her case for the first time, we know precisely why: we have watched her quest for respect proceed from the smallest animal spirit and nerve through all her exquisite delicacy and sensibility to a full knowledge of herself. As Clarissa and her maker further know, internalisation is impossible without an analogue, whether stated or implied, of body and mind. But we would falsify matters if we continued to believe that such an analogue owed its birth to the mid eighteenth century; in fact it was already fairly mature in Shaftesbury's formative years in the first decade of the eighteenth century.[25] Smollett's analysis of his last and greatest hero, Matt Bramble, couched in words well-meditated at the level of unconscious assumption only, could be the epigraph of all writers from Richardson to the Marquis de Sade: 'I think his peevishness', says his nephew Jery Melford, 'arises partly from bodily pain, and partly from a natural excess of mental sensibility'.[26] And Goldsmith's account of Sir William Thornhill (Mr Burchell in disguise) in *The Vicar of Wakefield*, the man who saved the Vicar and his family from destruction, and who is perhaps Goldsmith's most genuinely benevolent character, loses no opportunity to ground itself in a body-mind analogy that was old by 1766: 'Physicians tell us of a disorder', says Goldsmith, 'in which the whole body is so exquisitely sensible, that the slightest touch gives pain: what some have thus suffered in their persons, this gentleman felt in his mind. The slightest distress, whether real or fictitious, touched him to the quick, and his soul laboured under a sickly sensibility of the miseries of others'.[27] Body-mind analogies could not have become conventional in sentimental literature without an antecedent theory of nervous diseases widely disseminated throughout the culture, and this theory ultimately owes little to Burton, Bacon, Thomas Browne, and other seventeenth-century anatomists of melancholy. It is as if the infinitely expanding universe, upon which Addison and Pope had dwelt at such length, had to close up again, this time involuting itself on man's inner universe, before the process of internalisation could come full circle at the end of the eighteenth century.

But we can also begin to understand why that most puzzling of

[25] A list like this perhaps raises questions about Defoe and Fielding: were they not exposed to the same ideas as Richardson? Were their nerves any less sensible? Yes, Fielding received similar exposure—everyone did—but his physiology, the era of Mrs Donnellan would have argued, was much less exquisite than Richardson's. The truth is of course more elaborate than this but, however crude, her answer is an approximation, and we see it splendidly mirrored in Johnson's estimate of Fielding as a 'barren rascal'.

[26] *Humphry Clinker*, London, 1771; J. Melford to Sir Watkin Phillips, 18 April.

[27] In *Collected Works*, ed. Arthur Friedman, 5 vols., Oxford, 1966, IV, 29,

modern enigmas, Romanticism, was in turn the heir to a heritage of the cults of sensibility, thereby going beyond the best all-encompasing definition we thus far have, that of Harold Bloom. For if one accepts his enticing idea that it is proper to speak of Romanticism in literature only at the moment when conventional motifs of 'the quest' are internalised,[28] then we can start to see why the intricate process of internalisation itself required a specific neurological legacy. It is not true that Romanticism, understood in this way, could have occurred at any time. First a revolution in knowledge about man, set in motion by certain paradigmatic works, had to occur; and then the diverse cults of sensibility, religious, social, moral, literary, even fashionable, had to play themselves out. While they did, theories about man became increasingly internalised and it was no longer important to pretend, as Swift had, that man could or even ought to be merely a cerebrating creature. Imaginative writers could now return to 'the quest', then centuries upon centuries old, and internalise it—that is, accommodate their feelings to a new set of ideas about it—as readily, as naturally, as scientific thinkers of every persuasion had been internalising philosophical theories about the nature of man throughout the eighteenth century.

---

[28] Such is Bloom's theory in *The Visionary Company: A Reading of English Romantic Poetry*, New York, 1961; rev. and enl. edn, 1971. Bloom, taking his cue from Northrop Frye, titles his first chapter 'The Heritage of Sensibility'.

Philosophie et Littérature

Yvon Belaval

Entre l'expression que nous appelons—depuis quand?—littéraire et l'expression philosophique, il ne semble pas y avoir de différence essentielle; maints exemples le prouveraient: le poème de Parménide, ou de Lucrèce, le théâtre à thèse, le conte ou le roman philosophique (sans oublier les utopies), le réalisme militant sous toutes ses formes. Il arrive que l'œuvre littéraire se voue, didactique, à exposer un système: le *De Natura rerum*. Parfois elle introduit dans son récit une moralité, une réplique, un discours, une page, transcrite ou récrite, d'un philosophe: Ainsi, au début de *Gil Blas*, on entend qu'un flatteur vit aux dépens de celui qui l'écoute, Thomas Mann n'arrête pas de philosopher par la bouche de ses personnages —écoutez le Settembrini du *Zauberberg*—Sade pille Fréret, Voltaire, d'Holbach,[1] et l'on peut repérer, dans Heidegger, la source d'un passage de *La Nausée* sur le surgissement de l'existence. Parfois encore l'écrivain cache son jeu: dans *Le Mur*, Sartre combine les observations du Dr Gualino sur les condamnés à mort et la polémique sur le mensonge entre Kant et Benjamin Constant; personne ne devinerait dans *Le Chiendent* de Raymond Queneau le projet primitif de traduire le *Discours de la méthode* en français populaire, ni, malgré le titre, une substructure hégélienne dans *Le Dimanche de la vie*. Parfois enfin l'auteur s'inspire ou est censé s'inspirer d'un penseur dont il ne retient que la thèse en négligeant les arguments: on a parlé du bergsonisme de Marcel Proust.

Pourtant un philosophe n'écrit pas, ne pense pas comme un littérateur; un littérateur n'écrit ni ne pense comme un philosophe. Apparaît une différence essentielle d'abord inaperçue. C'est que le philosophe n'écrit pas pour produire un effet; il pense par concepts (même contre les concepts); s'il traite de sentiments, d'images ou d'actions, ce n'est pas pour les peindre et les donner à vivre, mais pour les analyser, les expliquer ou les comprendre en leurs essences.

---

[1] Jean Deprun, 'Quand Sade récrit Fréret, Voltaire, et d'Holbach', pp. 331-40 dans *Roman et lumières au XVIII⁰ siècle*, Paris, 1970.

Nous voici loin du 'donner à voir' du poète. On ne déduit pas une action, on la raconte. Ecoutons Diderot: partout, estime-t-il, on constate la

> décadence de la verve et de la poésie, à mesure que l'esprit philosophique a fait des progrès. . . . Platon chasse les poètes de la cité. L'esprit philosophique veut des comparaisons plus resserrées, plus strictes, plus rigoureuses. Sa marche circonspecte est ennemie du mouvement et des figures. Le règne des images passe à mesure que celui des choses s'étend. Il s'introduit par la raison . . . une sorte de pédanterie qui tue tout. . . . L'esprit philosophique amène le style sentencieux et sec. . . .[2]

Il n'est pas bon, pour une œuvre littéraire, que la philosophie saille trop, comme 'ce maudit écorché', pour citer encore Diderot, sous les nus de la peinture académique. Quand même une telle œuvre contiendrait une philosophie sous-jacente, il n'est pas nécessaire de connaître cette dernière pour apprécier, voire pour bien juger le mérite de l'art: que serait un psychanalyste qui ne séparerait pas de la psychanalyse le plaisir de contempler un Chagall? La vérité philosophique est évidemment essentielle à la philosophie, mais non à la littérature. On ne prend pas *Jacques le Fataliste* pour l'*Ethique*, ni *Candide* pour la *Théodicée*.

Où en sommes-nous? Il nous avait d'abord semblé, sur des exemples, que la lecture littéraire et la lecture philosophique pouvaient se confondre; à présent, il nous semble que l'une chasse l'autre, comme imager exclut percevoir ou l'inverse. Comment cela est-il possible? Une réponse générale demanderait un livre. Et qui l'écrirait? C'est sans doute un effet du paradoxe où se forme notre question, que les 'littéraires' se montrent les plus enclins, mais les philosophes les plus circonspects, à faire de l'intention, volontaire ou involontaire, de l'écrivain, une intention philosophique. Nous cherchons seulement quelques éléments de réponse. Ils peuvent n'être pas sans conséquences sur l'orientation de la critique littéraire. Où les trouver? Par chance il existe un siècle où les philosophes se sont voulus écrivains et les écrivains philosophes. Il facilite notre enquête. Avec ses lumières, le dix-huitième siècle nous permettra de mieux éclairer la différence de deux disciplines qui, tantôt paraissent s'unir, et tantôt se séparent.

Le progrès des sciences de plus en plus incontestable et la secousse révolutionnaire ont amené le dix-huitième siècle à prendre, le

---

[2] Salon de 1767; dans *Œuvres complètes*, tom. VII, Paris, 1970, pp. 165-6. Et l'abbé Trublet (1735) écrivait déjà: 'La sorte d'esprit qui fait qu'on sent toute la beauté d'un roman est bien différente de celle qui fait qu'on entend aisément et qu'on s'arrange nettement dans la tête un système philosophique' (*Essais sur divers sujets de littérature et de morale*, Paris, 1739, tom. I, première partie, chap. V).

premier entre tous les siècles, conscience de son originalité.[3] Il s'est voulu expréssement 'philosophique', mais par opposition à tout ontologie: en démarquant un mot célèbre, on dirait assez bien qu'alors la philosophie est descendue du ciel sur la terre; c'est en cela qu'elle a pu devenir littéraire. Mais avant d'en venir—et pour mieux en venir—à la littérature, suivons, à vol d'oiseau, le passage du ciel des dogmatismes au sol des empirismes.

Le dogmatisme croit que ses concepts lui font connaître l'absolu. Jusqu'à Descartes, dans une tradition platonicienne, les essences, que peut intuitionner le regard de l'esprit, sont—estime le dogmatique—hors de nous, dans les lieux des intelligent, ou τόπος εἰδῶν, dont notre monde participe. La révolution cartésienne les rend immanentes à notre esprit sous la forme d'idées innées que Dieu a imprimées en nous, comme un ouvrier imprime sa marque en son ouvrage: ces idées n'en gardent pas moins, dans la connaissance que nous pouvons avoir du monde et de l'homme, une valeur ontologique, garantie par la véracité divine. Avec Locke—sautons les intermédiaires—cette idée, toujours immanente, perd sa valeur ontologique; Voltaire la définira: 'une image qui se peint dans notre cerveau'; la voici subjective, rien de plus que psychologique; produite—et garantie—par le seule expérience des sens, il serait désormais contradictoire de lui attribuer l'innéité. Il n'y a donc de *connaissance* que des *phénomènes*. Par les idées, notre raison n'accède pas à l'absolu et doit se borner au savoir, relatif aux sens, qu'elles lui proposent. En revanche, l'analyse de ces idées acquises, et, par conséquent, la recherche de leur origine, nous permettra, par leur liaison au sensible, de progresser en un savoir de plus en plus efficace sur le monde et sur l'homme. En d'autres termes, la théorie lockienne de l'idée ouvre le champ des sciences expérimentales de la nature, dans une perspective newtonienne et, quant à l'homme, la voie à l'*idéologie*: 'cette science', dit fort bien l'auteur anonyme du *Tableau littéraire de la France*

> n'a rien, ou presque rien de commun avec l'ancienne métaphysique. En renonçant à celle-ci, on a cherché dans le XVIII e siècle, ce qu'on ne s'était pas encore avisé de chercher: le rapport des idées avec les signes, du raisonnement avec le langage. Le métaphysique n'était auparavant ni une science ni un art, car des hypothèses ne constituent pas une science et des

---

[3] Roland Mortier vient de le prouver en publiant un inédit tout à fait remarquable, *Le 'Tableau littéraire de la France au XVIIIe siècle'. Un épisode de la 'guerre philosophique' à l'Académié française sous l'Empire (1804-1810)*, Bruxelles, 1972. Ce *Tableau* est une pièce, non couronnée, d'un concours académique proposé dès 1804. L'auteur reste anonyme. En le présentant, Roland Mortier observe (p. 13): 'L'idée même de faire, au tournant d'un siècle, le bilan d'un centenaire est déjà un phénomène curieux et nouveau dont on ne trouve le précédent ni en 1700, ni auparavant'.

méthodes vicieuses ne forment point un art, mais on sent, à présent, qu'elle peut devenir l'une et l'autre, par l'observation et l'analyse des facultés. (pp. 117-18)

Si, pour notre anonyme, Condillac, en suivant les traces de Locke, sauve la métaphysique, ce n'est qu'au sens où Lazare Carnot, par exemple, parle de la *Métaphysique du calcul infinitésimal*.

L'idée de Dieu, elle aussi, se psychologise. Du coup, que démontrerait-elle? Ni pour le dogmatique ni pour le sceptique, la raison n'a jamais prétendu démontrer la Révélation: au mieux en admettra-t-elle la possibilité. Tout ce à quoi il lui est légitime de prétendre ne dépasse pas la théologie naturelle—le dieu des philosophes. Cette théologie n'exige que nos lumières naturelles. Mais, de tout évidence, l'appellation 'naturelles' n'a plus la même signification selon que l'on invoque une raison qui tire sa nécessité, ou son libre-arbitre logique d'une transcendance divine, ou bien une raison qui ne saurait qu'induire, avec plus ou moins de vraisemblance, à partir de ses idées acquises, expérimentales. Les 'Lumières' du dix-huitième relèvent d'une autre nature que le *Lumen naturale* de la théologie et du dogmatisme traditionnels. Pour l'expérience sensible, l'idée de l'infini n'est jamais que l'idée d'un indéfini. Pour une raison empirique l'absolu échappe à toute idée et, comme elle n'est plus, par doctrine, éclairée par un *Lumen supernaturale*, ni la Révélation ni les miracles n'entrent parmi les faits historiques dont elle pourrait faire une preuve expérimentale. Au résultat, l'idée psychologique de Dieu n'autorise que le déisme—ou l'athéisme: Voltaire et Rousseau—ou d'Holbach et Sade.

Un dernier mot sur cette connaissance par idées acquises. On l'a nommée (plus tard): sensualisme. Si l'on s'en tient à l'habitude de la définir par la vieille maxime 'il n'y a rien en notre entendement qui ne vienne des sens', on ne voit pas ce que le dix-huitième siècle apporte de nouveau à l'affaire. Voici le nouveau: dans le contexte traditionnel, les Idées ne sont pas des tableaux inertes, des images-copies, mais des Formes et, par suite, l'entendement lui-même n'est pas une table rase, indifférente, mais une activité qui collabore avec les 'choses' pour mettre en forme les sensations qu'elle en reçoit; le nouveau du sensualisme au dix-huitième siècle est que son refus de l'innéisme des idées entraîne—jusque'à Kant—le refus des structures de l'entendement.

Nous n'avons parcouru que la moitié de notre tour du monde philosophique. C'est l'innéisme des *idées* qui est exclu par Locke, et non celui du *sentiment*. Le scepticisme caractérise la théorie de la connaissance; quelque dogmatisme du 'cœur' commande peut-être l'action. Certes, dans la mesure où l'on estime qu'une opinion, un sentiment, une conduite ne s'organise que par la finalité d'une idée, il n'est jamais inné si l'idée est toujours acquise. Ainsi, 'l'instinct n'est rien', affirme Condillac, il se ramène à l'habitude. Allons plus loin que Condillac: supposons héréditaire l'habitude ou même, sans nous déclarer sur ce point, faisons naître l'action directement du corps, alors l'instinct est une fonction organique—et à tout être son corps est inné—en ce sens la raison, prolongement de l'organisme humain, devient, pour Diderot, un instinct. Il vaut la peine de noter, en passant, que le formalisme dont on privait l'entendement reparaît subrepticement avec le fonctionnement spécifique d'un organisme—et si l'on organicise la nature, fût-ce par la dynamique, il se cache dans la nature. En définitive, l'utile, qui circonscrit tout, n'est pas seulement l'avantage que nous obtenons par calcul en nous servant d'outils et d'échanges sociaux, il est aussi celui des 'vues de la nature'. Ici encore, l'auteur anonyme du *Tableau littéraire de la France* distingue fort bien:

> Il en est de cette volupté morale qu'occasionne la lecture d'un ouvrage bien pensé, bien écrit, comme de cet autre plaisir que nous fait éprouver, au physique, la satisfaction des besoins qui contribuent à la conservation et à la reproduction des êtres: Ce plaisir, dans les vues de la nature, n'est qu'un attrait pour arriver à d'autres fins: il en est de même en littérature.
>
> (p. 99)

Par le principe du plaisir, la nature nous guide selon ses fins: en termes de société nous recherchons tous le bonheur. D'où l'utilité des passions. Mais souvent les fins de la nature correspondent si peu à nos idées, qu'elles nous déconcertent, nous paraissent monstrueuses et énigmatiques: Ainsi sommes-nous contraints d'admettre l'utilité profonde du nuisible apparent, l'intérêt des grands crimes, la méchanceté du génie, ce médium de la nature. Souvent encore, en remontant à l'origine de nos facultés, nous devons reconnaître à la passion sa part obscure: à l'origine du langage, par exemple, les onomatopées imitent sans dessein pré-établi, les cris et les exclamations suivent la courbe émotionnelle des besoins et des sentiments élémentaires, se psalmodient, se mélodient, s'articulent sur elle. Pas d'esthétique—le mot apparait au milieu du siècle—qui n'invoque un *nescio quid* dont le secret s'enveloppe dans la nature, en-deçà de nos idées. C'est surtout en morale que, dès ses premières années, le dix-huitième a dénoncé les insuffisances de l'intellectualisme. La question semblait insoluble puisqu'elle consistait à tirer de l'expérience toujours muable, singulière, subjective, une morale immuable, universelle, objective. Locke pensait encore que, sans l'existence de Dieu, la morale était impossible; Shaftesbury, son élève, pensait, au contraire, qu'elle devait se suffire par elle-même; dès lors, si tout nous vient des sens, il faut qu'un sixième sens intervienne, le sens moral (on a aussi parlé d'un sens du beau) dont la spécificité tienne lieu d'universalité et qui, comme tout sens, ne s'éveille qu'avec l'expérience. Dans le vocabulaire de Georges Gurwitch, nous avons là une morale de *sens commun sentimental*. Avec Rousseau, nous nommerions dans le même vocabulaire, une morale de *l'intuition sentimentale*. Au fond, Rousseau, quand il définit l'homme d'avant la société, l'homme naturel, par la 'perfectibilité', c'est-à-dire par la raison en puissance, renvoie, traditionnellement, à l'essence métaphysique d'un être raisonnable; et comme, non moins traditionnellement, une essence ne comporte rien de contradictoire qui la rende impossible, l'homme est bon, heureux par nature. L'accident se produit par la naissance de la société et, avec elle, de l'histoire. Voilà l'expérience malheureuse: Ce n'est plus celle de la nature; elle actualise par contrainte la raison et fait de l'homme qui médite 'un animal dépravé', un animal dont 'l'instinct divin', l'intuition sentimentale, de sa vraie nature, exige toujours une ascèse.

A ce parcours, à vol d'oiseau, qu'avons-nous aperçu? 1. Que la philosophie, au dix-huitième siècle, se sépare des ontologies dogmatiques; elle rejette la métaphysique des grands systèmes. 2. Qu'en refusant d'admettre des idées innées, elle réduit la raison aux certitudes et aux limites du bon sens. 3. Qu'en regard de ce scepticisme dont elle se fait gloire ('apprendre à bien douter'), elle nourrit, en son culte de la nature, une sorte de dogmatisme du sentiment, qui, en fait, avant tout, une philosophie pratique (du sens commun).

Lorsque, participant au concours académique de 1804, Eusèbe Salverte écrit: 'Le XVIIIe siècle a pris et ne peut plus perdre le nom de Siècle de la philosophie. Les philosophes du XVIIIe siècle appartiennent presque tous à la littérature',[4] nous savons maintenant quelle philosophie s'adresse à la littérature et nous devinons quelle aide la littérature, avec la diversité de ses genres, et la force de ses expressions peut, en retour, apporter à cette philosophie populaire.

Cette philosophie a renoncé à la recherche de l'absolu dont elle croit la raison incapable: elle s'en tient au relativisme des apparences que nous offrent les sens et l'imagination. Observer et décrire ces apparences, voilà donc la première tâche. N'est-ce-pas à une tâche analogue que se consacrent la littérature, les beaux-arts et même, pour le dix-huitième siècle, la musique? Il leur fait *peindre* la nature humaine ou physique, telle qu'elle apparaît, imiter le sensible, imager, imaginer. Nous avons dit 'tâche analogue' et non pas 'identique': dans l'un et l'autre cas, on ne procède point par

---

[4] Cité dans *Tableau littéraire*, p. 79.

concepts *a priori* et l'on se défie de l'abstrait, mais l'imagination du philosophe doit se soumettre à la nature, celle de l'écrivain ou de l'artiste doit se soumettre la nature, l'une s'impose en fait, l'autre transpose le fait: là on s'applique au vrai, ici au vraisemblable. Analogiquement, des deux côtés, on observe, on décrit, on encyclopédise, et l'on finit souvent par se rejoindre: Le Jardin des Plantes a ses peintres au service de la science, comme les amateurs d'art ont les leurs, souvent aussi exacts, au service du beau, et Diderot, en s'habituant aux *Salons*, invente un nouveau regard d'écrivain qui va modifier le portrait romanesque (Balzac naît à la fin du siècle); les *Voyages* forment un genre intermédiaire entre le rapport scientifique et le récit d'aventures, comme les *Mémoires* entre l'histoire et le roman. Mais décrire ne suffit pas, il faut sauver les phénomènes, les lier entre eux par des lois. Newton devient alors le modèle idéal aussi bien pour le philosophe qui, à la manière de Hume, rêve d'être le Newton du monde moral, que pour le romancier, car 's'il est une ambition', commente Jean Sgard, 'qui définit, à partir de 1730, l'écrivain éclairé, c'est celle de découvrir dans l'univers ou dans l'histoire un ordre rationnel, un sens, des lois. . . . L'ordre social ou l'ordre international apparaissent comme des ensembles régis par des lois aussi rigoureuses que celles de Newton: où l'on cherchait les destins particuliers et l'étoile, on cherche maintenant des gravitations'.[5] Pour expliquer un phénomène, on l'analyse, c'est-à-dire on le décompose, mentalement ou expérimentalement, pour remonter à ses éléments simples ou supposés simples: la perception en sensations, la société en individus; après quoi on le recompose. Cette méthode est génétique. Cette genèse a ceci de particulier au dix-huitième siècle qu'elle ne peut partir ni d'un Dieu créateur, ni d'un principe inné, l'innéisme étant rejeté. L'analyse doit suppléer au manque de Dieu et d'inné: elle fait du dix-huitième le siècle qui s'interroge sur l'origine. Ici encore, le philosophe et l'écrivain conçoivent l'origine, chacun à sa manière: ce n'est pas en romancier que Rousseau imagine l'origine des langues, de l'inégalité parmi les hommes ou de la société légitime. Que l'on traduise *genèse* par *histoire,* on verra mieux à la suite la différence et l'identité analogique de la philosophie et de la littérature. Lorsque Voltaire intitule 'philosophie de l'histoire' sa première Préface à l'*Essai sur les mœurs*, il l'entend, à peu près, au sens de *Natural philosophy*; quant à l'histoire elle-même, il sait que pour en faire une science, il doit l'arracher aux dialogues, aux discours, aux portraits par lesquels, sous prétexte de la rendre plus vivante, on la rapprochait du roman. A l'inverse, pour l'écrivain, le

---

[5] 'Aventure et politique: le mythe de Bonneval', in *Roman et lumières,* p. 416.

roman doit se présenter comme une histoire—que de titres en 'histoire de . . .'! —dont on feint de faire passer l' 'au vraisemblable' pour du vrai. Au total, l'exclusion par Locke des idées innées impose au philosophe l'analyse des idées acquises pour en retrouver la genèse; transposée à la littérature, cette analyse devient l'histoire éducative d'une formation, un *Bildungsroman:* A l'intersection de la philosophie et de la littérature, on placerait l'analyse psychologique, conduite par l'idéologue ou par le romancier.

Une fois dégrisés, par l'expérience, des illusions métaphysiques, il ne nous reste plus qu'à cultiver notre jardin. Attachons-nous à l'étude du monde pour en exploiter les richesses. Attachons-nous à nous connaître pour mieux mesurer nos limites et nos pouvoirs. Les théories sur le monde et sur l'homme ne nous importent que liées ou liables à la pratique. Dans toute pratique on a finalement affaire à la Nature, où s'enracinent nos besoins et, par là même, nos idées: 'La nature, c'est-à-dire nos facultés déterminées par nos besoins', écrit Condillac en son *Traité des sensations.* Elle devient pour la philosophie du dix-huitième siècle, le nouvel universel nécessaire, le principe régulateur qui remplace l'ancienne raison dogmatique. Elle règle nos jugements. Elle décide de la vérité de nos opinions droites. La véritable religion est naturelle, le véritable droit est naturel, la véritable économie consiste à laisser faire, à laisser passer la nature, nos véritables sentiments sont naturels, et ainsi de suite: c'est toujours à la lumière naturelle que le philosophe doit analyser les passions qui nous meuvent et les institutions qui nous obligent. Bien entendu, cette thèse fondamentale est aussi celle de l'écrivain, de l'artiste, du musicien: il faut imiter la nature. Rousseau insiste sur l'universel nécessaire de la passion par delà les événements historiques des *Confessions* ou romanesques d'*Emile et Sophie.* Le philosophe écrit: 'Et qu'on n'objecte pas que n'étant qu'un homme du peuple, je n'ai rien à dire qui mérite l'attention des lecteurs. Cela peut être vrai des évenemens de ma vie: mais j'écris moins l'histoire de ces éve[ne]mens en eux-mêmes que celle de l'état de mon ame, à mesure qu'ils sont arrivés';[6] puis il passe la plume au romancier qui répète: 'ce n'est pas ici l'histoire des événemens de ma vie; ils valent peu la peine d'être écrits; c'est l'histoire de mes passions, de mes sentimens, de mes idées'.[7] Diderot ne veut pas montrer autre chose dans son théâtre des conditions où les conditions ne changent rien—tout au contraire de ce que soutiendrait aujourdhui le théâtre militant d'un marxiste—à l'universel des passions. Nous pouvons généraliser: C'est parce qu'elle se veut plus

---

[6] *Œuvres complètes*, éd. Bernard Gagnebin et Marcel Raymond, tom. I, Paris, 1959, p. 1150.
[7] Ibid., tom. IV, Paris, 1969, p. 890.

pratique que théorique, ce qui signifie en définitive plus politique, que la philosophie du dix-huitième siècle élabore les thèmes directement utilisables par la littérature en ses imitations de la nature et de l'expérience de la vie. Est-il besoin de rappeler ces thèmes et de les classer selon l'antithétique où l'innéité de la nature s'oppose à la convention sociale? Mettrons-nous en regard l'égalité et les privilèges, la liberté et l'esclavage, la bonté et la méchanceté, la fraternité et la lutte, le bonheur et l'inquiétude, le sauvage et le policé, la communauté des biens naturels et la propriété de l'argent et des terres, l'amour libre et l'amour contraint, la simplicité primitive et le luxe, la pureté des mœurs et le vice sous l'habit de soie, l'utile et le nuisible, le bon sens et le déraisonnable, le langage d'action et le langage de convention, le droit naturel et le droit positif, la religion naturelle (ou déisme) et la superstition, la tolérance et le fanatisme? On pourrait allonger la liste. A chaque terme, à chaque opposition, ou à toute autre combinaison de termes, on associerait aisément une œuvre philosophique et une œuvre littéraire et l'on se trouverait souvent dans la difficulté de distinguer l'un de l'autre le philosophe et l'écrivain. C'est que l'un et l'autre travaillent sur un propos commun: instruire et éduquer, servir la 'vraie' morale, interroger sur le progrès.

D'un autre point de vue, en abandonnant le latin et le vocabulaire scolastique pour la langue de l'honnête homme, le philosophe ne pouvait que devenir un écrivain. L'astronomie elle-même est enseignable aux dames en style galant; Fontenelle, auteur d'*Eglogues* devenues illisibles, le prouve par ses *Entretiens sur la pluralité des mondes*.[8] Fénelon n'écrit pas seulement le *Traité de l'existence de Dieu*, mais aussi il passe pour le créateur du poème en prose par ses *Fables*, surtout par son *Télémaque*; et à propos des occupations de l'Académie traite du style, en particulier pour l'histoire. Buffon aussi traite du style, et, dans son *Histoire naturelle*, 'Il a créé', dit l'anonyme du Concours académique de 1808, 'une sorte d'éloquence poétique, différente de celle des mouvements et des passions. Nul autre, avant lui, n'avait eu ce genre d'éloquence qui, comme écrivain, constitue son originalité'.[9] D'Alembert se veut écrivain, traduit, collectionne des synonymes. Inversement, le jeune écrivain Voltaire va se changer en philosophe. Une fois la philosophie devenue morale, politique, polémiste, ses thèmes sont repris par la poésie, parfois didactique (Delille, Chénier), le théâtre (Voltaire, Diderot, Sedaine, etc.), le roman, le conte, les pamphlets, les articles

---

[8] J'ai voulu traiter la philosophie d'une manière qui ne fût point philosophique . . . ni trop sèche pour les gens de monde, ni trop badine pour les savants' (début des *Entretiens*).
[9] *Tableau littéraire*, p. 117.

du journalisme naissant. La littérature exprime la philosophie: elle a mis au point la *maxime* qui se frappe en vers ou en réplique sur la scène; elle anime les *dialogues*; elle disserte par la bouche des personnages; elle se répand dans les *Lettres* du roman épistolaire (par exemple, la *Nouvelle Héloïse*, Partie IV, Lettre X et Partie V, Lettre II, expose des principes économiques). Il arrive que le philosophe romancier ou le romancier philosophe, Diderot, montre les coulisses de son roman, *Jacques le Fataliste*, pour en dénoncer le fictif, et en dévoiler le vrai. Dans un autre domaine, la doctrine (philosophique) sur l'origine des langues inspire les récitatifs de l'opéra-comique. Il s'est trouvé au dix-huitième siècle que les plus grands entre les écrivains aient été tous des philosophes.

Reste à se demander quel genre de lecture philosophique permet une œuvre littéraire du dix-huitième siècle.

Si l'on ne veut pas trahir l'esprit d'un siècle qui proscrit la métaphysique, il faut exclure, semble-t-il, le recours à l'ontologie des grands dogmatismes, même quand l'écrivain les tourne en dérision. Les a-t-il réellement étudiés? Il est douteux que Diderot ait lu l'*Ethique*. Souvent l'écrivain se contente d'un article de Bayle ou de Brucker. Serait-il remonté au texte original, peut-être ne l'aura-t-il parcouru qu'en créateur et non en philologue. Enfin, dès qu'on ne voit en un système qu'un roman de métaphysique, on n'en fait plus, en quelque sorte, qu'une lecture effaçante.

De toute manière, l'écrivain ne saurait reprendre un système philosophique qu'en lui faisant subir une transposition littéraire; cette transposition rappelle l'embarras de la critique picturale: on a beau parler de peinture, on ne parle pas la peinture. Certes, nous l'avons déja indiqué, au lieu de transposer, de traduire, un auteur insère souvent dans son œuvre des tirades philosophiques, au besoin découpées dans les pages d'un philosophe: mais alors il faudrait les extraire de l'œuvre où elles ont été insérées pour effacer les traces de leur transposition, dans un contexte littéraire; une philosophie dans le boudoir devient une philosophie de boudoir. Un système ne vaut que par l'unité qui le referme sur lui-même; un roman par la variété qui l'ouvre sur le monde.

Levy-Bruhl observait que, pour opposés qu'ils puissent être dans leurs principes, comme les stoïciens et les épicuriens, les philosophes d'une même époque et d'un même milieu, aboutissaient pratiquement à la même morale. En effet, tout se tient: un siècle se reflète et s'exprime dans toutes ses productions et il est assez aisé, à un certain niveau de généralités, de faire se correspondre sa philosophie et sa littérature. Cependant, on peut mettre quiconque au défi, s'il ne connaissait rien de Spinoza ou de Leibniz, de remonter de *Jacques le Fataliste* à l'*Ethique* ou de *Candide* à la *Théodicée*. Le critique est victime d'une illusion lorsqu'il projette ce qu'il sait d'un de ces systèmes dans le roman ou dans le conte. Plus il s'efforcera de reconnaître, d'autant plus il s'égarera. Qu'il se garde de détailler. Il faut dire ces choses en gros et se borner à invoquer d'un mot le fatalisme ou l'optimisme. Non pas le système qui est et ne peut être que la suite de ses enchaînements, mais son sens, sa thèse générale (le plus souvent commune à d'autres systèmes).

Le problème change en passant de la métaphysique à la philosophie pratique dont se réclame le dix-huitième siècle. Son domaine est essentiellement moral et politique. Elle se pose les questions à l'actualité. Certes, elle n'est pas en elle-même poétique, théâtrale, romanesque: ici encore Diderot et Rousseau nous préviennent: 'une maxime est une règle abstraite et générale de conduite, dont on nous laisse l'application à faire . . . mais celui qui agit, on le voit, on se met à sa place ou à ses côtés . . .'; et Rousseau: 'Toutes les fois que dans un roman l'on pei[n]t une action particuliére, il ne s'agit pas de la question morale, mais de l'imitation de la nature; il ne s'agit pas de savoir si Julie a bien ou mal fait de se marier, mais si, libre de sa foi, dans la situation donnée et conséquemment à son caractère, le parti qu'elle a dû prendre étoit celui d'obéir à son père, ou, après l'avoir vu à ses genoux verser des torrens de larmes, de braver son désespoir, sans jamais se laisser fléchir'.[10] Mais pour différentes que soient la maxime et son application, elles ont le même fond psychologique et s'expriment à si peu près dans la même langue que l'on n'a guère à traduire l'une dans l'autre. Le langage commun, s'il rapproche de notre vision les objets de l'histoire naturelle, avec Buffon, encore mieux en rapproche-t-il les objets du monde moral: le philosophe peut avoir une visée littéraire et le littérateur une visée philosophique—et les deux points de vue tendent à se confondre lorsque le philosophe a assez de sens littéraire pour ne pas déduire l'action romanesque, et l'écrivain assez de sens philosophique pour ne pas faire une copie de la philosophie, mais s'inspirer seulement d'un de ses thèmes. D'autant plus pauvre sera l'argumentation philosophique, d'autant plus libre et plus vivante sera l'action romanesque, manipulât-elle des marionnettes comme *Candide*.

Quelques remarques pour conclure. Selon nous, le critique s'expose à deux erreurs complémentaires quand il donne une interprétation philosophique d'une œuvre littéraire, soit que dans le thème directeur, par exemple le fatalisme, il veuille retrouver le détail du système dont il est pris, soit qu'il ne se demande pas si ce

---

[10] Lettre de Rousseau à Bastide, de 1762 (*Corresp. Gén.*, éd. Théophile Dufour, tom. VI, Paris, 1926, p. 17; cité par Lecercle dans *Roman et lumières*, pp. 277-8.

thème avait alors le sens qu'il a pris aujourd'hui. On se trompe aisément encore quand, pour prouver la présence entière d'un système, on en reconstruit la structure à partir d'éléments littéraires: c'est oublier que la matière numérique sur laquelle s'exerce la virtuosité combinatrice du mathématicien n'est pas celle des idées, des mots, des valeurs dont traite le critique et que, par conséquent, l'objectivité structurale n'a pas ici et là, la même force. De plus, la lecture critique qui observe, s'arrête, reprend, analyse, suscite toutes sortes de relations, n'est pas la lecture pour le plaisir; elles n'ont pas le même rythme; l'une a le temps de dessiner une philosophie que l'autre—y compris l'auteur—ne faisait qu'esquisser. A ce propos, on s'interrogerait sur l'analyse stylistique grossissante produite par les ordinateurs. Elle nous livre une pensée qui n'a jamais été pensée à cette échelle. On veut encore que la forme littéraire exprime intentionnellement la philosophie prise pour modèle: ainsi, le désordre apparent des phénomènes ou des hasards de l'existence se traduira par le décousu du récit; et de même que le philosophe cherche sous le désordre apparent un ordre nécessaire, de même sous le décousu de *Jacques le Fataliste*, on doit reconnaître la nécessité spinoziste; —cela revient à dévaloriser les effets esthétiques du décousu, sciemment, savamment calculé par l'auteur pour plaire à un public déterminé, et à lui substituer un décousu philosophique qui ne s'attacherait plus à plaire, mais seulement à instruire, plus propre à exciter une réflexion solitaire que les réactions d'un public, et qui devrait être, bien entendu, de surplus, homogène au fondement philosophique, le *fatum spinosanum*. Mais nous ne voulions qu'indiquer.

Nous avons borné notre enquête au dix-huitième siècle parce qu'il s'est lui-même nommé le siècle des philosophes. Elle nous a confirmé la différence irréductible de la philosophie et de la littérature. Elle nous a montré que cette différence s'atténue lorsqu'on descend du ciel de la métaphysique sur le terrain de la pratique et qu'on renonce à une langue scolastique savante pour une langue littéraire. Mais n'oublions pas le risque d'erreur que nous venons de dénoncer: les réponses que nous suggère le dix-huitième siècle, dans quelle mesure sont-elles valables aujourd'hui, en un siècle où, précisément, tant de philosophes sont venus à la littérature et, plus encore à la critique littéraire, et où tant d'écrivains se veulent engagés et militants?

Nichol Smith's Oxford Book Reappraised

William B. Todd

In this seminar, and particularly in this the third triennial convention, it is altogether fitting and proper to reconsider, after some fifty years, David Nichol Smith's *Oxford Book of Eighteenth Century Verse*. By its very nature, Nichol Smith's own anthology in the Oxford series does not rank among his enduring contributions to scholarship; yet of all his work it is the one book known around the world, the one most susceptible to the ravages of time, and the only one where—cognisant of ever changing tastes—the editor himself appears to invite some later review.

That Nichol Smith should have been slightly apprehensive about his choice of the better poems in the eighteenth century, and possibly even about presenting any at all, is perhaps a little difficult for us now to understand. Today almost everyone is fully persuaded that the eighteenth is incomparably the best of all centuries. In Nichol Smith's day, however, even the most dedicated scholar of our period could not readily dismiss all that was said against it. Just before he came to Oxford, and when he had already published works on Boileau and Dryden, Nichol Smith may well have had occasion to peruse *A Seventeenth Century Anthology*, edited by the formidable Alice Meynell. The introduction to this abruptly concludes (p. vii): 'The Elizabethan poetry is the apple blossom, fine and fragrant, the seventeenth century the apple, fragrant and rich. The change from the sixteenth to the seventeenth is a process, while that from the seventeenth to the eighteenth is a catastrophe'. Should Nichol Smith have missed reading this accolade in 1904, he would have found it again cited in 1926, just ten months before he issued his own anthology, and then as something which 'all should memorise'.[1]

[1] C. Lewis Hind, 'The Best Anthologies', *The Bookman*, LXIX (February

If Nichol Smith had any doubts at Oxford about the reception of his work they were certainly shared by his great contemporary at Cambridge, Sir Arthur Quiller-Couch. Several years before Q, vastly annoyed by his students' attitude toward the period, set about to bludgeon them out of their stupidity.

> I find, Gentlemen, when you read with me in private, that nine out of ten of you dislike the 18th century and all its literary works. As for the Women students, they one and all abominate it. You do not, I regret to say, provide me with reasons much more philosophical than the epigrammatist's for disliking Doctor Fell. May one whose time of life excuses perhaps a detachment from passion attempt to provide you with one? If so, first listen to this from Mr and Mrs Hammond's book *The Village Labourer*, 1760-1832:
>
> 'A row of 18th century houses, or a room of normal 18th century furniture, or a characteristic piece of 18th century literature, conveys at once a sensation of satisfaction and completeness. The secret of this charm is not to be found in any special beauty or nobility of design or expression, but simply in an exquisite fitness. The 18th century mind was a unity, an order. All literature and art that really belong to the 18th century are the language of a little society of men and women who moved within one set of ideas; who understood each other; who were not tormented by any anxious or bewildering problems; who lived in comfort, and above all things, in composure. The classics were their freemasonry. There was a standard for the mind, for the emotions, for taste: there were no incongruities. . . .'
>
> You do wrong, I assure you, in misprising these men of the 18th century. They reduced life, to be sure: but by that very means they saw it far more *completely* than do we, in this lyrical age with our worship of 'fine excess.' Here at any rate, and to speak only of its literature, you have a society fencing that literature around—I do not say by forethought or even consciously—but in effect fencing its literature around, to keep it in control and capable of an orderly, a nice, even an exquisite cultivation. Dislike it as you may, I do not think that any of you, as he increases his knowledge of the technique of English Prose, yes, and of English Verse I (do not say of English Poetry) will deny his admiration to the men of the 18th century.[2]

I have quoted Q at length so as to reach his final pronouncement that, while there is apparently in his view no eighteenth-century *poetry*, eighteenth-century *verse* is worth studying at least for its

---

1926), 250. Nichol Smith has inscribed his *Oxford Book* (National Library of Australia, DNS 4757) as 'Early copy 18 Nov: 1926'; publication, as indicated in a prospectus, was scheduled for 25 November.

[2] *On the Art of Reading*, Cambridge, 1920, pp. 202-3.

technique. Despite this very faint praise, uttered like all of Q's opinions with the greatest assurance and finality, Nichol Smith still dared to follow Q by issuing six years after this pronouncement another anthology in the Oxford series: one which later proved to be so popular that, excepting Q's own *Oxford Book of English Verse*, it alone of the series appeared for a while not only in regular but in India paper issues. Still, as already observed, passing time eventually requires a re-evaluation, and now that Dame Helen Gardner has isued a new anthology which may, perhaps, supersede Q's selection, we may reconsider what Nichol Smith has done.

The first consideration is the kind of verse to select, whatever the given period. Now Q, ranging over all times, was intent only upon numbers either 'lyrical or epigrammatic', a limitation which at least in the first part, the lyrical, excludes much of eighteenth-century poetry and sets aside all that is often found there—the occasional, the satiric, and even the didactic. Nichol Smith necessarily avoids any such restriction, allowing as his single criterion only what is of 'intrinsic merit', as this excellence may be found, he says, either among his own favourites, among those of the public, or among those suddenly discovered by friends or chance. Like Matthew Arnold, however, he would reject those poems which are only of historical interest, or known only because of certain popular associations; for, as he says, the florist then would degenerate into the botanist and become little more than a curator of dried specimens. Yet Nichol Smith does not choose to invoke—as Arnold would, and Q also—an invariable, immutable 'touchstone' of excellence: the choice for him, it seems, still remains, ultimately, a personal and hence a fallible one.

Secondly, whatever the criteria guiding his choice, the anthologist must, alone or with some assistance, endeavour to collect all that falls within his range, and indeed—so that further choice can be made—far more than his book may finally accommodate. This act of collecting, though denigrated by several writers of the time as nothing more than 'organized theft',[3] is of course a necessary process that may be pursued in various ways. One, the most laborious, and probably the least effective, is to search out and read through practically every available source. Norman Ault, in preparing his edition of *Elizabethan Lyrics*, perused upwards of 2000 printed books and nearly 300 manuscripts of the sixteenth and seventeenth centuries, eventually assembled some 2300 lyrics as possibilities

---

[3] Laura Riding (Jackson) and Robert Graves, *A Pamphlet against Anthologies*, London, 1928, p. 35. Chapter 3 of this work (so far as I am aware the only one on the subject) appeared as 'The Anthologist in Our Midst', *Calendar*, April 1927, pp. 22-36.

for inclusion, and finally decided upon 640. Out of all these, he triumphantly declared, ten (only ten!) were to be printed for the first time. Another, very simple, and entirely parasitical way, is to read nothing other than previous anthologies: the mode recommended and followed by C. Lewis Hind.[4]

Still another, and perhaps the most efficient mode for surveying any of the principal authors from Chaucer to Cowper, is to read Chalmers's massive compilation, *The English Poets*. In the preface to his *Golden Treasury* (1861), that famous Victorian anthology, Francis Palgrave states that he not only *twice* read through this, but twice systematically read 'the whole works of all accessible poets not contained in it and the best Anthologies of different periods'. Moreover, Palgrave was 'aided throughout by two friends of independent and exercised judgment, besides the distinguished person addressed in the Dedication'. That person was none other than Tennyson, the Poet Laureate, who (as we know from another report)[5] during a ten-day conference with Palgrave, examined all the poems suggested for inclusion and 'read each one aloud twice before passing final judgment'. It is not surprising, therefore, that through this persistent search, this repeated scrutiny and, not the least of tests, this oral delivery twice performed, Palgrave had indeed found what Arnold was later to call a 'touchstone', that he had through these various means, and by all this assistance, found the 'best' that could be redeemed out of much dross, and that this 'best' was *permanently* assessed. No wonder, then, that when Palgrave brought out an extended issue in 1883, and his second edition in 1891, he found no occasion to withdraw any of his earlier selections, but only to add certain 'after-gleanings', many of them again upon the 'advice of that distinguished Friend, by whom the final choice has been so largely guided'.

Unlike Palgrave, Quiller-Couch, in a summary preface, acknowledges no debt to Chalmers's vast repository, but admits that the *Golden Treasury* cannot be erased from his mind, nor indeed several of Bullen's 'treasuries', to which he owns 'a more advised debt'. Also mentioned are eight other anthologies, 'though my rule

---

[4] *The Bookman*, LXIX, 249. This practice enabled him to select, in his judgment, the *100 Second Best Poems* (London, 1925) and the *100 Best Poems* (London, 1926).

[5] Sir Charles Tennyson, *Alfred Tennyson*, London, 1949, p. 329. As Sir Charles further notes (p. 330), in reference to a *Times* article of 13 October 1930, 'The absence of any poem by Donne or Blake [in *The Golden Treasury*] is evidence of the remarkable change of taste which has occurred during the last 80 years'. It should be remarked, however, that four Blake poems were added in the 1883 impression, these and others on the advice of Palgrave's 'distinguished Friend', and that a single poem by Donne ('Present in Absence') was included in the second edition of 1891.

has been to consult these after making my own choice'. Any help derived from them, he continues, 'bears but a trifling proportion to the labour, special and desultory, which has gone to the making of my book'. As for personal assistance, no one is mentioned. Eleven years later, in presenting his *Oxford Book of Victorian Verse* (1912), Q's personal opinions, or his uncited 'touchstones', still remain infallible. 'The reader will allow me to pursue my old rule to the end; and when he re-greets in this volume many a poem that adorned the former one, he will understand that by excluding these I should have condemned myself to anthologizing the second-rate and clearing the ground for an *Oxford Book of the Worst Poetry*.' Twenty-six years after that, in the new edition of his original *Oxford Book* (1939), he again confidently, almost arrogantly, insists that all should remain essentially the same, that he now only repairs 'the old structure with a stone here, a tile there'. (Actually, as Dame Helen Gardner indicates in the preface to her *New Oxford Book*, among Q's 883 original selections, only some forty items were omitted and some forty added.) Thus where Palgrave over the years constantly sought advice, and constantly solicited oral delivery, Q as persistently rejected any oracle save his own.

Nichol Smith's own indebtedness is vaguely, and disappointingly, expressed only in the final sentence of his preface: 'At an early stage he had the support of Mr. H. V. Elwin's company through several volumes of Chalmers's *English Poets*, and at the last stage he had the skilled and unremitting assistance of Mr. F. Page and Mr. C. Williams'. Doubtless these several persons were, like Palgrave's two unnamed friends, 'of independent and exercised judgment'; but nothing is said here about twice reading through Chalmers, twice perusing all other accessible poets, or twice having a final arbiter read every choice aloud. Though Tennyson was long since dead, the poet designated as the official spokesman of the time lived only a few miles away at Boar's Hill: Robert Bridges. Again, then, I have the uneasy feeling that, as with Q's, Nichol Smith's selection was perhaps a little too hastily amassed, insufficiently controlled, and inadequately tested by other authorities.

No less important than the mode of selecting texts is the order of their presentation, and here the disparity between Palgrave and other anthologies is even more apparent. For his *Golden Treasury* Palgrave chose the 'most poetically effective order'; this, as C. Day Lewis rightly observes, so that 'each poem gains from its context and throws light upon those around it'. A proper disposition, Day Lewis continues,

> is the supreme gift of the anthologist. In no other way do taste, sensibility, learning, and a fine ear for subtle shades of meaning

so clearly reveal themselves. A satisfying arrangement of poems requires a special talent which can be fairly called 'creative.' ... [Palgrave's] grouping of his material into successive but overlapping themes ... was done with great delicacy, is never obtrusive, and enables the reader both to get more from individual poems and to receive general impressions about the style and poetic interests of each period.[6]

Thus in his third book, covering the eighteenth century, Palgrave begins with a commingling of Gray's 'Ode on the Pleasure arising from Vicissitude', Pope's 'The Quiet Life', Cibber's 'The Blind Boy', again Gray 'On a Favourite Cat, Drowned in a Tub of Goldfishes', then Ambrose Philips's 'To Charlotte Pulteney'. Among the next five selections the titles alone clearly indicate that we have now moved on to an unvarying theme: 'Rule Britannia', 'The Bard', 'Ode Written in 1746', 'Lament for Culloden', and 'Lament for Flodden'. For this latter group my omission of the names (respectively Thomson, Gray, Collins, Burns, Elliot) merely emphasises the fact that Palgrave, here and everywhere, considers the poet less significant than the work and so consistently identifies him only after the poem is presented. To him Pope is no more important than Jane Elliot, Gray of no greater consequence than Henry James Pye, Thomas Flatman, Stephen Duck, or even Jeremy Feeble.

For the happy disposition of his material Palgrave is perhaps partly dependent upon the precedent of certain earlier arrangements, especially those anthologies entitled *Beauties* or *Gems*, or the long-running compendium called *Laconics*. Whatever the dependence, it must also be observed that, while he was once subject to rigid pedagogic disciplines, Palgrave himself did not become an academic until 1885, twenty-four years after publication of his *Treasury*, and then as Professor of Poetry at Oxford was required to give only an occasional lecture. Hence in his anthology he escaped from the routines always adopted by literary historians, and pursued always in their courses, where authors are considered in succession and their works studied in a fixed chronological scheme. There priority is given not to the poem but to the poet; his name comes first, often followed by some little commentary, then—as so many pendants—his verse. In Palgrave the gradation is reversed, title large, text typographically one point less, author last, in least degree and to one side.

As against Palgrave, then, I would say that most anthologies, and all those in the Oxford series (these I believe without exception) are affected by an academic bias, one that regards all poetry of a

---

[6] F. T. Palgrave, *The Golden Treasury*, ed. C. Day Lewis, London, 1954, pp. 15-16.

given period as a kind of versified history or biography. Where Palgrave is always concerned with mood or subject—five poems first alternating between joy and sorrow, then five more on strife and battle—Nichol Smith starts his stiff parade with Pomfret, Defoe and John Philips (one poem each), then Walsh and Lady Chudleigh (two), then Congreve (four), then Prior (nine) and so on, poet by poet, in strictly temporal array. This is an unimaginative and mechanical arrangement, quite adequate (perhaps even necessary) for the schoolroom, but quite unappealing for the casual reader.

Now that we have paraded with Nichol Smith part way through his book, let us break ranks and consider at random what is offered the common reader. One poem by Gay, one of the eleven allotted at his predetermined position, is his 'Mr. Pope's Welcome from Greece Upon his having finished his translation of Homer's Iliad'. This is not to be found in any of the later anthologies I have examined and thus, on that count alone, might now be withdrawn as in disfavour even among the academics. Still, there it is, and one can only wonder what prompted the choice originally. It begins simply enough:

> Long hast thou, friend! been absent from thy soil,
>   Like patient *Ithacus* at siege of *Troy*;
> I have been witness of thy six years toil,
>   Thy daily labours, and thy night's annoy,
> Lost to thy native land, with great turmoil,
>   On the wide sea, oft threat'ning to destroy:
> Methinks with thee I've trod *Sigæan* ground,
>   And heard the shores of *Hellespont* resound.

Here of four italicised words—*Ithacus, Troy, Sigæan, Hellespont*—the gentle reader may possibly understand the first two but remain somewhat ignorant of the two last. The second stanza is much easier going (only *Homer* here), the third easier yet (*Thames, Kent, Essex*), but thereafter familiar personal and place names such as *Pope, Gay, Burlington, Prior* or *Gravesend, Tilbury, Greenwich, Deptford*, soon become lost in a welter of incomprehensible references. Who then, who now, can immediately identify (in order of appearance) *Disney, Watkins, Lewis, Laughton, Craggs, Carlton, Chandois, Jervas, Dartneuf, Maine, Cheney, Wanley, Evans, Booth, Mawbert, Frowd, Titcomb,* and *Digby*? No wonder later anthologists avoid the poem: this ejaculation requires an extensive apparatus every other line, and any such intrusion here would, of course, be intolerable to the casual peruser. Nonetheless, to compound this confusion, Nichol Smith, though twice abridging the poem, still insists on giving us fifteen stanzas, or 120 lines altogether. The academic has become relentless in his pursuit, so relentless here as to forget his own resolve about avoiding matters purely historic or only of local association. Here at least, if we may revert to his own prefatory image, Nichol Smith has become a mere botanist, a curator of dried specimens.

Even in simpler verse, mere length, I would now suggest, may soon fatigue one not fully attentive, one easily distracted by other things. Remember that the reader is not in a classroom, not under any duress to attend. Four of the poems here are considerably longer even than Gay's: Smart's 'Song to David' (516 lines), Chatterton's 'Bristowe Tragedie' (392), Cowper's 'Diverting History of John Gilpin' (252), and Burns's 'Tam o' Shanter' (224). Unlike Gay's, all these are found in later anthologies, and this sign of later approval, albeit from other academics, should not be disregarded. Moreover with these Nichol Smith does relent, ever so slightly, providing seven brief notes for the Smart and translating 68 words in the Burns. Even so, within the comparatively brief compass of an anthology, and the briefer span accorded any one author, we may occasionally be allowed too much. Smart's one poem takes up 18 of the 20 pages given him and Chatterton's 15 of his 21. On the other hand, the two less extensive poems do not overly encroach upon the allotted space, Cowper's running to nine of 35 pages, and Burns—given the most sway of all—only to eight of 52.

The emphasis upon Burns, I would add, betrays a pervasive characteristic of Nichol Smith's whole collection. This Ayrshire poet, represented almost entirely in his native Scottish dialect, is matched only by Pope, with 53 pages; Cowper and Thomson outrank Swift 35 and 30 to 26; and Gray, Chatterton, Smart, and Collins all, to our great surprise, completely overwhelm even Samuel Johnson, 25, 21, 20, 18, to 9. A decade later, and persistently thereafter, Nichol Smith was to acclaim the merits of Johnson's poetry; but in this collection of 1926 the Great Cham receives very short shrift. Once beyond Pope the tendency at this earlier time is always toward Burns, or verse of the personal and romantic Burnsian drift, a predilection early set, I suspect, by Nichol Smith's native origins.

If there is any doubt that Nichol Smith is, at this earlier date, ever looking for pre-romantic tendencies, for some relief from the aphoristic, the didactic, the heroic couplet and anything else that may be held against the eighteenth century, the statistics cited above find verbal expression in his own Preface. There he says that the poetry of the time is 'rich in conscious echoes; but it is richer in anticipations'. Then he immediately cites two passages (the only excerpts given in his Preface), one from Akenside as heralding Wordsworth, and one from Thomas Russell as the equal of any

Lake poetry. In short Nichol Smith seems to have been avoiding any direct approach to the subject of his volume and any sustained account of it. Perhaps James Sutherland had this anthologist directly in mind when, in his own book-length *Preface*, he observed that

> with one or two notable exceptions, few modern critics . . . have written about eighteenth-century poetry with their eye fixed steadily on the object, or even with any apparent eagerness to study it. To those who have written at large on English poetry, the hundred years from the death of Dryden to the publication of *Lyrical Ballads* have usually appeared as a rather dull plain lying between two ranges of Delectable Mountains, to be hurried across with all convenient speed. Even those who have made a more special study of the period have too often reserved their praise for what is least characteristic of it. Their eyes have been fixed continually on the horizon; and any faint glimmerings of pre-romanticism have been extolled at the expense of the more characteristic and central achievements of the century.[7]

But whether or not Nichol Smith is to be counted among Sutherland's 'one or two exceptions', the one or two steadfast adherents to the eighteenth century, is still a moot question, for it is known that as early as 1913, thirteen years before the publication of his anthology, he had advised the Clarendon Press that an edition of Samuel Johnson was under way. Though this edition was not finally produced, with the assistance of Edward L. McAdam, until 1941, it is readily apparent in his *Shakespeare in the Eighteenth Century* (1928), produced shortly after the anthology, that it is in the eighteenth century, indisputably, that his interests really lie. Burns may occupy 52 pages in his early anthology, Johnson only 9, but in the library he finally assembled the volumes relating to Burns number only two while those by Johnson extend to 194. (It must be remarked, however, that the Burns (2 vols., 1974) is then and now about all that any collector of moderate means could ever hope to acquire.)

Moreover it is safe to speculate that, while for practically all of his poets, the choice may have been in large measure, as he intimates, determined by the Chalmers compendium, the text comes usually from the copies in his study. Whether these copies represent the right texts are matters which of course we cannot at present decide, and Nichol Smith gives us no clue as to how he, or the Clarendon Press, may treat their accidentals. Palgrave says that he has selected 'the most poetical version, wherever more than one

[7] *A Preface to Eighteenth Century Poetry*, Oxford, 1948, pp. v-vi.

exists' and regulated to the best advantage all spelling and punctuation. Q also states that he has preferred 'the more beautiful to the better attested reading' and comments less explicitly on the orthography. On these several counts Nichol Smith is silent, indicating only the date of the chosen text; but his general appreciation of textual authority as manifest in his other works is surely no less than his predecessors', possibly commensurate with McKerrow's, and only less stringent than Greg's or, in later times, Bowers's. Even in this *Oxford Book* his own copy exhibits convincing testimony of his continuing concern. Against some forty-five editions there cited Nichol Smith has subsequently listed as many more alternative texts, an appreciable number of them in periodicals of earlier date. Also, in rechecking either his own sources, or those later brought to his attention, he has recorded scores of variants, substantive and accidental, many of them possibly of greater authority than those he allowed in print.

What he has produced, then (albeit imperfectly), what all the Oxford editors have produced (saving only one), is what Bowers would call a 'practical text', one that presents 'to a broad audience as sound a text (usually modernised and at a minimum price) as is consistent with information that may be procurable through normal scholarly channels and thus without more special research than is economically feasible'.[8]

In what I believe to be a solitary exception to all the Oxford 'practical texts', John Hayward's *Oxford Book of Nineteenth-Century English Verse* (1964), the preface lays down two principles which should hereafter determine the procedure of all.

> As a general rule [Hayward states], the text (too seldom treated with respect for authority and accuracy in anthologies) reproduces that of the first edition in book form—the version, that is to say, originally approved by the poet for publication and so presented to his earliest readers. Exceptions to this rule are indicated in the list of Contents, where the primary printed source of every poem and extract is given.

Only Helen Gardner's *New Oxford Book* (1972) seems to approach this requisite by depending, in general, upon 'the author's final version'; but unlike Hayward's first editions, which can readily be determined, the final version for many authors still remains unknown and, in Dame Helen's 'Notes and References' (pp. 946-53) is undeclared. Nichol Smith at least specifies his copy, whether or not it is the correct one.

In enunciating his second principle Hayward again looks askance

---

[8] 'Practical Texts and Definitive Editions', in *Two Lectures on Editing* by Charlton Hinman and Fredson Bowers, Columbus, Ohio, 1969, p. 26.

Plate XI Thomas Rowlandson, 'Departure from Wakefield', *The Vicar of Wakefield*, London 1817 edition, Plate 3 (Huntington Library and Art Gallery).

Plate XII Thomas Rowlandson, 'The Welcome', *The Vicar of Wakefield*, London 1817 edition, Plate 5 (Huntington Library and Art Gallery).

at earlier performances: 'In view of the deplorable practice of some anthologists of representing poems with lines and even whole stanzas surreptitiously and silently cut out in order to "improve" them, it may be well to conclude with an assurance that the textual integrity of every poem or passage in this collection has been strictly observed'. The titles supplied for extracts are thus bracketed in his edition and all omissions clearly marked. Unhappily this admirable procedure, not followed before, has not been followed since, for Dame Helen among others silently imposes her own titles above excerpts and, like the earlier anthologists, Nichol Smith included, as silently transposes both these and the newly-created first lines of verse into her several indexes.

Finally some comment is necessary both on the question of excerpting and on the inclusion of minor poets. The *OED* defines an anthology as 'a collection of the flowers of verse, i.e. small choice poems, *esp.* epigrams, by various authors'. Johnson's *Dictionary* (1755) offers a more orderly sequence of meanings: (1) 'a collection of flowers'—this reverting to the original Greek sense of a flower-gathering; (2) 'a collection of devotions in the Greek Church', and (3) 'a collection of poems'. Now as we will all immediately realise, especially on surveying the more expansive verse of the eighteenth century, one can rarely conflate Johnson's sense 3 with sense 1, that is, to regard a collection of poems as invariably also a collection of flowers, all bright and luxuriant, every blossom—if I may re-echo Alice Meynell—full and fragrant and rich. No, we must concede, on the very heights of Parnassus the flowers cannot grow, on any one patch, in great profusion. In one area, 'The Castle of Indolence', Nichol Smith eventually finds no fewer than six passages he considers worth excerpting. In each of two others, 'An Essay on Man' and Dyer's 'Ruins of Rome', he comes upon as many as five. In each of three more, 'Epistle to Dr. Arbuthnot', 'The Deserted Village', and Cowper's 'The Task', he decides to select only four. And in twenty more he must be content only with two or three passages.[9] Among all these twenty-six longer poems, it is interesting to observe, not one of the selections made comes at the very beginning of the slowly unwinding verse: all are discovered somewhere within. Only once, where more than one excerpt is given, does the first choice represent the opening lines—in Thomson's 'Winter'—and in this only one further passage is offered. So then, as any anthologist is bound to do, the flowers are snipped where they may be found, either in large or small clusters, among the broad expanses of eighteenth-century verse.

[9] Items 50-1, 52-3, 54-5, 61-3, 77-9, 84-5, 94-5, 140-1, 157-8, 159-61, 162-4, 190-1, 201-2, 206-7, 208-9, 225-6, 232-3, 290-2, 300-2, 367-8.

Once we descend from Parnassus, however, and on lesser slopes look for single blooms—the solitary excerpts or short poems presented in full—we move further away from any consensus. Among the 450 poems in his anthology, Nichol Smith, sometimes from his reading of Chalmers but more often from his reading elsewhere, selected 133 verses (in whole or in part) which are not to be found in the later collections I have inspected.[10] One of these, Gay's versified praise of Pope's Homer, has already been rejected, on my own fiat, as an abominable piece to be foisted upon any unsuspecting reader. All the others, similarly excluded in subsequent anthologies, were submitted to several of my colleagues, who joined me in the opinion that in thirteen instances the exclusions were fully justified: the poems are without merit.[11] Concerning 37 other selections we held differing views.[12] But for 81 more we agreed that Nichol Smith's early judgment is still acceptable and may prevail against all the later editors.[13] This latter group of 81 represents practically all the minor authors, all capable of writing—as Nichol Smith discovered—some memorable verse, but all generally ignored by pedagogic editors concerned only with notable figures. The very presence of these lesser poets, and in such considerable numbers, constitutes I should say the best recommendation of Nichol Smith's work.

Were he here today Nichol Smith certainly would, like most other anthologists, avail himself of an opportunity to introduce some poems earlier disregarded. As I have intimated, he might even

---

[10] In order of appearance these anthologies are: *A Collection of English Poems: 1660-1800*, ed. R. S. Crane, New York and London, 1932; *English Poetry of the Eighteenth Century*, ed. C. A. Moore, New York, 1935; *Poets of the English Language*, ed. W. H. Auden and N. H. Pearson, New York, 1950, Vol. III: *Milton to Goldsmith*; *Early Eighteenth Century Poetry*, ed. James Sutherland, London, 1965; *Poetry of the Landscape and the Night*, ed. Charles Peake, London, 1967; *18th-Century English Minor Poets*, ed. M. L. Jarrell and W. Meredith, New York, 1968; *Eighteenth-Century English Literature*, ed. Geoffrey Tillotson, Paul Fussell Jr, and Marshall Waingrow, New York, 1969; and *Poetry of the Augustan Age*, ed. Angus Ross, London, 1970. The survey also extended to a collection published just before Smith's: *The Shorter Poems of the Eighteenth Century*, ed. I. A. Williams, London, 1923. As some of these collections are imperfectly indexed, the accounts given in succeeding notes are probably not free of error.

[11] Items 17, 27, 49, 198, 243, 259, 261, 281, 332, 380, 432, 446, 449. In this and the following tallies I wish particularly to acknowledge the careful appraisal of Professors Leo Hughes and W. R. Keast.

[12] Items 2 6, 22, 45, 57, 111, 112, 121, 125, 131, 132, 133, 134, 137, 145, 166, 167, 171, 179, 188, 199, 205, 211, 214, 227, 229, 260, 275, 277, 319, 322, 323, 327, 328, 376, 431, 445.

[13] Items 3, 7, 10, 21, 46, 47, 60, 64, 74, 75, 87, 97, 99, 100, 138, 193, 204, 213, 216, 219, 220, 221, 222, 231, 241, 242, 263, 264, 265, 267, 268, 269, 270, 274, 280, 283, 284, 307, 308, 309, 310, 312, 315, 316, 317, 318, 333, 334, 335, 341, 349, 350, 355, 365, 366, 369, 370, 371, 390, 400, 401, 402, 404, 406, 412, 419, 427, 428, 429, 430, 433, 435, 437, 438, 439, 440, 441, 442, 443, 444, 447.

reorder his entries according to the theme or subject model of Palgrave and thus depart from the chronological precedent established by Quiller-Couch. Finally, as a careful editor of literary texts, he would take cognisance of Hayward's admirable practice and, so far as they are applicable, subscribe to the principles of Greg, Bowers, and others in his determination of copy. In this *Oxford Book* much that Nichol Smith has done he has done well, but as he would be the first to concede, all things can be done better.

Integrity and Life in Pope's Poetry

S. L. Goldberg

I

In the Preface to his edition of Shakespeare, Pope remarked that Shakespeare's work was 'inspiration indeed; he is not so much an imitator as an instrument of Nature; and 'tis not so just to say that he speaks from her, as that she speaks through him'.[1] It is easy to see what he meant. One mark of a very great writer is to present us with not so much a particular view of the world, as a 'world' itself—an imagined reality so large, so substantial, so free of any merely personal bias, that it seems continuous with our own. Things, places, actions, people assume an independent density and vigour; every particular seems alive; and the whole seems at once self-subsistent and yet everywhere animated by the same protean energy. As Pope said of Homer, 'What he writes is of the most animated nature imaginable; everything moves, everything lives and is put in action'.[2] It is what we call 'dramatic' power in its highest manifestation.

Pope himself is not often credited with this kind of power. He does seem to offer us a particular view of the world, and consequently it is his Augustanism that draws most attention. But to leave the emphasis there seems to me a critical mistake, for it is surely Pope's 'dramatic' power that ought most to concern us. Whatever Pope's conscious moral or philosophical intentions, he did not merely reflect his world, represent or 'imitate' it artistically, and comment critically on it. As he matured, he also came (as I think he saw) to 'represent' it in the other sense of embodying its ideal possibilities of self-awareness and self-criticism. His world really 'speaks through him': to realise as he did the significance of so many of its details was also to make their reality visible—visible and felt in all their stubborn but fascinating actuality. Like all

---

[1] *Literary Criticism of Alexander Pope*, ed. Bertrand A. Goldgar, Lincoln, Neb., 1965, p. 161.
[2] Ibid., p. 108.

great 'dramatic' writers, he makes his world conscious of itself and thereby (as he suggests of Shakespeare) he partly re-creates it. In fact, I think Pope re-creates his world more substantially, ranges in it more widely, and engages with it more profoundly, than any English writer between Shakespeare and Dickens. It is a remarkable achievement for one who wrote so much formally in his own voice (Chaucer's is perhaps the only comparable case in English); and if Arnold had been able to appreciate what the great novelists of his own age were doing, or had even understood the relationship between his own criticism of life and Pope's, he might have discerned one or two important truths in his otherwise silly remark that Pope is a classic of our prose. If Pope's affinities reach back to early seventeenth-century drama as well as to seventeenth-century poetry and prose, they also reach forward to the nineteenth-century novel and to nineteenth- and twentieth-century poetry and criticism.

One such affinity is perhaps too obvious to have been much noticed, though the nineteenth century's myths about Augustanism did not help anyone to appreciate it, nor do the twentieth century's own myths about the 'dissociation of sensibility' or the genealogy of 'modernism'. For Pope is not only an intensely 'dramatic' poet, he is also an intensely self-conscious one. By this I do not mean merely that he was a deliberate craftsman (though of course he was), nor that he deployed his various self-images with masterly skill (though he did), nor even that references to himself form part of a quite remarkable number of his poems (though they do). More than that, he was so serious about being a poet that he obviously had something like a sense of vocation about it—a consciousness from first to last that his destiny, his very self, was essentially that of a poet and Wit. He knew the power of genius in himself; it was only half a joke, for example, to assert that *The Dunciad* 'was not made for these Authors, but these Authors for the Poem'.[3] But as we might expect, the degree to which he actually understood himself corresponded exactly to the degree of his understanding of other people and of the ways in which their lives were also fated. His view of himself and his view of the objective world corresponded; and he clearly came to see this himself. But I think he also increasingly sensed that to realise the objective world was simultaneously to realise, to fulfil, and thereby to define himself—and vice versa.

These may sound odd terms to apply to Pope, as though he were some kind of prophet of Romanticism or a secret crypto-modernist. But it is worth remembering that Shaftesbury, for example, even in 1710 could advocate 'soliloquy', as he called it, or 'inward colloquy'

---

[3] *The Poems of Alexander Pope*, ed. John Butt, London, 1963, p. 433. Henceforth cited as *Poems*.

—essentially, the creative *dramatisation* of inner conflicts and possibilities—as a way of achieving moral self-consciousness.[4] As for poetic self-consciousness, the Romantics may have been the first to philosophise about it systematically, but they didn't after all invent it. Nor did self-definition become a problem only for writers in the nineteenth and twentieth centuries, despite the way some critics of modern literature talk. To look no further back, it was problem enough for some of Shakespeare's tragic heroes, or for Donne, or Marvell, or even for Milton; and it was no less so for Pope. Of course it is more usual to regard his art, like so much else in his age, as strictly—indeed, consciously—impersonal, and to talk of his use of artistic *personae* rather than different manifestations of his self. His age is supposed to have rested upon a commonly accepted, stable, comprehensive, and objective order of moral values, natural laws, and social institutions, in which no man needed to be much perplexed about who *he* really was or where *he* properly belonged; and Pope, it is assumed, simply adopted a number of recognised traditional *personae*—the social Wit, the easy Horatian Moralist, the philosophic Sage, the happy and virtuous Recluse, the dignified Poet and Critic of life, and so on—which are taken as devices, impersonal techniques, whereby Pope could get his personal self out of the way and bring traditional and impersonal values to bear on the present.

However much truth there may be in this view, it is not really adequate to Pope. For one thing, while it is obviously true that each of his poems is a created object in its own right, not a direct personal confession, it is also true that it is created by, and embodies, a particular mind, not some impersonal rhetorical process. In the second place, it is hard not to agree with Irvin Ehrenpreis in his suspicion of the term *persona* as applied to Pope. No one at the time thought the Alexander Pope inside the poems was a quite different creature from the Alexander Pope who published them; indeed, it is often the very point of the poems that they are the same. Clearly, it would be absurd to identify Pope with any one of his self-images; nevertheless, as Ehrenpreis argues, 'through his masterpieces a man defines—not hides—himself', and this, I think, was Pope's own view of it too.[5] Moreover, a term like *persona*

[4] See 'Soliloquy, or Advice to an Authour', in *Characteristics*, ed. J. M. Robertson, 2 vols., 1900; repr. Gloucester, Mass., 1963, I, 101-234, esp. p. 211. Also p. 136: 'The moral artist who can thus imitate the Creator, and is thus knowing in the inward form and structure of his fellow-creature, will hardly, I presume, be found unknowing in himself . . .'. Cf. Walter Jackson Bate, 'The Sympathetic Imagination in Eighteenth-Century English Criticism', *ELH*, XII (1945), 144-64.

[5] 'Personae', in *Restoration and Eighteenth-Century Literature*, ed. Carroll Camden, Chicago, 1963, p. 33.

suggests that he was more assured of the certain certainties of his age, and more self-possessed in confronting his material, than he really was. His 'wit' constantly played over those certainties; real self-possession—a full, measured, and secure self-understanding as a poet—was something he had continually to strive towards and win. And for a mind like his, as Johnson so well describes it, 'active, ambitious, and adventurous, always investigating, always aspiring', every success could be only partial and temporary.[6] In one sense, Maynard Mack is obviously right to insist that the satiric speaker in Pope's poems is a fiction. 'We may call this speaker Pope, if we wish', he says—though I cannot see what else we can call him, even while agreeing with Mack's general point that we can call him Pope 'only if we remember that he always reveals himself as a character in a drama, not as a man confiding in us'.[7] I doubt if the matter is finally quite as clear-cut as that, but in any case it is Pope the 'dramatist' that matters, and the relevant kind of impersonality to seek in his work is that manifested in the greatest dramatic 'masterpieces'—an integrity and plenitude of dramatic *and* personal realisation.[8]

II

The impulse towards such self-possession appears long before the obvious cases of the 1730s and 40s. In every one of his major poems up to 1717, Pope tries, more or less successfully, to locate the self who writes the poem by defining it in relation to his own personal experience on the one hand, and to the particular subject of the poem on the other. The reference to himself at the end of the *Essay on Criticism*, for example, hardly warrants even the term *persona*: it is little more than a conventional gesture imitated from Boileau, a tactful claim to modesty and moral integrity. But the actual spirit of the poem is much less conventional; it corresponds rather with the pervasive Longinian strain in its argument. Words like *life, force, vigour, motion, fire, ardent, teeming*, and so on, play against two other sets of words. One comprises such terms as *glittering, chaos, gaudy*, and the like. The other is an even more significant group: *dull, malignant, slow, creep, sleep, lumber, dust, dullness*. Pope once remarked that 'of the two extremes one could sooner pardon frenzy than frigidity';[9] and the similarly contrasting

---

[6] *Lives of the English Poets*, ed. G. B. Hill, 3 vols., Oxford, 1905, III, 217.
[7] 'The Muse of Satire', *Yale Review*, n.s. XLI (1951-2), 88. Cf. Donald Greene, ' "Dramatic Texture" in Pope', in *From Sensibility to Romanticism*, ed. Frederick W. Hilles and Harold Bloom, New York, 1965, pp. 31-53.
[8] My argument in this paper develops some points made in an earlier article, 'Alexander Pope', *Melbourne Critical Review*, No. 7 (1964), 49-65.
[9] *Literary Criticism* (ed. Goldgar), p. 123.

terms of the *Essay on Criticism* point forward to his explicit understanding later on in *The Dunciad*: that it is essentially the 'Elasticity' and 'Fire' his own verse represents that is the measure of the fools and dunces.[10] Another interesting example is a passage he wrote as a young man to add to Wycherley's *Panegyrick on Dulness*, where he states, in a merely 'witty' and theoretical way, an insight that he fully realises only in the last Book of *The Dunciad*: that the poet's 'wit', the very principle of life in him, actually depends upon Dulness, not only as the substance it seeks to transform and enliven, but as that in which it 'last must end'. Being 'satisfy'd, secure, and innocent', Dulness is a reality both within and outside the self; being 'fit for all Stations', it is paradoxically the very element in which life manifests itself.

The consciousness of a power in himself less sedate, less controllable, less socially amenable, and far less modest, than a young man could fully understand, let alone express, is clearly part of the self that writes these early poems. It peeps out in *The Temple of Fame* (1711), for instance, where Pope measures the personal cost of seeking poetic fame. Once again, the opposition he sees there— between seeking a conscious moral integrity (which might well necessitate a psychic *retreat* from the world) and a conscious claim to public recognition (which is virtually the need to *master* the world)—is still rather crude, rather notional, in comparison with his later sense of the strains and difficulties involved. The finest of his early poems, *The Rape of the Lock* and the 'Epistle to Miss Blount, on her leaving the Town, after the Coronation', do realise their conflicting values with real vivacity and a delicate, even tender, sharpness; and Pope does hold them in a fine balance. All the same, he achieves that balance only because his sense of the opposing forces, and of what must be sacrificed in balancing them, is limited—limited in ways that Marvell's sense of them in 'The Garden', for instance, is not. 'Annihilating' is not a word Pope seems to need in either poem; nor does Clarissa's 'good humour' quite answer to the fate of those wretches who hang that jurymen may dine.

Where Pope does reach out in these early poems towards such harsher, less tractable aspects of life, his sense of them inevitably corresponds to the extent and coherence of his self-understanding. *Windsor Forest*, for example, remains a mess; his exercises in the 'pathetic' mode remain far more pathetic than passionate. As Aubrey Williams has noted, in *The Rape of the Lock* Pope was concerned with 'a "type" of human experience . . . in which loss

---

[10] *The Dunciad* I, 186 (p. 729).

must be suffered if . . . gain is to be at all achieved'.[11] In both 'Eloisa to Abelard' and the 'Elegy to the Memory of an Unfortunate Lady' he is concerned with the same thing within the individual; and as his obvious self-identification with both unfortunate ladies suggests, he is trying not only to express the centre of their fates, the centre of each self as it confronted the world, but also to explore how far it is also a centre to which his own sense of himself could cohere. Certainly he now realises the distinction between the self and the world is more complex than it appeared in *Windsor Forest*. There is no conventional cant about 'home-felt Quiet', 'observing a Mean', 'soft retreats', and the like. As he sees, human life asks more than 'the world forgetting, by the world forgot'. But both poems remain so merely rhetorical because what Pope realises, at their centre and in his own self, is less the need and the capacity to commit one's life to a genuine passion than the *consciousness* of that need and capacity. He sees his subject-matter with a constricting kind of self-consciousness, as though it were enough to indulge in emotional rhetoric about it rather than to take emotion and rhetoric as means to discover it. His sense of himself has a correspondingly external pathos—a not very engaging mixture, in fact, of self-pity and self-congratulation on being a poet. And once again it hardly encompasses the harsher, more hostile feelings which give the poems such life as they have, and which spring from a quite different part of himself. One of the most revealing sentences in the Preface to his 1717 volume contains a metaphor that often recurs in his work: 'the life of a Wit', he remarks, 'is a warfare upon earth'. The word 'life', we may notice, is as significant as 'warfare'.[12]

This other side of him begins to take conscious form in 'The Universal Prayer', which he first wrote in 1715, or in the 'Hymn Written in Windsor Forest' of 1717. One stanza of the 'Prayer', for example, deals with a temptation that surely very few people can have felt strongly enough to think it warranted a place in a 'universal' prayer:

> Let not this weak, unknowing hand
> Presume Thy Bolts to throw,
> And deal Damnation round the land,
> On each I judge thy Foe.

Looking back from Pope's later work ('Yes, I am proud; I must be proud to see /Men not afraid of God afraid of me'), we can see why he might have been troubled by some elements in himself.

---

[11] 'The "Fall" of China and *The Rape of the Lock*', *Philological Quarterly*, XLI (1962), 424. (The article is reprinted in *Essential Articles for the Study of Alexander Pope*, ed. Maynard Mack, rev. and enl. edn, Hamden, Conn., 1968).
[12] *Poems*, p. xxvi.

Clearly, the simple integrity of innocence, retirement, identification with the conventional ethical virtues, was impossible to one whose genius had to take him into the world. Eventually, the losses he had to accept as the other side of this destiny prompted a fuller, if more difficult, understanding both of the world and of himself, rather than driving him to moral retreat or emotional indulgence.

III

Such integrity did not come just from Pope's wanting it, however, nor was he always right in thinking he had achieved it. He was only the first to think (as some scholars still do) that his mature work is really animated and shaped by the values to which he consciously attached himself: reason, good sense, taste, nature, order, and so on. But as a number of critics have pointed out, his imagination draws most of its vigour from the disorder, folly, irrationality, dullness, grotesque and fantastic distortions and extremes, that it realises as active forces in the world around him. If Pope eventually came to see this himself, he was not very clear about it at first. His confusions in the *Essay on Man*, for example, are most revealing. In so far as the *Essay* has any poetic life, it does not lie in Pope's repeated and rather strident assertions of a cosmic plan, or his attacks on 'pride', or even in his occasional perceptions of a scale of being in nature.[13] His mind most fully realises itself in realising the strange forms, the ambivalent energies, the self-entangled contradictions of the world: the realities he tries to fix within the bounds of a single cosmic idea. To annihilate all that's made to a thought is to be able to identify it as a whole, and therefore in some sense to possess it all. Equally, it is to possess all the possible forms of the self in a single thought too—the self that can reach out sympathetically to realise other forms of life and in doing so fulfil itself, partly at least. Nevertheless, it is an annihilation. Things are drained of their actuality; the mind, in order to rest in one ultimate idea, must (as Pope continually insists) 'cease' some of its activity. It must 'desist' from curiosity and aspiration; indeed, it must voluntarily surrender part of its life to fulfil a mysterious and impersonal order outside itself. Pope's theme in the *Essay* has been called 'constructive renunciation';[14] yet what is 'constructed' becomes less real precisely as the 'renunciation' becomes more insistent. The vehemence with which he tries in the *Essay* to assert an objective order—tries, that is, to possess all possible experience and

---

[13] Cf. Patricia Meyer Spacks, *An Argument of Images: The Poetry of Alexander Pope*, Cambridge, Mass., 1971, Chap. 3.

[14] *The Poems of Alexander Pope*, Vol. III, i: *An Essay on Man*, ed. Maynard Mack, London, 1950, p. lxx.

thereby secure both the world and himself within one self-sufficient and demonstrable object of thought—seems to be the reaction of a mind made insecure, even anxious, by its very capacities. In beating down 'pride', he seems to be beating down an uneasy (and never quite acknowledged) sense of the restlessly active, various, outflying, centrifugal force of his own imagination. He seems determined to rope the self down within the confines of a single, recognisable identity, and to find in large, indisputable abstractions an imposing bastion, an impregnable centre, from which to command all the confusions of life.

What I am suggesting is more than an attraction in Pope towards chaos, disorder, and eccentricity, quite as powerful as that towards order, form, and moral rationality.[15] It is more, too, than a local conflict of the sort Reuben Brower points to, between Pope's philosophy and his sensibility.[16] It is an unavoidable problem within himself—one that drew him forward to his later work. For he cannot help responding to a value in the disorder he sees. Its energy and substance remain for him an irreducible part of life; but if it prompts, it also seems to withstand, every formal paradox, every set of opposing terms, in which he tries to comprehend it in a larger whole. Consequently he is driven to seek a centre within himself where sympathetic responsiveness, as well as true understanding, authoritative judgment, and virtuous intent, all coincide. The search for objectively 'real' values in the world is also the search for 'real' identity—for a self that can and must and should acknowledge the impersonal authority of those values.

Thus the problem Pope stumbled into in the *Essay on Man* is not simply to reconcile such opposing ideas as A. O. Lovejoy has traced all through Western culture. For one thing, the opposition Lovejoy saw between 'otherworldliness' and 'this-worldliness' ramifies much further than he noticed. Not only has the One been set against the Many, order against plenitude and diversity, peace and concord against abundance and fullness of being, the Idea against physical reality, universal Reason against idiosyncrasy, and so on. Because all of these have ethical implications, they have been accompanied by other opposites. Contemplation has been set against action, retirement against public life, country against city and court, the individual self against the fragmentations of society, rest against movement and aspiration, self-sufficiency against involvement with and dependence upon others, self-preservation and withholding against giving and self-consumption, character against sensibility,

---

[15] Cf. the discussion of Pope's 'oscillations' in Peter Dixon, *The World of Pope's Satires*, London, 1968, Chaps. 8 and 9.
[16] *Alexander Pope: The Poetry of Allusion*, Oxford, 1959, pp. 206ff., 241.

sincerity against being tactful and accommodating, fixed identity against fluidity and the manifold potentialities of the self, the capacity (which Coleridge saw in Milton) to attract 'all forms and things to himself, into the unity of his own IDEAL', against the capacity (which he saw in Shakespeare) to dart forth, and pass 'into all the forms of human character and passion, the one Proteus of the fire and the flood'.[17] As Lovejoy suggests, such oppositions have generally been taken as dilemmas, terms that exhaust all the possibilities between them, and the Western mind has generally tried either to reduce one to the other or to reconcile both in some 'higher' third term. Moreover, the oppositions themselves have generally been taken as an inter-related set: any one opposition has tended to melt into others. This suggests, of course (as has been increasingly obvious since the early nineteenth century), that such oppositions are wholly or in part polarities of thought; the opposing terms are inter-dependent, so that to conceive the one is to conceive the other. But it also underlines another reason why Pope's difficulties were not merely local, philosophical ones. The opposing terms are more than 'ideas' in Lovejoy's sense. Their significance lies in their experiential content; and if for no other reason, this makes it necessary to distinguish (as many scholars, including Lovejoy, do not) between the different ways such oppositions may present themselves in literature. They may indeed appear as conceptual 'ideas', merely expounded or alluded to; but they may also appear as conflicts betrayed or exhibited by a work, or choices explored in it, or (as some Romantics wanted of all art) aspects of life that are absorbed in, and transcended by, the poetic imagination. We may recall Coleridge's famous description of the imagination as a power that, while activated and continuously controlled by the will and the understanding, 'reveals itself in the balance or reconciliation of opposite or discordant qualities'.[18] With regard to these oppositions, it would be truer to say that the imagination seeks not so much a 'balance' or 'reconciliation'—which may all too easily take a form *dictated* by the will and the understanding: a conceptual paradox or an idea in which the poet invests his conscious belief (*discordia concors*, for example)—but rather a wholeness of life, a 'unity of being', an integrity, which the imagination itself achieves in responding fully to all the complexities of life, but which it may also see as impossible to sustain in ordinary life. Another of Coleridge's observations is perhaps even more to the point, for as he says, the poet apprehending the world truly, 'brings the whole soul of man into activity, with the subordination of its

[17] *Biographia Literaria*, ed. J. Shawcross, 2 vols., Oxford, 1907, II, 20.
[18] Ibid., II, 12.

faculties to each other, according to their relative worth and dignity'.[19]

On one side, then, the temptation is to suppose order and value are merely data in the world, obscure but given facts of life to which the individual consciousness must submit, rather than possibilities of the world realised by the mind *in* its activity, forms in which the individual realises his identity as at once an individual, an inhabitant of a particular society, and a member of the human race. On the other side, the temptation is to equate an integral wholeness of being with a visible, objective simplicity. It is all too easy to think we have located our 'true' self when we have only lopped our experience back to some 'essential' or 'natural' pattern supposedly underlying all complexities: locating it, for instance, in the consciousness of our continuous and sincere attachment to a number of basic virtues. Pope's struggle to get free of both these temptations marks his artistic development through the 1730s and 1740s.

IV

It is interesting to see the change from the *Essay on Man* in (say) the *Imitation* of Horace's first Epistle of Book I, published in 1738. Here, Pope speaks of the imprudence of galloping his Pegasus to death, of the folly of writing at all, and of the inconsistencies he shares with the victims of his satire. But the poetry in which he speaks of all this is anything but a Pegasus 'devoid of fire, or force', and anything but incoherent. He talks as if inside the public Poet there was a simple, virtuous, wholly self-possessed Man struggling to get out—one who might say what he says elsewhere, 'Let Us be fix'd, and our own Masters still'.[20] But both the public and the private selves here turn out to be only manifestations of a yet deeper self: the one that looks at the other two, laughs at the contrast, and actually is its 'own master still', but *without* being 'fixed'. Bolingbroke may be most fully himself in 'never' (as Pope puts it) 'changing one muscle of his face' at the inconsistencies of other men; the integrity Pope realises in the poem is of a different (and more valuable) kind. For the self that writes these lines must laugh at his other two manifestations, not only because they are false, but also because they are not wholly false. Each does simplify, and so reduce, the whole of Pope's identity, but neither is insincere or a mere 'mask' or *persona*. As the writer sees, the only way he can realise his whole self is in the vivacious, critical, and coherent per-

---

[19] Ibid.
[20] 'The Second Satire of the Second Book of Horace, Paraphrased', line 180 (*Poems*, p. 624).

ception of those aspects of it—and of the social and personal facts to which those aspects are the only honest, sincere answer he can make in the real world.[21]

All the *Imitations of Horace* and both the *Epistle to Arbuthnot* and the *Epilogue to the Satires* are built, more or less securely, on a similar interplay between the public self (in his various forms—the Wit, the Critic, the Sage, the Moralist, and so on), the private 'real' self beneath that (in his various forms—lisping in numbers, stooping to truth, practising virtue, or piddling along with broccoli and mutton), and the writer of the actual poem in which the other two are portrayed and defended. One common mistake with these poems is simply to equate all three figures, which unfortunately tends to make Pope look something of a hypocrite at times, or rather priggish, or pompously self-important. Another is to separate the three figures altogether, which unfortunately tends to leave him with no specific identity at all. But it is not always clear just how the three figures are related to one another—largely because Pope the writer was not always clear about it either. The *Epistle to Arbuthnot* is a case in point, where the end of the poem seems quite at odds with the rest. As a personal apologia, the *Epistle* really depends on the brilliant 'fire' of its poetry and the protean but steady 'force' of its insight and judgment: on an imaginative wholeness, that is, of which only a part consists in the 'wit' and honesty of the public self, and another part in the conscious moral intent of the private self. This is clear enough even in lines not directly about himself:

> You think this cruel? take it for a rule,
> No creature smarts so little as a Fool.
> Let Peals of Laughter, *Codrus!* round thee break,
> Thou unconcern'd canst hear the mighty Crack.
> Pit, Box and Gall'ry in convulsions hurl'd,
> Thou stand'st unshook amidst a bursting World.
> (lines 83ff.)

The writer of these lines is obviously not one who could stand unshook amidst a bursting world; indeed, he demonstrates his lack of folly in his very responsiveness to Codrus's nature. His 'wit' lies in seeing that the ability to stand in unshaken self-possession in all circumstances and *not* to feel threatened or excited by the outside world, is the mark of an ultimate lack of spirit and intelligence. Obviously the writer here is not the public figure, whose only wish

---

[21] Pope's tone earlier, in his correspondence, is significantly different from that of the Imitation of Horace, Bk I, Ep. i; see, e.g., *Correspondence of Alexander Pope*, ed. George Sherburn, 5 vols., Oxford, 1956, I, 185-6, 201-3 (on inconsistency and activity); II, 141 (on retirement); II, 315 (on folly).

is to 'maintain a Poet's Dignity and Ease'. Nor is he the private man, who in the final section of the poem claims that he only wishes to 'live my own! and die so too!' (line 261) and to be like his 'innoxious' father, who 'held it for a rule /It was a Sin to call our Neighbour Fool' (lines 382-3). This latter self is quite sincere, of course, in wanting only to 'rock the Cradle of reposing Age /With lenient Arts extend a Mother's breath'; but in the final section of the poem, the writer has come simply to identify himself with the private man; and in doing so, he has stamped flat all the vital antitheses in his own being—the being who could respond with such insight and such controlled, 'unlenient' art to Codrus, for instance, or to Atticus, or to Sporus: 'And he himself one vile Antithesis'. The last section of the poem fails to sustain the bite and integrity of passages like those.

Pope's impulse to 'fix' an identity that he could *know* was continually at odds with his very capacity to know anything—with his appetite for life, his mobility, and his vivacious intelligence and wit. On the other hand, he could not simply define himself as a bundle of contradictions either: he was conscious of a more significant kind of coherence than that. Thus, although he was often led to identify himself in rather conventional terms, this does not mean that the impulse to do so represented something merely conventional in him. It does mean, however, that he is not reducible to any one of the self-images he projects in his verse. In his satires of the 1730s, for instance, he is not, as Maynard Mack and others tend to assume he is, 'really' the virtuous Horatian Recluse, standing aside from a corrupted society and opposing to it his ideal vision of social life. Pope's poetry represents that world too, quite as much as (if not more than) those who corrupt it; and Mack's argument in *The Garden and the City* seems to me based on an insufficiently wide and critical grasp of the poetic facts.[22] As a matter of biographical fact, Pope's retirement from the city in the 1730s was obviously sincere; nor was there anything ignoble in wanting to withdraw from a corrupt society and to denounce its corruption. The long tradition of such 'retirement' to some simpler and loftier bastion of the spirit testifies to the perennial need behind it. But it is also important to notice that Pope denounces that society *to itself*. To identify him with any one aspect of him is to mistake only one aspect of his poetry for the whole. It is also to miss what his critical imagination achieves at its greatest moments. The poet that Mack depicts is hardly the one, for example, who in the *Epilogue to the Satires* penetrates with such searching and creative disgust, into the ambiguities of retirement:

[22] *The Garden and the City*, Toronto, 1969.

> There, where no Passion, Pride, or Shame transport,
> Lull'd with the sweet *Nepenthe* of a Court . . .
>
> (lines 7ff.)

Mack does observe, in a footnote, that Pope tends to take himself for a subject in the poems of the 1730s, and that 'his favorite image of himself' owes a 'transparent debt to Montaigne as well as Horace'.[23] He dismisses the matter as a 'subject that has not so far been adequately explored', and indeed it has not. Yet this way of putting it is no less misleading than Mack's own emphasis. For if the best of Pope's poetry is not written by a virtuous Recluse, neither is it written by a man who (as Pope claims) loves 'to pour out all myself, as plain /As downright *Shippen*, or as old *Montagne*'. As he says, 'Fools rush into my Head, and so I write',[24] but the actual writing is certainly no pouring out of the self nor the exercise of some favourite self-image. Because the cast of Pope's imagination is so thoroughly dialectical, the impulse to 'fix' his true character is not merely a misguided attempt to identify himself with some consciously chosen *persona* or image, nor even a wish to play every role in the text like Bottom the weaver. It is the necessary reaction to the *out*going imagination, an attempt to find the centre in himself from which the imagination darts forth and to which it returns, the point where the personal fuses with the impersonal, each giving life, definition, and authority to the other.

V

The full integrity of his own life was something Pope could realise only 'dramatically' (as he does in most of *Arbuthnot*, for example, or in the ending of the *Epilogue to the Satires*),[25] but I think his greatest poetry is dramatic in a more direct sense: where his imagination, his 'whole soul', turns completely outwards to the lives of other selves, and realises its own integrity only in realising that of its object.

I have deliberately used the word 'integrity' because it embraces various inter-related meanings, which we need to be clear about in order to understand Pope's real achievement and importance. In its most obvious sense, 'integrity' refers to *moral* wholeness or consistency. An individual has 'integrity' in possessing a single, unyielding ethical core. That is, the word pertains to the understanding and the will; to lack integrity in this sense is to be insincere, or

---

[23] Ibid., p. 234, n. 4.
[24] 'The First Satire of the Second Book of Horace, Imitated', lines 51-2, 14 (*Poems*, pp. 615, 614).
[25] For a different view of the *Epilogue to the Satires*, see Thomas R. Edwards, *Imagination and Power*, London, 1971, pp. 106ff.

weak, or just morally stupid. With an eye to Pope's rather confused ideas on the subject, we might also notice that the word 'character' can have pretty much the same meaning as 'integrity' here: 'a man of integrity' is 'a man of character'.

In a second sense, 'integrity' refers to *psychological* wholeness or consistency—the particular pattern of motives and causes that determine the individual's feelings, attitudes and behaviour. Even a villain may have a human 'integrity' in this sense; to lack it is to be mad, or unstable, or an incomprehensible mystery. And once again 'character' can have much this same meaning too: as in Pope's line, 'Most Women have no Characters at all'.[26]

In yet a third sense, 'integrity' refers to the realised *identity* of an individual—the completeness with which he is the particular human being he is, his coherence, his Total disposition, as a single being. Since this comprises all of his particular ways of being alive in the world, as distinct from those of any other person, the word now includes what is meant by the existentialists' term 'authenticity'. To lack this kind of integrity is to fail in some vital respect to be an individual at all, or to be oneself only incompletely, to live (as the existentialist would put it) in 'bad faith'. What makes the corresponding sense of 'character' hard to define is that sometimes we regard a person's disposition as something he chooses, the effect of an unconscious will in him to be what he is, while at other times we regard his capacity to choose as finally dependent on his disposition, so that his 'character' seems less the visible effect of his choice than the visible sign of his fate or destiny. Nevertheless, there is a relevant sense of 'character' here: if, for example, a man acts gratuitously, he negates his 'character' in the first sense I mentioned, and in another way the second sense too, but he affirms it in this third sense. Thus Macbeth's 'character' (or 'integrity') lies in *everything* he chooses to his fate to be—although, as we see it, this is also everything he is destined to choose.

But at this point the three senses of the word obviously begin to coalesce. In the last analysis, we cannot separate destiny and choice, constancy and freedom; and we therefore give 'integrity' or 'character' a composite meaning to embrace all the ways that impersonal facts and forces and values shape the individual person, and are in turn given visible shape and significance by the whole, integral activity of the person. At the very roots of consciousness, and *a fortiori* of self-consciousness, impersonal causes seem both to determine, and yet to be transformed into, personal motive and choice;

---

[26] 'Epistle II: To a Lady', line 2 (*Poems*, p. 560). Cf. the prose argument to the poem: 'the Characters of *Women* . . . are yet more inconsistent and incomprehensible than those of Men' (p. 559).

impersonal social traditions and pressures seem to condition, and yet to be subject to, the personal will that accepts or rejects them; the possibilities of an impersonal order in the objective world seem to be realised only in the personal activity of apprehending them.[27] In the end, the 'integrity' of any individual is nothing less than his 'whole soul' in active and passive engagement with the whole of the not-self. It is the complex but elusive sense of 'character' corresponding to this that Shakespeare was concerned with (as in *Macbeth* or *King Lear*); so, in different ways, have the great novelists of the nineteenth and twentieth centuries been concerned with it too, as in some of Dickens's so-called 'caricatures', for instance, or (more consistently) in *The Brothers Karamazov*, or *Daniel Deronda*, or *Nostromo*, or in *Women in Love* and *Ulysses*. The tragic writer is most aware of how *much* a man may choose to experience in order to be what he is; the comic writer (and theories of 'humours' or the like are very much to the point) is most aware of how *little* a man need choose to experience in order to be what he is; but obviously these are not mutually exclusive points of view: indeed, in Pope it is almost impossible to distinguish them at times. But it is finally in Pope's concern with human 'character' in this sense that I see the basis of his stature and importance.

He tries to explain his ideas about it mainly in the first of the *Moral Essays*, on the 'Ruling Passion', and it is not hard to see why so few readers have taken him seriously. All of Johnson's objections, for example, are thoroughly justified; Pope's argument is confused, and does look like 'a kind of moral predestination' doubly confused with an absurdly simplified psychology.[28] Nevertheless, it is worth asking if Pope was not driving at something rather different from what he seems to be saying, or even from what he thought he was saying. He talks about both causes and motives, but muddles them together; he talks about inconsistencies both of behaviour and of valuation, but muddles these together too; he claims that social forces condition the individual's 'manners', but he also claims that social phenomena are shaped and coloured by the 'manners' of the individual perceiving them. But if I have rather laboured the meaning of the term 'integrity' or 'character', it is because it may help us see Pope's confusion here as the result less of incompetence than of an insight he could not quite express in the conceptual vocabulary available to him. As I see it, his real concern is not to reduce human behaviour to a single psychological cause, nor (like

---

[27] This last point is discussed quite suggestively by Patricia Spacks in *An Argument of Images*, Chaps. 2 and 4.
[28] *Lives* (ed. Hill), III, 174-5.

Shaftesbury, and even Montaigne perhaps)[29] to try to reduce all the individual's ethical activity to a single centre where it assumes rational consistency. Nor is he merely after a formula for depicting an individual's unique identity. His own principle, that 'all Manners take a tincture from his own', applies to his analytic 'manner' here. The awareness of his personal inconsistencies and fluidity impelled him to try to 'fix' his full integrity in some concept of himself; just so, his very responsiveness to others' inconsistencies impels him to try to fix their full integrity: to fix the point at which men's 'Manners with Fortunes, Humours turn with Climes', which is also the point where those fortunes and climes become destinies men choose for themselves in choosing to obey their pressure. The 'ruling passion' is the name Pope gives the point at which the individual is most intensely, most passionately, alive *as himself*; and since it also *delimits* his being, it is like the 'lurking principle of death' he receives at 'the moment of his breath'.[30] Thus the term includes all its psychological, moral, and even philosophical meanings, since it is what we might call a 'dramatic' principle: for Pope, the 'ruling passion' is the shaping and animating principle of an individual life as a dramatist would conceive it simultaneously from within and from outside.[31] Not surprisingly, Pope's meaning emerges far more clearly in the way his imagination actually sees particular cases (in the examples at the end of the poem) than in the way his intellect tries to expound the idea. With Helluo, whose 'fate' was a salmon's belly, as with the miserly old crone, or poor vain Narcissa, or any of them indeed, the individual's integrity—which is nothing less than the very principle of life in him and therefore nothing less than his whole destiny—can be seen as comic or heroic or tragic or (as Pope sees it here) something of all three at once. But either way, Pope's 'Characters' here and elsewhere—Atticus, say, or Sporus, or Villiers, or the main figures in the fourth Book of *The Dunciad*—are distinguished from those of any writer of 'Characters' before him precisely by this kind of integrity: the integrity of his imagination comprehending (and so also judging) the integrity of the individual as at once an ethical

---

[29] Cf. Shaftesbury, 'Soliloquy', in *Characteristics* (ed. Robertson), I, 197-212, and Montaigne, 'Of the Inconstancy of our Actions', in *Essays*, II, i.

[30] *Essay on Man*, II, 133-4 (*Poems*, p. 520).

[31] On the background meanings of 'ruling passion', see Mack's Introduction to the *Essay on Man*, pp. xxxviff.; Bertrand A. Goldgar, 'Pope's Theory of the Passions: the Background of Epistle II of the *Essay on Man*', *Philological Quarterly*, XLI (1962), 742-3; and Benjamin Boyce, *The Character-Sketches in Pope's Poems*, Durham, N.C., 1962, Chap. 6. The similarity of Pope's sense of 'character' and Shakespeare's is briefly mentioned by Reuben Brower, *The Poetry of Allusion*, pp. 298 and 301; cf. p. 305 on the 'sensitive point' in Pope himself, where 'taste' and moral judgment meet.

Plate XIII Thomas Rowlandson, 'The Lord of the Manor receiving his Rents', drawing (Huntington Library and Art Gallery).

Plate XIV Thomas Rowlandson, 'Attendance on a Nobleman', *The Vicar of Wakefield*, London 1817 edition, Plate 18 (Huntington Library and Art Gallery).

being, a social or psychological type, and a unique consciousness, sensibility, and will.[32]

Pope's judgments are therefore far more complex and searching than any reference to conscious Augustan norms would suggest. Some of the finest examples come in the second *Moral Essay*, on 'the Characters of Women'—examples all the more interesting for the hints here and there of a conscious relationship between the subject and Pope himself. Flavia, the 'Wit', whose whole being desires 'while we live, to live', has so much fire and force that she can only 'die of nothing but a Rage to live'. She has authenticity, we might say, but no moral centre. The cases that immediately follow have a moral centre, a 'fixed' character, but lack a necessary mobility or 'fire'. With Atossa, Pope actually echoes the phrase he had used of himself: 'with herself or others', she 'finds all her life one warfare upon earth'. She

> Shines, in exposing Knaves, and painting Fools,
> Yet is, whate'er she hates and ridicules.
> (lines 117-18)

'*Madame Atossa, c'est moi*'. It is as if Pope is realising in himself the *self*-laceration he sees as Atossa's 'character'. Again, at some points he tends to think of women (rather simplistically) as 'chameleons' that cannot be accurately painted in 'white and black' —with the clear implication, of course, that he has to be something of a chameleon himself to get them 'right'. At the end, however, turning to Martha Blount, he sees not a chameleon, but a 'blend' of the best (but opposing) qualities of each sex: 'Fix'd Principles, with Fancy ever new', and so on. Heaven 'shakes all together and produces—You'. Once again the self-implication is clear. If Heaven gave her sense and good humour, it also gave her a poet whose own character—chameleon-like, but not without 'fixed principles'—can realise the nature and value of hers. Pope makes the point about himself very delicately—and of course long before Keats used the same word, chameleon, for the 'dramatic' poet's lack of a fixed identity.

Nevertheless, oppositions like that between 'chameleon' and 'fixed principles' are hardly adequate to Pope's very greatest poetry, here or elsewhere: for example, the passage here that begins, 'Yet mark the fate of a whole Sex of Queens!', and ends with 'Alive ridiculous,

---

[32] Benjamin Boyce (*Character-Sketches*, p. 82) briefly notes some of the qualities that distinguish Pope's portraits: his remarkable 'inward' sense of character; his continuous interest in human 'inconsistency'—i.e. in the nature of the individual's unique identity (pp. 96, 114, 125); and the 'intensely emotional perception' that unifies the details in his finest 'Characters' so that 'the imagination can accept [the result] as a dynamic organism' (p. 128).

and dead, forgot' (lines 219-48). At first, the lines do turn on the opposition between the 'foreign glory, foreign joy' that women seek—the outgoing movement of life, against its integrating movement inwards towards a stable centre: 'Peace or Happiness at home', a 'well-tim'd Retreat' from the world, and so on. Yet (as always with Pope) the word 'fate' introduces a more profound kind of insight and judgment, which transcends such polarities: 'As Hags hold Sabbaths' . . . 'their merry miserable Night' . . . 'Ghosts of Beauty' . . . 'haunt the places where their Honour dy'd' . . . 'See how the World its Veterans rewards'. Compared with the way Pope saw human 'fate' in *The Rape of the Lock*, this passage is not only more substantial, more deeply observed, felt, and considered; his object here, in all of its personal, social, and even metaphysical dimensions, wholly contains his response to it in all of *its* dimensions. Here, 'fixed principles' *are* 'fancy ever new', and 'sense' and 'good humour' the other side of horror and compassion. To know that the life of a Wit is a warfare upon earth can amuse him, but it can also lacerate him with the consciousness of his being not just an elusive chameleon but a scarred and vulnerable veteran of the world too. But it is the *life* of the Wit, wholly realised in seeing what it means for these women to be no more than veterans of the world, that finally prevents him from also being 'alive, ridiculous, and dead, forgot'.[33]

A comparable passage is the ending of the third *Moral Essay* (to Bathurst), 'Of the Use of Riches'. Whatever argumentative function the story of Sir Balaam has in the Essay as a whole, I think Pope's instinct was right to end with it, for it collects and fuses together all the various attitudes towards money and the power of money that go before. The Balaam passage is at once a 'life', a tale, a criticism of society, a brilliantly funny tragedy, a religious parable—a whole drama, one might say, or rather a whole novel, concentrated under intensely creative power into a mere sixty-four lines. It is surely one of the greatest things in the language; certainly, it is characteristic of nobody but Pope. In theory, of course, his account earlier in the poem of the Man of Ross (lines 250-82) represents his ideals—the norm against which he claims to be judging the commercialisation of society. In fact, it represents only what he thought his central norm was. The difference in actual effect between that passage and the account of Sir Balaam could hardly be more striking: with the Man of Ross, rhetorical questions and vaguely

---

[33] It is worth noticing that the central metaphor of 'veterans' was absent from the first version of these lines, which began, 'Not as the World its pretty Slaves rewards': see *The Poems of Alexander Pope*, Vol. III, ii; *Epistles to Several Persons (Moral Essays)*, ed. F. W. Bateson, London, 1951, p. 67, note to lines 243-8.

general nouns, the verse deliberately flattening out its characteristic tensions and antitheses to correspond with an ideal peace, an ideal singleness of purpose, and a human identity so ideally simple that it is no more than the sum of its virtuous deeds—and £500 per annum; with Balaam, verve, spirit, a tone responsively alive to every manifestation of life—'an added pudding', 'farthings to the poor', 'his gains were sure', 'rouz'd by the Prince of Air, the whirlwinds sweep /The surge', 'lo! two puddings smoak'd upon the board', 'Behold Sir Balaam, now a man of spirit', 'Things change their titles, as our manners turn'. All through the passage, the rhythms evoke and comment simultaneously; the nouns are specific, and they gather metaphoric generality like an electrical charge. Pope's attitude is no less complex than the complex relationship he sees between having one's soul 'secured', and 'being a man of spirit' and 'wit'; between being acted upon and choosing to be acted on; between 'biting' and being 'bit'; between 'manners' and names and 'titles'. The energy of the verse is that of the world it evokes, even that of the Prince of Air who enters this society through the soul Balaam opens to him. Pope really *enjoys* Balaam. His detachment includes a certain complicity; his contempt is mixed, though not diluted, with pity. The writing is more buoyant, less compassionate than the passage on women; but the same edge of dismay under the precision, the bitter taste of loss and futility that gathers under the moralist's relentless logic, make the last few lines on Balaam's end far more adequate a response to this society than all the talk about moderation, general use, reconciled extremes, and the 'thrice happy' Man of Ross. Here, the choices and deeds and understanding of men (including Pope's own) are seen as conditioned by inescapable forces—psychological, social, moral, and metaphysical—and conversely those forces are seen as manifesting themselves for good or evil only in the individual's life—in personal choices, deeds, and understanding.

The greatness of the final *Dunciad* lies in this kind of dramatic insight and power, much more than in its forceful application of Augustan norms to Augustan society and culture. Not that the two features are wholly distinct, of course: like Balaam's life, the life of Pope's poetry obviously depends on the norms to which he gives real (not merely notional) assent. It is significant, for instance, that *Dunciad* IV harks back (sometimes in a seriously ironic way) to some of his earlier works;[34] the poem itself announces the personal

---

[34] Reuben Brower has noted the structural likeness to *The Temple of Fame* (see *The Poetry of Allusion*, p. 354); but the central insight echoes the early lines on Dulness for Wycherley's *Panegyrick on Dulness* (*Poems*, pp. 272-3), and the ending that of the early *Messiah*.

implications right at the start. The poet prays to the mysterious powers he celebrates and to which Time is also taking him: 'Suspend a while your Force inertly strong, /Then take at once the Poet and the Song' (lines 7-8). As he sees it here, Dulness is not just a possibility in the world he inhabits, a 'Seed of Chaos, and of Night', but an actual reality: it is the buzzing energy, the inert power, the weird and crazy forms of the life Pope also shares. It is the operatic singer, for example:

> Joy to great Chaos! let Division reign:
> Chromatic tortures soon shall drive them hence ...
> One Trill shall harmonize joy, grief, and rage,
> Wake the dull Church, and lull the ranting Stage ...
> (lines 54ff.)

It is the bard and blockhead marching side by side; the schoolmaster transforming boys into pedants; pedants transforming verse into prose again; the chef transforming 'Hares to Larks, and Pigeons into Toads'; the florist transforming the flowers of nature (including its human flowers: 'Each Maid cry'd, charming! and each Youth, divine!'); the fop transforming the education of taste into the mere eduction of tastes; and so on. The verse is alive with their activity, dense with their mental 'density', and integrated by their creation of 'one mighty Dunciad of the land'.

Obviously, part of the joke is that Pope (and we) realise perfectly well what he is doing here in transforming the Dunces' life into something else. The poet's creative 'character' is realising itself in realising theirs. His wit pounces on their activities as the material of its own. It too is buzzing with energy, vivacious, gaily—indeed, hilariously—responsive to every crazy object, exultant in its power to dart forth anywhere and everywhere so quickly and accurately. But it realises 'madness' and 'chaos' for what they are only because it sees them by the light of its own sanity and order, its own integrity. Pope, we should notice, does not now suppose that sanity and order are objective realities outside himself, divinely given facts merely obscured by a 'maze' of appearances. The world he sees and recreates here is not one of mere appearances, any more than the values by which it is judged are absolutes shining clearly behind the clouds. The sun itself is 'sick'; it is precisely because Dulness is real and alive that it is so much of a threat to the fullest realisation of life. Moreover, it is a double threat. On the one side, the chaotic plenitude of 'madness', its ever-multiplying forms, its 'bursting world', draw the mind (Pope's mind, our minds, the Dunces' minds) outwards, spinning the wits away from any stable integrity, any morally coherent, psychologically whole, personally authentic being.

On the other side, its force is that of inertia; it continually pulls the wits back, in towards the single, fixed, impregnable centre of rest, of *inaction*.

In Pope's whole sense of it, the threat of Dulness lies in the 'one trill' that 'harmonizes joy, grief, and rage' as much as in its 'chromatic tortures', in the 'dull Church' as much as 'the ranting Stage'. The hour in which Dulness triumphs is quite properly the 'all-composing' hour. Peace, concord, and unity are achieved in the 'one mighty Dunciad of the land'. If Dulness is the necessary element of the poet's life as a Wit, and all the figures in the poem like parodies of himself (and of the understanding reader), it is also a 'resistless' power, one the Muse must also 'obey'. It is the power that finally composes everything in an all-inclusive unity, in imperturbable self-possession, in absolute integrity: in short, in the undivided, unviolated chaos of boredom, sleep and death. The final joke—and Pope clearly appreciates it to the full—is that (like any man, but more objectively than most) he realises his own life, his own 'character', in triumphing (with the fullest and most passionately committed activity of his 'wit') over the 'resistless' triumph he proclaims. Although the poem portrays the 'all-composing' power of Dulness, the kind of 'all-composing' power it actually embodies, the creative power of human 'wit', remains to confront the triumph of Dulness with a very different kind of composure, energy, and integrity.[35]

VI

If there is any substance in the view of Pope I have been advancing here, it has some more general implications, of which I shall mention only two. In the first place, it supports G. K. Hunter's conclusion that in Pope's *Imitations of Horace*, Pope is far more personal, more 'Romantic' as Hunter puts it, than his original.[36] More than that, we also find in Pope hints of the idea of the poet-as-outcast (as William Empson has put it),[37] and even a self-reflexive irony, both of which are usually regarded as specifically Romantic characteristics. Again, Pope exhibits the kind of interplay

---

[35] Several illuminating discussions of *The Dunciad* have appeared in the last decade or so: Murray Krieger, 'The "Frail China Jar" and the Rude Hand of Chaos', *Centennial Review*, V (1961), 176-94; H. H. Erskine-Hill, 'The "New World" of Pope's Dunciad', *Renaissance and Modern Studies*, VI (1962), 49-67; Tony Tanner, 'Reason and the Grotesque: Pope's Dunciad', *Critical Quarterly*, VII (1965), 145-60; Emrys Jones, 'Pope and Dulness', *Proceedings of the British Academy*, LIV (1968), 231-63. (The first three are reprinted in *Essential Articles*, ed. Maynard Mack, 1968.)

[36] 'The "Romanticism" of Pope's Horace', *Essays in Criticism*, X (1960), 390-404.

[37] *The Structure of Complex Words*, London, 1952, p. 96.

between a 'chameleon' self and a 'central self' that Patricia Ball sees as a crucial feature of Romantic and Victorian poetry.[38] To say all this, however, is not to claim that Pope was 'really' a Romantic, nor merely to repeat (what everyone knows) that 'Augustan' and 'Romantic' are very slippery terms. But it does suggest that the English Romantics differed from Pope less in *exhibiting* these characteristics, than in being philosophically conscious of them and of their fundamental importance, and so taking them as a conscious *program* for poetry. Indeed, it may well be argued that it was just this philosophic and programmatic self-consciousness that limited nineteenth-century poetry. No matter how wide and subtle one's self-consciousness, to 'fix' it in *any* conceptual terms is to make it that much harder to sustain a full integrity of being; and this applies to the Romantics, who understood the point and worried about it, as much as to Pope, who never saw it in those terms. Perhaps the nineteenth-century novelists could achieve this kind of integrity more readily than the poets because they looked at the world more objectively, more dramatically; inasmuch as they were 'fixed' only upon seeking the full integrity of other people's lives, they could more fully realise their own.

As for the second implication, its relevance is illustrated in some recent works by two influential critics, F. R. Leavis and Lionel Trilling. Leavis, for example, has made some very large claims for Blake. He sees Blake's 'rebellion' against Augustanism as 'a vindication' of all that cannot be treated in abstract or quantifiable terms 'since it is "there" only in individual lives'; where, according to Leavis, the Augustans saw man only as a social being, Blake insists that 'a man is an individual, and his individuality is his reality'.[39] This dichotomy of 'abstract' and 'social' on the one side, and 'individuality' and 'particularity' on the other, surely rests on far too conventional a view of the Augustan age; indeed, if my view of Pope is at all tenable, it shows that the Augustan age could, and did, transcend the dichotomy altogether, and it also suggests that, if Blake could not transcend it, this can hardly be regarded as altogether a strength in him.

Much the same objection also applies to Lionel Trilling's recent book, *Sincerity and Authenticity*.[40] For Trilling, the two words in his title represent different stages of moral consciousness, and the shift from one to the other in the late eighteenth century represents one of the most important revolutions in the European mind be-

[38] *The Central Self*, London, 1968.
[39] *English Literature in Our Time and the University*, London, 1969, p. 106. The view of Pope implicit in this passage seems cruder than that in Leavis's earlier (and classic) essays on Pope in *Revaluation* and *The Common Pursuit*.
[40] London, 1972.

tween the sixteenth century and the present. This is not the place to discuss Trilling's argument as a whole, but it does seem to be based on a view of each literary period that, however valid for French or German literature, is little more than a conventional stereotype for English literature. To put it bluntly, English literature from Shakespeare onwards has been more profoundly and more continuously concerned with what I have tried to indicate with the word 'integrity' than with, firstly, 'sincerity' alone, and then 'authenticity' alone. The polarity—or rather the quasi-Hegelian dialectic—that Trilling sets up with these terms seems to me not only false to the history of English literature, but misleading even about his main focus of interest: the nature and genesis of 'modernism'. Anyone interested in modern literature must inevitably look at earlier literature in the light of that interest, but he has to look more sharply, more perceptively, and with fewer preconceptions than Trilling seems to; and this applies especially to those writers whose very stature lifts them beyond the commonplace attitudes of their day. It applies pre-eminently to Shakespeare, for example, and it also applies to Pope. It may well be that literary history—which is a form of cultural history—can hardly proceed, as E. H. Gombrich has suggested, without some quasi-Hegelian presuppositions about the field, or some quasi-Hegelian terms such as I have been using myself. But as Gombrich goes on to say, these have to be continuously *tested* in application, continuously brought up against a critical attention to the facts they are supposed to explain.[41] If any conclusion is beginning to emerge from recent critical studies of eighteenth-century literature, it is that the old, essentially nineteenth-century stereotype of 'Augustanism' will no longer do, nor will any history of English literature based upon it. The relationship between integrity and life in Pope's poetry is a case in point. If we look at it critically and without preconceptions about Pope's art, it surely invites a rather different view of English literature from Trilling's pretty conventional one, or Leavis's, and of English literature not merely in the eighteenth century, but in the nineteenth and twentieth centuries as well.

---

[41] *In Search of Cultural History*, Oxford, 1969, esp. pp. 42ff.

Allusion: The Poet as Heir

Christopher Ricks

I

Augustan poetry is remarkable for its literary allusion; the poetry creates meanings, comprehends judgments, and animates experiences, by bringing into play other works of literature and their very words. This is 'the Poetry of Allusion', to cite the subtitle of Reuben Brower's *Alexander Pope*.[1] I should like to consider the implications of J. B. Broadbent's words: 'Literary allusion can be a lesson in the abuse of authority, as well as in the generous spending of an inheritance. We need an essay on "The poet as heir".'[2]

My argument is that literary allusion is a way of dealing with the predicaments and responsibilities of 'the poet as heir'; that there are features of late seventeenth-century history and literary history, and of Dryden's biography (Dryden, the father of literary allusion for the Augustans), which parallel such predicaments and responsibilities; and that many of the most telling instances of allusion in Augustan poetry have to do with the poet as heir. We should notice when the subject-matter of an allusion is at one with the impulse that underlies the making of allusions at all, because it is characteristic of art to find energy and delight in an enacting of that which it is saying, and to be rendered vigilant by a consciousness of metaphors and analogies which relate its literary practices to the great world.

There are many ways in which allusion can be self-delightingly about allusion, can catch fire from the rapidity of its own motion. Pope:

> Back to the Devil the last echoes roll,
> And 'Coll!' each Butcher roars at Hockley-hole.
> *(The Dunciad B, I, 325-6)*[3]

[1] *Alexander Pope: The Poetry of Allusion*, Oxford, 1959.
[2] *Paradise Lost: Introduction*, Cambridge, 1972, pp. 100, 102.
[3] Quotations from Pope are from *The Poems of Alexander Pope*, ed. John Butt, London, 1963, which I follow in citing as *The Dunciad* A the edition of 1728-9, and as *The Dunciad* B the edition of 1742-3.

Dryden:

> Echoes from *Pissing-Ally*, *Sh*— call,
> And *Sh*— they resound from *A*— Hall.
> (*Mac Flecknoe*, lines 47-8)[4]

Pope's echoes reverberate, re-sound, because they depend on the allusion's echo; and the movement is not 'Back to the Devil' but gratefully back to Dryden. Again:

> But gentle *Simkin* just reception finds
> Amidst this Monument of vanisht minds.
> (*Mac Flecknoe*, lines 81-2)
> Which some the *Monument of Bodies*, name;
> The Arke, which saves from Graves all dying kindes;
> This to a structure led, long knowne to Fame,
> And cald, The Monument of vanish'd Mindes.
> (Davenant, *Gondibert*, II, v, 36)

Dryden's geniality is a matter of his allusion's alluding to itself, its saying to Davenant that he spoke too soon and yet spoke more wisely than he knew. What survives from Davenant rather gives the lie to any grand claim of 'long knowne to Fame'; and yet it does survive, and it was a good phrase, and Dryden is suitably grateful. The allusion is charmingly self-referring; the scale of it is appropriate to the scale of Davenant.

When a greater poet than Dryden alludes to a poet incomparably greater than Davenant, the scale is altogether grander, but the allusion still owes its fineness to its self-reference.

> *The Dunciad* B, II, 9-12:
> His Peers shine round him with reflected grace,
> New edge their dulness, and new bronze their face.
> So from the Sun's broad beam, in shallow urns
> Heav'ns twinkling Sparks draw light, and point their horns.
> *Paradise Lost*, VII, 364-6:
> Hither as to thir Fountain other Starrs
> Repairing, in thir gold'n Urns draw Light,
> And hence the Morning Planet guilds her horns.

Pope's allusion is doing truly what it contemplates in a travesty: it is gratefully drawing light from an even greater source of energy and illumination (Milton, the Sun); it is new-edging itself, and pointing itself, by means of a 'reflected grace'. To say this is not to smooth away the edged and pointed animosity in 'twinkling

---

[4] Quotations from Dryden's poems are from *The Poems and Fables of John Dryden*, ed. James Kinsley, Oxford, 1962, except that the translation of Virgil is cited from *The Poems of John Dryden*, ed. James Kinsley, 4 vols., Oxford, 1958.

Sparks'; but the feeling is of Pope and Milton ('Peers' in a true sense) standing assuredly together against such mere sparks. The result is a genuine 'grace' in Pope's sense of Milton; Pope is both graceful and gracious in the respect which he evinces for Milton, a respect perfectly compatible with an affection which knows that it risks impudence in thus turning such great poetry to its purposes, an affection that twinkles filially and not vacantly. In short, not only do Pope's lines describe the nature of a true allusion in the act of making one, they breathe the right spirit, 'the generous spending of an inheritance'.

Likewise, there is a special preposterousness of geniality at the moment in *Mac Flecknoe* when Fleckno's adjuration to Shadwell so amply refers to himself in the third person:

> Nor let false friends seduce thy mind to fame,
> By arrogating *Johnson*'s Hostile name.
> Let Father *Fleckno* fire thy mind with praise,
> And Uncle *Ogleby* thy envy raise.
> (lines 171-4)

The breadth of Dryden's humour here is a matter of the allusion to Virgil:

> ecquid in antiquam virtutem animosque virilis
> et pater Aeneas et avunculus excitat Hector?
> (*Aeneid*, III, 342-3)

This is not the mere employment of Virgil as a wheel to break a butterfly; it is precisely the risk of such an easily destructive comparison which the poetry has to fend off, and it succeeds in doing so because Dryden's lines are themselves about the allusive habit and the poet as heir. For it is Father Virgil who here properly yet modestly fires Dryden's mind with praise, in lines splendidly free from that 'envy' to which they allude. Dryden, humane and unsaintly, speaks often about the possibility of envy in the poet, and about a generous recognition of succession:

> Auspicious Poet, wert thou not my Friend,
> How could I envy, what I must commend!
> But since 'tis Natures Law in Love and Wit
> That Youth shou'd Reign, and with'ring Age submit,
> With less regret, those Lawrels I resign,
> Which dying on my Brows, revive on thine.
> ('To Mr Granville, on his Excellent Tragedy', lines 1-6)

Literary allusions to fathers (or to uncles) are liable to suggest a paternal-filial relationship between the alluded-to and the alluder, since the alluder has entered upon an inheritance; the great instances of allusion are often those where that to which allusion is liable ceases to be any kind of liability and becomes a source of energy and gratitude. As with the Virgilian allusion in one of Dryden's best poems, 'To the Memory of Mr. Oldham':

> Once more, hail and farewel; farewel thou young,
>   But ah too short, *Marcellus* of our Tongue.
>   (lines 22-3)

Dryden's translation of the *Aeneid* had discussed different interpretations of the lines at the end of Book VI:

> 'Tis plain, that *Virgil* cannot mean the same *Marcellus*; but one of his Descendants; whom I call a new *Marcellus*; who so much resembled his Ancestor, perhaps in his Features, and his Person, but certainly in his Military Vertues, that *Virgil* cries out, *quantum instar in ipso est!* which I have translated,
>   *How like the former, and almost the same.*[5]—
>   His Son, or one of his Illustrious Name,
>   How like the former, and almost the same.
>   (*Aeneid*, VI, 1194-5)

The beauty and the propriety of the Virgilian allusion in 'To the Memory of Mr. Oldham' derive from the gentle confidence that to Virgil, Dryden would be 'one of his Descendants'. If we had to sum up in one line both a true lineage and the true poetic lineage manifested in the art of allusion, it would be hard to better the similarity within difference of

> How like the former, and almost the same.

Two recent books are apt, though neither speaks of allusion: Walter Jackson Bate's *The Burden of the Past and the English Poet* and—a book which acknowledges its inheritance from Bate—Harold Bloom's *The Anxiety of Influence*.

'What is there left to do?': this cry animates Bate's book, in the belief that it has animated most poetry for the last three centuries.

> The central interest of the eighteenth century is that it is the first period in modern history to face the problem of what it means to come immediately after a great creative achievement.
> If Restoration England, through its delayed but now ready embrace of the neoclassic mode, at once secured standards that permitted it to avoid competition with the literature of the immediate past, this was especially because it could do so with that authority (in this case classical antiquity) which is always pleasing to have when you can invoke it from a distant (and therefore 'purer') source; pleasing because it is not an authority looming over you but, as something ancestral rather than parental, is remote enough to be more manageable in the quest

[5] *The Works of Virgil*, London, 1697, p. 633.

for your own identity. . . . For that matter, the ancestral permitted one—by providing a 'purer', more time-hallowed, more conveniently malleable example—even to disparage the parent in the name of 'tradition'. And in the period from 1660 to about 1730 there were plenty of people ready to snatch this opportunity. If their ranks did not include the major minds and artists, there were enough of them to justify us in recognizing this as the first large-scale example, in the modern history of the arts, of the 'leapfrog' use of the past for authority or psychological comfort: the leap over the parental—the principal immediate predecessors—to what Northrop Frye calls the 'modal grandfather'.[6]

For Bate, the crisis of Augustanism (with its heroic self-renewal) in the mid eighteenth century is a parental and ancestral burden of the past:

In short, the poet was now becoming flanked, in his own effort, on both sides—the parental as well as the classical-ancestral. At the same time, in a deeply disturbing way the features of the dead parent (more removed now and therefore most susceptible to the reverential and idealizing imagination) seemed to be settling into a countenance more like that of the ancestor. Almost—to the mid-eighteenth-century poet—the parental and ancestral seemed to be linking arms as twin deities looming above him.[7]

Harold Bloom's book, *The Anxiety of Influence*, seeks to further Bate's argument by making much more of the parental. 'I am afraid', says Bloom with the gloomy frisson that those words always promise, 'I am afraid that the anxiety of influence, from which we all suffer, whether we are poets or not, has to be located first in its origins, in the fateful morasses of what Freud, with grandly desperate wit, called "the family romance".'[8]

But Bloom's literary history too much plays at—and not just notices—leapfrog. He keeps saying 'post-Enlightenment English poetry', where 'post-' has the effect of a grand eliding; he says nothing about Dryden and Pope, but vaults from Milton to the Romantics, hovering only briefly over Gray. Yet a comprehension of Dryden and Pope, and of 'the family romance', could be greatly aided by such an observation as this by Bloom:

If one examines the dozen or so major poetic influencers before this century, one discovers quickly who among them ranks as the great Inhibitor, the Sphinx who strangles even strong

[6] Cambridge, Mass., 1970, p. 12. To illustrate Bate's point: Charles Churchill, for example, tried to escape oppression from Pope by leaping back to Dryden.
[7] *The Burden of the Past*, p. 43.
[8] Harold Bloom, *The Anxiety of Influence*, New York, 1973, pp. 56-7.

imaginations in their cradles: Milton. The motto to English Poetry since Milton was stated by Keats: 'Life to him would be Death to me'.[9]

But English poetry since Milton was—first of all—Dryden and Pope, and it is unfortunate that the great Inhibitor has inhibited Bloom from attending to Dryden. Not that he can dismiss Dryden from his mind, as a repeated allusion attests:

> Shakespeare belongs to the giant age before the flood, before the anxiety of influence became central to poetic consciousness.
>
> Yet there was a great age before the Flood, when influence was generous (or poets in their inmost natures thought it so), an age that goes all the way from Homer to Shakespeare.[10]

Bloom is inheriting from his father, Bate, the lines by Dryden which provide the epigraph to the first chapter of *The Burden of the Past*, the lines from 'To my Dear Friend Mr. Congreve' which proclaim of our poetic sires that 'Theirs was the Gyant Race, before the Flood'. Bate sees Dryden's greatness as intimately related to the shrewd generosity with which he recognised his predicament and its opportunity:

> In confronting a brilliantly creative achievement immediately before him in his own language, different from the mode he himself was to exploit, Dryden's situation as a seventeenth-century poet was almost unique. He is the first great European (not merely English) example of a major writer who is taking it for granted that the very existence of a past creates the necessity for difference—not for the audience, not *sub specie aeternitatis*, but for the writer or artist himself. It is typical of both his good sense and his courage as an artist—indeed one of the marks of his greatness—that he felt no defensive need to argue otherwise.[11]

II

When Johnson called Dryden 'the father of English criticism', his tribute (filial in its way) may have been partly to this very way of speaking. For Dryden is pre-eminently the critic who conceives of poetic creation and influence as paternal. It is a natural way to speak; yet there are a great many important critics who have not found it a valuable way to speak, and there are some literary periods where it is more ubiquitously apt than others. For Dryden, it is an essential figure of speech:

> Shakespeare was the Homer, or father of our dramatic poets

[9] Ibid., p. 32.
[10] Ibid., pp. 11, 122.
[11] Bate, *The Burden of the Past*, p. 31.

> . . . those two fathers of our English poetry [Waller and Denham].
> Homer the common father of the stage [as well as of the epic].¹²
> . . . as he [Chaucer] is the father of English poetry, so I hold him in the same degree of veneration as the Grecians held Homer, or the Romans Virgil.¹³

Dryden does not merely adopt the figure of speech, he pursues it:

> Milton was the poetical son of Spenser, and Mr Waller of Fairfax; for we have our lineal descents and clans as well as other families: Spenser more than once insinuates that the soul of Chaucer was transfused into his body; and that he was begotten by him two hundred years after his decease.¹⁴

What may seem a casual metaphor—'This is that birthright which is derived to us from our great forefathers, even from Homer down to Ben'¹⁵—is crucial to the burden of the past, to the anxiety of influence, and to the son's need not to be oppressed by his father's greatness:

> And this, Sir, calls to my remembrance the beginning of your discourse, where you told us we should never find the audience favourable to this kind of writing till we could produce as good plays in rhyme as Ben Jonson, Fletcher, and Shakespeare had writ out of it. But it is to raise envy to the living, to compare them with the dead. They are honoured, and almost adored by us, as they deserve; neither do I know any so presumptuous of themselves as to contend with them. Yet give me leave to say thus much, without injury to their ashes, that not only we shall never equal them, but they could never equal themselves, were they to rise and write again. We acknowledge them our fathers in wit; but they have ruined their estates themselves before they came to their children's hands. There is scarce an humour, a character, or any kind of plot, which they have not blown upon: all comes sullied or wasted to us: and were they to entertain this age, they could not make so plenteous treatments out of such decayed fortunes. This therefore will be a good argument to us either not to write at all, or to attempt some other way. There is no bays to be expected in their walks: *tentanda via est, qua me quoque possum* [for *possim*] *tollere humo*.¹⁶

---

¹² Quotations from Dryden's criticism are from *Of Dramatic Poesy and Other Critical Essays*, ed. George Watson, 2 vols., London, 1962; abbreviated hereafter to Watson. Here, 'Of Dramatic Poesy'; Watson, I, 70. 'Discourse Concerning Satire'; Watson, II, 150. 'To John, Lord Marquess of Normanby'; Watson, II, 229.
¹³ 'Preface to *Fables*'; Watson, II, 280.
¹⁴ Ibid., p. 270.
¹⁵ 'The Author's Apology for Heroic Poetry'; Watson, I, 206.
¹⁶ 'Of Dramatic Poesy'; Watson, I, 85.

But 'the sons of Ben'? The implication of the metaphor there was that Jonson had many sons, sibling-poets. The one thing that there wasn't was a son of Ben. But the preoccupation in Dryden's criticism, as in seventeenth-century life, is rather with succession, with primogeniture, with a burden that is a crown or a prophetic mantle which falls to you with or without a double portion of your father's art. The supremacy of Milton, and then of Dryden, and then of Pope, is not something to which there is an earlier counterpart; Shakespeare did not enjoy the same sort of supremacy as Pope, and nor did Jonson. Moreover, the striking thing about 'the sons of Ben' is not just the singularity of the instance (of whom else do we use the formula?), but also that this formula was so soon to be inapplicable and even unthinkable. Milton had a greater influence than Jonson, and yet no one thinks of 'the sons of Milton'; something meanwhile had happened either to poetic influence or to the sense of what a family was or to both. Bloom is right:

> We remember how for so many centuries, from the sons of Homer to the sons of Ben Jonson, poetic influence had been described as a filial relationship, and then we come to see that poetic *influence*, rather than *sonship*, is another product of the Enlightenment.[17]

By 1727, sonship is for boobies:

> Who sees not that *De F—* was the Poetical Son of *Withers*, *T—te* of *Ogilby*, *E. W—rd* of *John Taylor*, and *E—n* of *Bl-k-re*?[18]

Dryden was sceptical about the long-lived sons of Ben ('They can tell a story of Ben Jonson, and perhaps have had fancy enough to give a supper in Apollo that they might be called his sons');[19] he took the idea of sonship seriously, in his sense of the antagonisms inseparable from emulation both with one's contemporaries (siblings) and with one's great fathers.

> 'Tis not with an ultimate intention to pay reverence to the *manes* of Shakespeare, Fletcher, and Ben Jonson that they commend their writings, but to throw dirt on the writers of this age: their declaration is one thing, and their practice is another. By a seeming veneration to our fathers they would thrust out us, their lawful issue, and govern us themselves, under a specious pretence of reformation....
>
> These attack the living by raking up the ashes of the dead; well knowing that if they can subvert their original title to the

[17] Bloom, *The Anxiety of Influence*, p. 26.
[18] *Of the Art of Sinking in Poetry*, London, 1727, p. 38.
[19] 'Defence of the Epilogue'; Watson, I, 181.

stage, we who claim under them must fall of course. Peace be to the venerable shades of Shakespeare and Ben Jonson! None of the living will presume to have any competition with them: as they were our predecessors, so they were our masters. We trail our plays under them; but (as at the funerals of a Turkish emperor) our ensigns are furled or dragged upon the ground, in honour to the dead; so we may lawfully advance our own afterwards, to show that we succeed; if less in dignity, yet on the same foot and title.[20]

This was best said when it was not his immediate predecessor but his great forefathers in whose steps—'on the same foot and title'— he was advancing. Of his translation of the *Aeneid* he remarked:

I would say that Virgil is like the Fame which he describes: mobilitate viget, viresque acquirit eundo.

Such a sort of reputation is my aim, though in a far inferior degree, according to my motto in the title-page: *sequiturque patrem non passibus aequis*.[21]

The praise of Virgil is effected through an allusion to him as a father, Virgil himself speaking of a father. Likewise *Fables Ancient and Modern* (1700) offers this as its epigraph, in the year of Dryden's death:

Nunc ultro ad Cineres ipsius & ossa parentis
(Haud equidem sine mente, reor, sine numine divum)
Adsumus.
Virg., Æn. lib. 5.

Pope said: 'To follow Poetry as one ought, one must forget father and mother, and cleave to it alone'; and again: 'To write well, lastingly well, Immortally well, must not one leave Father and Mother and cleave unto the Muse?'[22] But the father whom it is well-nigh impossible (or altogether impoverishing) to forget or to leave, is one's poetical father. Pope could not forget or leave his poetical father, Dryden; he dealt with this both by embracing it ('And win my way by yielding to the tyde')[23] and by a respectful good humour such as re-created Dryden not as his father but as his benign elder brother. Dryden had no less severe strain from his relation to such predecessors as Jonson, Shakespeare and Milton.

Fame then was cheap, and the first commer sped;
And they have kept it since, by being dead.

[20] 'To Lord Radcliffe'; Watson, II, 159, 160.
[21] 'To John, Lord Marquess of Normanby'; Watson, II, 244.
[22] To Jervas, 16 August 1714; to Bolingbroke, 9 April 1724; quoted by Maynard Mack, *The Garden and the City*, Toronto, 1969, pp. 112-13.
[23] Pope, 'The First Epistle of the First Book of Horace Imitated', line 34 (Poems, ed. Butt, p. 626).

> But were they now to write ...
> ('Epilogue to the Second Part of *Granada*',
> lines 11-13)
> Due Honours to those mighty Names we grant,
> But Shrubs may live beneath the lofty Plant:
> Sons may succeed their greater Parents gone;
> Such is thy Lott; and such I wish my own.
> ('To Sir Godfrey Kneller', lines 120-3)

Harold Bloom quotes three apophthegms, each apt to the predicament of poets since Dryden:

> 'He who is willing to work gives birth to his own father.'
> (Kierkegaard)
> 'When one hasn't had a good father, it is necessary to invent one.' (Nietzsche)
> 'All the instincts, the loving, the grateful, the sensual, the defiant, the self-assertive and independent—all are gratified in the wish to be *the father of himself*.' (Freud)[24]

This last calls to mind a profound jibe against Colley Cibber—profound because it sees Cibber as a travesty or parody of the poet-hero, not as quite unrelated:

> And that he did not pass himself on the world for a Hero, as well by birth as education, was his own fault: For, his lineage he bringeth into his life as an Anecdote, and is sensible he had it in his power *to be thought no body's son at all*: And what is that but coming into the world a Hero?
> (*The Dunciad* B, 'Aristarchus, of the Hero')

III

No poet-critic has found it as natural as Dryden to think in terms of succession. But then no English poet has ever had a more intimately professional relation with a king of England (indeed, with kings—and this in an era when kingship was a pondering of succession).

Dryden was involved in those successions. His 'Heroique Stanza's, Consecrated to the Glorious Memory of his most Serene and Renowned Highnesse *Oliver* late *Lord Protector*' (1659); his *Astræa Redux. A Poem On the Happy Restoration and Return of His Sacred Majesty Charles the Second* (1660): from those early poems through to *Threnodia Augustalis: A Funeral-Pindarique Poem Sacred to the Happy Memory of King Charles II* (1685), and *Britannia Rediviva: a Poem on the Birth of the Prince* (1688), Dryden occupied himself with kingship and succession. And even

---
[24] Bloom, *The Anxiety of Influence*, pp. 56, 64.

thereafter, since (as William J. Cameron has most notably shown) Dryden's translation of the *Aeneid* is among other things a prudent remonstrance to William III:

> William need only model himself on Dryden's hero, and he would automatically become a true monarch 'so as to gain the Affection of his Subjects, and deserve to be call'd the Father of his Country'.[25]

But then Dryden's greatest poem is about the succession to the throne. As George de F. Lord has said:

> It is appropriate that *Absalom and Achitophel*, a poem dealing with threats to the Stuart dynasty and to the principle of succession, should embody in every way the principles that underlie succession.[26]

Yet the force of the poem lies in the congruity between such political principles and its literary principles and practice, since the legitimate use of literary allusion (upon which *Absalom and Achitophel* so warrantedly relies) is itself a matter of a principled literary succession, an inheritance neither grudgingly withheld (as by a literary Bill of Exclusion) nor irresponsibly squandered.

The felicity for which Dryden hopes is embodied in the word 'succeed' itself; so *The Medall*, in speaking of the politics of 'Our Temp'rate Isle', can assert that

> The wholesome Tempest purges what it breeds;
> To recommend the Calmness that succeeds.
> (lines 254-5)

—where 'succeeds' is at once 'ensues', 'takes up the succession', and 'effects success'; the word recurs eighteen lines later ('Yet, shou'd thy Crimes succeed', line 273), and finally, sixteen lines later, Dryden plays 'Succession' beautifully against 'fail':

> If true Succession from our Isle shou'd fail . . .
> (line 289)

Once upon a time, fathers and kings were one and the same:

> When Empire first from families did spring,
> Then every Father govern'd as a King.
> (*To His Sacred Majesty*, lines 93-4)

Yet the realities of the parallel between king and father survive for Dryden, and they include the realities of succession and inheritance. 'To my Dear Friend Mr. Congreve, on his Comedy,

---

[25] 'John Dryden's Jacobitism', in *Restoration Literature: Critical Approaches*, ed. Harold Love, London, 1972, p. 297.
[26] ' "Absalom and Achitophel" and Dryden's Political Cosmos', in *John Dryden*, ed. Earl Miner, London, 1972, p. 171.

call'd The Double-Dealer' tightens these relationships, with a freedom from repining which constitutes an image of that true succession of which *Mac Flecknoe* is the grotesque travesty.

> Well then; the promis'd hour is come at last;
> The present Age of Wit obscures the past:
> Strong were our Syres; and as they Fought they Writ,
> Conqu'ring with force of Arms, and dint of Wit;
> Theirs was the Gyant Race, before the Flood;
> And thus, when *Charles* Return'd, our Empire stood . . .
> (lines 1-6)
> All this in blooming Youth you have Atchiev'd;
> Nor are your foil'd Contemporaries griev'd;
> So much the sweetness of your manners move,
> We cannot envy you because we love . . .
> (lines 31-4)
> Oh that your Brows my Lawrel had sustain'd,
> Well had I been Depos'd, if You had reign'd!
> The Father had descended for the Son;
> For only You are lineal to the Throne.
> Thus when the State one *Edward* did depose;
> A Greater *Edward* in his room arose.
> But now, not I, but Poetry is curs'd;
> For *Tom* the Second reigns like *Tom* the first.
> But let 'em not mistake my Patron's part;
> Nor call his Charity their own desert.
> Yet this I Prophesy; Thou shalt be seen,
> (Tho' with some short Parenthesis between:)
> High on the Throne of Wit; and seated there,
> Not mine (that's little) but thy Lawrel wear . . .
> (lines 41-54)
> Let not the Insulting Foe my Fame pursue;
> But shade those Lawrels which descend to You:
> And take for Tribute what these Lines express:
> You merit more; nor cou'd my Love do less.
> (lines 74-7)

IV

Inheritance binds together so much which mattered to Dryden and his time that it constitutes more than a manner of speaking. The affiliation is more than verbal between the lines in *Astræa Redux* which speak of political despair—

> We thought our Sires, not with their own content,
> Had ere we came to age our Portion spent.
> (lines 27-8)

—and those in *Of Dramatic Poesy* which speak of a literary predicament: 'We acknowledge them our fathers in wit; but they have ruined their estates themselves before they came to their children's hands'.²⁷

Ian Watt has described the Augustan tradition:

> The defensive postures of the landed interest and of Augustan literature can themselves be seen as having the same essential movement: to survey the broad acres of the human inheritance, to value them duly, and to unite for their preservation.²⁸

Augustan poetry is an art of 'the human inheritance', an art therefore especially alert to that human inheritance which is literary allusion. What was metaphorically true for poets (genuinely but metaphorically true) was simply true, legally true, for the Augustan gentleman. For it is the late seventeenth century which witnesses the creation of the strict settlement, designed to see that fathers do not ruin their estates before they come into their children's hands. H. J. Habakkuk does not speak of literature, but much of what he says as an economic historian is apt to an age which was preoccupied with literary as well as legal inheritance—an age which in choosing the advantages of the strict settlement was also choosing to be burdened or pinioned by the past and by inheritance.

> In the early eighteenth century, the arrangements by which the English aristocracy and gentry commonly provided for their families conformed to a standard pattern, the strict settlement, in which the essential questions were settled at the marriage of the eldest son. Not only was his immediate maintenance fixed and his wife's jointure, but the provision for the children of the marriage—how much they were to receive, in what form and when—was decided at the same time. In its essentials, the marriage settlement first secured that the family estate should in each generation descend to the eldest son. It did this by limiting the interest in the estate of the father of the husband, and, after him, of the husband himself, to that of a life-tenant, and entailing the estate on the eldest son to be born of the marriage.
>
> About the middle of the seventeenth century the invention of a highly technical legal device, trustees to preserve contingent remainders, removed what had hitherto been the main deficiency in the more stringent forms of settlement, by protecting the interest of the unborn son of the marriage. By the use of this device it was possible for a landowner to settle an estate for life on his eldest son at marriage and prevent him enlarging his interest. A landowner could now ensure that the estate remained intact until the male issue of the marriage

---

27 Watson, I, 85.
28 'Two Historical Aspects of the Augustan Tradition', in *Studies in the Eighteenth Century*, ed. R. F. Brissenden, Canberra, 1968, pp. 83-4.

became twenty-one; the eldest son, being only a life-tenant, could not frustrate the provision for his sisters and younger brothers, and had himself to specify the provision which would, in fact, be made for his own younger children—for a life-tenant could mortgage his estate only for purposes and amounts laid down in the deed which created his life-tenancy.

Strict settlements employing this device were widely adopted in the later seventeenth century, and by the early eighteenth century they were the typical way of settling estates and providing for the children among landowning families. (Note: 'The earliest example I have found is dated 1647'.)[29]

That much of this is apt to the subject-matter of Augustan literature (say, Dr Johnson's 'Short Song of Congratulation') is evident enough; and it is apt to the principles and proceedings of Augustan literature, preoccupied with literary inheritance.

V

One further aspect of the father-son pressures of which the Augustan poet was especially conscious asks mention: the patron. The patron is a father; the King is the supreme patron—except that he himself has an even greater patron.

> Such were the pleasing triumphs of the sky
> For *James* his late nocturnal victory;
> The pledge of his Almighty patron's love ...
>   (*The Hind and the Panther*, II, 654-6)[30]

The Augustans were sensitive to the duties and the defections of the patron, and the finest Augustan poems ponder a crisis of patronage. The assurances and the dubieties of patronage were among the father-son parallels that pressed (sometimes benignly) upon the Augustan poet, making him alert to the implications of a central metaphor—the father—which was also variously an actuality (a king, an actual father, a patron, a literary progenitor). Dryden links patron, parent, emperor, and literary father in his note to his *Aeneis* V:

> *Virgil* seems to me, to have excell'd *Homer* in all those Sports, and to have labour'd them the more, in Honour of *Octavius*, his Patron; who instituted the like Games for perpetuating the Memory of his Uncle *Julius*. Piety, as *Virgil* calls it, or dutiful-

---

[29] From 'Marriage Settlements in the Eighteenth Century', *Transactions of the Royal Historical Society*, 4th ser., XXXII (1950), 15-30. I am grateful to Keith Thomas for drawing my attention to this.

[30] Geoffrey Hill has a fine poem on God and the patron, 'To the (Supposed) Patron' (*For the Unfallen*, London, 1959).

ness to Parents, being a most popular Vertue among the Romans.³¹

Similarly the note to *Aeneis*, VI, 1143-6:

> [Embrace again, my Sons, be Foes no more:
> Nor stain your Country with her Childrens Gore.
> And thou, the first, lay down thy lawless claim;
> Thou, of my Blood, who bear'st the *Julian* Name.]
>
> *Anchises* here speaks to *Julius Cæsar*; And commands him first to lay down Arms; which is a plain condemnation of his Cause. Yet observe our Poet's incomparable Address: For though he shews himself sufficiently to be a Common-wealth's man; yet in respect to *Augustus*, who was his Patron, he uses the Authority of a Parent, in the Person of *Anchises*; who had more right to lay this Injunction on *Cæsar* than on *Pompey*; because the latter was not of his Blood. Thus our Author cautiously veils his own opinion, and takes Sanctuary under *Anchises*; as if that Ghost wou'd have laid the same Command on *Pompey* also, had he been lineally descended from him. What cou'd be more judiciously contrived, when this was the *Æneid* which he chose to read before his Master?³²

But does this fatherhood of patronage connect with inheritance, the poet as heir? One of Dryden's most marked insistences is that patronage is itself a dual inheritance.

> Yet I have no reason to complain of fortune, since in the midst of that abundance I could not possibly have chosen better than the worthy son of so illustrious a father. He was the patron of my manhood when I flourished in the opinion of the world; though with small advantage to my fortune, till he awakened the remembrance of my royal master. He was that Pollio, or that Varus, who introduced me to Augustus.
>
> You are acquainted with the Roman history, and know without my information that patronage and clientship always descended from the fathers to the sons; and that the same plebeian houses had recourse to the same patrician line which had formerly protected them, and followed their principles and fortunes to the last. So that I am your Lordship's by descent, and part of your inheritance. And the natural inclination which I have to serve you adds to your paternal right, for I was wholly yours from the first moment when I had the happiness and honour of being known to you.³³
>
> *My LORD*
>   Some Estates are held in *England*, by paying a Fine at the change of every Lord: I have enjoy'd the Patronage of your

---

³¹ *The Works of Virgil*, pp. 630-1.
³² Ibid., p. 633.
³³ 'To Hugh, Lord Clifford'; Watson, II, 217, 221-2.

Family, from the time of your excellent Grandfather to this present Day. I have dedicated the Lives of *Plutarch* to the first Duke; and have celebrated the Memory of your Heroick Father. Tho' I am very short of the Age of *Nestor*, yet I have liv'd to a third Generation of your House; and by your Grace's favour am admitted still to hold from you by the same Tenure. I am not vain enough to boast that I have deserv'd the value of so Illustrious a Line; but my Fortune is the greater, that for three Descents they have been pleas'd to distinguish my Poems from those of other Men; and have accordingly made me their peculiar Care. May it be permitted me to say, That as your Grandfather and Father were cherish'd and adorn'd with Honours by two successive Monarchs, so I have been esteem'd, and patronis'd by the Grandfather, the Father, and the Son, descended from one of the most Ancient, most Conspicuous, and most Deserving Families in *Europe*.[34]

VI

'I have enjoyed the Patronage of your Family, from the time of your excellent Grandfather to this present Day.' And Dryden's sons —whose patronage did they enjoy? Dryden had three sons; one named after his king (Charles, born 1666, died 1704), one after himself (John, born 1668, died 1703), and one half-named after his father (Erasmus-Henry, born 1669, died 1710).[35] Dryden's sons enjoyed in the first place the patronage of the royal patron:

> The King . . . seems to have been gracious enough to Dryden when his influence became a substitute for money. He had provided Dryden's eldest son a King's Scholarship at Westminster School; and we can be sure that upon the petition of the poet, he appointed, within a few months of this time, the second son, John, to a King's Scholarship, which he took up probably in the summer. The youngest son, Erasmus-Henry, was approaching his thirteenth year, and with two boys already at Westminster on scholarships it was perhaps too much to ask that the third be accorded the same honor. Consequently, Dryden petitioned the King to nominate the youngest boy to a place at the Charterhouse. On February 28 [1682], Charles recommended to the Governors of the founda-

---

[34] 'Dedication of *Fables*'; quoted from *Poems*, ed. Kinsley, p. 515.
[35] Naming in this way was commonplace, yet it is true too that Dryden was interested in naming:
>> Un-nam'd as yet; at least unknown to Fame:
>> Is there a strife in Heav'n about his Name?
>> Where every Famous Predecessour vies,
>> And makes a Faction for it in the Skies?
>>   ('Britannia Rediviva: a Poem on the Birth of the Prince',
>>   lines 192-5).

None of Dryden's sons married, an unusual circumstance at that date.

tion that 'Erasmus Henry Dryden' be elected and admitted one of the children of that foundation 'on the first Vacancy'. [He was admitted to the Charterhouse, 5 February 1683.][36]

But their later patron was a figure even more important to them: their father. Dryden was the father as patron as well as the patron as father. Is there any other English poet who has published his poetry within the same volume as poetry by two of his sons? That the poetry was translation (Charles Dryden translated Juvenal VII; and John Dryden Jr, Juvenal XIV) only intensifies the sense of a poetic inheritance—as does the wry coincidence that Juvenal XIV should have the subject it does: 'Since Domestick Examples easily corrupt our Youth, the Poet prudently exhorts all Parents, that they themselves should abstain from evil practices . . .'. Of the other contributors to his Juvenal, Dryden said: 'let their excellencies atone for my imperfections, and those of my sons'.[37] But not only was Dryden happy to figure alongside his sons as a translator,[38] he was happy to make a kindly assimilation; for the filial contribution was also to Persius. Of his Persius II, Dryden noted:

> What I had forgotten before, in its due place, I must here tell the Reader; That the first half of this Satyr was translated by one of my Sons, now in *Italy*: But I thought so well of it, that I let it pass without any Alteration.[39]

Motteux, in his journal for February 1691/2, was aptly impressed:

> Poetry is it seems hereditary in his Family, for each of his Sons have done one Satyr of *Juvenal*, which, with so extraordinary a Tutor as their Father, cannot but be very acceptable to the world.[40]

So there is a felicity in all the circumstances surrounding the publication of *The Husband His own Cuckold* by John Dryden Jr in 1696. First, there was the epigraph from the *Aeneid*: *Et pater Æneas et avunculus excitat Hector*, which Dryden himself had so deftly rotated in *Mac Flecknoe*:

> Let Father *Fleckno* fire thy mind with praise,
> And Uncle *Ogleby* thy envy raise.
>
> (lines 173-4)[41]

---

[36] Charles E. Ward, *The Life of John Dryden*, Chapel Hill, 1961, pp. 178-9.
[37] 'Discourse Concerning Satire'; Watson, II, 152.
[38] See also 'Preface to *Sylvae*'; Watson, II, 33: 'Some of them [fellow-contributors to *Sylvae*] are too nearly related to me to be commended without suspicion of partiality'—said, apparently, of Latin verses by his son Charles.
[39] *The Satires of Decimus Junius Juvenalis. Together with the Satires of Aulus Persius Flaccus* (1693), p. 28 of the Persius pagination.
[40] Quoted by Ward, *The Life of John Dryden*, p. 255.
[41] The link was observed by William Frost, *Dryden and the Art of Translation*, New Haven, 1955, pp. 63-4.

The Virgilian line is reinstated, since for John Dryden Jr the true father is Father Dryden and the true uncle is—literally—the man to whom he dedicated the play, Sir Robert Howard (Dryden's brother-in-law). Second, the Dedication to Howard, by Dryden's son, widens the family of a poet by descent:

> I am confident I cou'd not chuse a more indulgent Foster-Father; and tho' my very Name bears an accusation against me, yet I have the honour also to be related to the Muses by the Mothers side; for you yourself have been guilty of Poetry, and a Family Vice is therefore the more excusable in me, who am unluckily a Poet by descent.

Third, there is 'the Preface of Mr. Dryden, to his Son's Play', which ends: 'Farewell, Reader, if you are a Father you will forgive me, if not, you will when you are a Father'. Fourth, there is Dryden's Epilogue to the play, an act of paternal patronage which incorporated a good-humoured pun on 'the Puny Poet'. Fifth, there is the Prologue, by Congreve, which ends:

> Hither an Offering his First-Born he sends,
> Whose good, or ill success, on you depends.
> Yet he has hope some kindness may be shown,
> As due to greater Merit than his own,
> And begs the Sire may for the Son attone.
> There's his last Refuge, if the PLAY don't take,
> Yet spare Young Dryden for his Father's sake.

How satisfying that it should have been Congreve who wrote this for Dryden's son (and for Dryden) in 1696; Congreve, to whom two years earlier Dryden had written as his true son by poetic inheritance:

> Oh that your Brows my Lawrel had sustain'd,
> Well had I been Depos'd, if You had reign'd!
> The Father had descended for the Son;
> For only You are lineal to the Throne.
> ('To my Dear Friend Mr. Congreve', lines 41-4)

VII

Dryden honours fathers, and finds foolish the belief that they were fools:

> A Tempting Doctrine, plausible and new:
> What Fools our Fathers were, if this be true!
> (*The Medall*, lines 111-12)

His religion is likewise imbued with a disdain for

ALLUSION: THE POET AS HEIR

> Disdain of Fathers which the daunce began.
> (*The Hind and the Panther*, III, 407)
> If not by Scriptures how can we be sure
> (Reply'd the *Panther*) what tradition's pure? . . .
> How but by following her, reply'd the Dame,
> To whom deriv'd from sire to son they came.
> (Ibid., II, 212-13, 216-17)

So his scorn is in wait for those who offer only a travesty of pious succession; the Hollanders and the Spanish for instance:

> They cheat, but still from cheating Sires they come;
> They drink, but they were christ'ned first in Mum.
> Their patrimonial Sloth the *Spaniards* keep,
> And *Philip* first taught *Philip* how to sleep.
> ('Prologue to *The Spanish Fryar*',
> lines 25-8)

But the likeness of that last line to a later severity—

> For *Tom* the Second reigns like *Tom* the first.
> ('To Mr. Congreve', line 48)

—suggests again the affiliation of the patrimonial to the literary. The association had been strong for Dryden from the start; his first poem, 'Upon the death of the Lord Hastings' begins:

> Must Noble *Hastings* Immaturely die,
> (The Honour of his ancient Family?)

—passes, after his real sires, through his imaginary sires, whom he would have outdone (Seneca, Cato, Numa, Caesar):

> Must all these ag'd Sires in one Funeral
> Expire? All die in one so young, so small?
> (lines 73-4)

—and arrives naturally enough at a literary metaphor, in urging Hastings's widow:

> With greater than *Platonick* love, O wed
> His Soul, though not his Body, to thy Bed:
> Let that make thee a Mother; bring thou forth
> Th' *Idea's* of his Vertue, Knowledge, Worth;
> Transcribe th' Original in new Copies . . .
> (lines 97-101)

But my argument is not simply that Dryden was preoccupied with fathers and poetic lineage, but that the parallel with the nature of allusion—the poet as heir—lent particular life to this preoccupation, his most creative allusions being those of which the quick is paternity and inheritance. Let us juxtapose two passages which end poems by Dryden and which invoke the same ideas and images:

> But to write worthy things of worthy men
> Is the peculiar talent of your Pen:
> Yet let me take your Mantle up, and I
> Will venture in your right to prophesy.
> "This Work by merit first of Fame secure
> "Is likewise happy in its Geniture:
> "For since 'tis born when *Charls* ascends the Throne,
> "It shares at once his Fortune and its own."
> ('To My Honored Friend, Sr Robert Howard',
> lines 99-106)
> Sinking he left his Drugget robe behind,
> Born upwards by a subterranean wind.
> The Mantle fell to the young Prophet's part,
> With double portion of his Father's Art.
> (*Mac Flecknoe*, lines 214-17)

The throne, mantle, fame and prophecy in the world of Sir Robert Howard are so much less telling than those in Fleckno's. The explanation is not just that *Mac Flecknoe* calls upon allusion, but that the particular allusion upon which it calls is an evocation of a true lineage such as a true allusion has itself to embody:

> And it came to pass, when they were gone over, that Elijah said unto Elisha, Ask what I shall do for thee, before I be taken away from thee. And Elisha said, I pray thee, let a double portion of thy spirit be upon me.
> . . . and Elijah went up by a whirlwind into heaven. And Elisha saw it, and he cried, My father, my father . . . He took up also the mantle of Elijah that fell from him . . .
> (2 Kings, ii, 9-13)

Dryden's art of allusion derives its energy and acumen from the fact that allusion itself is something which falls to his part and which he has to employ with double art.

Which is why the best study of Dryden's allusions—that by Michael Wilding—finds itself drawing our attention so often to allusions of paternity, succession and poetic inheritance. It is not just that *Mac Flecknoe* is about these things, but that its allusions are at once given point and protected against too easy a pointedness by themselves continually being engaged—as a matter of principled literary procedure—with that paternity, succession and poetic inheritance of which they speak. Not just the concluding lines of *Mac Flecknoe*, but—another of Wilding's illuminations[42]—the way

---

[42] 'Dryden and Satire', in *John Dryden* (ed. Miner), p. 199. (This essay is in part a revision of 'Allusion and Innuendo in *Mac Flecknoe*', *Essays in Criticism*, XIX (1969), 355-70.)

ALLUSION: THE POET AS HEIR

in which Milton is at work within Dryden's line, 'Sh— alone my perfect image bears' (line 15). For whereas the Son of God is 'the radiant image of his Glory' (*Paradise Lost*, III, 63), and Adam and Eve shine with 'The image of thir glorious Maker' (IV, 292), the 'perfect image' is that which Satan narcissistically loved in his daughter Sin:

> Thy self in me thy perfect image viewing
> Becam'st enamourd.
>
> (II, 764-5)

Dryden here writes as a true son of a true poet, about a false son of a false poet, and the words 'perfect image' bear a perfect image of this filial allusion.

Likewise with Wilding's comment on:

> At his right hand our young *Ascanius* sate
> *Rome's* other hope, and pillar of the State.
>
> (lines 108-9)

Wilding writes:

> The allusions to Aeneas have a force additional to the simple provision of a heroic context for the enthronement, through a play on the word 'author', the categorization of Aeneas in those lines of the *Aeneid* alluded to in lines 106-9 of *Mac Flecknoe*:
>
> > *Then issu'd from the Camp, in Arms Divine,*
> > Aeneas, *Author of the* Roman *Line*:
> > *And by his side* Ascanius *took his Place,*
> > *The second Hope of* Rome's *Immortal Race.*
> >
> > (XII, 251-4)

Yet the authentication of the allusion is that it does itself keep alive Rome's immortal race in a second, other, way; Dryden himself is here an 'Author of the *Roman* line'. The word 'line' is a fertile one for him, since it compacts the actual and the literary geniture;

> And from whose Loyns recorded Psyche sprung
>
> (line 125)

is a telling line because, as Earl Miner[43] has pointed out, 'loins' was then pronounced as 'lines'.

The same considerations underlie the great passage from *Absalom and Achitophel* which Reuben Brower chose as his instance of Dryden's allusive mode.

> Yet, *Corah*, thou shalt from Oblivion pass;
> Erect thy self thou Monumental Brass:
> High as the Serpent of thy mettall made ...
>
> (lines 632-4)

---

[43] *Dryden's Poetry*, Bloomington, 1967, p. 92.

Brower excellently relates Corah's brazen effrontery to its literary allusion ('a preposterous parody of Horace's *Exegi monumentum Aere perennius*') before gathering in the other associations:

> our hero is worthy of a 'monumental brass' in an English church, the rude command implying that this monument, contrary to decent custom and the laws of gravity, will rise of its own power.[44]

But what binds all this together is the relation of lineage to the poetic inheritance: Horace's line is itself shown to be as lasting as it had hoped, since it is present to be piously and reprovingly used; the church's monumental brass would be a pious tribute to lineage; and yet Corah's erection is hideously uncreating. 'Erect thy self thou Monumental Brass': I think of the brazen Colley Cibber: 'he had it in his power *to be thought no body's son at all*: And what is that but coming into the world a Hero?'[45]

The allusion involving fatherhood, then, can be a particularly potent allusion, because it can question, or corroborate, or qualify the nature of literature itself, so frequently and so aptly conceived of, and especially by the Augustans, as a profound geniture. Dryden himself was much drawn to one Biblical allusion, Noah's cursing of Ham for seeing him naked in his drunkenness. Noah's curse is recalled in the Preface to 'Religio Laici'; in the 'Preface to Ovid's Epistles', where Ovid 'gives occasion to his translators, who dare not cover him, to blush at the nakedness of their father';[46] in 'The Character of St Evremond' ('As I am a religious admirer of Virgil, I could wish that he [St Evremond] had not discovered our father's nakedness')[47] and in the 'Second Part of Absalom and Architophel':

> But, tell me, did the Drunken Patriarch Bless
> The Son that shew'd his Father's Nakedness?
>   (lines 384-5)

So it is not surprising that the best use of an allusion turned against Dryden should not only involve one of Dryden's favourite allusions but should itself depend upon the peculiar power of an allusion to discriminate the truly filial from the falsely so; I am thinking of the closing words of John Fowler's acute essay on 'Dryden and Literary Good Breeding', and of the severe equality with which the father of English criticism is rebuked for his condescension to the father of English poetry, Chaucer:

---

[44] *The Poetry of Allusion*, p. 6.
[45] *Poems* (ed. Butt), p. 718.
[46] Watson, I, 266.
[47] Watson, II, 57.

Only the dress was wanting, and Dryden out of disinterested veneration for that founder of English poetry who 'in the beginning of our language' laboured so well to write good things—Dryden, the restorer, is charitably willing to cover the nakedness of this Father.[48]

VIII

A son, especially a gifted son, needs to contain his father, and in more senses than one. A poet needs to do the same, and allusion is a way of containing one's predecessors. They could overshadow all one's potentialities.

> Due Honours to those mighty Names we grant,
> But Shrubs may live beneath the lofty Plant:
> Sons may succeed their greater Parents gone;
> Such is thy Lott; and such I wish my own.
> ('To Sir Godfrey Kneller', lines 120-3)

Dryden is the first major poet in English to allude extensively to poetry in English; not just using it as a source, or unconsciously, but creating his own meanings by bringing into play the meanings of other English poets. He does so without malignity or belittling, and yet to do so is necessarily to do something about what might otherwise be the crippling burden of the past; for to allude to a predecessor is both to acknowledge, in piety, a previous achievement and also is a form of benign appropriation—what was so well said has now become part of my way of saying, and in advancing the claims of a predecessor (and rotating them so that they catch a new light) the poet is advancing his own claims, his own poetry, and even poetry. By an open recognition of the predicament of the poet as heir, and of the burden of the past, by embracing rather than merely failing to evade the predicament, the poet can be saved by allusion, by being an alert and independent dependant. 'And win my way by yielding to the tyde' (Pope, *The First Epistle of the First Book of Horace Imitated*, line 34).

Through allusion, Dryden and Pope were enabled to cope with their immediate predecessors; and of these the most giant-like, in all his power to enable or to disable, was Milton—the poet whom Harold Bloom has called the great Inhibitor. Yet he did not inhibit either Dryden or Pope. Pope had the advantage of a certain distance and of the mediation of Dryden, but Dryden had to face the full glare of Milton's immediate and gigantic genius. Yet Dryden's gifts, far from being inhibited, were never more truly

[48] In *Restoration Literature* (ed. Love), p. 245.

exhibited than when, with dignity and without presumption, he recognised Milton's genius by making it serve his purposes in allusion.

'*This Man* (says *Dryden*) *Cuts us All Out, and the Ancients too*':[49] Dryden's reported reaction to *Paradise Lost* is compounded of awe and dismay. His feelings about Milton were always made up of many strains and strands; he could write with a sheerly unenvying generosity about Milton's heroic achievement, but he could also manifest a resistance to Milton which was less than disinterested but was also forgivable in a poet fighting for survival, for breathing-space. 'Milton's *Paradise Lost* is admirable; but am I therefore bound to maintain that there are no flats among his elevations . . .?'[50]—where Dryden speaks the truth but does at the same time convey a sense that something personal was binding him to maintain it. 'As for Mr Milton, whom we all admire with so much justice, his subject is not that of an heroic poem, properly so called . . .';[51] this last is from the discussion of the possibilities for epic (in *A Discourse Concerning Satire*), where, as George Watson has pointed out, there is a strange blankness or wilfulness about Dryden's urgings as to the kind of epic of which we stand in need. 'The reference to *Paradise Lost* . . . seems long delayed: Dryden is reluctant to admit that his proposal for an epic combining classical and scriptural imagery has already been fulfilled'.[52] And is it a coincidence, or a jockeying, that when Dryden proffers a subject for such an epic, it should be one—King Arthur—which 'Milton had considered as a young man'?[53] Again: 'And Milton, if the Devil had not been his hero . . .; if . . .; and if . . .':[54] the reservations obdurately unroll. And then there is of course the whole preposterous squandering of talent which converted *Paradise Lost* into *The State of Innocence*; Milton, who had no cause to fear Dryden, could be laconically civil:

> Jo: Dreyden Esq. Poet Laureate, who very much admires him, & went to him to have leave to putt his Paradise-lost into a Drama in Rhyme: Mr. Milton received him civilly, & told him he woud give him leave to tagge his Verses.[55]

Marvell was aware of the shadow of the impure motive in Dryden:

---

[49] Recorded by Jonathan Richardson; see *The Early Lives of Milton*, ed. Helen Darbishire, London, 1932, p. 296.
[50] 'Preface to *Sylvae*'; Watson, II, 32.
[51] *Discourse Concerning Satire*; Watson, II, 84.
[52] Watson's note, II, 91.
[53] Watson's note, II, 92.
[54] 'To John, Lord Marquess of Normanby'; Watson, II, 233.
[55] Recorded by John Aubrey; see *The Early Lives of Milton* (ed. Darbishire), p. 7.

Plate XV Thomas Rowlandson, 'The Vicar Preaching to the Prisoners', *The Vicar of Wakefield*, London 1817 edition, Plate 23 (Huntington Library and Art Gallery).

Plate XVI Thomas Rowlandson, 'The Weddings', *The Vicar of Wakefield*, London 1817 edition, Plate 24 (Huntington Library and Art Gallery).

> Jealous I was that some less skilful hand
> (Such as disquiet alwayes what is well,
> And by ill imitating would excell)
> Might hence presume the whole Creations day
> To change in Scenes, and show it in a Play . . .
>
> Thou hast not miss'd one thought that could be fit,
> And all that was improper dost omit.
> So that no room is here for Writers left,
> But to detect their Ignorance or Theft.
> ('On Mr. Milton's *Paradise Lost*',
> 1674, lines 18-22, 27-30)

'So that no room is here for Writers left': here, or anywhere, after Milton and Shakespeare? Dryden's genius was to make room from this very fact, with the help of allusion. It is not that he was grudging towards Milton, but he needed room for himself; and it is to the point that when in a subsequent edition of *Paradise Lost* (1688) Dryden followed Marvell's example by providing commendatory verses, his fervid 'Lines on Milton' appeared without attribution; they were not printed as Dryden's until well after his death (in *Miscellany Poems*, 1716).

'So that no room is here for Writers left': Marvell meant only here within this subject, but it is a resonant thought. And if I had to pick a single reason why Dryden was so importantly and so unusually a late-developer as a poet (for all his precocity)—*Annus Mirabilis*, which is immature and patchy, did not appear until he was thirty-five, and he was fifty when he published *Absalom and Achitophel*—it would be the shadow of Milton, a shadow which became a shelter, and a kind of shading, only after the death of Milton in 1674. Within ten years of Milton's death (the death of a poetic father sometimes being as enabling to a poet as can be the death of his actual father), Dryden had magnificently come into his inheritance, as the poet of *Absalom and Achitophel*, *The Medall*, *Mac Flecknoe*, and 'To the Memory of Mr. Oldham'.

That Milton continued to be a fatal as well as a fertile fascination, and that the imitative and allusive mode converts into generous energies what can be mean-spirited or blundering impulses, is clear from *Of the Art of Sinking in Poetry* in 1727:

> As *Virgil* is said to have read *Ennius*, out of his Dunghil to draw Gold; so may our Author read *Shakespear*, *Milton*, and *Dryden*, for the contrary End, to bury their Gold in his own Dunghil. A true Genius, when he finds any thing lofty or shining in them, will have the Skill to bring it down, take off the Gloss, or quite discharge the Colour, by some ingenious Circumstance, or Periphrase, some Addition, or Diminution,

> or by some of those Figures the use of which we shall shew in our next Chapter.
>
> The Book of *Job* is acknowledg'd to be infinitely sublime, and yet has not our Father of the *Bathos* reduc'd it in every Page?
>
> IMITATION is of two Sorts: the First is when we force to our own Purposes the Thoughts of others; The Second consists in copying the Imperfections, or Blemishes of celebrated Authors. I have seen a Play professedly writ in the Stile of *Shakespear*, wherein the greatest Resemblance lay in one single Line,
>   And so good Morrow t'ye, good Master Lieutenant.
> And sundry Poems in Imitation of Milton, where with the utmost Exactness, and not so much as one Exception, nevertheless was constantly *nathless*, embroider'd was *broider'd*, Hermits were *Eremites*, disdain'd was *'sdeign'd*, shady *umbrageous*, Enterprize *Emprize*, Pagan *Paynim*, Pinions *Pennons*, sweet *dulcet*, Orchards *Orchats*, Bridge-work *Pontifical*; nay, her was *hir*, and their was *thir* thro' the whole Poem. And in very Deed, there is no other Way by which the true modern Poet could read to any purpose the Works of such Men as *Milton* and *Shakespear*.[56]

But the force of irony here derives from the fact that by 1727—after *Mac Flecknoe* and *The Rape of the Lock*—there was manifestly another way by which the true modern poet could read to some purpose the works of Milton. Dryden and Pope wrote poetry 'in Imitation of Milton'; the imitation is not parasitic or servile, it is allusive, and the allusions derive their geniture from the very nature of allusion, its sense of the paternal and filial. The alternative was 'our Father of the *Bathos*'.

Dryden, of Shimei:

> During his Office, Treason was no Crime.
> The Sons of *Belial* had a glorious Time.
>   (*Absalom and Achitophel*, lines 597-8)

Milton:

> And when Night
> Darkens the Streets, then wander forth the Sons
> Of *Belial*, flown with insolence and wine.
>   (*Paradise Lost*, I, 500-2)

The flare, pungency and propriety of the allusion are alive because in speaking of 'the Sons of *Belial*' Dryden is acknowledging Milton, without 'insolence', as his father; Dryden shares in the truly 'glorious', the glory of Milton.

---

[56] pp. 39, 41-2.

Likewise, Pope:

> She saw old Pryn in restless Daniel shine,
> And Eusden eke out Blackmore's endless line.
> *(The Dunciad* A, I, 101-2)

Milton:

> Beyond compare the Son of God was seen
> Most glorious, in him all his Father shon
> Substantially express'd, and in his face
> Divine compassion visibly appeerd,
> Love without end, and without measure Grace,
> *(Paradise Lost*, III, 138-42)

The allusion itself shines, and—modestly—it ekes out, and thus it contributes to a truly 'endless line' (not the interminable maundering of Blackmore, but a true poetic succession); and the shining of the allusion is dependent upon Pope's establishing ('Substantially express'd', as it could not be in the Dunces' poetry) a filial and independent relationship with Milton such as is a counterpart of Milton's Son and Father—and such as blasts the travesty of divine progeny which is 'Blackmore's endless line' (not Milton's 'Love without end').

Less richly, but not less tellingly, there is in Pope the ghost of Dr Busby, headmaster of Westminster School:

> His beaver'd brow a birchen garland wears,
> Dropping with Infant's blood, and Mother's tears.
> *(The Dunciad* B, IV, 141-2)

Milton:

> First Moloch, horrid King besmear'd with blood
> Of human sacrifice, and parents tears.
> *(Paradise Lost*, I, 392-3)

Dr Busby is a travesty of a paternal-filial relationship; Pope's relation to Milton manifests the alternative, an affectionate and independent respect.

Dryden's respect for Milton was not less real, but it was necessarily more imperilled, its animation overlapping with animus. So his greatest allusion to Milton, *Absalom and Achitophel*, implies a repudiation of Milton's politics while gaining energy from Milton's poetic energy; the partial repudiation left room for Dryden to breathe. Here too there is a parallelism between heavenly fathers, royal fathers, political fathers, and poetic fathers; as Leonora Leet Brodwin says:

> To turn Milton's poetry against the party of his political heirs while using it to dignify his style would have been a brilliant enough point of wit to justify Dryden's use. But

fortunately, there were points at which *Paradise Lost* paralleled contemporary events. In *Paradise Lost*, Satan is first incited to rebellion because of his refusal to accept the decree of God exalting the Son to a position of sovereignty over all the angels next only to Himself. As soon as contemporary events are seen in this light, any questioning of the legal succession or hierarchy of power becomes Satanic. . . . But if allusion to *Paradise Lost* provides Dryden with his satiric norm, it also makes for his most devastating satire on Milton's political heirs. For is it not the highest point of satire to tell a faction that is opposing the legal succession on the religious grounds of opposition to James's Catholicism that it is Satanic, and to prove it to them by invoking a parallel to the greatest work of their greatest literary exponent?[57]

The mention of James—not son succeeding father, but brother succeeding brother—calls to mind a further, complicating, strain in Dryden's relationship with Milton. For while Milton stood in something of a paternal role to Dryden as a poet, the strain was exacerbated by the fact that he stood too in the role of an elder brother. He was, after all, not quite twenty-three years older than Dryden. Dryden, like his contemporaries, was very aware of the grievances of younger sons (just as he praises James for being so free from envy of Charles), and he naturally found the word brother coming to his pen when speaking of poetic emulation and of poetic lineage:

A native of Parnassus, and bred up in the studies of its fundamental laws, may receive new lights from his contemporaries; but 'tis a grudging kind of praise which he gives his benefactors. He is more obliged than he is willing to acknowledge; there is a tincture of malice in his commendations. For where I own I am taught, I confess my want of knowledge. A judge upon the bench may, out of good nature, or at least interest, encourage the pleadings of a puny counsellor; but he does not willingly commend his brother serjeant at the bar.[58]

> Nature is old, which Poets imitate,
> And for Wit, those that boast their own estate,
> Forget *Fletcher* and *Ben* before them went,
> Their Elder Brothers, and that vastly spent:
> So much 'twill hardly be repair'd again,
> Not, though supply'd with all the wealth of *Spain*.
> ('Prologue to *The Wild Gallant*', lines 43-8)

---

[57] 'Milton Allusion in *Absalom and Achitophel*', *JEGP*, LXVIII (1969), 28.
[58] 'To John, Lord Marquess of Normanby'; Watson, II, 230-1.

IX

Dryden's greatest poems—*Absalom and Achitophel* and *Mac Flecknoe*—are witty and humane explorations of the truths and falsities of paternal-filial relationship. Almost every line of *Mac Flecknoe* bears upon—and is borne upon by—the considerations of inheritance (literary and actual) which especially compact themselves in the art of allusion. Let me refresh the matter with the opening of *Mac Flecknoe*:

> All humane things are subject to decay,
> And, when Fate summons, Monarchs must obey:
> This *Fleckno* found, who like *Augustus*, young
> Was call'd to Empire, and had govern'd long:
> In Prose and Verse, was own'd, without dispute
> Through all the Realms of *Non-sense*, absolute.
> This aged Prince now flourishing in Peace,
> And blest with issue of a large increase,
> Worn out with business, did at length debate
> To settle the succession of the State:
> And pond'ring which of all his Sons was fit
> To Reign, and wage immortal War with Wit;
> Cry'd, 'tis resolv'd; for Nature pleads that He
> Should onely rule, who most resembles me:
> *Sh*— alone my perfect image bears,
> Mature in dullness from his tender years.
> *Sh*— alone, of all my Sons, is he
> Who stands confirm'd in full stupidity.
>
> (lines 1-18)

The poet who subsequently matured the concept of dullness, and who was of all the sons of Dryden the true heir, with a generous adroitness created room for himself by establishing a fraternal relation with Dryden. Pope's notes to *The Dunciad*, and especially 'Appendix VI: A Parallel of the Characters of Mr. Dryden and Mr. Pope, as Drawn by Certain of their Contemporaries', establish a fraternity free from the usual parental-filial intimidations. Some such large-minded room for honourable manoeuvre was essential to Pope; after all there has at no other point in English literature been a poetic succession where the features of a poet were, at first glance, so astonishingly like those of his distinguished predecessor. Fraternity was one way of dealing with the less welcome aspects of this similarity. Pope, again, was fortunate both in his confidence that he possessed a greater genius than Dryden and in the fact that this confidence was justified. But a corroborative strength of his poetry is that it uses its allusions to Dryden precisely to embody this sense of the succession, of Pope's being Dryden's heir and sharing many of his lineaments. Take the conclusion of the introductory paragraph of *The Dunciad* A: what is it that the Muses must say?—

> Say from what cause, in vain decry'd and curst,
> Still Dunce the second reigns like Dunce the first?
>> Alluding to a verse of Mr. *Dryden*'s not in *Mac Flecno* (as it is said ignorantly in the Key to the *Dunciad, pag.* 1.) but in his verses to Mr. *Congreve*.
>> And Tom *the Second reigns like* Tom *the First.*

It is an important allusion, the first to *Mac Flecknoe* in this poem which proffers itself as the son of *Mac Flecknoe* or *Mac 'Mac Flecknoe'*; and it is a penetratingly proper allusion because it so simply enacts its own enterprise. It is because Pope, without belittling or patronising Dryden's line, can so deftly turn it to new purposes, both literary and public (George II had recently succeeded George I), that we can have the equally amused confidence that what we are witnessing is not a Dunce or a Tom succeeding a Dunce or a Tom, but a true poetic majesty reigning as its predecessor had done. Pope is a King the Second who indeed reigns like a King the First, and pays tribute in the act of saying so in those very words. Dryden's previous couplet had said something that would prove true about the reign of Dryden and of Pope:

> Thus when the State one *Edward* did depose;
> A Greater *Edward* in his room arose.
>   ('To Mr. Congreve', lines 45-6)

For Pope, it was subsequently a God-given providence that furnished Colley Cibber with a son Theophilus, and so furnished Pope with a Bentleian footnote:

> this Poet being the only one who was universally known to have had a Son so exactly like him, in his poetical, theatrical, political, and moral Capacities, that it could justly be said of him
> *Still Dunce the second reign'd like Dunce the first.*
>   BENTL.[59]

Likewise with many of Pope's best allusions, themselves demonstrating their right to that true succession which indicts the Dunces' travesty of succession.
    Pope:

> Much she revolves their arts, their ancient praise,
> And sure succession down from Heywood's days.
>   (*The Dunciad* A, I, 95-6)

---

[59] Introductory note to *The Dunciad* B, Book I (*Poems*, ed. Butt, p. 720).

Dryden:
>   And setl'd sure Succession in his Line.
>   (*Aeneis*, I, 8)
>   Th'immortal Line in sure Succession reigns.
>   (*Georgics*, IV, 303)

Pope's conclusive tribute to Dryden was the ending of his translation of the *Odyssey*, with its mandate from an earlier ending:

>   So *Pallas* spoke: The mandate from above
>   The King obey'd. The Virgin-seed of *Jove*
>   In *Mentor's* form, confirm'd the full accord,
>   "And willing nations knew their lawfull Lord".

Dryden:

>   He said. Th' Almighty, nodding, gave Consent;
>   And Peals of Thunder shook the Firmament.
>   Henceforth a Series of new time began,
>   The mighty Years in long Procession ran:
>   Once more the Godlike *David* was Restor'd,
>   And willing Nations knew their Lawfull Lord.
>   (*Absalom and Achitophel*, lines 1026-31)

The beauty of Pope's assimilation is its openness, its recognition of a due gratitude. Once more Dryden is restored. A series of new time begins, and yet it does not break faith with the old series. Pope's concluding and conclusive allusion has 'confirm'd the full accord' of his relation to his predecessor; Pope, as willingly as the nations, knows the lawful lordship of Dryden—and this without any mock self-subordination. Dryden, the mentor, is acknowledged 'in *Mentor's* form'.

But let me end not with Pope's Homer, but with its predecessor, the last great enterprise of Dryden's life, his translation of Virgil. The lines are those which I have already quoted, since by alluding to them in 'To the Memory of Mr. Oldham' Dryden was exemplifying the nature of allusion, and of the poet as heir, in the very act of making the allusion:

>   His Son, or one of his Illustrious Name,
>   How like the former, and almost the same.
>   (*Aeneis*, VI, 1194-5)

It is characteristic of Pope not just that he should allude to Dryden but that he should allude to a passage which had furnished Dryden with a memorable allusion. Pope:

>   All as the vest, appear'd the wearer's frame,
>   Old in new state, another yet the same.
>   Bland and familiar as in life, begun
>   Thus the great Father to the greater Son.
>   (*The Dunciad* A, III, 31-4)

In alluding to Dryden, Pope speaks as the greater son of a great father ('Sons may succeed their greater Parents gone'); in modifying that line—'How like the former, and almost the same'—which epitomises the art of allusion, its likeness-in-difference for the poet as heir, Pope has again, and most creatively, manifested that of which he speaks, since 'Old in new state, another yet the same' is itself old and new, sharing but modifying the illustrious lineaments of

>How like the former, and almost the same.

Augustan Prose Fiction and the Romance Tradition

Henry Knight Miller

A brief prolegomenon on literary history may introduce my topic. Among the various patterns firmly imposed upon the study of literary history during the nineteenth century was the conception of a rise and evolution of literary modes.[1] This is a pattern which has proved so gloriously self-serving to each succeeding age that it appears unlikely we shall soon rid ourselves of the notion that, just as there has been a steady evolutionary progress through the long history of the major anthropoids—which may itself, from time to time, seem a dubious proposition—so too there must have been such an evolution in the major literary modes. When a given mode conveys the impression that it has become stabilised, fixed at its 'highest' development, this pattern will particularly be appealed to, explicitly or implicitly. And so it has been, until quite recently, with the so-called 'realistic novel'. The triumphant achievement of the nineteenth-century novel (actually, of course, an extraordinarily various thing) seemed at the time genuinely to validate an evolutionary theory of prose fiction, representing a final stage in an obvious progression from the 'primitive' romance form to a 'sophisticated' and ultimate form, the realistic novel.

Clearly, it has been rather more difficult to validate such assumptions in the case of the drama, where the examples of Greek tragedy and of William Shakespeare have rather inhibited evolutionary criticism, whose proponents would suggest that Shakespeare's achievement, for example, is representative of a primitive and tentative striving toward the mastery exhibited by the realistic 'well-made play'. Nor does the problem arise with the epic, which

---

[1] On the popularity of the 'teleological' approach to literary history in the nineteenth century, see my essay, 'The "Whig Interpretation" of Literary History', *Eighteenth-Century Studies*, VI (1972-3), 60-84. The analogy to the life of a man, through childhood, maturity, and old age, is of course much more ancient.

—as a form not indigenous to bourgeois culture—rather tends to be viewed as the sublime dinosaur of literary history, an evolutionary end-product in itself. But in prose fiction, the last two hundred years unquestionably did produce something really remarkable, and this has made the invocation of an evolutionary or teleological pattern considerably more plausible.

Given this kind of assumption, then, two procedures followed naturally enough: *histories* of prose fiction emphasised each faint anticipation of a full-blown 'realism' in works primitive by definition, ignoring, when they did not condemn, those elements of the whole which could not be so categorised; and *criticism* of prose fiction assessed—or better, judged—primitive works in terms of the Rules for the realistic novel, finding them successful artistically as they most clearly approached that ideal. This has been the required procedure from at least the time of John Dunlop's *History of Fiction* in 1814,[2] and, if we look about us, it would appear to be still the reigning mode in literary history and criticism, despite various and increasing critiques of such 'novel-centered' thinking.[3]

For myself, I have no intention of subverting such a pleasing and profitable enterprise. All I really wish to do is to suggest that, as the anthropologists are learning to see what we call 'the savage mind' rather in terms of its own complex and fully developed logic than as a merely primitive or childlike approximation to the *soi-disant* 'civilised' mind of modern Western culture, so there may be certain rewards even for the 'novel-centered' mind in trying to see early prose fiction as nearly as possible in terms of its own assumptions and conventions, rather than in terms of later laws that it knew nothing about and that automatically insist upon its inferiority to those modern instances which more faithfully obey the rules. We shall not any the less perhaps—in either case—refrain from our habitual use of the term 'barbarian' to describe those who, in the root sense of *barbaros*, are different from us; but we may at least enjoy the learned pleasure of submitting ourselves for the moment to different cultural presuppositions.

What I should like to do here, then, is merely to sketch the outlines of such a historical—or anthropological—approach, and to suggest some of the advantages that it might offer. I shall use the

[2] 3 vols., Edinburgh, 1814; revised, as *History of Prose Fiction*, with notes by Henry Wilson, 2 vols., London, 1906. Despite its critical deficiencies, Dunlop's history, like that by F. M. Warren (*A History of the Novel previous to the Seventeenth Century*, New York, 1895), offers a better survey of the romance tradition as a whole than Ernest Baker's *History of the English Novel*, 10 vols, London, 1924-39; supplementary volume, 1968, or any subsequent history.

[3] See especially Northrop Frye, *Anatomy of Criticism*, Princeton, 1957, pp. 303-4 and *passim*, and *The Nature of Narrative*, New York, 1966, by Robert Scholes and Robert Kellogg.

term 'romance' in one of its normal current senses, as a generic term for all prose fiction of some length prior to the eighteenth century, and the term 'novel' for all, or almost all, prose fiction subsequent to the eighteenth century. Because, as we have long recognised, the eighteenth century is the period when the gradual change from one reigning style of fiction to another does indeed occur. And whether one calls this 'the rise of the novel' or 'the decline of the romance', the fact is the same: older fictive conventions were modified, qualified, or rejected, in favour of other conventions more suitable to a middle-class audience that offered, particularly in its female population, a market to be exploited.[4] Now, it is obvious enough that under the catch-all term 'novel' we are accustomed to herd together many different breeds of cattle;[5] and yet, there has been in fact what Wittgenstein would have called a 'family resemblance' in most of the works so designated, a set of shared conventions and assumptions. It is my belief that the same may be said of the romance over a much longer period of time, from its origins in the Roman and later Grecian era up to at least the Renaissance (for, as I shall argue, the seventeenth-century French *roman heroique* so modifies or expands the conventions it inherits as to become almost another thing altogether). There is, to be sure, an enormous variety in this romance tradition; the *Aethiopica* of Heliodorus, the pastoral *Daphnis and Chloe* of Longus, the Christian saints' lives (which are authentic romances), Chrestien de Troyes and the rich flood of medieval chivalric and homiletic romance, the peninsular cycles of Palmerin and Amadis de Gaule, the so-called 'epic romances' of Boiardo, Ariosto, and Tasso, Spenser's *Faerie Queene*, Sidney's *Arcadia*, John Lyly's *Euphues*—all these romances, indifferently in verse or prose, surely represent an extraordinary range of attitudes and procedures, stemming from different centuries, different countries, different audiences, and different authors. And yet, once again, there is a 'family resemblance', a core of shared conventions and assumptions —not least, that of a providential universe, whether it is τὸ χρέων of Heliodorus (not for nothing later imagined to be a Christian bishop) or the watchful overlooking in Sidney. Even the separate but parallel mode of the comic romance, from Petronius, Apuleius,

---

[4] See Ian Watt, *The Rise of the Novel*, London, 1957, pp. 35-59 and *passim*.
[5] Including new versions of the Romance itself. See, for instance, Richard Chase, *The American Novel and Its Tradition*, Garden City, N.Y., 1957, which sees the American novel 'inevitably, as springing from England, but as differing from the English tradition by its perpetual reassessment and reconstitution of romance within the novel form' (p. viii).

Lucian, and Achilles Tatius,[6] through Pulci, Rabelais, and Cervantes, though it may be thought of as 'anti-romance', preserves many of the conventions and assumptions of the form that it is reducing, demythologising, or mocking.

Thus the commentator who wished to stress the infinite variety of this romance tradition would face no serious difficulties; but my task is perhaps more problematic, for I wish to take a 'synchronic' view (as we say) that stresses rather its continuity in motif and structure, its *likenesses* over the entire range. Before I turn to that, however, I should like to mention one important exception, which I think is highly significant for the future paths taken by prose fiction.

This, as I have suggested, is the so-called *roman heroique* of seventeenth-century France—'those voluminous Works', as Henry Fielding said, 'commonly called *Romances*, namely, *Clelia, Cleopatra, Astraea, Cassandra,* the *Grand Cyrus,* and innumerable others which contain, as I apprehend, very little Instruction or Entertainment'.[7] The 'heroic romance' was unquestionably a summation of and a variant upon the chivalric romance, particularly as the latter appeared in the extravagant sixteenth-century French continuations of *Amadis de Gaule*[8]—and Madeleine de Scudéry even claimed inspiration from classic Heliodorus.[9] But there was one crucial and all-pervasive difference in the seventeenth-century romance: it was primarily a plaything for a group of rather extraordinary women. The famous salons of Mme de Rambouillet and others of the *précieuses* circles were the inspiration for (and frequently the subject matter of) these lengthy productions;[10] and

---

[6] For the argument that Achilles Tatius belongs to the tradition of comic romance, see Donald Blythe Durham, 'Parody in Achilles Tatius', *Classical Philology,* XXXIII (1938), 1-19, seconded by Ben Edwin Perry, *The Ancient Romances,* Berkeley and Los Angeles, 1967, pp. 106-7, 114ff.

[7] Preface to *Joseph Andrews,* ed. Martin C. Battestin, Oxford, 1967, p. 4. Fielding's apparent animus against the 'romance' can be referred almost entirely to his distaste for the effeminate salon romances of the seventeenth century; it was the contempt into which the art of fiction had been brought by such performances, he said in the prefatory essay to his ninth book in *Tom Jones,* 'that hath made us so cautiously avoid the Term Romance, a Name with which we might otherwise have been well enough contented'.

[8] See John J. O'Connor, *Amadis de Gaule and Its Influence on Elizabethan Literature,* New Brunswick, N.J., 1970, pp. 10-23 and *passim.*

[9] Both in the preface to her *Artamène, ou le Grand Cyrus* and in that to *Ibrahim, ou l'illustre Bassa.*

[10] As the greatest and most influential apologist for the salon romance observed: 'The Ladies were first taken with this Lure: They made Romances their Study; and have despised the Ancient Fable and History . . . The Men, in Complaisance, have imitated them' (Pierre Daniel Huet, *The History of Romances,* Paris, 1670, tr. Stephen Lewis, London, 1715; in Ioan Williams (ed.), *Novel and Romance 1700-1800,* London, 1970, p. 53). See Thomas P. Haviland, *The Roman de longue haleine on English Soil,* Philadelphia, 1931, for a

it would in fact be more descriptive to call them 'salon romances' than 'heroic romances'—for, whereas the primary matter of most earlier romances had been such subjects as chivalric heroism or the perilous journey, and love had been only its secondary matter (despite later scholarly emphases), the equation was reversed with a vengeance in the salon romances,[11] which, for all their well-described battle scenes, were most notably marked by long debates on *questions d'amour*, were almost exclusively of the Platonic variety; wire-drawn punctilios of 'honour' (primarily having to do with female virtue); the elevation of the impeccably chaste lady to a position of awful distance, with the power of life and death over her adoring servant; and minute analyses of the internal state of the 'heart'.[12] Interestingly enough, despite the swelling and expanding of the topoi of the romance tradition, the authors of these ingenious monoliths firmly believed that their work was more *vraisemblable* than that of their predecessors;[13] and, if we may judge from the response of such readers as Dorothy Osborne, the tales were indeed felt as 'realistic' by their own generations.

It was these salon romances that led, on the one hand, to the

---

valuable comment upon the essentially 'feminine' nature of these *précieuses* romances, despite the fact that some of the best were written by such a gallant soldier as Le Sieur de la Calprenède.

[11] So Huet: 'In short, [Epic] *Poems* make some Military Act, or Politic Conduct, their Theme, and only descant upon Love at Pleasure; whereas *Romances*, on the contrary, have Love for their Principal Subject, and don't concern themselves in War or Politicks, but by Accident. I speak of Regular *Romances* [i.e. the seventeenth-century *romans heroiques*], for those in Old *French*, *Spanish*, and *Italian*, have generally more of the Soldier than Gallant' (Ioan Williams, *Novel and Romance*, p. 47).

[12] Many of these elements have been attributed to (or read back into) the medieval romances; but, aside from the obsessive degree of emphasis, not to say extravagance, in the salon-romances, it would also appear that they presented with total seriousness an attitude toward 'love' and toward women that had been (if recent scholarship is correct) largely ironic, a learned jest, in medieval writings. Among various corrections of nineteenth-century scholarly myths about medieval attitudes toward love, see E. Talbot Donaldson, 'The Myth of Courtly Love', *Ventures*, V (1965), 16-23; D. W. Robertson Jr, 'Some Medieval Doctrines of Love', in *A Preface to Chaucer: Studies in Medieval Perspectives*, Princeton, 1962, pp. 391-503; and some of the discussions in *The Meaning of Courtly Love*, ed. Francis X. Newman, Albany, N.Y., 1970.

[13] Thus La Calprenède (or his continuator) declared: '... au lieu de les appeler des romans, comme les *Amadis* et autres semblables, dans lequel il n'y a ni vérité ni vraisemblance, ni charte, ni chronologie, on les pourrait regarder commes des histoires embellies de quelque invention, et qui par ces ornements ne perdent peut-être rien de leur beauté' ('Avis au lecteur', prefatory to *Faramond*, Paris, 1661-70; cit. Vivienne Mylne, *The Eighteenth-Century French Novel*, Manchester, 1965, p. 22). And the English translator of La Calprenède's *Cassandre* admiringly said of the heroine: 'Her ten years story is so artificially [i.e. artfully] contrived, and with such exact decorum, that the truth whereon it is grounded, appears the greater fiction ...' ('To the Reader', *Cassandra*, tr. Sir Charles Cotterell, London, 1664, sig. A4ᵛ).

English heroic plays and, ultimately, the 'she-tragedies',[14] and, on the other hand, into the vulgarised erotic-pathetic ladies' books of the early eighteenth century written by such interesting personages as Mary Delariviere Manley and Eliza Haywood.[15] And both these modes have been well documented as being among the major stimuli that led an ageing printer of genius, named Samuel Richardson, to produce the first 'psychological' novel,[16] and to provide one major emphasis for the English novel of later centuries. It was also the salon-romances, I might add, that initiated a confusion, not yet straightened out, concerning the romance tradition in general. For eighteenth-century English writers normally took the French *roman heroique* as the very type of the romance (the older romances were frequently called 'histories'); and when the medieval romance was first treated in a scholarly, antiquarian way toward the end of the century, it was often assimilated to and coloured by the characteristics of the salon-romance (this is even more true of popular criticism at the time), thus initiating a set of critical and scholarly myths that would have a long and imaginative history.[17] Moreover, once its seventeenth-century vogue was past, the *roman heroique* came to be for later writers an emblem of narrative extravagance and

---

[14] See, for example, L. N. Chase, *The English Heroic Play*, New York, 1903, and H. W. Hill, *La Calprenède's Romances and the Restoration Drama*, Reno, Nevada, 1911. Kathleen M. Lynch, in *The Social Mode of Restoration Comedy*, New York, 1926, traces the *précieuse* tradition of 'Platonic love' in England from its importation by Henrietta Maria and her creatures to its varied treatment in Restoration drama. The 'Cavalier' poets played the game of Platonic love, but usually kept tongue firmly in cheek. In Sir John Suckling's tragicomedy, *Aglaura*, the ladies are all Platonics, the men anti-Platonics.

[15] See John J. Richetti, *Popular Fiction before Richardson: Narrative Patterns 1700-1739*, Oxford, 1969, for an excellent study of the literary and sociological implications of the erotic-pathetic formula.

[16] The praise of Richardson by his circle of ladies almost precisely echoes that of 'the great and incomparable Urfé' by (probably) Georges de Scudéry nearly a century before: 'But amongst many rare matters, that which I most esteem of is, that he knows how to touch the passions so delicately, that he may be called the Painter of the Soul; he goes searching out in the bottom of hearts the most secret thoughts; and in the diversity of natures, which he represents, eve[r]y one findes his own pourtrait . . .' (Preface to *Ibrahim, or the Illustrious Bassa*, tr. Henry Cogan, London, 1652; 1674 edn, sig. A3. As Fielding's *Joseph Andrews* was both a parody of the values of salon-romance in Richardsonian guise, and at the same time a comic presentation of an alternative romance tradition, so *Tom Jones* has elements of parody that look to the 'vulgar Romances' of the salons, but is primarily a restatement (an allusion to) the major romance tradition as it had existed from classic times through the Renaissance.

[17] Among these myths was the notion that the kind of Platonising 'idealised' love motif found in the salon-romance was also a normal medieval characteristic; but as Arthur Johnston accurately observes, 'To be called "romantic", love had to have the characteristics with which it is associated in seventeenth-century French romances, not those which are found in the Peninsular or medieval romances' (*Enchanted Ground: The Study of Medieval Romance in the Eighteenth Century*, London, 1964, p. 201). The upright soul of Mme de

obsessive emphasis on questions of love.[18] This, of course, is what the adjective 'Romantick' normally means in the eighteenth century; and the disrepute into which the whole romance tradition was brought by this most recent example of the genre unquestionably worked with other factors to encourage a new style of fiction that would be more down to earth.

But the new styles in fiction represent ground that has been trodden many times: our critical and scholarly interest, as I have observed, has been primarily in 'realism', and the search for precursors has been pushed all the way back to Petronius and Longus and even, indeed, to Homer. Doubtless the search will—and should —continue; for since each age or generation emerges with a new conception of 'realism', each age has to make a somewhat different kind of search, and useful things get turned up in the process. My own present interest, however, is in the romance.

For despite the bad odour into which the term itself had fallen because of the *roman heroique*, and despite the growing influence of modes of fiction that would concentrate upon ordinary people in ordinary surroundings, the romance influence (both classic-chivalric *and* salon versions) was by no means nugatory in the new fiction of the Restoration and the eighteenth century. Narrative artists still tended to follow the structural patterns of romance, the motifs employed in romance, the modes of character presentation found in romance. And this strong leavening of the anti-mimetic, anti-literal, anti-psychologising dimension in romance given to stories otherwise concerned with the portrayal of the ordinary, makes eighteenth-century fiction a special kind of creation, with a potent interest of its own. It has, currently, a peculiarly picquant, if adventitious, interest for the American reader, because some of the most striking recent American fiction exhibits much the same kind of mixture.[19]

Rather than demonstrate at length (which I scarcely have time here to do) the continuing operation of romance modes of narrative

---

Rambouillet would have been scandalised at the forthrightness of such medieval heroines as Rimenhild or Josian or Belisaunt. And it will be remembered that even the 'ideal' Princess Oriana bears a child out of wedlock to the heroic Amadis de Gaule—scarcely the behavior of a 'Platonist'.

[18] As William Wotton declared: 'In short, *Durfe* and *Calprenede*, and the rest of them, by over-straining the String, have broke it: and one can as soon believe that *Varillas* and *Maimbourg* wrote the Histories of great Actions just as they were done, as that Men ever made Love in such a Way as these Love-and-Honour *Men* describe' (*Reflections upon Ancient and Modern Learning*, London, 1694; in J. E. Spingarn (ed.), *Critical Essays of the Seventeenth Century*, 3 vols., London, 1908, III, 221).

[19] See the interesting study by Raymond M. Olderman, *Beyond the Waste Land: a Study of the American Novel in the Nineteen-Sixties*, New Haven, 1972.

in such authors as John Bunyan, Aphra Behn, Daniel Defoe, Samuel Richardson, Henry Fielding, I have chosen merely to sketch an 'ideal type' (in Max Weber's sense of an artificial construct) of the romance, a kind of polarised model which, though never perhaps actually realised, may serve as a heuristic device—and may also suggest why the so-called 'realism' of eighteenth-century writers has been thought imperfect from a later perspective. The first general point to make is, that the romance is essentially an 'epic' mode of narrative—and, of course, epic and romance disappear at roughly the same time in literary history. When both were alive, there were many critics to argue that there was no essential distinction between them,[20] and that therefore the romancers who followed Homer and Virgil and Statius belonged to the same narrative tradition—a postulate supported, incidentally, by a distinguished modern classicist, who has flatly declared: 'Romance and epic are basically the same genre, as much so as ancient and modern drama'.[21] But even if one wished for particular purposes to distinguish somehow between them, the epic would yet remain the dominant narrative model and literary point of reference during the period in which romances were written; and later emphases upon a dramatic model,[22] or (particularly) upon the post-Romantic model of the subjective lyric, have tended to obscure the fundamentally 'epic' nature of the romance, at no little cost to the proper comprehension and appreciation of its narrative conventions.

The second general point has to do with historical context. The romance, from Heliodorus to the Renaissance, is the literary product of a pre-democratic, pre-scientific, pre-industrial, pre-Lockeian (hence, in effect pre-psychologising) world, and its ideals and struc-

[20] This was a commonplace of continental criticism from at least the time of the great sixteenth-century masters, Giangiorgio Trissino and Giraldi Cinthio, and J. C. Scaliger (who anticipated Sir Philip Sidney in calling the *Aethiopica* of Heliodorus a prose epic) and Torquato Tasso; followed by Lopez Pinciano in Spain, seconded by Cervantes, and by many others, on through the influential *Traité du poème épique* (Paris, 1675) of René Le Bossu. There were counter-arguments, of course (see H. T. Swedenberg Jr, *The Theory of the Epic in England, 1650-1800*, Berkeley and Los Angeles, 1944, *passim*); but this is an impressive array. See also L. G. Salingar, 'Don Quixote as a Prose Epic', *Forum for Modern Language Studies* (St Andrews), II (1966), 53-68.
[21] Perry, *The Ancient Romances*, p. 45.
[22] R. F. Brissenden cites Congreve's preface to *Incognita* and the analogy with the drama made by the commentator on character-writing, Henry Gally, as precedents for Richardson's own emphasis on a dramatic model (*Clarissa: Preface, Hints of Prefaces, and Postscript*, Augustan Reprint Society, Publication No. 103, 1964, p.v). Of course, even Fielding, and later Goldsmith, were dramatists as well as novelists; and one cannot make a pure distinction between 'epic-fictions' and 'dramatic-fictions', although they point to different poles and emphases. But the Greek romances themselves, despite their epic reference, are not unrelated to Euripidan drama and New Comedy.

tures tend to reflect a hierarchical, patriarchal and aristocratic environment and an 'oral' literary tradition of public and non-subjective discourse. (All this, incidentally, makes the romances totally 'unromantic', because the great Romantic Age subscribed to ideals and structures quite the antithesis of these at every point: a fiat should probably be issued prohibiting the use of the adjective 'romantic' for romances written before the latter half of the eighteenth century.[23])

But the phenomenon that anthropologists call 'cultural lag'—and the phenomenon that literary historians call 'the chapbook'[24]— assured that for a considerable period after the epic and the chivalric romance had ceased to be written, their influence would persist. Indeed, the use of romance techniques by major writers of prose fiction in the eighteenth century gave them a fresh life that would in turn influence many of the so-called 'realistic novels' of later ages. This disturbed such 'realists' as Henry James and Ford Madox Ford, among others, but it is one of those features of literary continuity that should be set against the academic (or pedagogic) tendency to emphasise breaks in the tradition and to elevate gradual change to the status of sudden apocalyptic rebellion.

Nevertheless, the two general points that I have stressed—the epic dimension and the hierarchical and oral context—will serve adequately, for the moment, to differentiate romance from novel, and to account for many of the features that an 'ideal type' of the romance would tend to exhibit. And it is to this ideal type that I shall now turn, for if one is to orient oneself to see valid romance elements in eighteenth-century fiction, the proper perspective is neither the erroneous one of looking for 'romantic' (that is, nine-teenth-century) qualities of which the romance knew nothing, nor

[23] There is, to be sure, a form of 'romantic romance' (not redundant, given the facts of literary history) to be found after the Romantic Period, particularly in America, as Chase has indicated (see n. 5); and this 'genre' exhibits many elements of genuine continuity in structure and motifs, despite the fact that it issues from a totally different world-view from that which lies behind the original romance tradition.

[24] Restoration printers like Francis Kirkman and John Shurley turned a great many of the medieval and peninsular Romances into abbreviated chapbooks that would appear to have had an enormous circulation. Steele's Bickerstaff found that his little godson, by reading in *Don Belianis of Greece*, *Guy of Warwick*, and *Bevis of Hamptoun*, 'had his thoughts insensibly moulded into the notions of discretion, virtue, and honour' (*Tatler*, No. 95; ed. G. A. Aitken, 4 vols., London, 1898-9, II, 316); and Sterne's Uncle Toby would later recall 'when Guy, Earl of *Warwick*, and *Parismus* and *Parismenus* and *Valentine* and *Orson*, and the *Seven Champions of England* were handed around the school' (*Tristram Shandy*, VI, xxxii; ed. James A. Work, New York, 1940, pp. 460-1). Johnson and Burke battened upon romances in their youth, and Richard Brinsley Sheridan continued to prefer Sidney's *Arcadia* to the new 'realism' of Fielding and Smollett (Letter of 30 October 1772 to Thomas Grenville; cited in William Fraser Rae, *Sheridan: A Biography*, 2 vols., New York, 1896, I, 234-5).

even the legitimate identification of such obvious features as the battles and castles and dungeons and enchanted ground that Christian meets in the romance of *Pilgrim's Progress*. The influence of romance is both more subtle and more pervasive. And the major facets of that influence tend very sharply to conflict with the goals later prescribed for bourgeois realism.

II

The romance, pre-scientific in outlook, makes no sharp demarcation between 'fact' and 'invention': its structure (and this is my first topic) is 'mythopoeic' in that, like myth and legend, it concerns itself more with the total shape of a morally symbolic or ritualistic action (hence the 'contrived' ending, the necessary and inevitable *telos* of the story) than with the plausibility or 'natural' coherence of individual episodes—although logical chains of causality are by no means ignored. The romance is essentially a 'panoramic' rather than a 'focused' creation (*Antony and Cleopatra* as opposed to *Hedda Gabler*)[25] and, at a lower level, its plots tend to seek striking effects, narrative 'turns' and surprises, and a pageant-like variety. Except for the shaping ritual pattern, a strict 'organic' species of unity is not ordinarily its ideal; instead it seeks fresh situations, illuminating fresh aspects of the theme or of the hero: for its narrative model and implicit norm is the epic, understood as a long narrative of varied episodes and circumstances. However, although those romances that very consciously imitate epic conventions (like the *Aethiopica* or Sidney's *Arcadia*) may even begin *in medias res*, the more popular form of plot is that of history and biography, the pattern of an individual life-cycle, focusing on the 'gestes' of the mature or maturing hero, Bevis of Hamptoun or Guy of Warwick or Libeaus Desconus, or focusing upon a particular episode from such a larger pattern, with its own beginning, middle, and end.[26] There is no 'typical' romance plot, but there are certain favoured archetypal actions, such as the mythic struggle between the forces of death or sterility and those of life and fertile vitality (the Battle of Winter and Summer); or the journey or progress through the wilderness of the world; or the 'discovery' of a hero in one apparently of low estate. The image of the human soul alienated from true reality, to which it can be admitted only by a ceremony of initiation, is as central to Apuleius's metamorphosed ass as it is to Sir Percival. The romance presents us with a 'daemonic' world of forces that impinge upon human experience for

[25] Cf. Alan S. Downer, *The Art of the Play*, New York, 1955.
[26] See Dieter Mehl, *The Middle English Romances of the Thirteenth and Fourteenth Centuries*, London, 1969, pp. 37-8 and *passim*.

evil or good (Fate or Fortune, as opposed to—though in a Christian context inevitably an aspect of—Providence); hence it is in essence 'magical' rather than scientific, as it is also exemplary rather than journalistic. The narrative aim is to unfold a plot that exhibits moral action and moral choice; and its strategy is normally to create a disequilibrium, to postulate a dilemma (like the 'fairy-tale' opening of *King Lear*), and to move through the moral action to a new equilibrium. As in the hierarchical, 'closed' societies that most of the romances mirror, the formal and the traditional are major desiderata—the shock of recognition rather than the lust for the new. And such literary conventions as peripeteia and anagnorisis in the action, the acceptance of 'coincidence' as an arbitrary divine intervention in the 'ordinary' course of affairs, the expansive use of digression sanctioned by epic and oral practice, the disguised personages (where dress is often morally emblematic), and the soliloquy as a mode of 'public' self-revelation, are persistent features of the romance from its beginnings. The mediation between such established conventions and the changing contextual order is, however, a source of no little pleasure in individual romances: the cumulative tradition offers, as it were, the *langue* or structure, to which individual representations relate as the *parole* or *praxis*. In general, the romance can be said to emphasise the 'formal' (in the Aristotelian sense) interpretation of experience, in terms of formal and final causes, or allegory and anagogy, as weightier than a 'material' interpretation in terms of efficient and material causes, of tropology and the literal.

The setting of romance, like the physical stage of Shakespeare's theatre, is relatively undifferentiated in place as well as time. When place becomes of significance (usually symbolic, as offering a meaningful context for moral or divine values, rather than just physically contextual), it may be identified at some length; and when time is of concern, as in the working out of a vow or a prophecy (the 'Triumph of Time', as Greene's *Pandosto* is subtitled), temporality will be kept present to our consciousness, though seldom with any great concern for precision. The landscapes are, once again, 'daemonic', charged with the energies of good and evil, which is to say that they are almost inevitably *paysages moralisés*, like the winter landscape through which Sir Gawain rides to meet the Green Knight. The *paradeisos*, as the good, secure, or sacred locus, has a rich variety of traditional representations,[27]

---

[27] See A. Bartlett Giamatti, *The Earthly Paradise and the Renaissance Epic*, Princeton, 1966; John Armstrong, *The Paradise Myth*, London, 1969; and Ernest Curtius, *European Literature and the Latin Middle Ages*, tr. W. R. Trask, New York, Bollingen Series XXXVI, 1953, Chap. X: 'The Ideal Landscape'.

and the road leading to it demands a *rite de passage* from the profane to the sacred, or from the merely existential to the essential. Various emblems of its opposite (the dark forest, the Dungeon of Despair) may serve as crucial points of reversal in the action, from a descending to an ascending vector. The world is visualised as a stage for human action (and contemplation), but it is normally thought of as supervised and ordered by a higher providential power: the universe is a moral universe, a structured universe, even though the action on the merely human stage may suggest (as in the *Metamorphoses* of Apuleius or the medieval *Athelston*) mere arbitrary chaos. At the level of detail the minute particulars of interest to a given audience may be described with loving care; but little attention is paid to the rest of the environing world, except as it impinges upon the hero. One is anchored in 'reality' in terms of local norms (usually the arts of civilised moral existence, even when the action lies in deserts or on oceans), rather than in 'solid' physical nature. That is, in the romances man occupies a world of symbolic and ceremonial 'reality' rather than of material and historical 'actuality'.

Character in the romance is most often expressed through significant action performed by a symbolic, and normally (though not inevitably) aristocratic community, centering in the hero. Surrounding characters are more likely to be typologically presented than detailed as 'psychological personalities'.[28] Although the private lives of the major characters are commonly treated, they tend to be seen in the perspective of their roles in society; and the characters interact in terms of what can be called a *reciprocité symbolique des types*, a 'field' of symbolic, ritualistic, hierarchical relationships and deeds, not in terms of conflicts between self-enclosed psychological worlds. The ritualistic shape of the total design defines the significance of the individual figures, rather than the other way about. The literary validity of the characters may be assessed in large measure by the 'decorum' of their roles, according to age, status, and the like; and their qualities and emotions (love, valour, beauty, or indeed, villainy and ugliness) tend to be heightened and 'idea-

---

[28] A number of quite independent intellectual pursuits in the modern era have converged to produce something of a fresh attitude toward the 'type', freeing us from the Victorian stereotype of the 'stereotype'. One may think of C. G. Jung's typologies, of Northrop Frye's archetypes, of E. H. Gombrich on the schemata of perception ('making comes before matching'), of E. D. Hirsch on the habit of implicit genre-reference, and so on. On the presentation of literary portraits in Chaucer by means of typological and iconographic detail, see Robertson, *Preface to Chaucer*, pp. 241-77, and *passim*. As Scholes and Kellogg observe: 'There is more of myth and of fiction in Don Quixote than in Isabel Archer. There is more of mimesis in her. She may be quixotic, but he is Quixote' (*The Nature of Narrative*, p. 161).

lised'—that is, brought to representative status. The poet's business, as Sidney observed, is to feign notable images of virtues and vices: and major characters in the romances are vehicles of ethical or metaphysical truth. Human nature exhibits itself, of course, in various guises,[29] but an essential underlying homogeneity is assumed (one can define man's 'essence') and the various individual shapes that this 'nature' takes are matters of accidental rather than substantial qualities. Hence 'motivation', although it was surely intuited by individual artists from actual experience, is typically expressed by conventions of logic and rhetoric, to illustrate moral being;[30] and character is conceived primarily in terms of the orientation of the soul and of the 'good' that the will consistently pursues. That is to say, we have here to do with a psychology in its root sense of 'Psyche-ology',[31] the logos of the soul, and with the emphasis upon the soul's free will. The romances are, as noted above, pre-Lockeian, hence there is little concern with the epistemological complexities of a perceiving mind in its problematic relationships with 'the Other'. The soul is, by whatever regnant philosophy, in some sense the 'form' of the material body and radically different from the natural world, with which it forms a kind of disjunctive symbiosis. Significant *change* in character, when it occurs, is seen as a ritual passage to a new state of being or as a transcendent 'conversion' experience—a change in the orientation of the soul—and it may occur with shocking rapidity. In other respects, the focus is less on change (or 'development') in character than upon the different meanings displayed in different contexts by a logically invariant character. Naming often seeks to identify this logical 'essence'; for names, as Angus Fletcher has said, 'are endowed with mana'.[32] (To Locke, although names did serve to preserve essences, they were merely arbitrary sounds.) To speak generally, the romance is an 'ontological' mode of fiction, concerned with being, rather than with a temporal becoming, thus concerned genuinely

[29] Angus Fletcher observes that 'for allegorical heroes life has a segmented character, and as each event occurs a new discrete characteristic of the hero is revealed' (*Allegory: The Theory of a Symbolic Mode*, Ithaca, N.Y., 1964, p. 35). Most of the romances are 'allegorical' in Professor Fletcher's sense of an anti-mimetic mode.
[30] Discussion of the romance techniques for projection of a character's psyche can be found in *The Nature of Narrative*, pp. 80ff., 171ff.
[31] I use the coinage of the great nerve-pathologist, Thomas Willis, after the *psychologia* of the theologians (see Richard Hunter and Ida Macalpine, *Three Hundred Years of Psychiatry 1535-1860*, London, 1963, p. 187). 'Psyche-ology' inevitably has a moral dimension and most often a theological dimension—which differentiates its focus quite sharply from that of 'Psychology'.
[32] *Allegory*, p. 50, n. 48. 'The intermediate stage between an image and an agent is a *name*, i.e., a *metonymy*. To fix the agent into a name is to bring it from motion into rest' (p. 86, n. 25).

with what E. M. Forster, in a different context, called 'life by values' rather than 'life by time'.[33]

The dianoetic reference of the romances, the significant meanings, can be abstracted from the actions, words, and so on, of the characters, or can indeed be abstracted from the structures themselves. The concern of the romance is normally with a pre-existent world of values, an emotionally charged body of religious or philosophical conceptions, that the invented action serves to dramatise and articulate. Thus the ancient distinction of form and content (or *significant* and *signifié*) is almost inescapable in discussing it: its structure is inherently binary. General ethical concerns (often, however, in contrast or counterpoint) are embodied in symbols or types; and the ideal or the symbolic is the ultimate goal—the 'real' conceived as lying in a dimension beyond the merely 'actual' world of appearances. The essential appeal, as Walter R. Davis has put it, is 'centrifugal', an appeal to the sense of being part of a larger structure:[34] hence the generic, the universal, is held to be more important than the 'particular', and myth and legend may appear to contain more certain 'truth' than specific or factual history (as Aristotle had suggested). Thus, too, the 'literal' may be less persuasive than the metaphorical or allegorical. The romance vision does not, of course, deny that the 'actual' world is full of mutability and fluctuation and chaotic particulars (indeed, these are usually the materials of its foreground action), but it normally seeks to transcend this merely present and mutable physical scene, to find values in a 'real' order that is unchanging and eternal: it seeks the 'intelligible world' known by intuitive reason (or, of course, by divine revelation), not simply the material world (the 'actual') available to sense experience. And the actions of its characters are inevitably assessed, with various degrees of detachment or involvement, by reference to that extratextual higher order. The 'truth' in romance may be called deductive and moral, presented in terms of norms, as opposed to the inductive and empirical 'truth' which is emergent from significant particulars. The romance contemplates human action from a transcendental or metaphysical perspective, hence its world is not one of historic time and scientific fact.

The language, both in narration and dialogue, of most 'literary' (as opposed to 'demotic') romance tends to be consciously stylised, 'rhetorical' and anti-mimetic;[35] the language is intended to be enjoyed for its own sake, for literature was, until the rise of positivist

[33] *Aspects of the Novel*, New York, 1927, p. 49.
[34] *Idea and Act in Elizabethan Fiction*, Princeton, 1969, Chap. I.
[35] In another sense of 'stylised', this would be true even of the 'demotic' romances, for like most literature close to the oral tradition, they exhibit highly stylised patterns of delivery.

currents, normally thought of as identical with language (and, of course, language was never conceived in scientific terms as a transparent glass that admitted an 'undisturbed' view of the phenomena). A number of possible styles and tones can be employed in a single romance, to achieve range and variety and 'decorum'; but the dominant voice of the narrator serves as a catalyst joining the other elements of the narrative in a unified totality of effect. And the narrator presumes a 'public' relationship, an 'I-Thou' relationship, with his audience or readers, that is part of the significant experience of his fiction.[36] Thus the romance, like the classical literature from which it stems, is essentially an 'oral' product, designed to be heard; not, as Mill said of (Romantic) poetry, to be 'overheard', to be 'scanned silently in private'.[37]

Other differentiations (and many qualifications of the foregoing) could surely be derived inductively from the great body of extant romances; but this will perhaps serve the present purpose. That my postulated 'ideal type' is neither a description of all romances nor a prescription for any romance will, I trust, go without saying. It should be remembered, incidentally, that 'the novel', as we ordinarily employ that term, also represents an implicit ideal type (whose centre is, or has previously been nineteenth-century 'realistic' fiction); and that under this cover have nestled such unlikely neighbours as *Animal Farm* and *Green Mansions* and *Light in August* and *The Forsyte Saga*. Such an intellectual construct—or, for that matter, the dichotomy of 'novel' and 'romance' itself—ultimately represents a falsification of the continuous history of prose fiction, with its varying emphases from one age to another. But if our categorisation is in the end a lie, it can at least be argued that it is a useful lie, a heuristic ruse. And it would also be my argument, though that is matter for another paper (or volume), that prose fiction from Bunyan to Smollett must be assessed in some such terms as these I have sketched for the 'ideal romance' (taking full note of differences and of new currents), if its coherent artistry within its own frame is to be appreciated and its moral and intellectual aims are to be understood. Such an assessment is essential, if criticism of eighteenth-century prose fiction is to offer other pleasures than self-congratulation at the distance we have travelled from the primitive.

[36] Fletcher says: 'By drawing attention to himself, or to an imagined spectator . . . the artist immediately starts a critical train of thought. One interprets the scene from the imagined spectator's point of view; the double view amounts to an allegorizing of an imitation' (*Allegory*, p. 102, n. 51).

[37] The latter phrase is that of Moses Hadas, distinguishing 'modern' habits of approaching fiction from earlier modes (*Ancilla to Classical Reading*, New York, 1954, p. 50); he adds: 'All classic literature, it may be said, is conceived of as a conversation with, or address to, an audience. . . . And the practice of oral presentation affected the nature of prose as it did of poetry' (pp. 50, 51).

Index

Achilles Tatius, 244
Addison, Joseph, 156
Akenside, Mark, 178
Amadis de Gaule, 243, 244
Apuleius, 243, 250, 252
Ariosto, Ludovico, 243
Armet, Catherine, 5n., 10n.
Armstrong, John, 251n.
Arnold, Matthew, 173, 186
Athenaeum, The, 122
Ault, Norman, 173
Austen, Jane, 70, 153
Austin, J. L., 99n.

Backman, Sven, 69n.
Bacon, Francis, 156
Bahner, Werner, 74n., 83, 86n., 92n.
Bailey, Nathan, 56
Baker, Ernest, 242n.
Ball, Patricia, 206
Balzac, Honoré de, 102, 165
Barber, W. H., 125n.
Barthes, Roland, 107n.
Bate, Walter Jackson, 187n., 212-13, 214
Bath, Guildhall Archives, 43n., 52n.
Baumgart, Fritz, 38n.
Bayle, Pierre, 168
Beaumont, Christophe de, 81
Beckett, Samuel, 103
Behn, Aphra, 248
Belaval, Yvon, 115
Bell, Colin, 38n.
Bell, Howard H., 58n.
Benveniste, Emile, 108n.
Best, G. F. A., 62, 66n.
Beuchot, A. J. Q., 127, 128n., 129n., 130
Bewley, William, 13
Birch, Thomas, 14, 15, 17
Blackmore, Richard, 216, 235
Bladud, 45
Blake, William, 174n.
Bloom, Harold, 157, 213-14, 216, 218, 231

Boerhaave, Hermann, 155
Boiardo, Matteo Maria, 243
Boileau-Despréaux, Nicholas, 171
Bordes, Charles, 81
Boswell, Alexander (father), 22
Boswell, Alexander (son), 24, 25-6
Boswell, Elizabeth (Bruce), 22
Boswell, Elizabeth (daughter), 26
Boswell, Euphemia, 25, 26
Boswell, Emily, 26, 27
Boswell, James, 1-5, 18, 19, 21-35
Boswell, James (grandfather), 22
Boswell, James (son), 24n., 25, 26
Boswell, James (grandson), 26-7, 28
Boswell, Janet Theresa, 26
Boswell, Jessie Jane (Cunninghame), 26
Boswell, John Douglas, 29
Boswell, Julia, 26, 27
Boswell, Margaret Amelia, 26
Boswell, Veronica, 26
Bowers, Fredson, 180
Boyce, Benjamin, 200n., 201n.
Bridges, Robert, 175
Brissenden, R. F., 141, 248n.
Broadbent, J. B., 209
Brodwin, Leonora Leet, 235-6
Brooks, Cleanth, 8
Brower, Reuben, 192, 200n., 203n., 209, 229-30
Browne, Thomas, 156
Bruce, Alexander, 21
Brucker, Johann Jacob, 168
Brunelleschi, Filippo, 37
Buchanan, David, 35n.
Buffon, Georges Louis Leclerc, Comte de, 167, 169
Bunyan, John, 248, 250, 255
Burke, Edmund, 5, 249
Burley Griffin, Walter, 54
Burney, Charles, 12
Burney, Fanny, 55
Burns, Robert, 176, 178, 179

Burton, Robert, 156
Busby, Richard, 235
Bute, John Stuart, 3rd Earl of, 5-6, 9, 10, 11, 12, 17, 18, 19
Butor, Michel, 107

Cameron, W. J., 219
Canguilhem, George, 150n.
Carnot, Lazare, 162
Carter, Elizabeth, 3
Catrysse, Jean, 95n.
Cervantes, Miguel de, 97, 103, 244, 248n., 252n.
Chagall, Marc, 160
Challe, Robert, 111
Chalmers, George, 174, 175, 179, 182
Chambers, Ephraim, 155
Charles II, 220, 224, 236
Chase, L. N., 246n.
Chase, Richard, 243n., 249n.
Chasles, Philarète, 122, 123, 126
Châtelet, Françoise Gabrielle, 127
Châtelet, Emilie le Tonnelier de Breteuil, Marquise du, 127, 128
Chatterton, Thomas, 178
Chaucer, Geoffrey, 174, 186, 215, 230
Chenier, André de, 167
Cheyne, George, 142, 151, 153, 155
Chudleigh, Lady, 177
Churchill, Charles, 14, 15, 17, 213n.
Cibber, Colley, 122, 124, 126, 127n., 129, 176, 218, 230, 238
Cinthio, Giraldi, 248
Clarke, Edwin, 146, 148n.
Coleridge, S. T., 193-4
Collier, Jeremy, 126, 134-5
Collins, William, 176, 178
Combe, William, 66n.
Condillac, Etienne Bonnot de, 162, 163, 166
Congreve, William, 123, 125, 127n., 177, 226, 248n.
Constant, Benjamin, 159
Constapel, H., 129n.
Cotterell, Charles, 245
Cowper, William, 174, 178, 187
Crane, R. S., 60, 142, 144
Cranston, Maurice, 93
Chrestien de Troyes, 243
Crocker, Lester G., 151
Cullen, William, 144, 147, 149
Curtius, Ernest, 251n.

D'Alembert, Jean le Rond, 80, 167
Darwin, Charles, 154
Davenant, William, 210
Davies, Herbert, 34
Davies, Tom, 3
Davies, Walter R., 254
Day Lewis, C., 175-6
Defoe, Daniel, 45, 65, 156n., 176, 216, 248
Delille, Jacques, 167
Deloffre, Frédérick, 111n.
Denham, John, 215
Deprun, Jean, 159
Descartes, René, 144, 147, 161
Destouches (Philippe Néricault), 127n.
Dewhurst, Kenneth, 149n.
Dickens, Charles, 65, 70-1, 186
Diderot, Denis, 95-120, 139, 160, 163, 165, 166-70
Dixon, Peter, 192n.
Dobrée, Bonamy, 130
Dobson, Austin, 55n.
Dodington, George Bubb, Baron Melcombe, 9
Donaldson, E. Talbot, 245n.
Donne, John, 174n., 187
Donnellan, Ann, 151-2, 153, 156n.
Doran, John, 121, 122, 126
Downer, A. S., 250n.
Driesch, H., 150n.
Dryden, Charles, 224
Dryden, Erasmus-Henry, 224-5
Dryden, John, 171, 209-40
Dryden, John (Jr), 224-5, 226
Duck, Stephen, 176
Dunlop, John, 242
D'Urfey, Thomas, 246n.
Durham, D. B., 244n.
Duvignaud, Jean, 37, 44-5, 45n.
Dyer, John, 181

Eco, Umberto, 98-9
Edwards, T. R., 197n.
Ehrenpreis, Irvin, 187
Einstein, Alfred, 154
Elliot, Jane, 176
Elphinston, James, 10
Elwin, H. V., 175
Empson, William, 205
Erämetsä, Eric, 141n.
Erskine-Hill, H. H., 205n.
Etherege, George, 122, 124, 125
Eusden, Lawrence, 216

INDEX

Fairfax, Edward, 215
Falk, Bernard, 63
Farmer, Richard, 8-10
Farquhar, George, 127n.
Faulkner, William, 255
Fénelon, François de Salignac de la Mothe, 167
Fenger, Heming, 124n., 127n.
Ficino, Marsilio, 46
Fielding, Henry, 152, 156n., 244, 246n., 248, 249n.
Fink, Eugen, 116n.
Fitzgerald, Percy, 123
Flatman, Thomas, 176
Fleming, John, 38n.
Fletcher, Angus, 253, 255n.
Fletcher, John, 215, 216
Fontenelle, Bernard le Bouvier, Sieur de, 167
Forbes, William, 25
Ford, Ford Madox, 249
Forster, E. M., 245
Foster, Michael, 149n.
Foucault, Michel, 137n., 138, 143
Fowler, John, 230
Frederick the Great, 75
Fredman, Alice G., 102n.
French, R. K., 149n., 150n., 153n.
Fréret, Nicholas, 159
Fréron, Elie, 129n., 130
Freud, Sigmund, 154, 218
Friedman, Arthur, 60n., 63, 66n.
Frye, Northrop, 140-1, 143, 157n., 242n., 252n.
Fulton, John F., 149n.

Gainsborough, Thomas, 153
Galen, 144, 146
Gally, Henry, 248n.
Galsworthy, John, 255
Gardner, Helen, 175, 180, 181
Garrick, David, 23
Gay, John, 177-8, 182
Gay, Peter, 139
Gay, Robert, 41
Gentleman, Francis, 18n.
George II, 4, 238
George III, 4, 5, 10, 75
George, Dorothy, 57, 58
Giamatti, A. B., 251n.
Goldgar, B. A., 200n.

Goldsmith, Oliver, 55-70, 156, 181, 248n.
Gombrich, E. H., 207, 252n.
Graffigny, Mme de, 127
Gray, Thomas, 176, 178
Greene, Donald, 18n., 188n.
Greene, Edward Burnaby, 18n.
Greene, Robert, 251
Greimas, A. J., 96, 102n.
Grey, W. W., 180
Grimsley, Ronald, 74-5
Gurney, Isabel (Lady Talbot), 27, 28, 33
Gurney, Samuel, 28n.
Gurwitch, George, 164
Guyon, Bernard, 78

Habakkuk, H. J., 221
Hadas, Moses, 255n.
Haller, Albrecht von, 142, 144, 147, 149, 150n., 152-3, 155
Hammond, J. L. Le B., 172
Handel, George Frederick, 153
Hardwicke, Philip York, 1st Earl of, 14, 17
Harvey, William, 146
Haviland, Thomas P., 244n.
Hawkesworth, John, 16-17
Hayes, John, 64n.
Hayward, Eliza, 246
Hayward, John, 180-1
Hecht, Jean, 57n.
Heidegger, Martin, 159
Heisenberg, Werner, 154
Heliodorus, 243, 244, 248, 250
Helvétius, Claude Adrian, 84
Hill, G. S., 2, 26
Hill, H. W., 246n.
Hind, G. Lewis, 171n., 174
Hippocrates, 46
Hirsch, E. D., 252n.
Hobbes, Thomas, 155
Hogarth, William, 37, 57-8, 64, 70, 122, 153
Holbach, Paul Henri Dietrich, Baron d', 159, 162
Hollis, Thomas, 2
Homer, 215, 216, 222, 234, 248
Howard, Robert, 226, 228
Hudson, W. H., 255
Huet, Daniel, 244n., 245n.
Hume, David, 9, 138, 139, 150, 155, 165
Hunter, G. K., 205

Hunter, Richard, 253n.
Hunter, William, 155
Hutcheson, Francis, 150, 153, 155
Huxley, Aldous, 85

Ibsen, Henrik, 250
Isham, Ralph H., 21, 31, 84
Isler, Hansruedi, 149n., 150n.
Isles, Duncan, 2n.
Ison, Walter, 38n.

Jakobson, Roman, 107n.
James II, 236
James, Henry, 249, 252n.
Janin, Jules, 123
Jenkinson, Charles, 19
Johnson, Samuel, 1-19, 21, 22, 23, 56, 58, 156n., 178, 179, 187, 188, 199, 222, 224, 249
Johnston, Arthur, 246n.
Jones, Emrys, 205n.
Jonson, Ben, 215-16, 217
Jung, C. G., 252n.
Juvenal, 225

Kant, Immanuel, 159, 162
Kempf, Roger, 95n.
Kennedy, John, 14
Kennicott, Benjamin, 6-7
Kerr, Joyce (Lady Talbot), 29-30, 32-3
Kierkegaard, Søren Aabyi, 218
Kincardine, Alexander Bruce, Earl of, 21-2
Kirkman, Francis, 249n.
Koyre, Alexander, 140n.
Krieger, Murray, 205n.
Kuhn, Thomas S., 137-43, 144, 149n., 153

La Calprenède, Gautier de Costes de, 245n.
La Fontaine, Jean de, 113, 116n.
La Mettrie, Julien Offroy de, 139, 147, 155
Lanson, Gustave, 126n.
Laslett, Peter, 57, 58, 62
Laufer, Roger, 96n.
Lavoisier, Antoine Laurent de, 139
Leavis, F. R., 206-7
Le Bossu, René, 248n.
Le Cat, Claude Nicolas, 139
Lee, John, 134

Leeuwenhoek, Antoine van, 146n.
Leibniz, Gottfried Wilhelm, 168
Lennox, Charlotte, 2
Le Normant, C. F., 92
Levi-Strauss, Claude, 143
Libeaus, Desconus, 250
Lifraud, Yvonne, 132
Locke, John, 41, 54, 138, 139-45, 149n., 150-2, 155, 161-2, 163, 166, 253
Longus, 243
Lonsdale, Roger, 58n.
Lord, G. de F., 219
Lovejoy, A. O., 192-3
Loy, J. Robert, 96n.
Lucian, 244
Lucretius, 159
Luxembourg, Duc de, 74
Lyly, John, 243
Lynch, Kathleen M., 246

McAdam, E. L., 179
McCrone, Robert, 28
MacKenzie, Henry, 154, 155
McKerrow, R. B., 180
McPherson, C. B., 41n.
Mack, Maynard, 188, 196-7, 200n.
Mahaffy, Elsie, 20n.
Malone, Edmond, 25
Malpighi, Marcello, 149n.
Mandeville, Bernard, 139
Manley, Mary de la Riviere, 246
Mann, Thomas, 159
Mannheim, Karl, 37
Marat, Jean-Paul, 139
Marvell, Andrew, 187, 189, 232-3
Marx, Karl, 37, 52-3, 92
Mauzi, Robert, 107
May, Georges, 110
Mehl, Dieter, 250n.
Merton, Robert K., 138n.
Meynell, Alice, 171, 181
Miles, D. H., 125n.
Mill, John Stuart, 255
Milton, John, 187, 210-11, 214, 215, 216, 217, 231-6
Miner, Earl, 229
Molière, Jean Baptiste Poquelin de, 122, 125, 132
Mortier, Roland, 161n.
Mounsay, George, 27
Murphy, Arthur, 10, 11-12, 15, 19
Murray, John, 28

INDEX

Navarre, Marguerite de, 111n.
Newbery, John, 3
Newton, A. Edward, 31
Newton, Isaac, 139, 140, 165
Nichol Smith, D., 34, 171-83
Niebyl, Peter H., 144n.
Nietzsche, Friedrich Wilhelm, 218
'Nipclose, Sir Nicholas', 18
Noble, George, 14n.

O'Connor, John J., 244n.
Ogilby, John, 216
Olderman, Raymond M., 247n.
Oliver, William, 39
Onians, R. B., 144n.
Oppé, A. P., 63
Orwell, George, 255
Osborne, Dorothy, 245
Osborne, Thomas, 11
Otway, Thomas, 128

Page, F., 175
Pagel, Walter, 145n.
Palgrave, Francis, 174, 175, 176-7, 179-80, 183
Palladio, Andrea, 37, 48-9
Palmerin, 243
Panofsky, Erwin, 37, 46-7
Parmenides, 159
Paulson, Ronald, 58, 65n.
Percy, Thomas, 8, 10, 11
Perkin, Harold, 41n.
Perry, B. E., 244, 248
Persius, 225
Petronius Arbiter, 243
Pevsner, Nikolaus, 38
Philips, Ambrose, 176
Phillips, John, 177
Pinciano, Lopez, 248n.
Pomfret, John, 177
Pommier, Jean, 108n.
Pope, Alexander, 4, 156, 176, 178, 181, 185, 207, 209-11, 213, 214, 216, 217, 231, 233-4, 235, 237-40
Pottle, Frederick A., 10, 32
Poynter, F. N. L., 144n.
Prior, Matthew, 177
Proust, Marcel, 159
Pruner, Francis, 96n., 103n., 107n., 114
Pulci, Luigi, 244
Pye, Henry James, 176
Pythagoras, 45
Queneau, Raymond, 113, 159

Quiller-Couch, Arthur, 172-3, 174-5, 180, 183
Quintana, Ricardo, 56

Rabelais, François, 104, 244
Rambouillet, Catherine de Vivonne, Marquise de, 244, 246-7n.
Rather, L. J., 150n.
Renouard, Antoine Auguste, 128n., 130, 132n.
Revue britannique, La, 122
Reynolds, Joshua, 12, 13, 15, 153
Richardson, Samuel, 141, 151, 152-6, 246, 248
Richet, Denis, 73n.
Richetti, John J., 246n.
Riding, Laura, 173n.
Ridley, Humphrey, 149n.
Riese, Walter, 145n.
Robertson, D. W., 245n., 252n.
Robinson, Nicholas, 155
Rose, William, 19
Rosenbach, A. S. W., 31, 32
Rothschuk, K. E., 144n.
Rousseau, George, 56n.
Rousseau, Jean-Jacques, 73-93, 100n., 139, 155, 162, 164, 165, 168-9
Rowlandson, Thomas, 55, 56, 58, 63-5, 68-9
Russell, Thomas, 178

Sade, Donatien-Alphonse-François, Marquis de, 154, 155, 159, 162
St-Evremond, Charles Marguetel de Saint-Denis, Seigneur de, 230
St James's Chronicle, 13, 15
Saintsbury, George, 55n.
Salingar, L. G., 248n.
Salverte, Eusèbe, 164
Sardou, Victorien, 132
Sarraute, Nathalie, 97
Sartre, Jean Paul, 96-7, 159
Scaliger, Julius Caesar, 248n.
Scholes, Robert, 242n., 252n.
Scott, Geoffrey, 32
Scudéry, Georges de, 246n.
Scudéry, Madelaine de, 244
Sedaine, Michel Jean, 167
Sgard, Jean, 165
Shaftesbury, Anthony Ashley Cooper, 3rd Earl of, 139, 142n., 143, 150, 153, 155, 163, 186-7, 199-200

Shakespeare, William, 185, 186, 187, 198-9, 214, 215, 216, 217, 233, 250, 251
Sharp, John, 9n., 10
Shaw, William, 10n., 14n.
Sheridan, R. B., 122, 130, 134, 249n.
Sheridan, Thomas, 10
Shurley, John, 249n.
Sidney, Philip, 245, 248n., 249n., 250, 253
Simpson, A. W. B., 42n.
Sir Gawain and the Green Knight, 251
Smart, Christopher, 178
Smith, Adam, 44, 138, 139, 150
Smollet, Tobias, 54, 153, 156, 249n., 255
Solmsen, F., 144n.
Sommelsdyck, Veronica van, 21-2
Sorel, Charles, 96
'South Briton, A', 15-16
Spacks, P. M., 191n., 199n.
Spencer, Joseph, 124n.
Spenser, Edmund, 215, 243
Spinoza, Benedictus de, 168
Staal de Launay, Marguerite Jeanne Cordier, Baronne de, 127, 128-9
Stahl, Georg Ernest, 147
Statius, 248
Steele, Richard, 249n.
Steno, Nicolaus, 149n.
Step to the Bath, A, 39
Sterne, Laurence, 102, 105n., 151, 153-4, 155, 249n.
Stothard, Thomas, 55
Stuart, James, 26
Suckling, John, 246n.
Summerson, John, 38n.
Sutherland, James, 179
Swedenberg, H. T., 248n.
Swift, Jonathan, 157, 178

Tableau littéraire de la France, 161-2, 163
Talbot, James Boswell (6th Lord), 27, 29, 31, 32
Talbot, Milo, 28
Talbot, Milo (7th Lord), 34-5
Talbot, Richard (5th Lord), 27, 28, 33
Tanner, Tony, 205n.
Tasso, Torquato, 243, 248n.
Taylor, John, 216
Temple, William, 25
Tennyson, Alfred, 174

Tennyson, Charles, 174n.
Thomson, James, 58, 176, 178, 181
Thrale, Henry, 18
Tinker, C. B., 21, 29, 30-1, 32, 33
Trilling, Lionel, 206-7
Trissino, Giangiorgio, 248n.
Trublet, Nicolas Charles Joseph, 160n.
Truffier, Jules, 132n.
Turner, Baptist Noel, 9, 10

Vanbrugh, John, 121, 122-3, 134-5, 126, 130-1, 132-3, 135
Van Helmont, Jean-Baptiste, 148
Varloot, Jean, 115n.
Vesalius, 148
Virgil, 211-12, 215, 216, 217, 222-3, 229, 233, 248
Voegelin, Erich, 144n.
Voltaire, 86, 121-35, 159-62, 165, 167, 169
Vuystinck, Gerrit, 22

Waller, Edmund, 214, 215
Walsh, William, 177
Ward, Ned, 216
Wark, Robert, 64
Warren, F. M., 242n.
Watson, George, 232
Watt, Ian, 152, 221
Weber, Max, 248
Wedderburne, Alexander, 11, 12
Whytt, Robert, 142, 144, 147, 149, 152-3, 155
Wightman, W. P. D., 145n.
Wilding, Michael, 228-9
Wiles, Roy M., 3n.
Wilkes, John, 14, 15, 16, 24
William III, 219
Williams, Aubrey, 189-90
Williams, C., 175
Willis, Thomas, 141-2, 143, 144, 145-6, 147-50, 151, 154, 155, 253
Wilson, Charles, 126n.
Wittgenstein, Ludwig, 243
Wittkower, Rudolf, 37
Wolf, E. C. J., 56n.
Wood, John, 38, 43-54
Wordsworth, William, 141, 178
Wotton, William, 247n.
Wycherley, William, 123, 124, 125

Young, Arthur, 55n.

www.ingramcontent.com/pod-product-compliance
Lightning Source LLC
Chambersburg PA
CBHW022214090526
44584CB00012BB/483